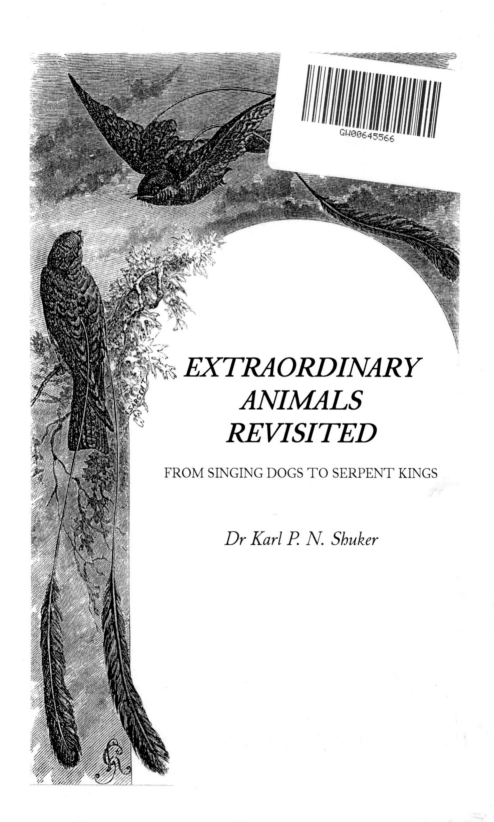

EXTRAORDINARY ANIMALS REVISITED

FROM SINGING DOGS TO SERPENT KINGS

Dr Karl P. N. Shuker

Typeset and Edited by Jonathan Downes
Scanned and proofed by Corinna Downes and Oliver Lewis
Cover design and Layout by Mark North for CFZ Communications
Using Microsoft Word 2000, Microsoft , Publisher 2000, Adobe Photoshop CS.

First published in Great Britain by CFZ Press 2007
Revised Impression 2008

CFZ Press
Myrtle Cottage
Woolsery
Bideford
North Devon
EX39 5QR

ISBN:978-1-905723-17-1

Dedication

To my mother, Mary D. Shuker, whose
lifelong interest in wildlife has guided
and encouraged my own since
my earliest days.

The mother's heart is the child's schoolroom

Henry Ward Beecher – *Life Thoughts*

By the same Author

Mystery Cats of the World: From Blue Tigers To Exmoor Beasts (Robert Hale: London, 1989)
Extraordinary Animals Worldwide (Robert Hale: London, 1991)
The Lost Ark: New and Rediscovered Animals of the 20th Century (HarperCollins: London, 1993)
Dragons: A Natural History (Aurum: London/Simon & Schuster: New York, 1995; republished Taschen: Cologne, 2006)
In Search of Prehistoric Survivors: Do Giant 'Extinct' Creatures Still Exist? (Blandford: London, 1995)
The Unexplained: An Illustrated Guide to the World's Natural and Paranormal Mysteries (Carlton: London/JG Press: North Dighton, 1996; republished Carlton: London, 2002)
From Flying Toads To Snakes With Wings: From the Pages of FATE Magazine (Llewellyn: St Paul, 1997)
Mysteries of Planet Earth: An Encyclopedia of the Inexplicable (Carlton: London, 1999)
The Hidden Powers of Animals: Uncovering the Secrets of Nature (Reader's Digest: Pleasantville/ Marshall Editions: London, 2001)
The New Zoo: New and Rediscovered Animals of the Twentieth Century [fully-updated, greatly-expanded, new edition of The Lost Ark] (House of Stratus Ltd: Thirsk, UK/House of Stratus Inc: Poughkeepsie, USA, 2002)
The Beasts That Hide From Man: Seeking the World's Last Undiscovered Animals (Paraview: New York, 2003)
Extraordinary Animals Revisited: From Singing Dogs To Serpent Kings (CFZ Press: Bideford, 2007)
Dr Shuker's Casebook: In Pursuit of Marvels and Mysteries (CFZ Press: Bideford, 2008)

Consultant and also Contributor

Man and Beast (Reader's Digest: Pleasantville, New York, 1993)
Secrets of the Natural World (Reader's Digest: Pleasantville, New York, 1993)
Almanac of the Uncanny (Reader's Digest: Surry Hills, Australia, 1995)
The Guinness Book of Records/Guinness World Records 1998- (Guinness: London, 1997-)

Consultant

Monsters (Lorenz: London, 2001)

Contributor

Fortean Times Weird Year 1996 (John Brown Publishing: London, 1996)
Mysteries of the Deep (Llewellyn: St Paul, 1998)
Guinness Amazing Future (Guinness: London, 1999)
The Earth (Channel 4 Books: London, 2000)
Mysteries and Monsters of the Sea (Gramercy: New York, 2001)
Chambers Dictionary of the Unexplained (Chambers: London, 2007)

Contents

Foreword
to the New Edition

I have been a professional cryptozoologist for nearly twenty years now, and an amateur one for more years than I care to remember. During my formative years as a cryptozoologist, and indeed in more recent times as well, there have been a handful of people who have been truly inspirational to me in my work in this field. I think that it is true to say that if it hadn't been for the books of Dr Karl Shuker, for example, I would never have been inspired to start the Centre for Fortean Zoology back in 1992. And it is certain that if it had not been for the kindness and friendship shown to me by him in the early days, the CFZ would have disappeared into the ether like too many other nascent organisations.

In fact, the more I think of it, I owe much of my career to Karl's patronage back in the early days (and most of the rest of it to the similar friendship shown to me by Tony `Doc` Shiels). If it wasn't for these two men, my life would almost certainly have taken a completely different path.

So - nearly two decades on - I can return the favour, by publishing this book. Except for the fact that I am not doing anyone any favours at all; this is a magnificent book! The original edition is probably the most obscure of any of Dr Shuker's writings, which is something that I have always thought was a great pity.

Karl and I - I think - were born about a hundred years too late. We should have been active during the heyday of Victorian natural history, rather than in the cold, grey days of the end-years of the 20th Century, and the grave new world of the 21st. This book confirms my thesis completely. For it is a 21st Century analogue of one of those glorious Victorian books of natural history containing a miscellany of apparently disparate facts and figures about the intricacies of God's creation, which nevertheless mesh together into a seamless and intriguing whole.

I love this book. It does exactly `what it says on the tin`, describing some truly extraordinary animals, mostly cryptozoolological, but sometimes not. My favourite chapter is actually *not* a cryptozoological one; the chapter on solifugids - gloriously bizarre invertebrates that I have always wanted to keep. But even these have a phenomenalogical aspect to them. Not only did they turn up in the third of the Harry Potter movies, but they have been the subject of one of the weirdest and most unpleasant quasi-fortean rumours to have arisen out of the recent war in Iraq. Truly the world is still a magnificently peculiar place.

One of the things that has always impressed me about Dr Shuker's research is the way that he unearths obscurities that nobody else has ever heard of. In this way he is like a truffle hound on some bucolic French farm, working away with dogged determination until he finally manages to uncover a rare and valuable nugget of information, and not resting until he has placed it firmly within the public domain. It is truly a wild talent (as Charlie Fort would no doubt have put it), and one which I sincerely hope that he continues to utilise for the rest of his professional life.

This is the first of (we hope) many books by Dr Shuker that we shall be publishing. When I started CFZ Press some years ago, my hope was that we would eventually become the definitive cryptozoological publishing house for the English speaking world. With the publication of this groundbreaking book we are another step along the way towards achieving our goal.

Watch this space!

Jonathan Downes
(Director, CFZ)
The Centre for Fortean Zoology,
Woolfardisworthy,
North Devon
July 2007

Introduction
to the New Edition

An engaging modern bestiary, chronicling a variety of forms of beast - imaginary, real and somewhere in between.

The Observer (London), 8 July 1991.

Compiled by cryptozoologist Karl Shuker, an author with an enthusiasm for delving into obscure literary and scientific journals in search of the unusual; and the unusual he has certainly found... an entertaining read packed with fascinating information.

Michael Bright - *New Scientist*, 31 August 1991

A handsome and interesting collection of accounts of zoological oddities of all kinds... Each of the creatures is discussed with admirable scientific precision. The scope and depth of Shuker's research is impressive, and covers a wide range of books and articles.

Ron Rosenblatt - *Strange Magazine*, November 1991

[A] fascinating pot-pourri of mythology, cryptozoology, and genuine natural history... The strength of this lively book lies in the intelligent assessment and explanation of the various mysteries propounded.

Professor John L. Cloudsley-Thompson - *The Biologist*, November 1991

Karl's sure grasp of his subject, and his thorough research, gather and retell fascinating facts and stories about a type of animal and the interesting or folkloric variations of it... It is easy to read, useful enough to become a valued reference, and surprisingly entertaining. What more could one ask from a non-fiction work?

Bob Rickard - *Fortean Times*, December 1991

A work of great interest to anyone curious about little-known mysteries and anomalies of the animal kingdom... Even readers knowledgeable about the animal kingdom will be amazed by how much material is unearthed on creatures ignored by mainstream wildlife books... Extraordinary Animals Worldwide is highly recommended, and I eagerly await Dr. Shuker's next work.

Mark Chorvinsky - *Fate*, November 1992

During the 16 years since its original publication back in 1991, my second book, *Extraordinary Animals Worldwide*, has acquired something of a cult status among readers, especially those interested in cryptozoology. Combining thought-provoking accounts of mysterious, still-controversial, unrecognised beasts with esoteric information concerning various formally-recognised but no less remarkable creatures, it offered readers access to all manner of truly extraordinary animals never previously given detailed coverage in a mainstream book, plus nowadays-forgotten but still-fascinating insights into how Western science first became aware of all manner of species now wholly accepted within the pantheon of contemporary zoology.

And to highlight this celebration of what used to be called 'romantic natural history', I purposefully selected wherever possible beautiful Victorian engravings and other eye-catching archive illustrations depicting the animals that I was documenting. What I was hoping to create was a delightfully anachronistic volume evoking those of Philip Gosse, Frank Buckland, and, more recently, Willy Ley - and hence a million aeons away from the standard glossy full-colour tomes of today, packed with exactly the same information and images as one another, and where anything remotely controversial and/or cryptozoological is ruthlessly eliminated.

Happily, my little book's bold tilt at the windmills of zoological correctness and conformity soon attracted more than a little positive attention and interest from an international audience, and even though it has now been out of print for several years I still receive correspondence from readers concerning the subjects covered in it. This in turn has encouraged me to prepare at last a new, second edition of *Extraordinary Animals Worldwide,* the result of which is the book that you are now reading. As suggested by its modified title, *Extraordinary Animals Revisited*, some of the chapters from the original edition that proved especially popular with readers reappear here, updated if need be but otherwise retaining their original content. To those are added a series of new chapters, variously based upon, expanded from, or inspired by articles of mine published in the past but which may not have reached as wide an audience back then as they would do now, plus a selection of charming additional illustrations to accompany them. In addition, and at the risk of upsetting those readers of a metric persuasion, I have retained here the imperial measurement units used in the original edition, not least of all because this new edition is aimed particularly at the American market, as the original version allegedly was not as readily available in the States as readers there would have wished.

So join me now, revisiting your favourite extraordinary animals from this book's original incarnation, and making the acquaintance of a veritable menagerie of fresh ones - from singing dogs to serpent kings, pseudo-plesiosaurs to quasi-octopuses, hounds with two noses and birds with four wings, the Sandwell Valleygator and New Mexico's medicine wolf, cobras that crow, and snake gods that dance, giant solifugids and rodent colossi, devil-birds and devil-pigs, furry woodpeckers and marsupial hummingbirds, archangel feathers and the scales of the Eden serpent, scorpion-stones and elephant-pearls, tales of the peacock's tail, parachuting palm civets, missing megapodes, blue rhinoceroses, glutinous globsters, anomalous aardvarks, a platypus from Colorado, man-sized spiders from the Congo, de Loys's lost Venezuelan ape, Margate's marine elephant, a flying hedgehog called Tizzie-Wizzie, a mellifluous mollusc called Molly, India's once (and future?) pink-headed duck, the squeaking deathshead, the vanquished bird-god of New Caledonia, and much much more – all waiting to amaze and amuse, a pageant of natural and unnatural history for your attention and entertainment. But wait - I hear something stirring in the shadows. The exordium is over, for the show has begun...

Foreword
to the Original Edition

by Janet and Colin Bord

Living in the country, as we are fortunate enough to do, surrounded by trees and with river valleys, mountains and forests close by, one soon becomes accustomed to natural events that once, when we first moved to this house, were new and exciting. The tawny owls, for instance, which live in our conifer plantation, and every year produce young which can be seen perching on the gate-posts or sitting side by side on a tree gazing down like Tweedledum and Tweedledee. Or the curlews, which every year return to the valley, their haunting calls echoing up the hillside. The arrival in early May of the house martins, without whose restless flight and endless chatter the summer would be dull indeed. (We disregard the marks on our windows and white walls - they are a small price to pay for our enjoyment of the birds' exuberant love of life.)

No doubt much goes on here that we do not know about. Going out on a winter's morning into the snow-covered garden, we see footprints everywhere, indicating that while we were asleep all kinds of animals have been active: if only our cats could talk! We see rabbits, of course, and sometimes hares; we see stoats and weasels, rats, mice, voles, moles and shrews. Pheasants are commonplace, feeding in our garden throughout the winter, and often a female will reward us come the spring by nesting on the ground, in a clump of daffodils by the front window for example. But the eggs never hatch: either she deserts the nest when there is activity in the garden, as we begin to repair the winter ravages; or the nest is discovered by a cat which wastes no time in breaking open the eggs and eating the contents.

It would be easy, if we didn't have to earn a living, to spend the whole of our days outdoors: apart from the work to be done, there is so much wildlife to discover and to watch. In addition to the larger creatures there are of course also many species of insect. In summer we become aware of the wasps building their nests in the toolshed; of the bees who have taken up residence inside the house wall, entering through a hole by the bathroom window, with their constant to-ing and fro-ing during the warm weather; of the many different kinds of spider and flies, beetles and caterpillars.

But although we see all these birds and beasts regularly, we know very little about them. We observe their behaviour, but we are seeing only a small fragment of their lives; and when we read up on any creature, be it spiders or bats, we cannot help but be amazed by the intricacy of their existence. Humankind is by nature egocentric, seeing all other forms of life as subordinate and of incidental importance, but as a species we will need to learn humility and tolerance if we are to survive on earth. Above all, we will have to learn to live in easy harmony with all other forms of nature, not constantly trying to subdue them. We are never keen to admit our dependence on the natural world, but we are a part of it and the sooner we come to terms with that fact and begin to treat nature sympathetically, the better it will be for everyone. We can begin by reawakening our awareness of the myriad life-forms with which we share the planet, and there is no better guide to the more extraordinary manifestations of nature than Dr Shuker. His forays into the backwaters of zoology have resulted in this collection of case-studies which will fascinate even the most experienced student of the natural world, and will cause us all to look at the world around us with a new sense of wonder.

Introduction
to the Original Edition

Indeed, what is there that does not appear marvellous when it comes to our knowledge for the first time? How many things, too, are looked upon as quite impossible until they have been actually effected?

Pliny the Elder - *Natural History, Book VII*

The above quotation is never more valid than when applied to the animal kingdom, and provides the theme of this entire book - because this book does *not* deal with commonplace creatures, or with familiar facets of animal behaviour or lifestyle. On the contrary, its subjects are ones that have stimulated wonder and curiosity, mystery and mythology, and, in many cases, surprising new discoveries and continuing controversy.

Drawing its material from a diverse array of sources - from forgotten treatises, obscure journals, and foreign-language accounts not previously made available in English, to the most recent scientific researches and media reports - and brought together for the very first time in a single volume, this is an investigation of some of the most extraordinary animals and astonishing episodes from the annals of unnatural history.

Such creatures include the blue rhinoceros, and the flying jackal; a 'terrible mouse' the size of a fox terrier, and a voracious, horse-eating terror bird taller than the ostrich; a mystery 'ape' of South America, and a giant Himalayan lungfish(?); Australia's electric platypus, and Africa's amazing lightning bird; a snake that not only bears a cockscomb but also crows like a cockerel, and another that miaows like a cat; a 40-ton 'earth shaker', and a 70-ft sea monster; the Father of Stenches, and the Whale-Headed King; the bird with two beaks, and the bird with four wings; a gliding frog, and a parachuting palm civet; the devil-pig, and the devil-bird; a New Guinea phoenix, and a yodelling dingo; serpent-kings, and snake-stone secrets; a pygmy tyrannosaur, and a giant bee; the squeaking deathshead... and many more.

In order to complement these animals' unusual nature with equally arresting illustrations, I have, whenever possible, drawn extensively upon what must surely be one of the most attractive artforms ever devised — the exquisite art of wood-engraving, sadly eclipsed by the advent of photography and largely forgotten today by all but its most avowed aficionados. Some of the engravings included in this book originally appeared in one or more of the following antiquarian wildlife works:

Brown, R. (ed), *Our Earth and Its Story,* 3 vols (Cassell, London, 1887-9)
Duncan, P.M. (ed), *Cassell's Natural History,* 6 vols (Cassell, London, 1883-9)

Figuier, L., *The Insect World* (Cassell, London, 1872)

Gesner, C., *Historiae Animalium, Liber I .. (apud* Christ. Froschoverum, Tiguri, 1551)

Lydekker, R. (ed), *The Royal Natural History,* 6 vols (Frederick Warne, London, 1894-6)

Newton, A., and Gadow, H., *A Dictionary of Birds* (Adam and Charles Black, London, 1896)

Pouchet, R.A., *The Universe* (Blackie and Son, London, 1873)

Taffs, A. (ed), *The World of Wonders* (Cassell, Petter, and Galpin, London, 1881)

Tennent, E., *Sketches of the Natural History of Ceylon* (Longman, Green, Longman, and Roberts, London, 1861)

Wood, J.G., *Illustrated Natural History,* 3 vols (Routledge, Warne, and Routledge, London, 1859-63)

This, then, is a book of extraordinary animals. However, lest anyone should despair of ever encountering such creatures personally (fearing that they must surely inhabit only the most remote reaches of the world, and that they all, by definition, must have strange forms, or bizarre histories) permit me to present without further ado this book's first example. For it provides an excellent demonstration that some truly extraordinary animals live in the most familiar of lands and are perfectly ordinary creatures - until, without warning, they reveal a totally unexpected facet of their nature.

The setting was the famous Exmoor wildlife sanctuary of noted naturalist Trevor Beer, one day in June 1988. Walking towards some ground-level vegetation, Trevor suddenly heard a series of very shrill cries, which seemed to be coming from the vegetation. Peering closely, Trevor spotted a stoat *Mustela erminea,* sitting on its hind legs and staring up at him. Mindful of the very wary nature of stoats, which will disappear from view at the slightest movement made by anyone fortunate enough to spy one of these handsome animals, Trevor paused, pleased to be able to observe it at such close range, but nonetheless expecting it to vanish at any moment.

The stoat did not vanish, however; instead, it remained sitting upright for a time, and then dropped on all fours, but immediately rose back up onto its haunches again, repeating the shrill cries that had first drawn Trevor's attention to it. And still it made no attempt to leave. Naturally, Trevor was quite perplexed by this very atypical behaviour for a species widely considered to be one of Britain's most elusive mammals. At first he wondered whether it might have some young hiding nearby, and was standing guard to ensure that he did not harm them, but then, as he recalled to me when recounting this most interesting episode afterwards, some indefinable instinct told him that it was important that he should take an even closer look nonetheless.

So he bent down towards the stoat, and it continued to stare at him, but still did not move away. And as he peered at it, Trevor suddenly noticed a thorn from a hawthorn bush embedded in one of the animal's forepaws. Considering the relatively large size of the thorn in proportion to the tiny size of the stoat's paw, there could be little doubt that it was inflicting a great deal of pain upon the unfortunate animal. Clearly, then, there was only one course of action open, so Trevor reached out towards the stoat in an attempt to pick it up and see whether he could pull the thorn out. Not too surprisingly, the stoat reacted by snapping at his hand, but eventually, with a balance of patience and speed, Trevor succeeded in gently catching hold of it. He was able to pull the thorn out quickly and easily, after which he placed the stoat back on the ground.

Even then the stoat did not run away. First of all it sniffed tentatively at its treated paw, and then licked it several times, no doubt to ease the pain and reassure itself that all was well with it once more. Only then did it finally turn around, and disappear amongst the nearby trees.

To this day, Trevor is sure that the stoat had been 'asking' him for his help, and in view of its unexpectedly fearless behaviour and overall attitude, who could disagree? Having said that, it is very fortunate that Trevor was the human to whom the stoat appealed; there are all too many who would have dealt with the unfortunate animal in a much less kindly manner. Trevor, however, is someone who has not only a great knowledge of his fellow creatures but also a great compassion and respect for them. Perhaps this is why the stoat made its presence known to him in this remarkable, Androclesian incident; as Shakespeare noted in *Coriolanus*: "Nature teaches beasts to know their friends".

There are many other thoroughly remarkable creatures awaiting attention and investigation in the following 24 chapters of this book. So venture now, if you will, into this menagerie of the marvellous and mysterious, to encounter creatures of reality and legend, to meet inhabitants of dreams and, occasionally, of nightmares - an assemblage of fascinating and, above all else, truly extraordinary animals. Or, to borrow from the Bard of Stratford-upon-Avon once again:

> *I would entreat thy company*
> *To see the wonders of the world.*

> William Shakespeare - *Two Gentlemen of Verona*

Chapter One
Aardvark Anomalies

Towards evening the Aard Vark issues from the burrow wherein it has lain asleep during the day, proceeds to the plains, and searches for an ant-hill in full operation. With its powerful claws it tears a hole in the side of the hill, breaking up the stony walls with perfect ease, and scattering dismay among the inmates. As the ants run hither and thither, in consternation, their dwelling falling like a city shaken by an earthquake, the author of all this misery flings its slimy tongue among them, and sweeps them into its mouth by hundreds. Perhaps the ants have no conception of their great enemy as a fellow-creature, but look upon the Aard Vark as we look upon the earthquake, the plague, or any other disturbance of the usual routine of nature.

Reverend J.G. Wood - *Homes Without Hands*

The aardvark is best known to many people as that peculiar beast that is inevitably the first creature to be dealt with in any alphabetically-ordered animal encyclopedia written in English - but in reality it has far greater claims to zoological fame than that. Indeed, there is every good reason for looking upon this African anomaly as a truly singular creature - in every sense of the word.

Encountering the Earth-Pig

In 1705, naturalist Peter Kolbe travelled to Cape Town, South Africa, and spent a number of years there, during which time he acquired a substantial knowledge of the area's wildlife, as later documented in his book *Caput Bonae Spei, i.e. a Complete Description of the African Cape of Good Hope* (1719). This contained accounts of many animal forms hitherto unknown to science - one of which was a strange 8-ft-long mammal referred to by the Boers as the aardvark or erdvark, translating as 'earth-pig'. It derived these names from its subterranean domicile, and from its meat - said by the Boers to taste rather like pork.

Certainly, it was *not* named for any overall resemblance to a pig, because in truth the aardvark bears scant resemblance to *any* other, *single* modern-day creature known to humanity. If anything, it is best likened to an animated association of spare parts, randomly acquired from all manner of different creatures and almost as randomly assembled, to yield a morphological muddle of very uncertain affinity and highly unlikely appearance - as underlined by the following account, penned by Professor P.M. Duncan in *Cassell's Natural History* (1883-89) and describing one of the first aardvarks to be exhibited in England, at London Zoo:

...in the evening, and sometimes in the morning, when the food is placed in

the cage...a long pair of stuck-up ears, looking like those of a gigantic Hare with a white skin and little fur, may be seen poked up above the straw; and, soon after, a long white muzzle, with small sharp eyes between it and the long ears, comes into view. Then a very fat and rather short-bodied animal with a long head and short neck, low fore and large hind-quarters, with a bowed back, comes forth, and finally a moderately long fleshy tail is seen. It is very pig-like in the look of its skin, which is light-coloured and has a few hairs on it. Moreover, the snout is somewhat like that of a Pig, but the mouth has a small opening only, and to make the difference between the animals decided, out comes a worm-shaped long tongue covered with mucus...and as it walks slowly on the flat of its feet and hands to its food, they are seen to be armed with very powerful claws. In Southern Africa, whence this animal came, it is as rarely seen by ordinary observers as in England, for there it burrows into the earth with its claws, and makes an underground place to live in, and is nocturnal in its habits, sleeping by day.

Its subterranean, daylight-shunning lifestyle could explain the aardvark's success in eluding scientific detection prior to Kolbe's arrival in Cape Town. As for its appearance - why, surely one could be forgiven for suspecting this extraordinary creature to be nothing more than a figment of someone's over-indulged imagination, with no basis in reality? And sure enough, following the publication of Kolbe's book this is precisely the response that the aardvark did elicit, and from no less a person than Count Georges Louis Le Clerc de Buffon - probably the 18th Century's foremost zoological authority.

Discounting the aardvark as an impossible composite, Buffon refused to countenance any possibility that such a beast was genuine - until 1766. This was when he learned that a fellow naturalist, Peter Simon Pallas, had obtained further details from South Africa regarding the aardvark and had also presented it with that most cherished manifestation of zoological respectability, a scientific name. In 1795 it was renamed by Prof. E. Geoffroy Saint-Hilaire, and so it was that as *Orycteropus afer* ('African digging-foot'), the Dark Continent's enigmatic earth-pig finally, if somewhat belatedly, entered the zoological catalogue.

In due course, moreover, scientists discovered that the aardvark existed far beyond the confines of southern Africa. For example, in Ethiopia a shorter-headed form was found - with smaller ears, a longer thinner tail, and a sparser pelage. Known locally as *abu-delaf* ('Father of Nails'), this northern aardvark was initially deemed to comprise a separate species, and was christened *O. aethiopicus*. Similarly, a russet-furred aardvark with even smaller ears, formally described in 1906 from the Ituri Forest (in what is now the Democratic Congo) by Prof. Einar Lönnberg, was also looked upon at first as a species in its own right, and was dubbed *O. eriksonii*.

However, it is now known that the aardvark has a vast (albeit localised) distribution range throughout much of Africa south of the Sahara - stretching from this continent's southernmost tip to Senegambia in the west, the Somali Republic in the east, and Eritrea in the north. Consequently, the Ethiopian, Congolese, South African, and all other modern-day aardvarks are nowadays classed together by the majority of workers as a single species, *O. afer*, which is generally divided into as many as 18 subspecies.

In Search of an Identity -
Unravelling the Mystery of Milk Teeth and Tube Teeth

Once science had finally accepted that the aardvark did indeed exist, and was not a hoax, it was then posed with the problem of deciding the aardvark's precise nature. What exactly was this bizarre beast? What were its closest relatives among other mammals? Its composite appearance lent itself to a number of different possibilities, each of which attracted due consideration and controversy at some stage.

The aardvark's principal diet consists of termites (often termed 'white ants', even though they are quite unrelated to true ants), which it obtains in great quantities by ripping open termite hills with its formidable claws in a somewhat bear-like manner (which has earned it the alternative name of 'ant bear'). It snares the hapless insects upon its extremely long, vermiform tongue, liberally coated with sticky mucus and able to flick through the narrowest termite corridors within their demolished edifices.

All of this closely compares with the feeding behaviour of the familiar South American anteaters or vermilinguas ('worm-tongues'), and as the aardvark does bear a vague morphological resemblance to these mammals too, some zoologists stated that it must represent an Old World branch of the anteater family. This was subsequently dismissed, however, as further studies revealed that the anteaters were a peculiarly New World group, nurtured in South America during its many millions of years of isolation as an island continent (an isolation that finally ended with the end of the Pliocene 2 million years ago, when South America became connected to North America via the emergence from the seas of the Panamanian isthmus).

As for the aardvark's morphological similarities to the anteaters, these were due not to any taxonomic relationship, but rather to its parallel lifestyle. Even though aardvarks and anteaters are not closely related to each other, their lifestyles are very similar, so they have evolved into similar forms - a phenomenon termed convergent or parallel evolution.

Another theory put forward was that the aardvark was related to the scaly anteaters or pangolins. Zoogeographically, this had better prospects than the anteater suggestion, because pangolins are indeed found in Africa. Once again, however, it was later abandoned, because the aardvark's overall anatomy did not substantiate an affinity with pangolins.

Clearly, its insectivorous diet was responsible for leading zoologists hopelessly astray in their search for the aardvark's taxonomic identity - and then a school of thought arose that totally ignored dietary considerations, only to offer an identity that seemed even more implausible than those already presented! The English mam-

Aardvarks

malogist Dr Elliot Smith was startled to discover that the aardvark's cranial structure bore noticeable similarities to that of a fossil beast called *Phenacodus*, belonging to a taxonomic order of very primitive, long-extinct hoofed mammals (ungulates) called condylarths. Even the aardvark's bear-like claws appeared, when closely examined, to be little more than highly specialised hooves, modified for digging.

An ungulate with claws? A clawed hoofed mammal? It seemed a contradiction in terms, yet was by no means unprecedented. An entire family of horse-related clawed ungulates known as chalicotheres once existed, which are thought to have used their claws for digging up roots and other vegetation, and survived until as recently as the mid-Pleistocene (1 million years ago) in Africa, their last stronghold. Moreover, based upon certain reports of Kenya's famous mystery beast the Nandi bear, some zoologists cautiously retain hope that the Dark Continent may yet reveal the presence of a *living* chalicothere. South America also once harboured some clawed ungulates, including the notoungulates *Protypotherium* (an interatheriid) and *Homalodotherium*.

Nevertheless, the idea that the aardvark was a primitive hoofed mammal seemed so radical that many scientists were disinclined to accept it; instead, they sought to reveal its identity by more traditional means. One of the greatest zoological authorities of all time was the late-18th Century expert Baron Georges Cuvier, and such were his talents for taxonomy that he confidently claimed he could discern the precise relationship of any species of mammal merely from an examination of its dentition. "Show me your teeth, and I will tell you what you are," are words attributed to him, and his unparalleled success in mammalogical systematics was ample proof that this was no idle boast. Other researchers practised his methods, and it was proved beyond a doubt that the dentition of mammals was a most important key to deciphering their taxonomic affinities. Inevitably, therefore, it was not long before the aardvark's teeth received close scrutiny, in the hope that they would expose its true nature. In reality, however, all that they did expose was a fresh indication of the aardvark's omnipresent singularity.

No incisors or canine teeth are present, just 18-20 chewing teeth (premolars and molars); but unlike those of all other mammals, the adult aardvark's totally lack enamel crowns, as well as roots. Their internal structure is unique too - instead of containing a pulp cavity, each tooth comprises a series of closely-packed vertical tubes, numbering between 1000 and 1500. In short, these are not really teeth at all, but are simply teeth vestiges - the last remnants of normal teeth that have degenerated over the course of millions of years of evolution, as the aardvark became ever more specialised for an insectivorous existence (in which teeth were of minimal importance). Accordingly, it was impossible to deduce anything concerning the aardvark's taxonomic persuasion from its teeth, much to the growing despair of scientists worldwide.

A spark of hope momentarily flickered when, in 1890, British Museum mammalogist Oldfield Thomas revealed that young aardvarks possess milk teeth, lost by the adults. Perhaps these would offer a clue? As it turned out, each member of the largest, rearmost pair of these milk teeth does possess a crown and root, but otherwise their structure is still the baffling tubicolous arrangement that had become only too familiar to taxonomists, so Thomas's expectations were in vain after all (*Proceedings of the Royal Society*, January 1890).

The aardvark was utterly unclassifiable. True, it did seem to share some slight similarities with ungulates, but even these did not appear sufficiently strong to justify its categorisation within any of the already-established taxonomic orders of ungulates, living or extinct. Only one option remained - to erect a brand new order, with the aardvark as its sole occupant. And this is exactly what was done, even before Oldfield Thomas's disappointment regarding its milk teeth, when in 1872 Prof. Thomas Huxley chose the aardvark's most distinctive feature as the basis for its order's name - Tubulidentata ('tube-toothed').

Even today, more than 130 years later, this classification still stands, with the aardvark being deemed to represent an early offshoot from those ancestral ungulates the condylarths, an offshoot that has followed a completely independent, highly-specialised course of evolution ever since, totally removed from all other ungulate lines.

A Medieval Madagascan and a Native New Worlder?

Discussing the aardvark in *Living Mammals of the World* (1955), Ivan T. Sanderson wrote:

> *This creature...stands quite alone in the mammalian tree of life, like a single green leaf caught adventitiously on a spider's thread.*

As already seen above, this is indeed true relative to the present day - but it was not always so. Palaeontologists have uncovered at least 13 fossil species of aardvark, providing our single modern-day form with a lineage dating back many millions of years.

The earliest known aardvarks are *Myorycteropus africanus* and a very small species named *Orycteropus* (=*Myorycteropus?*) *minutus*, both of whose remains have been found in Kenya and date from the early Miocene epoch, around 20 million years ago. By the mid-Miocene, 10 million years later, other members of the modern-day aardvark genus, *Orycteropus*, had appeared. These include *O. seni* of Turkey, and *O. chemeldoi* from Kenya. During the late Miocene, Gaudry's aardvark *O. gaudryi* (the first fossil aardvark species ever described) could be found on the Mediterranean island of Samos, and was somewhat similar in form to Africa's living species but rather smaller in size, measuring a mere 3 ft or so in total length. A related Upper Miocene species, *O. browni*, has been described from Pakistan's Siwaliks, plus *O. mauritanicus*, native to Algeria.

Remains of other extinct *Orycteropus* aardvarks have been uncovered in areas as disparate as Africa (inhabited by *O. crassidens* during the Pleistocene epoch 2 million years ago, *O. djourabensis* from Chad's Pliocene, plus *O. abundulafus* during the late Upper Miocene in Chad and *Leptorycteropus guilielmi* of Kenya from that same period), southern France (home to *O. depereti* from the Lower Pliocene), and Turkey (*O. pottieri* of the Upper Miocene). Also on record are some intriguing pygmy aardvark remains from the Middle and Upper Miocene of southern Namibia. Quite evidently, then, the aardvark order had a much greater range in earlier ages than it does today.

True to form, however, just like their single living descendant the fossil aardvarks have not been without their taxonomic tribulations and controversies. Take, for example, the so-called Madagascan aardvark *Plesiorycteropus madagascariensis*, officially described by Filhol in 1895. Its remains have been disinterred from several deposits on the central plateau of Madagascar as well as in its western and southwestern portions, as documented fully by Dr Bryan Patterson in a detailed review of fossil aardvarks (*Bulletin of the Museum of Comparative Zoology, Harvard University*, 1975), and are only about a thousand years old. In other words, *Plesiorycteropus* persisted well into historic times.

What makes this particularly important is that *Plesiorycteropus* was notably different from the African aardvark - due to its smaller size (only as big as a small domestic dog) and shorter skull, its even more specialised teeth (lacking altogether, in fact, in some specimens), and also (judging from the structure of its limb bones) to the likelihood that it was capable of much more versatile movements. Indeed, *Plesiorycteropus* may not only have been able to dig, but also to jump and even to climb - talents far surpassing those of the rigidly terrestrial *Orycteropus*. All in all, *Plesiorycteropus* presents itself as a decidedly 'un-aardvark-like' aardvark – and for a very good reason.

In 1988, Duke University zoologist Dr R.D.E. Macphee aired the view that this unusual species was not an aardvark at all, and should perhaps be placed instead within the taxonomic order Insectivora, alongside the shrews, moles, hedgehogs, gymnures, and related families. Then in 1994, he decided that it was most closely allied to ungulates after all, but sufficiently distinct from any of them (including the aardvark) to warrant its own separate taxonomic order – which was duly created, and named Bibymalagasia. Hence this enigmatic species is now known colloquially as a bibymalagasy. Moreover, based upon skeletal remains retrieved from a central Madagascan site, a second bibymalagasy species has lately been described – *Plesiorycteropus germainepetterae*.

Perhaps the most contentious of all aardvark-associated fossil forms, however, at least for many years, was *Tubulodon taylori* - for two quite different reasons. First described in 1932, and allied by some researchers with the aardvark due to the comparable tubular structure of its teeth, its remains date back to the lower Eocene, just over 50 million years ago, thereby pre-dating *Myorycteropus* and earning for itself the status of the world's earliest-known aardvark - if, of course, it truly were an aardvark.

What made this latter issue so controversial was the locality in which *Tubulodon*'s remains were discovered. Namely, Wind River, Wyoming - in the U.S.A. No other aardvark fossils have ever been obtained in the New World, but if those of *Tubulodon* were definitely of tubulidentate affinity, their antecedence of all other such fossils would indicate that this entire order of mammals actually originated here, and not in the Old World after all. If so, then aardvarks presumably migrated into Africa and other Old World continents at some later date, by way of the various land-bridges formerly connecting North America to them.

It would be quite a revelation if the aardvark were eventually shown to be a native New Worlder - yet another paradox in the history of this most bemusing beast. In reality, however, such a revelation was not to be. Subsequent studies have reclassified *Tubulodon* as a member of the order Pholidota, represented today by the pangolins or scaly anteaters - though they, too, have no modern-day New World members. (Also, Pholidota itself has lately been reclassified, demoted to the level of sub-order within the otherwise entirely extinct mammalian order Cimolesta, which includes such long-demised mammals as the tillodonts, didelphodonts, pantodonts, and taeniodonts.)

Aardvarks in Ancient Egypt?

Notwithstanding its more proliferate past, nowadays the aardvark order is represented exclusively by *O. afer*. However, there are some tantalising clues from the realms of iconography and mythology to suggest that, not so very long ago, even this last remaining species had a greater distribution range than it does today - a range that may have extended as far north as Egypt.

As mentioned by Dr Jonathan Kingdon in *East African Mammals, Volume I* (1971), there is a pre-dynastic Egyptian vase on record that depicts a number of unusual animals readily identifiable as aardvarks, thereby implying that in early historical times this creature ranged northwards as far as the Mediterranean region. Of course, a perfectly plausible alternative explanation for this vase's images is that they were inspired by descriptions of aardvarks - recounted back home in Egypt by some of that country's great travellers in those long-departed times, travellers who may well have journeyed through the aardvark's tropical African territory far beyond the southern limits of Egypt. However, there is another, equally thought-provoking piece of evidence favouring the existence of aardvarks in Egypt during historical times.

Set (Seth), one of the more significant deities of ancient Egyptian mythology, was usually depicted as a strange-looking creature whose specific zoological identity has still to be conclusively determined by scientists. Its most noticeable features were a long tubular snout, large upstanding ears, and a thick, rigidly-held tail. As discussed by H. TeVelde in his authoritative work *Seth, God of Confusion* (1967), a vast and varied spectrum of animals have been considered as likely (and unlikely) candidates for the Set beast's identity.

These range from the giraffe, hyaena, jerboa, camel, jackal, and electric elephant-trunk fish (mormyrid), to the crocodile, gazelle, hippopotamus, fennec fox, certain snakes and birds, ass, and wild boar. Intriguingly, following directly on the heels of its formal scientific discovery in 1901, even the okapi was offered up, by Dr A. Wiedermann (*Orientalistische Literaturzeitung*, 1902), as a possible explanation for this cryptic creature. And more recently, Michigan scientist Dr Michael D. Swords proposed that it may have been some mysterious form of dog still unknown to zoology (*Cryptozoology*, 1985). There is also one other candidate - the aardvark.

The description of the Set beast's head and tail certainly compares well with this distinctive animal. Moreover, according to Egyptian mythology the Set beast devoured the moon each month while assuming the guise of a large black boar; it was associated with the desert and desert life; and its rough skin was likened to the short-haired hide of an ass.

If briefly spied in moonlight during one of its predominantly nocturnal forays, the aardvark might well seem to resemble a large, dark-coloured pig-like beast; in the more arid expanses of its range, it does inhabit sandy desert-like stretches; and its skin is certainly rough, and clothed only with relatively short hair. All in all, there is more than sufficient accord between the Set beast and the aardvark to justify giving serious attention to the candidature of *Orycteropus* as a plausible contender for the identity of Set's arcane animal - which in turn lends important support for the likelihood that the aardvark did indeed exist in Egypt until at least as recently as the era of ancient Egypt's mighty civilisation.

Ant Bears, Nandi Bears, and a Verisimilitude of Vermilinguas?

Not only is the aardvark already a very sizeable mammalian mystery in itself, it may also be an unintentional participant in an even bigger one.

For countless decades, Western explorers and settlers in eastern Africa have heard tell from natives of a large and reputedly ferocious beast supposedly still unknown to science, and on occasion they have even apparently encountered it themselves. Bristling with all manner of different local names (including the chemosit, kerit, and gadett), in English this greatly-feared mystery beast is most commonly referred to as the Nandi bear, because rumours and stories concerning it are particularly prevalent in Kenya's Nandi region, and it is said by some to resemble a bear.

In *On the Track of Unknown Animals* (1958), Dr Bernard Heuvelmans carefully analysed a wide selection of Nandi bear reports, and came to the conclusion that several different, quite unrelated species of animal were collectively responsible for them. This was because the beasts described in the reports were far too dissimilar from one another in morphology and behaviour to be feasibly explained by any *single* animal species - known or unknown.

The principal components in the Nandi bear saga appear to be: all-black male specimens of the bear-like ratel (honey badger) *Mellivora capensis*; very large hyaenas, possibly aberrantly-coloured specimens or even the supposedly extinct short-faced hyaena *Pachycrocuta brevirostris*; extremely large baboons; the nefarious activities of native witch-doctors; and, just possibly, a surviving species of chalicothere, which, although not carnivorous, would resemble some of the unidentified beasts included within the heterogeneous Nandi bear category. Furthermore, judging from an extraordinary encounter documented in Charles T. Stoneham's *Hunting Wild Beasts With Rifle And Camera* (1933), it seems likely that at least one other creature has made an occasional contribution to the Nandi bear melange too.

The scene was one evening at Stoneham's trading station at Sotik, on the edge of Kenya's Lumbwa Reserve, when, after hearing a noise, Stoneham left his hut and gazed through the mist towards what seemed to be an approaching animal of undetermined form. Standing upwind of the animal and concealed by the mist and tall grass all around, Stoneham viewed the oncoming beast with great interest, knowing that it was unaware of his presence, and wondering what it could be. When it was within a dozen paces of him, the creature paused. Suddenly, the moon appeared from behind the clouds and illuminated it, revealing at last the appearance of Stoneham's unexpected visitor:

> *I received a dreadful shock. The beast was like nothing I had ever seen or imagined. It had a huge square head, and the snout of a pig; its eyes, two black spots, were fixed upon me in an observant stare. Large circular ears, the size of plates, stood up from its head, and they were transparent - I could see the grass through them. The creature's body was covered with coarse brown hair, its tail was the size of a tree trunk. There is an anteater in Kenya, a survival of the age when the cave bear and the woolly rhinoceros roamed the earth, but this beast, though like to that rare species, was not of it.*

After hearing his account, Stoneham's friends informed him that he must have seen a Nandi bear, but he believed that he saw "...some weird, hybrid ant-eater".

Needless to say, and as Heuvelmans recognised in his own coverage of this incident, Stoneham's account can be readily dismissed as merely a somewhat dramatic description of an aardvark. Its nocturnal lifestyle and noticeably shy, retiring nature ensure that the aardvark is rarely seen, hence an unexpected encounter with one of these extraordinary-looking animals may well come as a great shock to anyone not previously acquainted with it.

In any case, true anteaters (or, more correctly, vermilinguas) are exclusively Neotropical and belong to the order Xenarthra - which makes the following item especially intriguing. An early 20th Century explorer widely known as 'Stany' (in reality, the Marquis of Chatteleux) penned a series of travel memoirs collectively entitled *Loin des Sentiers Battus*, charting his journeys through the Dark Continent and containing some strange cryptozoological claims.

One of the most curious of these appeared in the first volume of his memoirs, published in 1951, in which he referred to a constant four-legged companion called Honoré, which he supposedly captured alive in Africa. What makes Honoré so amazing is that Stany categorically stated that he was a giant anteater *Myrmecophaga tridactyla* - a species endemic to South America! Even Stany's description of Honoré corresponded perfectly with this New World novelty. Accordingly, Dr Heuvelmans wrote to him for further details, politely questioning his identification of Honoré, and wondering (if his pet were indeed an anteater) whether he might have purchased Honoré from some importer of Brazilian beasts at an African port. However, in his letters of reply to Heuvelmans, dated 17 November 1953 and 9 December 1953 respectively, Stany unequivocally reiterated that Honoré was not an aardvark but a bona fide anteater, which he had personally caught in the African wilds. Nevertheless, as Stany's memoirs are far from reliable on other zoological matters, it seems safe to assume that whatever Honoré was and wherever he originated, he was not a native African representative of the vermilinguas.

Of Pigs and Pumpkins (but not Forgetting the Dodo!)

The burrowing skills of the aardvark are renowned and unrivalled among large mammals. It can readily outdig a 10-strong team of men, and as its immediate reaction to danger is to dig downward with all speed whenever possible, it is hardly surprising that this remarkable creature is extremely difficult to capture. Its burrow can be as long as 9-12 ft, and is usually about 16 in wide, with a rounded chamber at the innermost end where the aardvark spends its days asleep, and where the female gives birth to her single offspring each year in mid-autumn. Every eight days thereafter for the next six months, the female digs a new burrow and shares it with her baby; at the age of six months, the young aardvark begins digging burrows of its own.

Aardvark burrows are in demand not only from aardvarks but also from a surprising range of unrelated creatures, such as assorted owls, pythons, mongooses, lizards, hares, and even hyaenas. Others include the ant-eating chat *Myrmecocichla formicivora* (a species of thrush), the common slit-faced bat *Nycteris thebaica*, and, in particular, that pulchritudinally-challenged wild pig known as the wart-hog *Phacochoerus aethiopicus*.

Whereas many of the previous species listed above often inhabit aardvark burrows on a strictly temporary basis (sometimes merely as momentary hideouts in which to escape from a pursuing predator, or as sanctuaries in which to survive the terrible onslaught of a raging bush fire), the wart-hog looks upon them as highly desirable longterm residences, with entire families swiftly assuming possession once the burrows' original owners have abandoned them to move elsewhere. Indeed, so popular are these with wart-hogs that a good way of seeking such structures is to keep a lookout for a wart-hog family - because wherever there is a family of these pigs, the chances are that an aardvark burrow is not far away.

An even more unexpected but equally reliable indicator of abandoned aardvark burrows is the presence of a certain species of gourd-like plant called *Cucumis humifructus* - variously known locally (and for good reason) as the aardvark pumpkin or aardvark cucumber. Although the aardvark subsists principally upon termites and other insects, scientists have learned from various native tribes (after traditionally disbelieving their testimony as folklore!) that in arid areas, where water is scarce, it will consume the juicy underground fruits of this plant if encountered during its burrowing.

The aardvark is a clean animal as far as its own dwelling place is concerned, choosing not to defaecate inside its burrows but rather to deposit its droppings just outside, after which it buries them. As these naturally contain the seeds of *C. humifructus*, in due course the latter germinate, ultimately maturing into adult plants and marking the location of the aardvark's burrows. In fact, it seems that the time spent

South American giant anteater

passing through the aardvark's gut actually increases the seeds' fertility, thus providing a noteworthy example of a plant intimately dependent upon the action of a single species of animal for its survival and propagation.

Curiously enough, a markedly similar case to this is one that involved a tree and a very extraordinary bird. The reason for speaking of this case in the past tense is that the bird in question is now extinct - for it was none other than the famous dodo *Raphus cucullatus* of Mauritius. The case first came to attention in the mid-1970s, when botanists realised that one of Mauritius's native species of tree, *Calvaria major*, was now represented by no more than 13 living specimens - and all of these were over 300 years old, dating back to the very time of the dodo's extinction in the late 17th Century. Just a coincidence?

What was particularly curious about this situation was that these last surviving trees still produced perfectly-formed fruit, but the seeds never germinated. Indeed, judging from the synchrony of dates in relation to the dodo's extinction and the age of the living *Calvaria* trees, no such seeds had germinated since the death of the dodos. American biologist Stanley Temple was greatly intrigued by this mystifying affair, and pondered over the possibility that there was some direct but currently undisclosed link between the dodo and *Calvaria*. The seeds of *Calvaria* were encased within extremely thick, tough shells, and it was this feature that set him on the trail of their mystery's solution. Perhaps the seeds needed some external assistance to escape from their encapsulating shells - and perhaps it was the dodo that had traditionally provided that assistance. But how?

Temple was well-versed in dodo anatomy, which seemed to offer a reasonable answer to that question. The dodo had possessed a very powerful gizzard - a portion of the upper section of the gut in many birds, used for grinding up hard material. If it had included *Calvaria* fruit in its diet, the tough shells of the seeds would have been broken up when passing through its gizzard, thereby permitting the seeds to germinate when defaecated or regurgitated by the dodo. It all seemed to fit - but as there were no longer any dodos, how could Temple put his theory to the test?

By improvising - which in this instance involved the force-feeding of *Calvaria* seeds to a congregation of turkeys, which have similar gizzards to that of the dodo. When the variously excreted and vomited seeds were collected and planted, the dramatic result was the successful germination of three *Calvaria* seedlings. It has been claimed that these were the very first seedlings germinated since the dodo's extinction almost three centuries earlier.

In fact, although Temple's may have been the first to have received germination stimulation via avian gizzard abrasion since the dodo's demise, success in germinating *Calvaria* seeds without abrasion has also been achieved, but only rarely. It seems likely, therefore, that abrasion, although not obligatory, does enhance germination in *Calvaria* (also called the tambalacoque). Certainly, botanists today use turkeys, as well as gem-polishers, to erode the seeds' shells (endocarp) and thus stimulate germination (*Plant Science Bulletin*, vol. 50, 2004).

From Superstition to Super-Hero

It is inevitable that any creature as distinctive and mysterious as the aardvark should have inspired its fair share of native folklore and superstition, but like everything else concerning this bizarre beast, one of its most memorable contributions is nothing if not idiosyncratic.

To the witch-doctors of the Hausa people from West Africa, the aardvark is a very magical creature known as *dabgi*, whose nails, heart, and the skin of its brow are of great value to them when concocting a charm much sought-after by passionate paramours. Once the aardvark ingredients are ground up with the root of a certain tree, the resulting powder is wrapped up in another piece of pelt, and is secured against the purchaser's chest.

According to Hausa lore, the purchaser is now endowed with the useful ability to enter the private room of his lover without needing to seek her father's permission - all that he has to do is sit upon her roof, and he will instantly pass through it safely and silently. Similarly, a thief owning one of these aardvark amulets needs only to lean upon the wall of the house that he wishes to plunder amid the all-concealing darkness of evening, and the wall will very conveniently part, enabling him to pass through unseen and unheard by the house's owner.

And finally: if Africa's insectivorous ant bear makes an implausible ferocious Nandi bear, what can we say about the aardvark as a suave, macho super-hero? In fact, since the late 1970s this highly unlikely transformation has been very much a reality - thanks to a quite wonderful comic-book monthly by Dave Sim, entitled Cerebus.

Published by Aardvark-Vanaheim and commencing in 1978, its eponymous star is a laconic tubulidentate of short limbs and even shorter temper, given to saving the world (not to mention his own skin) at regular intervals, and all without ever needing a single top-up of termites!

The history of the aardvark is one of unparalleled paradox and perplexity. From milk teeth to tube teeth, misleading Madagascans to enigmatic Egyptians, ant bears to Nandi bears, and even from cucumbers to comic-book heroes, at every turn the aardvark effortlessly underlines its startling singularity, and, above all else, it emphasises its pre-eminent claim to be recognised as the most mysterious mammal alive today.

Chapter Two
The Curious Case of the Crowing Crested Cobra

A beast over which controversy rages at this moment is the 'crowing crested cobra', which, the natives say, is a snake, like a cobra, with a crest on its head and a loud, distinct cry like the crow of a cock.

Captain William Hichens - *Discovery* (December 1937)

Judging from Hichens's description, the above mystery beast must bear a close resemblance to the popular conception of a cockatrice - that mythical, cockscomb-crested, crowing serpent derived from an egg laid by a cockerel and hatched by a toad. Yet whereas the cockatrice is wholly fictional, a fabulous beast of Western legend, the existence of the crowing crested cobra is vehemently affirmed not only by native tribes spanning much of East and Central Africa, but also by a number of the Dark Continent's Western explorers, travellers, and settlers - notwithstanding the fact that by all the traditional tenets of herpetology, such a creature is a zoological impossibility.

Distribution, Description, and Lifestyle

Possibly the first Western account of this mysterious reptile was a short description included in Horace Waller's *The Last Journals of David Livingstone, vol. II* (1874), but many others have appeared since then. One of the most detailed is that of Dr J. Shircore, writing in 1944 from Karonga, Nyasaland (now Malawi), in *African Affairs,* which brings together much of what has been reported on this subject.

The alleged distribution of the crowing crested cobra is quite immense, covering some 800,000 square miles, from Natal northwards to Victoria Nyanza, and westwards to Lake Tanganyika and Zambia, and the Indian Ocean. Over this huge territory, it has acquired many names by the various tribes present. These names include: *bubu* (as noted by Livingstone) at Shupanga on the Lower Zambezi, *inkhomi* ('the killer') in Chi-ngoni and Chi-nkhonde, *hongo* in Chi-ngindo, *kovoko* in Kinyamwezi, *ngoshe* in Chi-wemba, *songo* in Chi-yao (Malawi), and *mbobo* by Zimbabwe natives. Also, in his checklist of apparently unknown animals (*Cryptozoology,* 1986), Dr Bernard Heuvelmans noted that it was referred to as *n'gok-wiki* by the Baya of the Central African Republic. And oddly, as reported by Henri Lhote and Helfried Weyer in their book *Sahara* (1980), there are even stories that this vast desert houses pythons with hairy necks!

Most recently, during the CFZ's 'The J.T. Downes Memorial Gambia Expedition 2006', the expedition team learned that the *ninki-nanka*, a reptilian Gambian mystery beast hitherto thought to be dragonesque in form, was actually likened by the locals to a huge crested snake.

The names may be different, but its description is fairly constant. Reputed to measure up to 20 ft (thus exceeding the dreaded king cobra or hamadryad *Ophiophagus hannah),* the crowing crested cobra is said to be a very formidable and extremely ferocious, vicious species, usually buff-brown or greyish-black but with a scarlet face, and of arboreal inclination despite its great size. Its 'cobra' appellation is something of a misnomer, as it does not possess a hood.

Instead, and distinguishing it instantly from all known snakes, it allegedly bears a prominent bright-red crest, resembling a cockscomb but projecting forwards rather than backwards. Both sexes have this crest, but the male additionally sports a conspicuous pair of red facial wattles, enhancing its similarity to a cockerel. The greatest correspondence between the latter fowl and this extraordinary snake, however, arises from the male's astonishing ability (according to eye-witness accounts) to crow loudly, just like a farmyard rooster! And to complete this remarkable parallel, the female apparently emits a hen-like clucking sound. In addition, both sexes can produce a distinctive warning note, best represented as *chu-chu-chu-chu,* repeated rapidly several times.

Just as curious as its appearance is its diet, for according to Shircore this huge snake subsists upon an almost exclusive diet of maggots, obtained from the dead bodies of other animals. Moreover, it reputedly kills animals for the express purpose of consuming the maggots that will emerge from eggs (laid by flies) present on the rotting carcasses - a trait, incidentally, also noted for certain smaller snakes, and even some rodents and cuckoos. Nevertheless, in view of its enormous size, it is highly unlikely that the crowing crested cobra could thrive solely upon maggots, and in his own account of this extraordinary creature in *Les Derniers Dragons d'Afrique* (1978), Heuvelmans notes that according to vet Dr Dennis A. Walker, specimens sighted in Southern Rhodesia (now Zimbabwe) prey upon hyraxes, those diminutive rodent-like hoofed mammals related to elephants. Walker also mentioned that in addition to their arboreal tendencies, these snakes could be found among kopjes (hillocks) and large rocks.

And if the huge red-crested serpent reported from the Congo region by animal collector Charles Cordier (*Zoo,* April 1973) is one and the same as the crowing crested cobra described from elsewhere, this mystery snake may also have aquatic inclinations, because the Congolese version can be found stretched out on trees alongside riverbanks.

The exceptional appearance of this huge but scientifically unrecognised serpent may be more than enough in itself to terrify anyone encountering it unexpectedly, but the principal reason for the absolute horror that it incites among the native tribes is due to the devastating combination of its unnerving willingness to attack people at the slightest provocation, and its deadly venom - so potent that a bite is supposedly followed almost instantaneously by death. According to Shircore, its usual mode of attack is to remain concealed upon branches overhanging a path, and then to lunge downwards at the head or face of any unwary person walking by underneath. Indeed, its Chi-yao name, *songo,* translates as 'that which strikes downwards and pricks the head'. Some natives have sought to safeguard themselves against its lethal onslaughts by carrying pots of boiling water on their heads when journeying through forested areas said to be inhabited by this highly dangerous creature; if the snake should then strike, it would burn or kill itself.

Interestingly, in his *Memories of a Game-Ranger* (1948), Harry Wolhuter recalled that some southern African natives tell of a similar mystery snake, crested and vocal, called the *muhlambela,* and measuring almost 12ft long. It too strikes at the heads of the unwary. However, its voice is a deer-like bleat rather than a cock-crow, and its crest is composed of feathers (though this odd feature may in reality have a surprisingly prosaic explanation, as will be explained a little later).

Some Identities and Some Relics

All of the above seems so fantastic, so nightmarish, that it should come as no surprise to learn that many zoologists are very sceptical as to whether such a macabre, phantasmagorical serpent as the crowing crested cobra could truly exist, still awaiting formal discovery and description by science. Surely it must be merely a particularly graphic example of primitive superstition and imagination, with no basis in corporeal reality? This issue has inspired heated debate, but has yet to be resolved.

Former game warden Lieutenant Colonel Charles R.S. Pitman believed the crowing crested cobra to be a non-existent composite entity, 'created' from the erroneous lumping together of reports appertaining to various totally different snakes. In his *Report on a Faunal Survey of Northern Rhodesia* (1934), Pitman stated that the Gaboon viper *Bitis gabonica* and the rhinoceros viper *B. nasicornis* (two highly venomous horned vipers inhabiting Zambia) have strikingly coloured heads, in keeping with the brightly hued face attributed to the crowing crested cobra. Furthermore, he noted that in Kawambwa the Gaboon viper is oddly claimed to be the

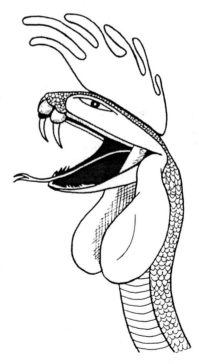

My reconstruction of the crowing crested cobra, as based upon eyewitness accounts

'crested snake which crows' (even though it isn't, and doesn't).

Pitman also noted that the natives inhabiting parts of the Barotse Valley allege that the male black mamba *Dendroaspis polylepis,* another deadly species, has a crest and is capable of crowing. Although the latter ability has yet to be proven, there is some truth in their allegations regarding a crest. In *African Wild Life* (December 1961), Umtali Museum worker Donald C. Broadley recorded that an old mamba sometimes experiences difficulty in shedding the skin on its head, pieces sticking to its nape instead of peeling off; after successive unsatisfactory sloughings, a distinct ruff or crest of unshed skin is thus acquired. Several 'crested' snakes caught for identification have proven to be black mambas adorned in this way - including a monstrous 14.5ft specimen described by the natives as bearing feathers on its head (explaining the *muhlambela*?), shot by J.A.W. Bennetts in Natal (*African Wild Life,* 1956). Also, in his *Last Journals,* Livingstone suggested that the *bubu* was the black mamba; and F.W. Fitzsimons noted in *Snakes* (1932) that black mambas in trees do lunge down at the heads of people below.

So could it be that the crowing crested cobra is nothing more than a confusion or conceptual pot-pourri of the most poisonous formally recognized snakes encountered by tribes in East and Central Africa? A wholly symbolic representation of all that they fear most in serpentine form, rather than a valid, distinct, flesh-and-blood species?

Without any complete or partial remains of crowing crested cobras, this hypothesis is quite tenable - however, some sundry remains of this extraordinary creature do appear to have been obtained. At the time of his report, Shircore owned what he believed to be the bony skeleton of the fleshy cockscomb, and a portion of the neck (containing several vertebrae), from one of these snakes. Describing the cockscomb:

> *Its skeleton consists of a thin lanceolate plate of bone (1.5 ins long by 0.5 in wide, at its broadest part) with a markedly rounded smooth ridge, 0.5 in wide, slightly overhanging both sides of the upper border, with a distinct voluted curve to the left. The lower border is sharp-edged and faintly ridged. The lateral surfaces are concave, throughout the long diameter. The whole fragment is eminently constructed for the insertion and attachment of muscles - much the same as the structure of the breast-bone of a bird. Some skin, part of which, spread smoothly above the base of the plate, on one side, is red in colour: and attached to the lower angle is a dark wrinkled bit, which appears to be a remnant of the head-skin - all of which should be valuable for purposes of identification. A small portion of the bone, tapering towards both ends, 0.5 in long by 0.5 in wide, is missing from the lower anterior border, including the tip - it was broken off for use as medicine by the witch-doctor, from whom the specimens were obtained.*

This structure is clearly something more than an artifact of unshed skin, and bearing in mind that its description is from the pen of a medical doctor, trained in meticulous scientific observation, we can have no doubt regarding its accuracy. As to the identity of the species from which these remains originated, no zoologist has so far reconciled them with any species currently known to science.

Shircore's report took the form of two notes, the second written some time later than the first, after which both were submitted to *African Affairs* and published as one. The above description appeared in the first note, but in the second he recorded that he had since obtained two further preserved specimens. One, from a relatively small crowing crested cobra, consisted of five lumbar vertebra, which were 7mm long and 5mm wide, with the concave, articulating face 2mm from top to bottom and 3mm across; two ribs 26mm in length along the curve; a 10 x 8mm piece of skin; and the laterally flattened, granular-textured skin-tip of its crest, measuring 6

Frilled lizard in threatening posture

mm long and 3mm wide at its base. The second specimen was a single dorsal vertebra, said to have been obtained from the remains of a huge crowing crested cobra that had killed a man; the vertebra's articulating surfaces measured an impressive 8 x 9mm.

Another very noteworthy report is that of John Knott (*African Wild Life,* September 1962). Driving home from Binga, in the Kariba area of Southern Rhodesia, during the end of May 1959, Knott accidentally ran over a large, jet-black snake measuring 6.5-7ft long. The snake was mortally wounded, so that, although still alive, it was incapable of escape or attack when Knott stepped out of his Land Rover to investigate. He was very surprised to discover that the snake bore a distinct crest on its head, perfectly symmetrical and capable of being erected by way of five internal prop-like structures.

This description recalls a very peculiar Australian reptile known as the frilled lizard *Chlamydosaurus kingii.* The first sighting of this species by a Westerner was made on 8 October 1820 by Allan Cunningham at Careening Bay, Port Nelson, in Western Australia. As he recounted in P.P. King's *Narrative of a Survey of the Intertropical and Western Coasts of Australia Between the Years 1818 and 1822* (1827):

> *I secured a lizard of extraordinary appearance, which had perched itself upon the stem of a small decayed tree. It had a curious crenated membrane like a ruff or tippet around its neck, which it spreads five inches in the form of an open umbrella.*

This lizard is totally harmless, eluding predators by sprinting away bipedally like a miniature dinosaur. If cornered, however, it expands its bizarre frill as a shock tactic. Interestingly, this frill is erected by means of bony structures extending into it from the lizard's mouth, thereby expanding whenever the mouth is opened wide. A comparable structural arrangement, operated by muscles attached to the prop-like components observed by Knott, could mobilize the crest of the crowing crested cobra.

So deadly a beast as this snake obviously does not inspire willingness on the part of natives to capture specimens for scientific study - a plausible enough reason for the scarcity of remains. However, there is another important reason for that. According to Shircore, this species is very closely associated with snake-worship by certain tribes (especially those referring to it as *inkhomi*). Its skin and crest are prized by its worshippers, and other parts of its body are essential ingredients for many charms and medical potions utilized in tribal witchcraft and witch-doctor activity.

Consequently, whenever such a snake is killed, its remains rarely if ever fall readily into the hands of anyone outside these tribes, Of course, if some ardent anthropologist were to serve an apprenticeship in one of these cults, he may then be given access to remains of this snake - but whether, under these conditions, he would ever be granted the opportunity to apply any scientific analysis to them is another matter entirely.

Judging from the above accounts, the crowing crested cobra would indeed seem to be real and distinct, at least on morphological grounds. But what about its strangest characteristic of all, its ability to crow? Is that genuine too, or is it unadulterated fantasy? Before attempting to examine this issue, let us first consider one further and extremely intriguing aspect of the crowing crested cobra case - the existence of a remarkable parallel to it many thousands of miles away.

Caribbean Counterparts

In his book *The Romance of Natural History, Second Series* (1867), naturalist Philip H. Gosse reported that a peculiar snake, wholly unknown to science, apparently existed on certain of the islands in the West Indies chain. Except for its much shorter length, this snake bears an uncanny resemblance to Africa's crowing crested cobra. In 1845-46, Gosse visited Jamaica, and while there:

> *I heard accounts of a wonderful animal occasionally seen in the eastern districts of the island, which was reported as a Snake with a cock's comb and wattles, and which crowed like a cock.*

Sounds familiar, doesn't it?

Yet surprisingly, in complete contrast to the attention attracted by Africa's crowing crested cobra, the Caribbean's counterpart seemed afterwards to sink into obscurity. In an attempt to rectify that sad situation, this chapter will provide all of the eyewitness accounts cited by Gosse in his book.

He received his first from a medical man of repute, who informed Gosse that:

> *...he had seen, in 1829, a serpent of about four feet in length, but of unwonted thickness, dull ochry in colour with well-defined dark spots, having on its head a sort of pyramidal helmet, somewhat lobed at the summit, of a pale red hue. The animal, however, was dead, and decomposition was already setting in. He informed me that the negroes of the district were well acquainted with it; and that they represented it as making a noise, not unlike the crowing of a cock, and as being addicted to preying on poultry.*

This remarkable reptile has also been recorded from the island of Hispaniola (Santo Domingo), where one of Gosse's friends, Richard Hill, learned of it. According to Gosse, when visiting one of his Spanish acquaintances in Haiti, Hill had been informed by him that he had seen one of these snakes in that country's far eastern section:

> *My friend's Spanish informant had seen the serpent with mandibles like a bird, with a cock's crest, with scarlet lobes or wattles; and he described its habits, - perhaps rather from common fame than from personal observation, - as a frequenter of hen-roosts, into which it would thrust its head, and deceive the young chickens by its imitative physiognomy, and by its attempts to crow, like their own Chanticleer. 'Il canta como un Gallo,' was*

the report in Hayti, just as in Jamaica.

Before Gosse's return to Europe, a Jamaican resident, Jasper Cargill, offered a sovereign for a specimen of this snake that he could present to Gosse. Unfortunately, Cargill was not successful in obtaining one, but Hill was later able to send Gosse details of two encounters with this snake in relation to Cargill, though no specimen was preserved on either occasion. The first had involved Cargill himself, some years before Gosse's visit to Jamaica:

> *...when visiting Skibo, in St. George's, an estate of his father's, in descending the mountain-road, his attention was drawn to a snake of a dark hue, that erected itself from amid some fragments of limestone-rock that lay about. It was about* four feet *long, and unusually* thick-bodied. *His surprise was greatly increased on perceiving that it was crested, and that from the side of the cheeks depended some* red-coloured flaps, *like gills or wattles. After gazing at him intently some time, with its head well erect, it drew itself in, and disappeared among the fragmentary rocks.*

Cargill's second account concerned an incident involving his son, which took place on or around 30 March 1850. According to Hill:

> *...some youngsters of the town came running to tell me of a curious snake, unlike any snake they had ever seen before, which young Cargill had shot, when out for a day's sport among the woodlands of a neighbouring penn. They described it as in all respects a serpent, but with a very curious shaped head, and with wattles on each side of its jaws. After taking it in hand and looking at it, they placed it in a hollow tree, intending to return for it when they should be coming home, but they had strolled from the place so far that it was inconvenient to retrace their steps when wearied with rambling.*

As it happened, one of the youths did return the following morning, but although he was sure that he had found the correct tree, there was no sign of the snake's body, leading him to conjecture that it had been taken by rats during the night. When this incident was recounted to Mr Hill, his godson Ulick Ramsay came to him to inform him that he too had spied such a snake only a short time earlier:

> *...not long previously, he had seen in the hand of the barrack-master-serjeant at the barracks in Spanish Town, a curious snake, which he, too, had shot among the rocks of a little line of eminences near the railway, about two miles out, called Craigallechie. It was a serpent with a curious shaped head, and projections on each side, which he likened to the fins of an eel, but said that they were close up to the jaws.*

That was the last report cited by Gosse. What are we to make of these Greater Antillean anomalies? Certainly they all seem to refer to the same species, but, just as certainly, one that is not recognized by science. Of course, it would be tempting to postulate that these West Indian reports are nothing more than derivations of the

African crowing crested cobra beliefs, resettled in these islands along with all of the other folklore and superstitions conveyed here by the countless African natives who were mercilessly transported from their homes as slaves during those terrible years of the slave trade period.

However, this cannot be the explanation, as such snakes have also been reported by Western observers, some of high standing (remember the well-respected medical man on Jamaica?). In fact, there is no greater reason for disbelieving the reports of West Indian crowing crested serpents than for disbelieving those of their African counterparts. All of this leads us again to that most fundamental obstacle to accepting such snakes' existence (whether in Africa or the Antilles). Namely, their much acclaimed ability to crow like a cockerel.

A Samoan Surprise

In the May 2007 edition of his online *BioFortean Review* journal, American crypto-zoologist Chad Arment revealed an additional, unexpected example of a crowing snake – reported from the Samoan island of Savai'i. Arment notes that at least two authors have referred to the existence here of such a serpent. One of these was Albert Barnes Steinberger. In his *Report on Samoa* (1874), he stated:

I saw the first reptiles in the islands at the village of Asou, in Savaii, and there learned of the 'crowing snake,' (Vivimi gata.) It is the subject of native songs. The testimony of both whites and natives points directly to the fact that they have a snake which crows like a cock. I did not see or hear one. The apparent physical impossibility of such an anomaly made me skeptical, but the unequivocal testimony of the missionaries to the existence of such a reptile seems too strong to be rejected.

Author #2 was Consul-General James H. Mulligan, who, in his *Consul Reports* for May 1896, commented as follows regarding this curious reptile:

There are persons whom I should regard as reliable, who stoutly maintain the existence in these islands of a very large serpent, which gives out a noise somewhat like the crowing of a cock - a serpent which I have heard spoken of as a crowing snake. Other persons of long residence speak of it as a myth. A party of labourers at work in a clearing near this town, not long since, were scattered by the appearance of a large serpent, which swung itself from the branch of one tree to that of another. The men united in the assertion that it made a crowing sound, was of enormous size, and moved with great rapidity. I vouch for none of these assertions, but give them for what they are worth; but the existence of the crowing snake is by some held to as firmly in Samoa as it is by others abroad believed to belong in these islands.

Apart from the apparent absence of a cockscomb and wattles (none is mentioned in these reports), this very vocal Samoan mystery snake is certainly more than a little reminiscent of the crowing serpents documented above in this chapter.

There is also a traditional legend of a crowing snake in the independent Pacific island state of Palau.

A Chinese Example?

There may even be a Sinian crowing crested cobra. In an email to me concerning various Chinese cryptids, former Chinese resident Paul B. Lu (now living in Spokane, Washington, USA) referred to 'rooster-crest snakes' of Shen Nong Jia. He also stated: "My grandma told me her mother's story of how such a snake was found in a local 'Tu Di' (earth god) temple in the rural Nanjing, Jiangsui Province, the snake didn't hiss, but sounded like [a] chicken, the locals thought it has a crest because it was old". This is of course reminiscent of old African mambas with crests.

Snakes that Bleat, Bellow, Purr, Bark, Cough ...and Chime!

The familiar hissing sounds of snakes are produced by air being forced through the glottis (the opening from the back of the throat's pharynx into the windpipe); the pitch of the hiss is controlled by the width of the glottis's aperture. In addition, as I learnt from Colin McCarthy, herpetological expert at the British Museum (Natural History), there are certain species, such as the North American bull snake *Pituophis melanoleucus,* with an unusually well-developed glottis flap (epiglottis) that increases these sounds as air is blown against it. Indeed, so effective is this that the bull snake's bovine grunt (earning it its name) can be heard up to 100ft away. But what about genuine cock-crows?

In his earlier-mentioned report on North Rhodesian fauna, Lt. Col. Charles Pitman offered a singularly original and quite unforgettable explanation - postulating as the likely answer what must surely be the most macabre form of ventriloquism ever conceived!

According to Pitman, in those incidents on record featuring a snake that seemed to its bemused observer to be crowing, the snake was not actually making the sounds itself; on the contrary, the sounds were the screams of a prey victim that the snake was in the act of swallowing alive! In support of this ghoulish hypothesis, in his book *A Game Warden Takes Stock* (1942) Pitman cited the case of an African naturalist who suddenly heard a strange squeaking cry nearby, and discovered to his great surprise that it was coming from a rhombic night adder *Causus rhombeatus* in the middle of a heap of stones. To his even greater surprise, he found that the adder contained a small toad, engulfed so recently that it was still alive, and which, in Pitman's opinion, was unquestionably responsible for the peculiar cries issuing from the adder's mouth.

Yet even if such an imaginative theory could be stretched to explain every single report of snakes that crow (which is itself highly unlikely, as the possibility of frequent encounters with snakes engaged in the very act of swallowing screaming prey victims must surely rate as exceedingly slim!) it is still unsatisfactory - because crowing cries are by no means the only unexpected type of sound to have been reported from African (and other) snakes. Also on file are accounts of snakes that bleat, roar, bellow, cough, purr, bark, and even emit metallic bell-like sounds.

A representative series of examples was provided during the interesting interchanges published in London's *The Times* newspaper during the latter half of 1929. It began on 22 August, with a letter by Captain Tracy Philipps, reporting the existence in Kabale (in Kigezi, Uganda) of a snake allegedly able to produce a single, sustained bell-like note like that of some Ethiopian horns; the natives informed him that this animal was known locally as *nkweta*. That elicited a largely sceptical response on 24 August from Alleyne Leechman (former Director of Tanzania's Agricultural Research Station at Amani), though he did concede that noted British herpetologist E.G. Boulenger had admitted that a snake might make a sound comparable to the notes produced by a gently struck tuning fork.

On 26 August, Jan H. Koens of the Royal Empire Society announced that he had seen a 24ft-long python raise itself up like a young tree and produce a deer-like bleat, and had heard an 11ft black mamba cough like a monkey; he felt that they purposefully imitated the cries of their prey to entice them to approach. Worth noting here is that many years earlier Livingstone had mentioned a snake in South Africa referred to by the natives as *nogo putsane* - 'kid snake' - because it reputedly bleats like a young goat.

Moreover, in his afore-mentioned *BioFortean Review* article (May 2007), Chad Arment noted a comparable African report documented by Charles John Andersson in his book *Lake Ngami* (1856):

> *The story of the cockatrice, so common in many parts of the world, is also found among the Damaras; but instead of crowing, or, rather, chuckling like a fowl when going to roost, they say it bleats like a lamb. It attacks man as well as beast, and its bite is considered fatal. They point to the distant north as its proper home. In Timbo's country it is termed 'hangara,' and is said to attain to twelve feet, or even more, in length, with a beautifully variegated skin. On its head, like the Guinea-fowl, it has a horny protuberance of a reddish colour. It dwells chiefly in trees. Its chuckle is heard at nightfall; and people, imagining that the noise proceeds from one of their own domestic fowls that has strayed, hasten to drive it home. But this frequently causes their destruction; for, as soon as the cockatrice perceives its victim within reach, it darts at it with the speed of lightning; and if its fangs enter the flesh, death invariably ensues. Timbo informed me that he once saw a dog belonging to his father thus killed. Moreover, the cockatrice, like the wild dog, wantonly destroys more at a time than it can consume.*

Also of relevance is a note by explorer Leonard Clark in his book *The Rivers Ran East* (1954) concerning the supposed existence in South America of a snake called *shushupe,* which allegedly emits a strange cry like that of a duck in distress to lure its prey within striking range.

Could this possibly be the formidable, highly-venomous bushmaster *Lachesis muta*? Certainly, as revealed in his book *More About Leemo* (1967), Stanley E. Brock has absolutely no doubt that this snake has vocal capabilities:

> *In my experience the bushmaster is the only snake in South America that I have heard emit any vocal sound. The noise is a high pitched, "chee-chee-chee-chee," one, and awesomely common (after you have learned what it is made by) in some forest areas. In Guyana, in the Kuyuwini, Kassikaitu, and Upper Essequibo River jungles, it is especially notorious. No doubt I would never have known what the noise was, although I had heard it often, if I had not been told by the Indians. They say it only makes the sound at dusk when it first moves off to hunt from its day-long sleep. I have never actually stood and watched a bushmaster chirp, but I suppose some hawk-eyed Indians must have in the past. Every time I hear it my Indians (very often different ones) call its name - "nan-amat" immediately, and so I am personally convinced that the fact is true.*

Of course, bearing in mind that Brock admits he has never personally witnessed a bushmaster vocalizing, it is possible that the chirping sound heard is made by some entirely different creature, and that the Indians are mistaken in their belief that the bushmaster is responsible for it, but as seen in this chapter, the bushmaster is far from unique as an alleged vocalizing serpent.

On 27 August 1929, a letter by Sir Hector Duff reminded readers of *The Times* of an episode included in his *Nyasaland Under the Foreign Office* (1903), concerning a long drawn-out sound, like the rather metallic note of a wire in the wind, heard by him in the hills near Zomba, and which his native servant declared to be the cry of a certain type of large snake.

On 31 August 1929, G.P.L. James recalled in *The Times* that he had encountered several cobras in India that would produce a deep cat-like purr just before striking at their prey or if disturbed. (In 1931, in his definitive *Snakes of the World*, herpe-tologist Dr Raymond Ditmars also noted this, describing the sound as a sharp sneeze-like hiss.) Then on 2 September, G.E. Davies suggested that the 'purr' was emitted to bemuse or 'fascinate' the prey victim - already mesmerized by the co-bra's expanded hood. Worth noting is that three years later, on 27 September 1932, a letter to *The Times* by David Freeman recorded that in Malaya he had heard co-bras uttering an exceedingly shrill note, which did not seem to have any warning purpose, but may have been related to mating.

On 30 December 1929, Captain Philipps expanded upon his earlier *Times* letter, adding that his mystery snake's local name, *nkweta,* meant 'I-you-am-calling', and that after encountering it and hearing it produce a sustained bell-like sound, he had recognised it as a puff adder. This corroborated a statement made by Captain G.B. Ritchie, who had noted in an *East Africa* article (September 1929):

> *Puff adders calling their mates at breeding time emit a beautiful bell-like note, audible for about 200 yards. Dr. G. Prentice, whose attention I drew*

to this matter, personally proved it.

In a letter to *The Times* of 7 September 1932, Philipps provided more details regarding this; he also noted that similar sounds produced by snakes had been heard by L.M. Nesbitt when crossing Ethiopia's Danakil desertlands in 1928 *(Geographical Journal,* 1930).

Probably the most astonishing letter of all, however, came from Mrs Duncan Carse, of Crowthorne, Berkshire *(The Times,* 5 October 1932), because her oddly vocal serpent was a specimen of *Natrix natrix,* the familiar European grass snake! One hot morning in summer 1932 she and her dog had spied a grass snake lying asleep in her garden. The dog froze:

> *...and at the same instant the snake 'spotted' us, and let out a clear bird-like call, obviously of alarm, and the next second had disappeared like a flash into the undergrowth. The 'note' of the snake was so loud that my husband, who was working in his studio several yards away, heard it distinctly, and came dashing out to see "what sort of a weird bird" had flown into our garden!*

Concluding her grass snake letter, Mrs Carse steadfastly maintained that:

> *...there is not the slightest doubt that this one screamed: a clear, peculiar, bird-like call, quite as loud as the note of a blackbird.*

While on the subject of snakes producing distinctive alarm calls, Indian zoologist B. K. Behura published a concise paper *(Journal of the Utkal University, Bhubaneswar,* July 1962) entirely devoted to non-sibilant vocal sounds produced by snakes, and, supporting his claim with several cases featuring species such as pythons and kraits, he concluded:

> *Normal healthy snakes can produce sounds other than hissing. When alarmed or under duress, they produce a sound resembling 'Umh' of a man in agony.*

Still with snake alarm calls: back in 1933, a Northern Rhodesian correspondent to the journal *East Africa* reported killing two snakes in his orange-packing warehouse that had emitted sounds that he described as 'hoooh', and which belonged to a species that the native people in the area claimed could crow.

All of this may seem quite unbelievable, but as mentioned by Heuvelmans, and also by Dr Maurice Burton when considering the matter in *More Animal Legends* (1959), reports describing virtually the same sounds for such snakes have emerged from many different localities, documented by eye-witnesses totally unknown to one another, and in completely separate publications, collectively yielding a formidable coincidence to explain away - unless these reports are truly based upon real incidents, involving snakes that really do produce these singularly unsnake-like sounds.

Not surprisingly, and in agreement with Heuvelmans's sentiments, I feel the alternative to this, that of supporting Pitman's hypothesis, would be somewhat rash - as the explanation that such snake-emitted sounds are actually due to sightings of snakes containing assorted goats, deer, cows, dogs, cats, and birds, all freshly engulfed and still alive (plus a goodly supply of self-ringing bells!) is in every sense extremely difficult to swallow!

Reasons Given in the Past for Dismissing Reports of Overly Vocal Snakes

And so we arrive finally at the crux of the whole crowing crested cobra problem. Can snakes really produce sounds other than their usual sibilant hisses? Diehard disbelievers have traditionally responded with two daunting arguments against this (as expressed in a long series of correspondence in *East Africa* during 1928). These are as follows:

Argument 1: *It would be pointless for a snake to have a voice, whether for communication or for any other purpose, because snakes are totally deaf, completely unable to detect airborne sounds.*

The ear of a snake is very degenerate in comparison with that of other terrestrial reptiles. It has neither an eardrum nor an air-filled middle ear cavity, but it is able to detect ground-borne vibrations, because with snakes, the ear bone known as the stapes (which conducts airborne sounds to the inner ear in lizards) is connected to the quadrate bone - present at the upper jaw's rear end, attached to the braincase, and articulating with the lower jaw. Thus, when a snake rests its head on the ground, any vibrations passing through the ground will be transmitted via the lower jaw, quadrate, and stapes into the snake's inner ear.

Relatively recently, however, and to the great surprise of herpetologists everywhere, it was shown that snakes could actually detect certain airborne sounds too. In 1960, researchers Drs E.G. Wever and J.A. Vernon reported that these supposedly deaf reptiles were really rather sensitive to airborne sounds within a frequency range of 100-500 Hz (*Journal of Auditory Research*).

These findings were later expanded by Dr P.H. Hartline (*Journal of Experimental Biology,* 1971), whose series of experiments testing the sensitivity of snakes to ground-borne and airborne vibration revealed that in relation to frequencies within the 150-400 Hz range, the snake's auditory system was more sensitive than the system of vibration detectors ('somatic hearing') present in its skin; moreover, between 200-400 Hz, the snake's hearing was more acute than that of a frog (which is very sensitive, though rather less so than that of mammals). In short, snakes are not deaf at all, and the findings of the above researchers lend credence to the possibility that future workers will unfurl evidence for even greater auditory ability among snakes.

Indeed, following the publication in 1991 of this present book of mine's original incarnation, *Extraordinary Animals Worldwide*, I received some remarkable confirmation of snakes' auditory abilities from noted Exmoor naturalist-conservationist Trevor Beer. Recalling to me some incidents from his boyhood nature rambles in the company of Jack, a gentleman poacher very knowledgeable in the ways of wild-life (as described by Trevor in his delightful book *Poachers Days*, 1985), Trevor mentioned that whenever Jack wanted to pick up a snake safely (regardless of whether it was a grass snake or an adder), he would tell Trevor to click his fingers. This invariably caused the snake to turn its head away from Jack, and towards the direction of the click, whereupon Jack would bend down swiftly and pick up the unsuspecting snake from behind. As far as I am aware, this remarkable ability of grass snakes and adders to detect the sharp sound of clicking fingers has not previously been documented; hence it greatly deserves formal scientific investigation.

Moreover, studies by Dr Bruce A. Young of Hollins College, Virginia, with king cobras suggest that they are well able to hear the unusually deep, growl-like hisses characteristic of their species and believed to be produced via pocket-like structures called tracheal diverticula, evaginating from the windpipe and functioning as low-frequency resonance chambers (*Journal of Experimental Zoology*, 1991). Young's researches into the auditory and sound-producing capabilities of snakes have more recently yielded an extremely informative, enlightening survey published in 2003 by the *Quarterly Review of Biology*, in which he confirms that snakes are actually more sensitive to airborne than to groundborne sounds, thus totally reversing the traditional view concerning snakes' auditory abilities.

Argument 2: *Snakes cannot possibly produce sounds other than the usual hisses, because they have no vocal cords.*

It is indeed true that although snakes have a voice-box (larynx), it does not contain any vocal cords. However, the same is also true for fishes, yet many species are known that are able to give voice to loud (sometimes quite stentorian) noises - as discussed in W.S. Berridge's *Animal Curiosities* (1922) and Burton's *More Animal Legends* (1959) among others. And remarkable as it may seem, those most versatile of animal vocalists the song-birds are also without vocal cords inside their larynx; their varied mellifluous and cacophonous outpourings are due instead to a special-ized structure called the syrinx, positioned some distance below the larynx. Clearly, the possession of vocal cords is not obligatory for a vertebrate to emit loud, distinc-tive sounds.

Nevertheless, the more recalcitrant sceptics of crowing crested cobra reports have continued to regard the snakes' lack of vocal cords as the last word on the matter, refusing to believe that without such structures snakes could ever crow (let alone bleat, bark, bellow, etc). If only, somehow, a snake could be formally discovered that could utter something more, much more, than a mere hiss (even of *Pituophis* power), thereby instantly, and audibly, annihilating for all time this obsolete obsta-cle to believing that a crowing serpent could truly exist.

It was a long time coming, but eventually such a find was indeed made, one that stupefied zoologists.

The Miaowing Snakes of Sarawak

In 1980, Phillp Chapman from Bristol's City Museum took part in what proved to be a herpetologically historic scientific exploration of the huge Melinau limestone cave system in Sarawak's Gunung Mulu National Park. During the expedition team's penetration of the largely unknown and predominantly lightless world of Clearwater Cave (up to 10,000ft underground), its members were suddenly confronted by a very loud and extremely eerie yowling sound, evidently coming from some animal just ahead. Very cautiously, almost fearfully, they shone their torches in its direction, to expose the originator of these disturbing noises, and saw to their amazement that they were being made by a snake!

As I learnt from Phil Chapman, the snake in question was coiled up on the cave floor (*not* hanging from the wall, as some reports have alleged) and was emitting a hoarse, yowling miaow, just like a cat. Very surprisingly, however, this singular serpent did not represent a new species. On the contrary, it belonged to a form already well-known - the Bornean cave racer *Elaphe taeniurae grabowskyi,* a slender, blue, non-poisonous subspecies known not only from caves but also from above-ground, and of comparable appearance wherever found (*Sarawak Museum Journal,* December 1985). Yet somehow its extraordinary vocal capability had never before been recorded, or even suspected, by science.

Moreover, the team soon learnt something equally mystifying concerning these strange snakes. Their prey comprised fast-flying, cave-dwelling birds called swift-lets - which, astonishingly, they could catch in total darkness, while the birds were still *in flight.* Yet the cave racers cannot see the swiftlets, and without limbs or other tactile organs they cannot make physical contact with them except when actually striking. So when the birds are in flight, how can the snakes know where they are, let alone be able to catch them on the wing? It may be relatively easy to snatch a swiftlet flying through a narrow tunnel, but what about in the great open spaces inside the main caves themselves? Perhaps the racers detect the birds by smell, or respond to their wings' vibrations carried through the air - or perhaps there is an even more ingenious method.

As the domain of the cave swiftlets is shrouded in continuous, absolute darkness they avoid collisions with one another, the cave walls, and other objects by carrying out echo-location, like bats, emitting shrill cries of extremely high frequency. Is it just a coincidence that their serpentine predator, the cave racer, is also able to give voice to a high, yowling cry? Could this be an attempt on the snake's part to mimic the birds' calls, in order to lure them within striking range, or perhaps even an attempt to disrupt their echo-location, to throw them off-course so that they fly towards the cave walls and thence to the waiting snakes?

Such suggestions as these, however, require one further assumption - for the snakes to mimic the swiftlets' cries, they must therefore be able to detect them. And if this is genuinely the case, then in addition to the above activities involving its own vocal powers such a snake could also make use of an approaching swiftlet's - by gauging the precise direction and timing of its strike according to the direction and volume of the echo-location cries emitted by the bird (which thus betrays its precise position). I realise that the concept of a snake sensitive to high-frequency airborne sounds must seem extremely radical, but we must never forget that not so long ago no one believed that snakes could detect any airborne sounds at all.

Crowing Crested Conclusions

The case of the Bornean cave racer, a snake totally unaware that its cat-like cries are little short of herpetological heresy, demonstrates emphatically that the crowing crested cobra is far from the zoological impossibility that it is generally held to be even today. True, estimates of its total body length may well be exaggerated, as people do tend to enlarge a creature in direct proportion to their fear of it. On the other hand, its crest, albeit dramatic in appearance, is no more impossible than the equally impressive erectile cape of the frilled lizard, or the wing-like gliding membranes of the famous flying 'dragon' *Draco volans* (which even has fleshy wattles too). And never again can its most controversial attribute, its diagnostic cock-crow, be raised as an insuperable objection to its existence.

Incidentally, although most of the unexpected sounds attributed to snakes in reports presented here genuinely seem to involve hitherto unsuspected vocal abilities on the part of these reptiles, there is one such category of sound that may be of a non-vocal nature. As far back as 1908 *(The Field,* 27 June), eminent British zoologist Dr Richard Lydekker noted that during the mating season the males of some species of American terrapin have two patches of horny tubercles on their hind legs, which, like crickets, they rub together to produce a very loud, musical note, apparently to attract mates.

According to Lydekker, similar sounds are also produced by *Teratoscincus* and *Ptenopus* geckos, via friction on their tails' horny rings. Moreover, egg-eating snakes *Daypeltis spp.* and the saw-scaled viper *Echis carinatus* can produce very audible rustling or rasping sounds by rubbing together strongly serrated scales on several lateral scale-rows of writhing coils. Could such a mechanism also be responsible for those reports of serpents emitting bell-like or other musical sounds? Worth remembering is Captain Ritchie's allegation that puff adders attract their mates by producing such sounds - instantly recalling Lydekker's terrapin disclosure.

Also well worth noting is that the common American garter snake *Elaphe quadrivittata* can produce a very audible, deep-toned, non-vocal hum via the rapid vibration of its tail's tip. According to a letter by F.A.T. Reuss (*Herpetologica*, vol. 7, 1951), in a quiet location this sound can be heard at a distance of 2-3 yards.

And Finally...

Ending this investigation of crowing crested conundra are two decidedly enigmatic cases – for very different reasons. A perplexing mystery beast called the Paraguayan barking snake was widely reported in 1972. As I noted, however, in a chapter reviewing classic animal misidentifications within my book *From Flying Toads To Snakes With Wings* (1997), the serpent in question, housed at Asuncion's Zoological Gardens, was merely an anaconda. Its barking prowess, moreover, was nonexistent, as this was due not to Nature but simply to a mistranslation of its local Guarani name, *mboi-yagua* ('jaguar-snake' - alluding to its rosette markings), which somehow became 'dog snake'.

More recently, an even more bizarre report was filed. North of St Petersburg, Russia, in the Vepskaya Heights is a small but much-dreaded, dense area of forested marshland, infamous for the discovery here of 16 naked human corpses since 1993, whose cause of death remains unknown. They showed no signs of violence, but they seemed to have gone mad before dying, as they had stripped all their clothes off, had eaten dirt, thrown away edible foodstuffs that they had been gathering in the forests, and replaced it in their baskets with their own clothes.

Several possible explanations have been aired by baffled investigators, including a serial killer, some strange form of fever, or the effects of ingesting toxic mushrooms or some other comparably deadly items while collecting their berries, fungi, etc. Perhaps the most intriguing suggestion of all, however, is that the dead people are the victims of a controversial, still-unidentified species of snake said to inhabit the bogs in this area.

According to local testimony collected since the 1980s, such snakes are readily distinguished by a fleshy growth on their head in male specimens that resembles a rooster's cockscomb. In addition, they have a lethally venomous bite, are often found in the trees here, and can leap great distances from tree to tree, so that they are nicknamed the flying monsters. Only one known species of snake can glide in this manner - the so-called flying snake *Chrysopelea ornata* of southeast Asia. Suddenly, one unsolved mystery - the explanation for the dead bodies - has become two, with a creature of cryptozoology having been cited as that selfsame explanation.

Chapter Three
Ameranthropoides loysi – The Strange Saga of a South American 'Ape'

Simia, quam similis turpissuma bestia, nobis!
[The ape, vilest of beasts, how similar to us!]

Ennius – *Cicero: de Natura Deorum,* Book I

One of the 20th Century's most contentious zoological events was the alleged discovery of an unknown species of ape in South America, an enigmatic episode that remains a unique controversy in the annals of zoology almost a century later.

Encountering an Enigma

From 1917 to 1920, Swiss geologist Dr François de Loys (1892-1935) and a team of colleagues had been conducting a scientific expedition through a little-explored forest-covered range of mountains called the Sierra de Perijáa, straddling the Colombia-Venezuela border.

It proved to be a forbidding, inhospitable region, with the hapless party beset by virulent tropical diseases, threatened by all manner of venomous fauna, and perpetually in fear of the highly hostile Motilone Indians with their deadly poison-tipped arrows. So harrowing were their experiences that by 1920 most members of the expedition were dead; upon his return to civilization later that year, a gaunt, haggard Dr de Loys was accompanied by less than a handful of the original 20-strong team.

Even then, however, their ordeal was far from over. Before the close of the 1920s, the expedition, and de Loys in particular, would be accused by many of perpetrating a deliberate, elaborate hoax - and all because of one very remarkable photograph.

According to an article by de Loys *(Illustrated London News,* 15 June 1929), his party had been exploring the untrodden forests along the Tarra River, a tributary of the Rio Catatumbo, in southwestern Lake Maracaibo, state of Zulia, Venezuela. Suddenly, near a bend in one of the Tarra's own, western tributaries, two strange creatures strode into view just ahead, resembling tall, hairy, tailless apes walking on their hind legs.

Approaching the party, they became increasingly violent, screaming wildly and ripping branches and foliage off nearby vegetation in anger. As a further gesture of their barely contained fury, they even defecated into their hands and threw their excrement at the explorers - who by then were not only astonished at the sight of such totally unfamiliar creatures, but were also thoroughly alarmed, fearing for their own safety.

Consequently, when what seemed to be the male member of the pair, leading its mate towards them, drew even closer, de Loys and party opened fire at it with their guns. Just as they did so, however, the male moved to one side, in order for his mate to approach alongside him. As a result, he escaped the majority of the shots, which hit the female instead, killing her instantly - whereupon the male turned and fled.

The female's body was closely examined by the explorers, who were all completely mystified by its singular appearance. So they sat it upright on a packing case, kept it erect by propping it up with a long stick placed underneath its chin, carefully measured it, and photographed it from the front (but *not* from the back - a critical component of this saga).

According to de Loys, most of those b/w photographs were tragically lost a little later, when their boat capsized in a river, but one superb photograph was saved. This is reproduced here in its familiar background-cropped form, but it also appears (artificially colourised) in its less familiar uncropped form on this present book's front cover.

The measurements recorded by de Loys, and the surviving photograph, imply a truly extraordinary creature. Fundamentally, it was most similar to the *Ateles* spider monkeys, possessing a number of features characterizing these familiar South American primates.

For example: each of its eyes was encircled by a prominent ridge of bone; its genital organs were very large; its thumbs were extremely small; its hands and feet were shaped like those of spider monkeys; the triangular patch of pale pigment on its forehead compared closely with that of the long-haired or white-bellied spider monkey *Ateles belzebuth* (a species itself known from the Rio Tarra valley, and referred to locally as the marimonda); and, like all New World primates, not just spider monkeys, its nostrils opened sideways and were separated from one another by a thick division of cartilage (the platyrrhine - 'flat-nosed' - condition).

Yet in stark contrast to spider monkeys, the largest of which never attain a total height much in excess of 3.5ft, de Loys's paradoxical primate allegedly measured a mighty 5 ft 1.75in - equalling all but the loftiest of chimpanzees. Also, its limbs appeared sturdier than those of spider monkeys - species specifically famed, and named, for their limbs' noticeably gracile, arachnine appearance. Similarly, its body seemed stockier, with broader shoulders.

And as pointed out by veteran cryptozoologist Dr Bernard Heuvelmans in *On the Track of Unknown Animals* (1958), its thorax seemed longer and flatter, more like that of an Old World ape than like that of a New World spider monkey.

Most significant of all: according to de Loys's testimony it was tailless (unlike *any* known species of South American primate), and only possessed 32 teeth (all known South American primates have 36, occasionally more).

De Loys's American 'Ape'

Following his return to Europe, de Loys consulted French zoologist Prof. George Montandon, and provided him with much information concerning his party's baffling discovery, plus the precious photograph, but was unable to offer any physical remains - though this is not as surprising as it may initially seem.

After all, the appalling conditions that the expedition had faced during its jungle forays had been more than enough to deal with, without the additional (and very considerable) problems that would have been posed by attempting to transport a hulking 5ft carcase all too soon to transform into a stinking mass of putrefaction.

Apparently, they did salvage the skull, but their party's cook ill-advisedly used it as a salt container. As a result it had completely disintegrated before their departure for Europe. (And a comparably regrettable fate allegedly befell the specimen's skin of greyish-brown fur too.)

Nevertheless, de Loys's testimony and the striking photograph sufficiently

De Loys's photograph (cropped) of Ameranthropoides loysi

Spider monkeys – identity of Ameranthropoides?

convinced Montandon that the creature had been something totally new and significant for him to publish a formal paper *(Comptes Rendus,* 11 March 1929), introducing it to the scientific world.

Moreover, so certain was he that it represented a South American counterpart to the Old World anthropoids, i.e. a New World species of comparable evolutionary status to the gibbons, gorillas, orang utans, and chimpanzees, that he named its species *Ameranthropoides loysi* - 'Loys's American ape'.

Monkeying Around with - and by - Montandon?

Scientists throughout the world were astounded - the concept of a New World ape seemed so alien to zoological tradition (in which apes were strictly confined to the Old World) that most found it impossible to accept. So it was not long before a variety of published opposition to Montandon's views materialized. Among these was the uncompromising contribution by British primatologist Sir Arthur Keith, who sternly pronounced in *Man* (August 1929) that *Ameranthropoides* was nothing more than an ordinary spider monkey (he personally favoured *Ateles paniscus*, the black spider monkey), and appeared very sceptical concerning its alleged absence of tail, great size, and depauperate dentition. In summary, he felt that at most it should merely have been named *Ateles loysi,* thereby allying it with the spider monkeys, and flatly rejecting Montandon's views that it was the Americas' answer to an anthropoid.

Similar, and sometimes even stronger, views were expressed by many other zoologists. One aspect that attracted much adverse criticism and suspicion was the supposed taillessness of de Loys's 'ape'. Some authorities clearly felt that it appeared tailless in the photograph only because its tail had been deliberately cut off, or hidden from view. Certain others, like Francis Ashley-Montague, writing in *Scientific Monthly* (September 1929), seemed willing to accept that its taillessness was genuine, but suggested that this may not have been a natural feature; instead, it could have resulted from an accident at early infancy (adult male monkeys have often been known to bite off the tails of their offspring).

Also engendering much heated discussion and dissension was the creature's impressive height. Once again, some suspected a hoax. Montandon, however, recorded that the standard size for petrol crates of the type supporting its body in the photograph was known to be 18 in, which thereby provided a standard measurement that could be used to estimate accurately the creature's total height from the photograph alone (i.e. independent of de Loys's measurements taken directly from the creature itself). Using this method, a total height of 5 ft was obtained, which agreed very closely with de Loys's result. To emphasize further the notable size of *Ameranthropoides,* and using identical crates to the example in de Loys's picture, Montandon even published a series of comparative photographs that showed men and spider monkeys sitting on the crates in the same pose as that of *Ameranthropoides* in the original photo. His critics, however, remained unconvinced - and ultimately they won the day.

In 1930, as a final attempt to silence and satisfy his opponents, Montandon's full scientific treatment of the anomalous *Ameranthropoides* was published, complete with a formidable list of pertinent references. It certainly *silenced* them, after a fashion - because it attracted no response at all. Time, though, has shown that it did not *satisfy* them – for in mainstream zoological circles *Ameranthropoides* is generally spoken of today (by those few such researchers who are actually aware of it or can still recall its history) as at best a monster of misidentification, based upon a specimen of *A. belzebuth* (which is the most robust species of spider monkey). At worst, it is summarily dismissed by them as a failed fraud.

Moreover, in recent years a very sinister, previously-unpublicised ulterior motive for Montandon's desire to acquire scientific recognition for *Ameranthropoides* as a bona fide South American ape has come to light, courtesy of research by American cryptozoologist Loren Coleman and French cryptozoologist Michel Raynal. In a revelationary article, (*The Anomalist*, autumn 1996), they brought to attention that Montandon had proposed and actively promoted an extreme, racist theory of human evolution called human hologenesis. Put simply, this theory claimed that instead of the modern-day multi-racial human species *Homo sapiens* having arisen from a single common ancestor, its various races had sprung up simultaneously but independently of one another, and with each having evolved (according to Montandon) from a different species of ape.

For example, he believed that Africa's black nations had arisen from the gorilla, whereas Asia's oriental nations had arisen from the orang utan. However, a major flaw for him was that he could offer no suitable ape ancestor for the native American nations – until, that is, *Ameranthropoides* had come along. Suddenly, Montandon had been presented with, in his view, the 'missing link' in his hologenesis theory, thus explaining why he was so insistent in supporting the claim of *Ameranthropoides* as a legitimate ape rather than a mere monkey.

Towards the end of World War II, however, Montandon was shot by the French as a traitor, and, with him, his objectionable theory of hologenesis died too. The controversy regarding the zoological identity of *Ameranthropoides*, conversely, persisted - albeit to a much lesser extent than before, and is nowadays largely restricted to cryptozoological circles – if only because the possible existence of such a beast is not wholly dependent upon the validity of de Loys's claims and photograph.

Similar Sightings, and Support from the Past?

On the contrary, mystery animal researchers are well aware that large ape-like creatures, walking bipedally and lacking tails, have been frequently reported by natives and Western explorers alike from many parts of South and Central America, where they are referred to variously as the *didi* (Guyana), *shiru* (Colombia), *vasitri* (Venezuela), *mono rey* (Bolivia), *sisimite* (Belize), *xipe* (Nicaragua), *tarma* (Peru), etc. This lends support to de Loys's account and the proposed status of *Ameranthropoides* as a genuine New World, platyrrhine equivalent of the Old World's anthropoid apes. Detailed documentation of such sightings lies outside the scope of this chapter, but one extremely noteworthy, representative encounter occurred as recently as 1987.

That was when New York Botanical Gardens mycologist Gary Samuels was crouching down on the forest floor in Guyana, investigating fungi. Looking up, he was very startled to see a 5-ft-tall hairy ape-man, walking by at close range on its hind legs but seemingly unaware of him as he stayed kneeling, concealed on the ground. This remarkable entity, which uttered an occasional 'hoo' cry as it passed by him, was presumably a *didi*.

Explorer Simon Chapman's book, *The Monster of the Madidi: Searching For the Giant Ape of the Bolivian Jungle* (2001), documented his search in Bolivia's Madidi region for the *mono rey*. Although he failed to find it, his book does contain a couple of tantalising snippets that were new to me. One was his claim that until recently, a local Bolivian actually owned a pelt from a *mono rey*, which was then purchased by "a gringo" (European) who took it home and sent it (or samples from it) off for DNA analysis, but the results (if any) were never revealed. No details were given in his book as to who the "gringo" was, where he came from, or where he sent the pelt/samples. The other snippet, which Chapman had apparently attempted unsuccessfully to substantiate, was that a living *mono rey* had allegedly once been exhibited at Bolivia's Santa Cruz Zoo! (This zoo is known in full as the Santa Cruz de la Sierra Municipal Zoo.)

At one time, a major stumbling block to accepting the possibility that *Ameranthropoides* was genuine was the absence of any fossil precedents. That all changed in 1995, however, with the publication of a paper by American anthropologist Dr Walter Hartwig in the *Journal of Human Evolution*, which documented the remains of a very sizeable Pleistocene monkey discovered in Brazilian cave deposits. In fact, this large-bodied species had originally been described as long ago as 1838, by Danish naturalist Peter Wilhelm Lund, who had named the extinct species *Protopithecus brasiliensis*. However, later publications concerning it did not examine the original fossils and underestimated this species' actual size.

In his paper, however, Hartwig rectified that error, and estimated that *P. brasiliensis* may well have been more than twice as massive as any living New World monkey. The accuracy of his estimate was swiftly confirmed, for just a year later he published a second *Protopithecus* paper (*Nature*, 23 May 1996), co-authored with Brazilian palaeontologist Castor Cartelle, this time describing a near-complete skeleton, which had been found in 1992 within Pleistocene cave deposits in Brazil's 60-mile-long Toca da Boa Vista, the longest cave in the Southern Hemisphere, located in the Brazilian state of Bahia.

Intriguingly, this skeleton revealed that the anatomy of *P. brasiliensis* combined a howler monkey-like vocal sac with a spider monkey-like cranium, and sported a robust body with limbs adapted for brachiation (arm-swinging locomotion), similar to both spider monkeys and woolly monkeys. This giant species, which would have weighed around 50lb, is now categorised within the spider monkey subfamily, Atelinae. Also found in that same cave at the same time was a near-complete skeleton of another, hitherto-unknown, species of giant Pleistocene ateline monkey, which was duly christened *Caipora bambuiorum*, and would have weighed around 45lb in life (*Proceedings of the National Academy of Science, USA*, 25 June 1996). And in 2000, after co leading a palaeontological expedition to Toca de Boa Vista, Hartwig announced that thousands of fossils, mostly from extinct mammals, had been unearthed - including the skull of a 55lb spider monkey, over twice the size of any species alive today.

Turning from palaeontology to archaeology, another problem facing de Loys's critics is explaining the existence of centuries-old carvings and statues depicting large, tailless, ape-like beasts, found among the crumbling relics from long-gone civilizations in various South American (and also Mexican) localities. Just coincidence – or representations of genuine creatures? There is even an unequivocally ape-like mask preserved at Chicago's Field Museum of Natural History, which had been carved in stone by Costa Rica's Guetar Indians and dates from 1200 to 1500 AD.

Accordingly, combining eyewitness testimony, palaeontological precedents, and archaeological artefacts with various anatomical features of *Ameranthropoides,* some cryptozoologists have looked favourably upon its credentials as a major new discovery. Indeed, Idaho State University anthropologist Dr Jeff Meldrum, who has a longstanding cryptozoological interest in man-beasts aside from his official research, deems it possible that *Ameranthropoides* represents a relict population of *P. brasiliensis.* Others, conversely, have denounced it utterly as a disgraceful deception.

Dr Heuvelmans, for example, proffered the unusually massive body and robust limbs of *Ameranthropoides* with (assuming the veracity of de Loys's report) its abnormally small number of teeth and absence of tail as evidence for its distinction from any known species of spider monkey, and as indications of morphological convergence towards the Old World anthropoids. On the other hand, in the opinion of Ivan T. Sanderson (a cryptozoologist and also, like Heuvelmans, a qualified zoologist), outlined tersely in *Abominable Snowmen: Legend Come to Life* (1961), its burly form was not the product of anatomical design, but rather the outcome of advanced decomposition inside its carcass - which had correspondingly swollen or 'blown' to yield a bloated body that would bear little resemblance to its form in the living state.

Furthermore, Sanderson did not believe that it was tailless, and he alleged that the type of petrol crate on which it had been photographed was not 18in high, but only 15.5in, which, if true, would decrease the creature's estimated height to within the range of *A. belzebuth*. Primate researcher Don Cousins also questioned the crate's size, and selected *A. belzebuth* as the likeliest identity for *Ameranthropoides (Wildlife,* April 1982). So who is right? If only we had more evidence to hand for evaluation – but perhaps we do!

A Lost Photograph...?

Tragically, as I pointed out in my book *The Lost Ark* (1993): "Today, de Loys's perplexing photo and the equally perplexing creature it portrays are largely forgotten, and are very rarely alluded to in wildlife literature". That is very true, for whereas this photograph may well be one of the most famous images in cryptozoology, you would be very lucky indeed to find half a dozen mainstream wildlife or zoology books currently in print that contain it. As a result, it is possible that a very remarkable, additional piece of evidence relevant to the question of whether or not *Ameranthropoides* is genuine has been overlooked by non-cryptozoological zoologists for many years, simply because they have been unaware of its significance.

What a tragedy that only a single photograph of this enigmatic beast survived the boat's capsizing. If only there could have been at least one other, especially one that portrayed some of de Loys's party standing alongside the carcase. That would have provided a much clearer guide to the creature's size. In fact, as I discovered to my great surprise while researching this cryptid, just such a photo might indeed have survived. Not only that, it may actually have been published - judging from the fact that I have on file the testimony of several wholly independent but highly qualified eyewitnesses who all claim to have seen it!

Dr Susan M. Ford is an Associate Professor and Director of Graduate Studies at Southern Illinois University's Department of Anthropology. During correspondence in November 1997 concerning *Ameranthropoides*, Dr Ford informed me that sometime in the early 1980s a student had shown her a popular-format wildlife book that included a spread containing an *Ameranthropoides* photograph - but not the one reproduced by me here in this present book's chapter, and which is the only such photo presently known to cryptozoologists. According to her recollection of the photo, it was:

> *...a black and white photo of the animal (looking a lot like a big spider monkey), dead, propped between two native males who were standing. They appeared to be adult but of possibly short stature; I recall no scale in the picture or reference in the text to the height of the humans. It was a chapter specifically dealing with this animal, in a book about unusual animal discoveries. I seem to recall it being hard bound with a dark cover, and not a large or thick book. It was small [in a separate communication she suggested that it was possibly 100 pages long, probably had an 8" x 6" format, and was a rather old book], the size perhaps of an average journal today. I recall neither title nor author of the book...I can visualize the picture quite clearly, however, and there were two males on either side of the dead monkey.*

The native men were presumably two of the geological party's local Indian helpers. As for the student who showed Dr Ford the book, she can no longer remember who this was.

Moving from one side of the Atlantic to the other, I also learned in 1997 from Scottish cryptozoologist Alan Pringle that one of his colleagues, education officer Jon Flynn at Cricket St Thomas Wildlife Park in Somerset, is convinced that several years ago he too saw a photograph of de Loys's ape that included some men standing on either side of it. Unfortunately, however, he cannot recall any details of the publication containing this picture.

Furthermore, in a letter to me of 15 January 1998, Steven Shipp, who was at that time the proprietor of the Sidmouth-based mail order book service Midnight Books, wrote:

> *I am certain that I too have seen a picture of this monkey flanked by two people! My first thought when I saw the photograph [the familiar cropped version] (before reading the text) was why has it been cropped, leaving out the people either side? Then I read the article and realised it was a different photograph! I believe that I saw the picture in one of those mysteries anthologies covering all aspects of the unexplained - probably during the time I would have been buying books for the catalogue [Steven's own mail order catalogue of books for sale] - so that pins it down to the last nine years! It may have been in an older book as Susan Ford says but I am sure it was in a big format, well illustrated book. Of course I cannot remember which. But I will certainly keep an eye out for it again and let you know immediately if I locate it. I don't believe this is a case of my memory deceiving me as I can clearly see the image in my mind's eye.*

Several months after receiving Steven Shipp's communication, I received a letter on this same subject from Lawrence Brennan, hailing from Liverpool, which (curiously) was dated June 31 1998! (I am assuming that he meant June 30.) Anyway: in his letter, Lawrence was adamant that he too had seen such a photograph - so much so that until reading my account on this subject, he had no idea that there was any mystery surrounding it. According to his testimony, he saw it in a book when he was aged around 13-15; and as he was 30 at the time of his letter to me, this means that the book had been published no later than the early 1980s. The photo depicted de Loys's 'ape' sitting upright on a crate, flanked by at least two humans - who were also sitting, one on either side of it, and likewise presumably on crates, as they seemed to be of comparable height to the ape. At least one of the humans may have been dressed in what Lawrence refers to as "full 'Great White Hunter' garb", with a rifle resting in his hands, but he was not absolutely certain of this because, as he pointed out: "The ape is obviously the thing you tend to concentrate on and remember!". He went on to say that there were possibly other persons, probably natives, standing behind, and he reiterated that the creature was of similar size to the humans.

As for the book that contained this photo: Lawrence claimed that his father had obtained it for him from the local library, and that its subject was man-beasts from around the world. He believes that the book was entitled something like "Giants Walk the Earth", or "There are Giants Among Us", and is certain that the word 'Giants' featured in it somewhere.

Needless to say, as soon as I read this, I immediately thought of the book by Michael Grumley entitled *There are Giants in the Earth*, first published in 1975, which is indeed a book surveying man-beasts worldwide, including de Loys's 'ape'. I lost no time in seizing my own copy of this volume from my cryptozoology bookshelves, and painstakingly going through it - how ironic (and embarrassing!) it would be if the 'missing' photo proved to be in a book that I actually owned! Consequently, it was with somewhat mixed feelings that I ascertained that it was not present in the book. True, the familiar photo of *Ameranthropoides* was included, but far from showing anyone standing alongside the ape, it had been so extensively cropped for publication in this particular book that the creature's hands, feet, and even the top of its head had been cut off! Another dead end.

In October 1998, I received a letter from Robert Hill of Cardiff, Wales, who claimed to have seen a photograph of de Loys's ape with two persons alongside it when he was younger than twelve, i.e. before November 1976. He is sure of this because he remembers seeing it while he was on one of his childhood holidays in Porthcawl, South Wales. He looked at it while inside a newsagent's shop or bookstore, and, interestingly, goes on to say: "It sticks in my mind because I had just bought (or had bought for me) a copy of *There are Giants in the Earth* by Michael Grumley (which I still have!)".

Robert's statement is important, demonstrating independently of my own search through it that Grumley's book and the book containing the mystery photograph are indeed different, notwithstanding Lawrence Brennan's thoughts regarding the latter's title. It also pinpoints Robert's sighting of the mystery photo to the years 1975-76 (1975 being the publication date of Grumley's book, which he had received *before* seeing the mystery book; and 1976 being the last year in which, until November, he was still less than 12 years old).

Robert believes that the publication in which he saw it was a wildlife book of some sort. Moreover, since seeing it he had always assumed (until reading my account) that the familiar photograph depicting the ape by itself was simply a cropped version of the picture that he had seen in the mysterious wildlife book encountered by him all those years ago in Wales.

Echoing comments by Steven Shipp and Robert Hill, when I first began investigating the mystery of the 'lost' *Ameranthropoides* photograph I too had initially speculated that perhaps the explanation was simply that the familiar *Ameranthropoides* photo was indeed a cropped image, which had originally contained people standing on either side of the animal, i.e. that the 'lost' photo was merely the original, uncropped version of the familiar one. However, I subsequently recalled having seen a print of the familiar picture in its rarely reproduced, uncropped form – it appeared in the 1995 reprint of Heuvelmans's *On the Track of Unknown Animals*, which contains several pictures not present in the original edition from 1958. As already noted, it also now appears, colourised, on this present book of mine's front cover - and as can readily be seen, there are no people in it.

In view of the above-quoted testimonies, I feel that there really could be a second 'missing' *Ameranthropoides* photograph somewhere out there, inconspicuously residing amid the vast worldwide library of wildlife literature - and also, I would assume, held (apparently without knowledge of its cryptozoological value) in one or two picture libraries. Who knows - there may even have been others too. As already noted, de Loys's own account of encountering the creature and its mate first appeared as an article in the *Illustrated London News* on 15 June 1929, with the famous photo as its illustration. One plausible scenario that comes to mind is that when de Loys sent in his article, he submitted with it not just one but a selection of photos from which the magazine's picture editor could select the most eyecatching example with which to illustrate it - a common enough occurrence in publishing. Judging from Dr Ford's account, the second, 'lost' photo, depicting the creature's dead carcase supported between two men, would be less dramatic, and certainly less photogenic, than the famous photo, depicting the creature by itself, deftly propped upright in quite a life-like pose by the long slender pole.

Consequently, if both of these images were indeed submitted (and perhaps others, too, maybe even depicting the geologists alongside it in similar poses to those adopted by the native men?), it can be readily appreciated why the now-famous photograph would have been the one selected for reproduction. The other(s) would presumably have been returned to de Loys.

There is, of course, another interpretation of this tantalising case, one with which devotees of the long-running saga of the missing thunderbird photograph (see my book *In Search of Prehistoric Survivors*, 1995) will be only too familiar. For, just as with that latter 'lost' crypto-image, sceptics will no doubt claim that such a photo never existed - that it is merely a figment of the imagination, or is a half-remembered, distorted memory of some superficially similar picture.

Certainly, just as there are many early pictures in existence of large birds with their wings outstretched that mirror the alleged thunderbird photograph, so too are there numerous early pictures of hunters standing alongside carcases or stuffed specimens of gorillas and other large primates that might conceivably be capable of generating false memories of *Ameranthropoides* images with some eyewitnesses. (Moreover, in a letter of 12 January 1998, Alan Gardiner of West Sussex, England, even nominated, as a possible false-memory trigger, a certain infamous hoax photo that depicts a supposed alien bipedal entity flanked by two government agents.)

Could a distant, confused or mis-remembered memory of one such photograph explain why my correspondents believe that they have seen a second, currently unknown photo of *Ameranthropoides*? An intriguing variation on this theme was proffered by Argentinian biologist Mariano Moldes in a letter to me of 2 February 1998. Discounting the false memory scenario, he suggested that what may have happened is as follows:

> *The book alluded to by them [the eyewitnesses of the missing photograph] probably existed and had a chapter on* Ameranthropoides loysi - *illustrated with a wrong photograph. It's quite common that laypeople in charge of editorial technical tasks mistake similar illustrations on a subject, and the frequency of such an event increases with decreasing general quality of the publication. Dr Ford says that it was a "rather old" book with forgettable author and title. It's true that the witnesses couldn't have mistaken an allusion to a well-known simian...But what if they saw a bad*

photograph of, say, a bonobo chimp (Pan paniscus) *or a siamang (genus Symphalangus) surrounded by misleading text? In the former case, an image from that region of South America showing black tribesmen instead of Indians wouldn't startle an anthropologist as there live many of the so-called bush Negroes (descended from runaway slaves) who have a way of life similar to their African jungle kinspeople instead of that of their assimilated or Creole compatriots of the same race, and look like them. In the latter case - besides from the ape being not so well-known - the assistants would have Southeast Asian racial features, very similar to those of American Indians.*

Although all of the above-proposed explanations undeniably have merit, in this particular instance I consider them unsatisfactory. After all, the missing photograph's eyewitnesses whose vocations are known to me include a wildlife education officer, a highly-qualified university anthropologist, and a dealer in cryptozoology books - hardly the kinds of eyewitness likely to suffer problems in distinguishing (or subsequently remembering) photos of gorillas and other extremely familiar primates from that of a highly distinctive, wholly unfamiliar beast resembling an exceptionally large ape-like spider monkey. Mariano Moldes's suggestion has more merit - I am certainly aware of many instances, especially in older wildlife books, in which photos have been wrongly identified, or a section of text concerning a particular species has been accompanied by a photo of the wrong species. Even so, I still consider it unlikely that those eyewitnesses with zoology-related expertise would fail to spot such a mistake.

Consequently, I am currently willing to believe that a second *Ameranthropoides* photo may indeed exist, concealed somewhere amid the world's vast archives of wildlife literature. Perhaps there is someone reading this present book who has seen a 'lost' *Ameranthropoides* photo, or knows where such an image has been published. If so, please send me any information that you can.

...and a Found Letter!

In the past, I have tended to look rather favourably upon the veracity of the *Ameranthropoides* episode as documented by de Loys, if only because I found it difficult to believe that a team of geologists - with no professional interest in zoology, and whose principal concern must certainly have been to escape with their lives from the horrors experienced during their ill-fated expedition - would have had the slightest interest in staging a scientific sham. Equally, after surviving the jungle's terrors, harassment and vitriolic accusations were without doubt the very last things wanted or needed by de Loys during his recuperation in the safety and peace of his European home.

In 2001, however, a publication appeared (though not widely-publicised even in cryptozoological circles) that I freely confess has somewhat shaken my faith in de Loys's testimony. Written by Bernardo Urbani, Ángel L. Viloria, and Franco Urbani, and published in *Anartia, Publicaciones Ocasionales del Museo de Biologia de La Universidad del Zulia*, this extensive paper presented a very detailed examination of the whole *Ameranthropoides* case history, after which its authors concluded that the entire episode was a blatant hoax - conceived as little more than a joke, but which with Frankensteinian vigour swiftly raged out of its creator's control, until in order to preserve his reputation as a serious geologist de Loys found himself unable to confess the truth.

Presented as a key piece of evidence supporting their conclusion was a hitherto-unpublished, unrevealed letter, written in 1962 by Enrique Tejera (1899-1980), a friend of de Loys in the field (as well as a decorated tropical physician and pathologist, ambassador, and minister in the Venezuelan government), to Guillermo J. Schael, who had published a report that same year of another encounter with de Loys's supposed species of South American ape, and once again in the Río Tarra vicinity. In his letter, Tejera claimed that the (in)famous 'ape' in the *Ameranthropoides* photograph was nothing more than a marimonda spider monkey that de Loys had adopted as a pet while in the jungle, and which, after it had died, had been detailed and then photographed propped upright as a joke. Unfortunately, as this letter was not made public until long after Tejera's death, it cannot be expanded upon. So whether Tejera was telling the truth or not will never be known, and therefore simply adds yet another layer of controversy to this complex, multi-tiered mystery.

Well over 250 different publications dealing with de Loys's 'ape' have been published since his own initial article back in 1929. Yet notwithstanding such a hefty archive of speculation, all that can safely be said about this notorious crytozoological subject is that *Ameranthropoides loysi* is evidently a mystery still awaiting a satisfactory, conclusive solution. It may yet metamorphose into a major zoological revelation; then again, it may not... In other words, it remains a classic open-and-shut case that, frustratingly, is all too common a scenario within the annals of cryptozoology.

Chapter Four
Introducing the First -
and Last – British Tinamous

At the turn of the [19th] century, many tinamous, mainly Pampas hens, were introduced and raised as game birds in France, England, Germany, and Hungary. After this initial success, however, all attempts to settle tinamous in Europe in the wild have failed.

Alexander F. Skutch – 'Tinamous', in *Grzimek's Animal Life Encyclopedia,*
Volume 7, Birds I

To aviculturalists, tinamous are well-known for being those nondescript, deceptively gallinaceous birds of the Neotropical Region that are in reality most closely related to certain of the giant, flightless ratites. Rather less well-known, conversely, is that at one time they seemed destined to become exotic new members of the English avifauna, as revealed here.

Tinamous are among the most perplexing and paradoxical of birds. Comprising some 40-odd species in total, and ranging in size from 8 in to 21 in, they closely parallel the galliform gamebirds in outward morphology, with small head and somewhat long, slender neck, plump body and short tail, sturdy legs, and rounded wings. Admittedly, their beak is generally rather more slender, elongate, and curved at its tip, and the tail is often hidden by an uncommonly pronounced development of the rump feathers, but in overall appearance they could easily be mistaken for a mottle-plumaged guineafowl, grouse, or quail (depending upon the tinamou species in question).

Even so, it would seem that their misleadingly gallinaceous morphology is a consequence of convergent evolution (i.e. tinamous filling the ecological niche in South and Central America occupied elsewhere by genuine galliform species, but having arisen from a wholly separate ancestral avian stock). For detailed analyses not only of their skeletal structure but also of their egg-white proteins and (especially) their DNA have all indicated that their nearest relatives are actually the ostrich-like rheas!

Nonetheless, the tinamous are nowadays classed within an entire taxonomic order of their own, Tinamiformes, because in spite of their ratite affinities they have a well-developed keel on their breast-bone for the attachment of flight muscles, and are indeed able to fly - although they are not particularly adept aerially. This is probably due to their notably small heart and lungs, which would seem to be insufficiently robust to power as energy-expensive an activity as flight. Equally paradoxical is the fact that although their legs are well-constructed for running, tinamous are not noticeably successful at this mode of locomotion either, preferring to avoid danger by freezing motionless with head extended, their cryptic colouration affording good camouflage amidst their grassland and forest surroundings.

Their outward appearance is not the only parallel between tinamous and galliform species. On account of the relative ease with which these intriguing birds can be bagged, in their native Neotropical homelands tinamous have always been very popular as gamebirds - a popularity enhanced by the tender and very tasty (if visually odd) nature of their almost transparent flesh. Accordingly, it could only be a matter of time before someone contemplated the idea of introducing one or more species of tinamou into Great Britain as novel additions to our country's list of gamebirds - a list already containing the names of several notable outsiders, including the red-legged partridge *Alectoris rufa* and the common ring-necked pheasant *Phasianus colchicus*.

The concept of establishing naturalised populations of tinamou in Great Britain was further favoured by the great ease with which these birds can be raised in captivity, enabling stocks for release into the wild to be built up very rapidly. So in 1884 the scene was set for the commencement of this intriguing experiment in avian introduction - the brainchild of John Bateman, from Brightlingsea, Essex.

The species that Bateman had selected for this purpose was *Rhynchotus rufescens*, the rufous tinamou or Pampas hen - a 16-in-long, grassland-inhabiting form widely distributed in South America, with a range extending from Brazil and Bolivia to Paraguay, Uruguay, and Argentina. In April 1883, he had obtained six specimens from a friend, D. Shennan, of Negrete, Brazil, who had brought them to England from the River Plate three months earlier. Bateman maintained them in a low, wire-covered aviary with hay strewn over its floor, sited on one of his homesteads; and by June, they had laid 30 eggs, most of which successfully hatched - and half of these survived to adulthood.

In January 1884, naturalist W.B. Tegetmeier paid Bateman a visit, and became very interested in his plans to release tinamous in England; on 23 February 1884, *The Field* published a report by Tegetmeier regarding this. However, the first release had already occurred (albeit by accident), for during the summer of 1883 a retriever dog had broken through the wire-roof of Bateman's tinamou aviary, resulting in the death of four tinamous, and the escape of seven or eight others onto Bateman's estate and thence to the Brightlingsea marshes. Only a small number of tinamous had remained in captivity but these had increased to 13 by the time of Tegetmeier's visit. As for the escapees, Bateman recognised that they were in grave danger of being bagged by persons shooting in the area (thereby ending any chance that they would succeed in establishing a viable population). So in a bid to thwart this, he issued a handbill, drawing to the attention of local people the basic appearance and habits of tinamous, and his plans for their naturalisation in England. The handbill read:

The tinamou, or, as it is called by the English settlers on the River Plate, "Big Partridge," is a game bird, sticking almost entirely to the grass land; size, about that of a hen pheasant; colour when roasted, snowy white throughout. When flushed, he rises straight into the air with a jump, about 15 ft., and then flies off steadily for about half a mile; he will not rise more than twice. Mr Bateman proposes, after crossing his stock with the tinamous in the Zoological Gardens, to turn them out on the Brightlingsea marshes, which are strikingly like the district whence they came, and he hopes that the gentlemen and sportsmen of Essex will give the experiment a chance of succeeding, by sparing this bird for the next few seasons, if they stray, as they are sure to do, into the neighbouring parishes, as they would supply a great sporting want in the marshland districts.

To supplement his captive stock, following Tegetmeier's visit Bateman obtained three more specimens of rufous tinamou from his friend Shennan, and also purchased three from London Zoo. In April 1885, he released 11 individuals onto the Brightlingsea marshes; these, together with 14 hatched from eggs, had increased to approximately 50 or 60 birds by September, according to a second, more extensive report by Tegetmeier (*The Field*, 12 September 1885).

Tegetmeier noted that throughout spring and early summer in Brightlingsea and parts of Thorington, the rufous tinamou's presence there could be readily confirmed by its very distinctive call, described as a musical 'ti-a-ú-ú-ú' in the case of the cock bird, and sounding unexpectedly similar to that of the blackbird *Turdus merula*. Illustrating this similarity is an entertaining anecdote contained in a letter to Tegetmeier from Bateman:

Mr Bateman, in his letter to me, states: "A passing gipsy bird-fancier hailed my keeper's wife, after listening attentively awhile, with 'That's an uncommon fine blackbird you've got there, missus,' alluding to the note.
'Yes,' she replied.

'Will you take five bob for him, missus?'
'No; I won't.'
'May I have a look?'
'Yes; ye may.'
'Well I'm blowed!'"
As he well might be, seeing what he regarded as the note of a blackbird proceeding from a bird as large as a hen pheasant.

Summing up his report of 12 September 1885, Tegetmeier offered the following words of optimism:

I cannot conclude without congratulating Mr Bateman on the success of

Rufous tinamou Rhynchotus rufescens

the experiment as far as it has yet proceeded. So much harm has been done by indiscriminate and thoughtless acclimatisation, that it is satisfactory to hear that one useful bird has a chance of being introduced under conditions in which other game birds are not likely to do well.

Of course, even if the threat to the tinamous' establishment from shooters could be prevented, there remained the problem of persecution from four-legged predators - most especially the fox, a major hunter of tinamous in their native New World homelands. Yet in his second report, Tegetmeier had dismissed the possibility that foxes would be a danger to them in England:

> *. . . there is no doubt that an English fox would not object to a bird that is as delicate eating as a landrail [corncrake Crex crex]. The young brood in Brightlingsea are, however, spared that danger, as the M.F.H. of the Essex and Suffolk hounds has, with that courtesy which always distinguishes the true sportsman, granted a dispensation for the season from litters of cubs in the parish.*

Tragically, however, Tegetmeier's expectation was not fulfilled; despite all precautions, the foxes triumphed very shortly afterwards, and the tinamous were exterminated. In less than a decade, Bateman's hopes for a resident species of tinamou in Britain had been promisingly born, had temporarily flourished, and had been utterly destroyed. (Moreover, as noted in this chapter's opening quote, similar attempts at around the same time to introduce tinamous elsewhere in Europe also ultimately ended in failure, no doubt meeting much the same vulpine-vanquishing fate.) By 1896, the entire episode had been relegated to no more than the briefest of mentions in the leading ornithological work of that time. Quoting from *A Dictionary of Birds* (1894-6) by Prof. Alfred Newton and Hans Gadow:

> *What would have been a successful attempt by Mr. John Bateman to naturalise this species,* Rhynchotus rufescens, *in England, at Brightlingsea in Essex . . . unfortunately failed owing to the destruction of the birds by foxes.*

A unique chapter in British aviculture was closed - or was it? In his *Introduced Birds of the World* (1981), John L. Long states:

> *It seems likely that a number of tinamous, other than the Rufous Tinamou, may have been introduced into Great Britain, but these attempts appear to be poorly documented.*

An event that may have ensued from one such attempt featured a tinamou far from the Brightlingsea area, but sadly the precise identity of that bird is very much a matter for conjecture. On 20 January 1900, *The Field* published the following letter from J.C. Hawkshaw of Hollycombe, Liphook, Hants:

> *On Dec. 23 last, while shooting a covert on this estate, a strange bird got up amongst the pheasants and was shot. On examination it proved to be a*

great tinamu [sic], or, as it is sometimes called, martineta. As Christmas was near, I skinned it myself, with a view of preserving it until I could send it to be set up, and found it to be in excellent condition, with its crop full of Indian corn, which it had evidently picked up in the covert, where the pheasants were regularly fed. The keeper on whose beat it was killed said that he had constantly seen it feeding with the pheasants. If you would be kind enough to insert the above in your columns I hope that I may be able to discover whence this stranger had strayed.

As a footnote to that letter, the editors of *The Field* briefly referred to Bateman's experiment at Brightlingsea, but confessed that they were unaware of any similar trials in Surrey, Sussex, or Hants (Liphook was sited on the border of those three counties) that might explain the origin of the specimen reported by Hawkshaw.

Not only was this tinamou's origin a mystery, so too was its identity. No description of its appearance was given; the only clues to its species are the two common names, 'great tinamu' and 'martineta', applied to it by Hawkshaw. Ironically, however, these actually serve only to confuse the matter further, rather than to clarify it. The problem is that they have been variously applied to at least three completely different species. Both names have been applied to the rufous tinamou (as in Dr Richard Lydekker's *The Royal Natural History*, 1894-6); but 'great tinamou' is also commonly used in relation to a slightly larger species, *Tinamus major* (native to northwestern and central South America, as well as Central America); and 'martineta' doubles as an alternative name for the elegant tinamou *Eudromia elegans* (inhabiting Chile and southern Argentina).

Was Hawkshaw's bird proof, therefore, of another attempt to introduce the rufous tinamou into Britain; or was it evidence of a comparable experiment with a different species? Perhaps its existence in the wild was wholly accidental, totally unplanned - simply a lone escapee from same aviary. Certainly, tinamous had been maintained in captivity in Britain, with no attempt made to release them for naturalisation purposes, by a number of different aviculturalists for many years before this event.

Today, even with such established exotica as flocks of ring-necked parakeets *Psittacula krameri*, ruddy ducks *Oxyura jamaicensis*, and golden pheasants *Chrysolophus pictus* surviving in widely dispersed areas of the U.K., it still seems strange to consider that had it not been for an all-too-formidable onslaught by the foxes of Brightlingsea just over a century years ago, Great Britain may well have become home to an entire extra taxonomic order of birds - that short-legged relatives of rheas and ostriches would have become a common sight by now in the fields and marshlands of England, far removed indeed from their original Neotropical world.

Chapter Five
Riddle of the Buru,
and the Lungfish Link

The lung-fishes constitute a sub-class of particular interest, inasmuch as they present many striking resemblances to the land-dwelling Amphibians (frogs, toads, etc.), and the original discovery of these fishes was followed by violent controversies concerning their true position in the animal kingdom.

J.R. Norman - Hutchinson's Animals of All Countries

Known scientifically as dipnoans ('double noses') because they have external *and* internal nostrils, lungfishes are undoubtedly among the most unusual of all modern-day fishes, with an air-bladder modified into lungs (either single or paired) richly supplied with blood, paired fleshy fins, an odd but characteristic pointed tail, and an overall appearance reminiscent of some strange hybrid of eel and overgrown newt. Little wonder, then, that they so greatly perturbed zoologists when first discovered.

Although lungfishes have an extensive fossil history, only six modern-day species are known, which exhibit a curiously dispersed distribution. The first species to be brought to scientific notice was the tiny-finned, eel-like *garamuru* or South American lungfish *Lepidosiren paradoxa,* when in 1837 Dr Johann Natterer captured two specimens - one in a swamp on the Amazon's left bank, and the other in a pool near Borba, on an Amazon tributary called the Madeira.

Next to be discovered were the four *Protopterus* species from Africa - *P. aethiopicus*, *P. amphibius*, *P. annectens*, and *P. dolloi* - slim-bodied with thin lengthy fins. And in 1870 the most primitive modern-day species was formally described from Queensland - *Neoceratodus forsteri,* the Australian lungfish. Much more robust than the others, with surprisingly sturdy, limb-like fins, and only a single lung (each of the other living lungfish species has a pair), *Neoceratodus* is considered sufficiently distinct to warrant its own taxonomic family; moreover, its teeth are so similar to those of the archaic fossil genus *Ceratodus* that it is thought of as a 'living fossil'.

These, then, are the *known* present-day lungfishes - which, seemingly for no good reason, lack any type of Asian representative. Or do they? In fact, it is possible that until quite recently there was an extra species, much larger than the others, inhabiting certain swamplands in the Assam region of the Outer Himalayas.

In 1948, news correspondent Ralph Izzard of the London *Daily Mail* accompanied explorer Charles Stonor on a unique expedition to an eastern Himalayan swamp valley called Rilo, close to Assam's Dafla Hills. The object of their expedition was to seek a mysterious creature called the *buru*, of which Stonor had learned during two trips made at the close of World War II with anthropologist J.P. Mills to another valley, to the north-east of these hills, called Apa Tani. According to the Apa Tani natives, the *buru* had been exterminated here when their ancestors had drained the valley's swamplands. In contrast, the Rilo natives maintained that it still existed in their valley's swamps.

Sadly, however, Stonor and Izzard failed to find any evidence for this assertion. Nevertheless, their searches were not wholly in vain. During the Apa Tani expeditions, Mills had meticulously recorded the detailed, quite matter-of-fact descriptions of the *buru* recounted by the Apa Tanis, which were based upon accounts passed down from their forefathers; and to those were added the largely comparable Rilo versions collected by Stonor and Izzard during their Rilo search. All of this information was carefully documented by Izzard in his subsequent book *The Hunt For the Buru* (1951), and the following is a summary of this animal's description.

The *buru* was elongate, and roughly 11.5-13.5ft in length - which included a 20in head with a greatly extended, flat-tipped snout, behind which were its eyes. Its teeth were flattened, except for a single pair of larger, pointed teeth in both the upper and lower jaws, and its tongue was said to be forked. Its neck was about 3ft long, and capable of being extruded or retracted. Its body was roundish, as was its tail, which tapered towards the tip, measured about 5ft, and bore broad lobes running along the entire length of its upper and lower edges. The appearance of the *buru's* limbs is somewhat uncertain: some of the natives attested that they were well-formed, roughly 20in long, with claws; others asserted that they were nothing more than paired, lateral flanges, so that the animal seemed rather snake-like. Its skin was dark blue with white blotches and a wide white band down its body's underside, and resembled that of a scaleless fish in texture.

As for the *buru's* lifestyle, it was reputedly wholly aquatic, rarely venturing on to land even for a short time, but sometimes extending its neck above the water surface to utter a loud, bellowing sound. It did not eat fish. Lastly, but of particular interest, the Rilo natives said that when the swamps dried up during the dry season, the *buru* remained in the layers of mud and sludge on the swamp bottom.

Izzard believed that the *buru* might have been a modern-day species of dinosaur. Since his book, few writers have mentioned this mystery beast, and its identity remains very much a matter of controversy. In *The Leviathans* (revised 1976), the late Tim Dinsdale, the world-renowned Loch Ness monster authority, postulated from its description that it could have been some form of crocodile. Cryptozoologist Dr Roy P. Mackal, though, in *Searching For Hidden Animals* (1980), favoured a large species of water-dwelling monitor lizard. The riddle of the *buru* has intrigued me for a long time, and, after having given the matter some considerable thought, in this present book's original incarnation, *Extraordinary Animals Worldwide* (1991), I offered a third contender - a giant lungfish. As I revealed, this identity provides a

African lungfish Protopterus

compelling correspondence relative to the *buru's* general appearance and behaviour.

One of the most awkward characteristics to explain when attempting to reconcile the *buru* with a large reptilian species is its tendency to remain ensconced within the swamp-bottom mud when the waters dry up during the dry season. Certainly it seems unlikely that either crocodiles or monitors would (or could) stay submerged in this manner for extended periods of time. In contrast, it is well known that *Lepidosiren* and two *Protopterus* species burrow into the mud when their streams dry out during the hot summer months, and remain duly encased, in a resting state called aestivation, until the water returns. Indeed, the first specimen of *P. annectens* brought to Europe from its native Gambia, in 1837, was transported here whilst still entombed within its cocoon of mud and secreted slime. If the *buru* is (or was) a lungfish, comparable behaviour could explain its otherwise anomalous actions during the dry season.

The *buru's* head was said to terminate in a great snout, flattened at the tip. This is a fair description of the head of *Lepidosiren* and *Protopterus,* whose eyes, moreover, are closely aligned behind the snout - another *buru* characteristic. The teeth of lungfishes consist of rows that yield connected ridges borne on thickened, fan-shaped plates, flattened in form and thus comparing closely with the flattened teeth described for the *buru*. In some species, smaller tooth-plates occur that are less flattened and separate - these could explain the pointed pairs of teeth reported for the *buru*.

Lungfishes do not have long necks. However, a modern-day species with the eel-like body of *Protopterus* or (especially) *Lepidosiren* but with pectoral fins positioned further back on its body (thus paralleling the condition present in some extinct lungfish species) could appear to the untrained observer to have a long 'neck', as described for the *buru*. The *buru's* round body and tapering tail are features exhibited by modern-day lungfishes, and the lobes of the *buru's* tail could be explained as merely a slight elaboration of the normal tail-fin possessed by all living lungfishes (a characteristically primitive, pointed type referred to as being protocercal). Furthermore, the tail-fin of *Protopterus* is indeed split dorsally into slight flukes.

South American lungfish Lepidosiren

As for the *buru's* limbs, the lungfish identity can provide a close correspondence whether they were true limbs with clawed feet (according to some native reports), or merely paired lateral flanges that made the animal seem snake-like (according to certain other native reports). On the one hand, Australia's *Neoceratodus* has sturdy flipper-like pelvic and pectoral *fins,* with rough spiny edges that do resemble claws. And on the other hand, the fins of *Protopterus* and *Lepidosiren* are indeed little more than paired lateral flanges with no real resemblance to limbs, thereby enhancing these fishes' anguinine appearance - to the extent that they could seem quite serpentine to a casual observer.

In actual fact, it is even possible that the *buru* had *both* types of limb (which would resolve the controversy regarding their shape). Like so many fish species, it might have been sexually dimorphic (i.e. possessing morphologically dissimilar sexes), with the limbs of one sex (probably the male) of more robust construction than those of the other.

The *buru's* skin allegedly resembled that of a scaleless fish; closely conforming once again, the scales of *Protopterus* and *Lepidosiren* are concealed under a soft outer skin, so that they appear superficially scaleless. Also, whereas *Lepidosiren* and *Neoceratodus* are mostly brown in colour, *Protopterus* is pale pinkish-brown with dark blue-black blotches, so that it would not require too drastic a change in colour scheme to produce the *buru's* bluish-brown shade and white blotches. Moreover, it is interesting to note that Africa's *Latimeria chalumnae,* that celebrated lobe-finned fish known as the coelacanth – one of only two known survivors of an ancient piscean lineage (the other is the recently discovered Indonesian coelacanth *L. menadoensis*) and classed by some as the lungfishes' closest living relative - is steely-blue in colour and dappled with numerous white blotches, only fading to a dull brown following its death.

The *buru* was alleged to be emphatically aquatic, rarely venturing onto land and never spending any length of time there. However, the natives stated that sometimes it had been seen raising its head up out of the water and making a bellowing noise. This scenario is one that has strong lungfish associations for me.

One of the most popular exhibits of the ichthyological practicals during my days as a zoology student at university was a living specimen of an African lungfish *Protopterus,* which was sometimes placed on display in order that we could observe its behaviour. As it happened, for much of the time there was actually very little that we *could* observe, because it would spend most of the practical resting motionless at the bottom of its tank. Every so often, however, and usually when everyone's attention was diverted elsewhere, it would solemnly perform its *pièce de resistance.* All at once, without any prior warning, it would raise the front part of its large body upwards, until its head just touched the surface of the water. Sometimes it would then simply nudge the tip of its snout above the water surface, but if we were lucky (by now, everyone would have rushed up to its tank to watch its celebrated performance) it would actually raise its entire head, after which it would remain in this position for several minutes, ventilating.

Although lungfishes have external nostrils, they breathe through their mouth, positioned at the very tip of the snout. This intake of air, readily perceived visually by the movements of its mouth and throat (proving that the lungfish is genuinely swallowing air) can also be very audible. The size of the *buru* was such that if it were truly a lungfish, the bellowing noise reported when its head was visible above the water might well have been the very audible result of its ventilation period.

According to native testimony, the *buru* was not piscivorous - in stark contrast to crocodiles and aquatic monitors. But what about lungfishes? It has been demonstrated that the diet of *Protopterus* depends upon its body size. Up to 1ft long, it eats only insect larvae; between 1 and 2ft, its diet is a mixture of insect larvae, snails, and the occasional fish; above 2ft, it eats only snails. Among the other lungfishes, crustaceans are also popular (as is plant material with *Neoceratodus*). Thus a

Australian lungfish Neoceratodus

diet in which fish is only an insignificant inclusion is typical for lungfishes.

All in all, there would seem to be only one noteworthy discrepancy between the *buru's* appearance and that of lungfishes - its forked tongue. This is a feature typical of monitors, certain other lizards, and snakes, but not of lungfishes. In view of the overwhelming degree of correspondence with lungfishes on other morphological grounds, however, it is quite probable that this feature was *not* a genuine component of the *buru's* make-up, but rather a fictional flourish - especially as it is common amongst primitive tribes from many parts of the world to ascribe a forked tongue to a creature (sometimes even to another tribe's members) that they fear or dislike.

In summary, on virtually every count a lungfish identity corresponds more than adequately with native descriptions of the *buru*. Overall, it seems to compare most closely with the elongate *Lepidosiren* or *Protopterus,* but its much larger size and possible *Neoceratodus-like* fins imply that it would have probably required a brand-new genus.

Worthy of brief mention is a second putative identity for the *buru* involving a strange type of freshwater fish (again previously unconsidered), a type which, although totally unrelated to lungfishes, provides some striking parallels with them,

South American arapaima – a bonytongue

and hence with the *buru*. Last survivors of an ancient line, the bonytongues or osteoglossids have an oddly discontinuous distribution, existing in northern Australia, south-east Asia, West and Central Africa, and eastern South America - thus almost precisely mirroring the distribution of the lungfishes, *except,* of course, for Asia. Moreover, they are long, cylindrical species, the most famous being the mighty 7-ft-long arapaima or pirarucu *Arapaima gigas* of South America, with flattened head and snout, oddly shaped fins, and, most intriguing of all, an air-bladder modified as a lung - all features again exhibited by the lungfishes.

Most striking of all in terms of parallel lifestyles, however, is the bonytongues' method of breathing. For most of the time they remain beneath the water surface, but every so often they raise their body upwards, and poke their mouth up through the surface to gulp air. Sounds familiar? On the other hand, unlike some lungfishes, bonytongues do not aestivate.

Nevertheless, it would require greater morphological changes to reconcile the *buru* with a bonytongue (even though there are already Asian forms) than with a lungfish. True, opponents of the lungfish identity might argue that the absence of *any* form of modern-day lungfish from Asia (though various fossil species have been found here) is a major obstacle to overcome. However, there is one final item of information that I have still to offer in favour of the lungfish identity, an item that could effectively provide this theory's missing segment of credibility.

During my correspondence with Dr Roy Mackal regarding the *buru,* he informed me that he has collected excellent anecdotal reports that point to the existence in Vietnam of a 6-ft-long species of lungfish. Apart from being a zoological sensation, the discovery of such a creature would provide very considerable support for the identity of the *buru* as a larger, related species.

Clearly, as was shown in 1930 when the sole specimen of the enigmatic Australian paddle-nosed lungfish *Ompax spatuloides* was exposed as a hoax (constructed from a *Neoceratodus* head, mullet body, and platypus beak!), the lungfishes have a continuing potential for inciting violent controversy among scientists.

Chapter Six
The Phoenix, the Paradise Birds, and the Archangel's Plume

In the Garden of Paradise, beneath the Tree of Knowledge, bloomed a rose bush. Here, in the first rose, a bird was born: his flight was like the flashing of light, his plumage was beauteous, and his song ravishing.

But when Eve plucked the fruit of the knowledge of good and evil, when she and Adam were driven from Paradise, there fell from the flaming sword of the cherub a spark into the nest of the bird, which blazed up forthwith. The bird perished in the flames; but from the red egg in the nest there fluttered aloft a new one - the one solitary Phoenix bird. The fable tells us that he dwells in Arabia, and that every hundred years he burns himself to death in his nest; but each time a new Phoenix, the only one in the world, rises up from the red egg.

The bird flutters round us, swift as light, beauteous in colour, charming in song. When a mother sits by her infant's cradle, he stands on the pillow, and, with his wings, forms a glory around the infant's head. He flies through the chamber of content, and brings sunshine into it, and the violets on the humble table smell doubly sweet.

But the Phoenix is not the bird of Arabia alone. He wings his way in the glimmer of the Northern Lights over the plains of Lapland, and hops among the yellow flowers in the short Greenland summer. Beneath the copper mountains of Fahlun and England's coal mines, he flies, in the shape of a dusty moth, over the hymn-book that rests on the knees of the pious miner. On a lotus leaf he floats down the sacred waters of the Ganges, and the eye of the Hindoo maid gleams bright when she beholds him.

The Phoenix bird, dost thou not know him? The Bird of Paradise, the holy swan of song! On the car of Thespis he sat in the guise of a chattering raven, and flapped his black wings, smeared with the lees of wine; over the sounding harp of Iceland swept the swan's red beak; on Shakespeare's shoulder he sat in the guise of Odin's raven, and whispered in the poet's ear "Immortality!" and at the minstrels' feast he fluttered through the halls of the Wartburg.

The Phoenix bird, dost thou not know him? He sang to thee the Marseillaise, and thou kissedst the pen that fell from his wing; he came in the radiance of Paradise, and perchance thou didst turn away from him towards the sparrow who sat with tinsel on his wings.

The Bird of Paradise – renewed each century - born in flame, ending in flame! Thy picture, in a golden frame, hangs in the halls of the rich, but thou thyself often fliest around, lonely and disregarded, a myth - "The Phoenix of Arabia."

In Paradise, when thou wert born in the first rose, beneath the Tree of Knowledge, thou receivedst a kiss, and thy right name was given thee – thy name, Poetry.

Hans Christian Andersen – 'The Phoenix Bird', in *Hans Christian Andersen's Fairy Tales*

Native to New Guinea, its outlying islands, and (in the case of four species known as riflebirds) the north-eastern perimeter of Australia, the dazzling, flamboyantly plumed birds of paradise first became known to a greater portion of the world during the 16th Century, when skins of these exquisite species were brought to Europe by one of Ferdinand Magellan's vessels. That, at least, is the *official* history of these birds.

Less well-publicised, however, is fascinating evidence which strongly implies that the birds of paradise were known beyond Australasia many centuries before this, and also that they may well hold the key to the identities of at least two spectacular and celebrated birds of ancient mythology.

The Egyptian Phoenix and the Miraculous Manucodiata

The Egyptian phoenix must surely be the most famous of all fabulous birds. According to its legend's most familiar version, every 500 years (or every century in certain other versions) it would construct its nest from twigs, cinnamon, myrrh, and perfumed herbs; then, as the heat from the intense Eastern sun ignited its nest, transforming it into a blazing pyre of conflagration, the phoenix would raise its outstretched wings and dance, before perishing utterly amidst the flames, which would flicker and burn as the years passed by until only ash remained. From this spent mass of cinders, a new phoenix would rise, reborn and whole, and wrap the remains of its nest in myrrh enclosed within aromatic leaves; it would then fashion this into an egg, and fly triumphantly to the temple of the Sun King at Heliopolis, Egypt, to place its egg on the temple's altar, before departing to construct a new nest and begin the cycle of self-immolation and resurrection all over again.

Most of this has traditionally been dismissed as imaginative fiction. Admittedly, scholars have attempted to identify the phoenix with various known species, ranging from the peacock, flamingo, and golden pheasant *Chrysolophus pictus* to (with somewhat less conviction) certain exotic parrots and other brightly plumaged cagebirds imported from the tropics, but none of these identifications is very satisfactory. Alternatively, certain species of perching bird, particularly some crows, seemingly experience a pleasurable sensation from fanning their wings over burning straw or twigs; sightings of this could have contributed to the phoenix legend - discussed by Dr Maurice Burton in *Phoenix Reborn* (1959).

As documented by Texas University researcher Thomas Harrison *(Isis,* 1960), there had even been suggestions by some of the early naturalists and poets that the phoenix could have been based upon a bird of paradise, but as the phoenix legend considerably precedes these birds' 'official', 16th-Century debut in the West, this possibility received short shrift - until 1957. But before we investigate this further, we should recall how the birds of paradise themselves first came to Western attention.

It was September 1522 when the survivors of the once-mighty expeditionary fleet of renowned Portugese explorer Ferdinand Magellan returned home to Europe, arriving in Seville, Spain, and bringing with them all manner of exotic treasures and relics from far-flung corners of the globe. Among these was a series of truly exceptional bird skins, which had been purchased from natives of New Guinea and various of its outlying islands. Their most immediately-striking features were their extravagantly flamboyant feathers - spectacular flourishes of gauzy, rainbow-hued plumes that billowed like dazzling fountains from beneath their wings and tail.

When examined more closely, however, these resplendent specimens revealed an even more remarkable characteristic - they were wholly devoid of flesh, blood, and bones. Their heads came complete with eyes and a beak, and their bodies had wings, but otherwise it seemed that these extraordinary birds were composed entirely of feathers - they did not even possess any feet! Yet there were no recognisable signs that the skins had been in any way tampered with, so the possibility of a hoax was discounted.

The belief in fabulous sylph-like creatures such as these recurs in mythology throughout the world, but never before had science obtained any hard evidence in support of their reality. Needless to say, therefore, zoologists were totally bemused, but at the same time thoroughly captivated, by these astonishing specimens, and concluded from their near-weightless, fleshless, and footless forms that they undoubtedly lived an exclusively aerial existence - spending their entire lives, from birth to death, drifting ethereally through the heavens, and presumably sustained solely upon an ambrosial diet of nectar and dew imbibed in flight.

To quote one zoologist of that time, they were nothing less than "...higher beings, free from the necessity of all other creatures to touch the ground". Not surprisingly, as birds that seemed to have originated from Paradise itself, their species ultimately became known as the bird of paradise, and also as the manucodiata ('bird of God').

Subsequent expeditions to New Guinea brought back more skins, again purchased directly from native tribes, and it soon became obvious that these exquisite creatures comprised many different species, delineated from one another by their distinct but all equally splendid plumages. No living specimens, however, were captured, and it was not until the 19th Century that Western scientists penetrated the dark New Guinea jungles to spy these gorgeous birds for themselves – one such encounter calling forth a paean of praise and wonder from the pen of naturalist Alfred Russel Wallace, who wrote in his diary:

> *The feelings of a naturalist who at last sees with his own eyes a creature of such extraordinary beauty and rarity so long sought after, would require a touch of the poet to reach full expression. I found myself on a remote island, far from the routes of the merchant fleets, I wandered through luxuriant tropical forests...And here, in this world, I gazed upon the bird of paradise, the quintessence of beauty. I thought of the long vanished ages during which generation after generation of this creature...lived and died - in dark, gloomy forests, where no intelligent eye beheld their loveliness. And I wondered at this lavish squandering of beauty.*

Only then did scientists finally expose these extraordinary birds' long-hidden secret. The skins that had been arriving back in Europe were incomplete ones - the

A selection of birds of paradise

New Guinea natives had developed to a fine art the immensely skilled process of skin preparation whereby the flesh, blood, bones, and feet of these birds were removed without leaving behind any readily-noticeable signs of their former presence. In short, the birds of paradise were not ethereal, everlastingly-airborne beings at all.

In fact, as ornithologists swiftly discovered when at last able to examine complete specimens, they were nothing more than gaudy relatives of the sombrely-plumaged rooks and ravens. Happily, however, their wonderful feathers were genuine, therefore offering at least a measure of consolation and compensation to scientists and poets alike for the otherwise traumatic transformation of the miraculous manucodiata into first-cousins (albeit very beautiful ones) of the crow family!

Upon the arrival of the first bird of paradise skins in Europe, their unparalleled beauty attracted equally unparalleled attention, not only from the scientific world, however, but also from the fashion industry, whose wealthier patrons yearned to be as glamorously decorated in these extravagantly beautiful plumes as the birds of paradise themselves. During the 19th Century, when Wallace and others finally spied living specimens in their native homelands, this insatiable demand set in motion a traffic in bird of paradise skins on so great a scale that it soon became evident to all that, if this trade continued for much longer, many species would become extinct within a very short space of time.

Accordingly, many countries banned all import of these skins, and in the 1920s New Guinea banned their export, thereby freeing the most famous and magnificent members of its avifauna from any further massacres in the name of fashion, and enabling their much-depleted numbers to recover. Nevertheless, a certain degree of skin trade still occurred *within* New Guinea, and in 1957 a team of Australian scientists set out to discover the extent of this traffic - never dreaming that one of the outcomes of their investigations would be the disclosure of a hitherto unknown facet of the Egyptian phoenix myth.

According to a detailed account in *Purnell's Encyclopedia of Animal Life* (edited by Dr Maurice Burton and Robert Burton, 1968-70), the scientists learned to their astonishment that the New Guinea native tribes had been killing the birds of paradise to obtain their skins for trade with visiting Western seafarers *long before* the 16th Century. In fact, this had been taking place as far back as 1000 BC, when bird of paradise skins were transported thousands of miles westwards to Phoenicia - birthplace of the phoenix legend. But that was not all.

To preserve the skins' delicate plumes during their long sea journey from New Guinea to Phoenicia, the tribesmen had presented them to the sailors carefully wrapped in a covering of myrrh skilfully fashioned into an egg-shaped capsule, in turn enclosed within a parcel of burnt banana leaves. If we equate the banana leaves of reality with the aromatic leaves of legend, the result is an extraordinarily close correspondence with the famous myth of the phoenix.

All that is missing is the blazing fire encompassing the bird on all sides - but this is the easiest aspect of all to explain via the bird of paradise hypothesis. One of the most magnificent and also one of the most abundant species (even during the height of the fashion trade, and even though it was especially sought-after due to its sumptuous plumes) is *Paradisaea raggiana,* Count Raggi's bird of paradise. A crow-sized species, the male is a truly resplendent sight during the breeding season, set apart by the breathtaking brilliance of the scarlet plumes that surge from each side of its breast, cascading all around like a blazing eruption of scorching flames. During the male's pre-mating display, moreover, it expands and elevates these huge sprays of plumes, and vibrates its body, so that the resulting effect is uncannily like that of a bird dancing in the midst of a coruscating inferno of flame!

Considering that the abundance, the gorgeous appearance, and the notable popularity among plume-hunters of Count Raggi's bird of paradise would ensure that it was well-represented in all series of skins sold by the natives to the Phoenicians, and that the natives undoubtedly regaled them with vivid descriptions of its striking courtship display, need we really look any further for the origin of the Egyptian phoenix, and its dramatic dance of death in the fiery heart of its blazing nest?

The Chinese Phoenix

Chinese mythology has its very own phoenix, commonly referred to in China as the *feng-huang.* Just like the Egyptian phoenix, it has been identified with a range of real birds, in particular the peacock and the ocellated pheasant *Rheinardia ocellata,* but in 1967, just a decade after the Australian team's bird of paradise revelations regarding the Egyptian phoenix myth, a Chinese researcher postulated that the birds of paradise may also have been the basis for the *feng-huang.*

In a lengthy paper written principally in Chinese (in the *Bulletin of the Institute of Ethnology of Taipeh, Academia Sinica,* autumn 1967), Tzu-Chiang Chou based his assertion upon four primary points, summarized as follows:

1. According to Tzu-Chiang Chou, in the Chinese hieroglyphics of the Shang Dynasty (1384—1111 BC), the shape of the Chinese character termed 'Feng', denoting the phoenix, resembled the typical, effusively-plumed *Paradisaea* birds of paradise more closely than any other proposed contender for this fabulous bird's identity.

2. The shape used for the character denoting the wind within this system of hieroglyphics was comparable to the Feng character, implying that the phoenix was in some way associated with the wind.

3. He offers many examples from ancient Chinese writings and from bird designs on the bronzewares of ancient China's pre-Chin period (i.e. prior to 221 BC) that suggest a *Paradisaea* species as their model.

4. He presents material that he interprets as evidence for believing that as recently as 1100 AD (during the Sung Dynasty), southern China was home to two *native* species of bird of paradise, which have since become extinct.

From the examples of Shang Dynasty hieroglyphics depicting the 'Feng' and 'Wind' that Tzu-Chiang Chou provides, a certain, but by no means unequivocal, similarity to at least two different birds of paradise (greater, *Paradisaea apoda*, and king, *Cicinnurus regius*) is present, but his claim that a third example specifically comprises a depiction of a composite bird of paradise (created from the most striking characteristics of a wide range of different species) is less convincing. As for the wind connection, he points out that in Chinese the birds of paradise are referred to as 'wind-birds', because they fly against the wind.

Within the ancient Chinese texts, the Chinese phoenix is described as having colourful plumage, long tufts of feathers sprouting from its flanks, a fondness for dancing, and communal behaviour - all features shared by the *Paradisaea* birds of paradise (whose males do display in groups rather than singly). Conversely, in more recent Chinese accounts a very different phoenix is described - a somewhat grotesque entity with a snake's neck, a tortoise's shell, and a fishtail - but Tzu-Chiang Chou believes that this image is wholly imaginary, not based upon observations of real forms.

So far, then, Tzu-Chiang Chou's evidence for the identification of the Chinese phoenix as a *Paradisaea* bird of paradise is quite persuasive, but his fourth point is much more contentious. Quoting from various early Chinese encyclopedias, he provides descriptions of two exceptionally handsome birds supposedly native to China in those long-departed days, at least according to the authors of the descriptions.

One bird, allegedly inhabiting Canton Province during the Sung Dynasty, referred to by the natives as the *feng-huang,* and said to have long sashes of red plumes on its flanks, beneath its wings, is identified by Tzu-Chiang Chou as the red bird of paradise *Paradisaea rubra*. This species is officially known only from the Western Papuan islands of Saonet, Waigeu, and Batanta (and perhaps Ghemien too).

The other mystery bird, reported from Kwangsi Province, again during the Sung Dynasty, and called the *u-feng* or black phoenix, was reputedly bluish-green and purple, with a head crest and an elongated tail with bunches of feathers at each end. Tzu-Chiang Chou considers this to be the long-tailed sicklebill bird of paradise *Epimachus fastosus* (formerly *magnus)*.

These identifications, however, are far from precise. Goldie's bird of paradise *Paradisaea decora* and the earlier-mentioned Count Raggi's also have sprays of long red plumes emerging from their flanks beneath their wings; and the sicklebills do not have crests - the equally long-tailed species of astrapia do, but (in common with the sicklebills) they do not have bunches of feathers at each end of their tails. In any event, I consider it highly unlikely that any genuine birds of paradise have ever been native to China, even if we accept Tzu-Chiang Chou's claim that in earlier days its climate was much warmer, and hence closer to the tropical temperatures of New Guinea.

Ornithological experts believe that the birds of paradise originated in the mid-mountain forests of New Guinea, and as the present diversity of species progressively evolved, the family's range gradually expanded, infiltrating north-eastern Australia as its distribution's southernmost limit and extending as far to the west as the Moluccas (home to Wallace's standardwing *Semioptera wallacei* and the paradise crow *Lycocorax pyrrhopterus*).

It is reasonable to suppose, therefore, that if the family were to send representatives beyond the Moluccas, ultimately reaching southern China, it would do so either via the Philippines, a handy series of stepping stones to the Asian mainland and thence China, or via a longer Sulawesi-Borneo-Vietnam course. Yet there is no evidence for the former existence of birds of paradise in any of these countries, thereby undermining support for their onetime occurrence further north-west, in China itself.

It is far more likely that early travellers visiting New Guinea arrived at China with preserved bird of paradise skins, and perhaps even some live specimens, whose outstanding appearance would guarantee their documentation in major Chinese texts of the day - their authors probably being unaware that these birds had originated from beyond China.

Another legendary Chinese bird that may conceivably have been inspired at least in part by bird of paradise skins or specimens is the vermilion bird. Totally distinct from the *feng-huang*, this noble and elegant bird is a mythological spirit creature, one of the four symbols of the Chinese constellations. Representing the south of China and the summer season, it is very selective where it perches and what it eats, and its gorgeous plumage incorporates many different hues of reddish orange.

Reverting from oriental to occidental examples: in his *Feather Fashions and Bird Preservation* (1975), Robin Doughty provides extra reasons for suggesting that bird of paradise plumes were known in the Levant long before Magellan's voyages. And in Peter Lum's *Fabulous Beasts* (1951), Roman emperor Heliogabalus (reigned 218-222 AD) is said to have *dined* upon a bird of paradise. Also, as V. Kiparsky noted in an *Arsbok-Societas Scientiarum Fennica* paper from 1961, basing his ideas upon accounts in ancient Russian literature tantalizingly comparable to bird of paradise descriptions (most notably the famous Russian firebird or *zhar ptitsa*), a trade in their plumes may have been taking place at a very early date in eastern Europe.

The Unexpected Phoenix of Little Tobago

A further case of birds of paradise far from home is a fully confirmed and totally unique modern-day example - a population of the greater bird of paradise *Paradisaea apoda* in residence on a tiny Caribbean island.

Native to southern New Guinea and the offshore Aru Islands, this species' numbers were depredated so severely for their cascading sprays of golden, gauze-like feathers during the fashion craze for these birds' plumes that *P. apoda* seemed surely destined for extinction. Someone who resolved to avert this disaster, however, was newspaper magnate Sir William Ingram. Deciding that the species' best hope lay in repatriation far beyond the threat of the plume industry, Sir William (not a person given to small measures) bought an entire islet - uninhabited Little Tobago in the

EXTRAORDINARY ANIMALS REVISITED

West Indies, whose tropical climate would provide a home-from-home environment - and established a warden-monitored colony of *P. apoda* there, comprising just under 50 immature birds captured alive during an expedition to the Aru Islands in 1909.

Many introductions of exotic species from one part of the world to another have failed dismally, but happily the birds of paradise seemed to thrive in their new home; and even though (thankfully) the introduction's original purpose had been rendered obsolete - the plume industry collapsed before this species could become extinct in its native lands - the West Indian contingent was permitted to remain on Little Tobago after Sir William's death.

Over the years, the population remained relatively constant, rarely exceeding or falling much below the 20-30 individuals mark. But then came Hurricane Flora, a meteorological monster that mercilessly lashed Little Tobago one devastating day in 1963, and remorselessly swept most of the hapless birds of paradise out into the rampaging waves, to their inevitable death. Only a handful remained alive, and most of those were males. The plucky little population was doomed - no specimen has been recorded from the islet for many years. The unexpected phoenix of Little Tobago had been extinguished not by flame, but by wind and water, and just as surely as if it had been exterminated by the plume-hunters back home in New Guinea.

A Plume from the Wing of an Archangel?

El Escorial, also known as the Escurial, is a palatial architectural masterpiece of such splendour that its countless admirers refer to it as the 8th Wonder of the World. Commissioned by King Philip II, constructed from 1563 to 1584, and situated in Madrid, Spain, it houses the monastery of San Lorenzo (St Lawrence), a basilica, a library, the Royal Pantheon, the palaces of the Bourbons and Austrians, and a magnificent collection of fine art by such masters as Titian, Tintoretto, Velasquez, El Greco, Rubens, Dürer, and Bosch.

El Escorial also contains 515 reliquaries, containing no fewer than 7,421 holy relics. One of these relics forms the subject of this chapter's final case, because it is of particular cryptozoological interest - and for good reason. Constituting a single, but very singular, feather of extraordinary beauty, it lays claim to an even more extraordinary identity - for according to traditional belief, it originated from one of the wings of the archangel Gabriel.

A few centuries ago, this remarkable plume was a celebrated religious treasure, famous throughout Europe, but today its existence - if indeed it still exists - is largely unknown. Indeed, when I wrote in January 2001 to the monastery of San Lorenzo, housed within El Escorial, requesting information concerning the Gabriel feather, the monastery's Keeper of National Heritage, Carmen Garcia-Frias Checa, wrote back denying all knowledge of it (see my book *Mysteries of Planet Earth*, 2001, for further details). Nevertheless, it definitely existed at one time. Perhaps its best known observer was William T. Beckford (1759-1844), an exceedingly wealthy

English author-traveller, who set forth on several extensive forays around Europe, visiting sites and buildings of religious significance in Spain, Italy, and Portugal.

During one such excursion, in 1787, Beckford journeyed to El Escorial, where he was privileged to see Gabriel's feather, and he subsequently documented it in one of his travelogues, *Italy, With Sketches of Spain and Portugal*, vol. 2 (1834). The publication of this work is of especial note, because it followed closely upon the formal description of a truly exceptional new species of bird that initially influenced scientific speculation concerning possible ornithological origins for the Gabriel feather.

The quetzal is indisputably one of the world's most beautiful species of bird. It is native to Central America, including Mexico and Guatemala, where it was deemed sacred by the Toltecs, Mayans, and Aztecs. Indeed, it is the national symbol of Guatemala even today, and this country's unit of currency is named after it too. Moreover, if a person stands in front of the mighty 1100-year-old Mayan pyramid of Kukulkan (El Castillo) at Chichén Itzá near Cancún, Mexico, at the base of its staircase, and claps their hands, the pyramid will emit a distinctive chirping echo - but not just any chirp. In 2002, Californian acoustical engineer David Lubman and a team of Mexican researchers revealed that it constituted a precise phonic replica of the quetzal's call (*National Geographic Today*, 6 December)! Some researchers, such as Ghent University mechanical construction specialist Dr Nico F. Declercq, have since questioned whether this acoustical anomaly was intentional on the part of the pyramid's Mayan designers and architects (*Journal of the Acoustical Society of America*, December 2004), but if not it is surely a formidable coincidence.

Belonging to an exclusively tropical taxonomic order of brightly-plumaged species known as trogons, and sporting a shimmering emerald-green plumage complemented by scarlet underparts, the quetzal is instantly distinguished from all other birds during the breeding season. This is when the male, whose body measures a mere 18in, grows a quartet of extremely elongate tail plumes, 2-3ft in length. These undulate as it flies, affording it the appearance of a feathery snake, and inspiring the Aztecs to associate it with their sky god Quetzalcoatl, often portrayed as a green plumed serpent.

Yet despite its flamboyant plumage, the quetzal's debut within the ornithological literature of the Western world was unexpectedly belated, and controversial too. In 1831, after receiving a description of the quetzal from Duke Paul of Würtemberg, the eminent French zoologist Baron Georges Cuvier stated that in his opinion this bird's astonishing tail plumes could not be genuine. Instead, they must have been created artificially, i.e. they were composite feathers, composed of several individual plumes artfully combined together. Interestingly, a skilfully-constructed composite feather is one identity that had already been aired by some naturalists as an explanation for the celebrated feather of Gabriel.

However, ornithologist Dr Pablo de la Llave was well aware of the quetzal's authenticity, because he had first become acquainted with this spectacular species prior to 1810, from examining over a dozen specimens obtained by natural history expeditions in Central America and maintained in the palace of the Retiro near Madrid.

The resplendent quetzal Pharomachrus mocinno

Accordingly, in 1832 he formally christened it *Pharomachrus mocinno* in the *Registro Trimestre* (a Mexican journal), honouring Mexican naturalist Dr J.M. Mociño.

Once the quetzal became known in scientific circles, it was inevitable that this species (now known specifically as the resplendent quetzal, thereby distinguishing it from five other, less spectacular quetzal species that all lack the long tail feathers of breeding male *P. mocinno*) would be mooted as a possible explanation for the Gabriel feather. Certainly the breeding male quetzal's tail plumes are exquisite enough to have inspired speculation, perhaps, by non-zoological theologians as to whether they might conceivably be of divine rather than merely mortal origin.

Moreover, in view of this species' eyecatching appearance, it is also possible that during the 1500s the Spanish conquistadors brought some preserved quetzal skins or plumes back home with them when they returned to Spain after conquering Mexico (which in those days incorporated Guatemala too). Needless to say, if one of these should thence have found its way into the collections of the newly-built Escorial, we would not need to look any further for an explanation of the Gabriel feather.

Unfortunately, however, this elegant solution has a fatal flaw, as ornithologists reading Beckford's travelogue, published two years after Llave's description of the quetzal, would soon discover. For in his account of the Gabriel feather, Beckford revealed that it was not green, but was in fact rose-coloured. Exit the quetzal from further consideration!

Yet if not a quetzal plume, from which bird could the Gabriel feather have originated? (Worth noting here, incidentally, is that the concept of angels possessing feathered wings is a relatively recent one, nurtured largely by Renaissance artists and hence dating back only a few centuries, with no foundation in early theological lore.)

'Rose-coloured' conjures up images of flamingos, but it is difficult to believe that plumes from species so familiar to European ornithologists as these leggy waterbirds could be lauded as divine feathers derived from the wings of archangels. In my opinion, a much more plausible option is that the Gabriel feather may indeed be of heavenly association - inasmuch as it might well be an example of the long exotic plumes borne during the mating season by male specimens of certain New Guinea birds of paradise. Those of Count Raggi's in particular are sumptuously adorned with vivid sprays of bright red or rose-coloured plumes - thus corresponding closely with the appearance of the Gabriel feather. Could it be, therefore, that the long-awaited solution to the mystery of this perplexing plume's identity is that a feather derived from a *P. raggiana* skin brought back to Spain from New Guinea four centuries or more ago has been ultimately elevated in status from that of a bird of paradise to that of a heavenly archangel?

I am continuing my investigations into this compelling subject, in the hope of uncovering the Gabriel feather's early history, e.g. when was it added to El Escorial's reliquaries, by whom, and from where, and possibly even obtaining a photograph of it - always assuming, of course, that this fascinating relic still survives. In addition,

I have learnt from Ted Harrison, a Fortean researcher specialising in stigmata and other religious phenomena, that he has heard rumours and reports of other angel feathers, and has promised to send me any details concerning them that he encounters. Equally, if any readers of this book have relevant information on this subject, I would very much like to hear from you.

Chapter Seven
The New Guinea Singing Dog, and other Canine Curiosities

Canis a non canendo.
[A dog *(canis)* so called from its not singing *(canens).*]

Varro - *De Lingua Latina*

One of New Guinea's most intriguing mammals is a dog that *does* sing, or at least yodel - just one of the odd and often controversial canine curiosities included in this chapter.

New Guinea Singing Dog – a Yodelling Dingo?

In addition to the many feral (run-wild) domestic dogs of relatively recent origin and varied appearance present throughout New Guinea, there exists in its eastern highlands a very primitive canine form of much greater antiquity and well-defined morphology. This resembles a small, thickset dingo, not only in general external appearance, but also in relation to certain cranial-dental ratios held to be of significance in canid classification. It was first made known to the western world as long ago as 1606, when Diego de Prado reported finding specimens in southeastern Papua, while voyaging through the Torres Strait separating Papua from Queensland, Australia. In 1957, Dr Ellis Troughton, Mammal Curator at the Australian Museum, classed it as a distinct species, dubbing it *Canis hallstromi,* in honour of Sir Edward Hallstrom (President of the Taronga Park Trust), and in an attempt to initiate further studies of this largely ignored form that would determine its precise taxonomic status. Troughton based his description of this new species upon a pair housed at Sydney's Taronga Zoo.

In 1971 he published another paper treating C. *hallstromi* as a valid species; but two years earlier, following detailed studies of its breeding and offspring, Dr W. Schultz had proposed that it should be incorporated within the domestic dog's species *(Zoologischer Anzeiger,* 1969). This was widely accepted, and today the creature is generally considered to be nothing more than a long-established but taxonomically insignificant feral breed of domestic dog (as is the dingo).

Nonetheless, Troughton's paper remains a very important contribution. It contains one of the most detailed accounts of this little-known dog currently available, documents early descriptions, details its relationship with the New Guinea natives (who look upon it as a valued food item), and, most memorable of all, reveals that it does not bark, but gives vent to a curious howling whine instead, likened by some other researchers to yodelling. This last-mentioned characteristic has earned '*C. hallstromi*' its most popular English name, the New Guinea singing dog, and has inspired many unusual myths concerning it.

According to some, these animals harbour the souls of dead tribesmen, who communicate with their living relatives via the dogs' yodelling. Moreover, the natives believe that by listening carefully to the specific tones of a given dog, the identity of the dead tribesman speaking with its voice can be instantly recognized. Also, their vocal abilities have inspired a legend in the mythology of Port Moresby's Motu tribe that attributes the gift of speech to these dogs. And in the vicinity of eastern New Guinea's Mount Hagen, the natives imitate this creature's whistling yodels as an effective means of communicating with one another over great distances.

Singing dogs are rarely seen beyond their New Guinea homeland, but on account of their name's musical association a pair was presented during the early 1960s as an undeniably original and delightfully appropriate gift to the eminent conductor Sir Malcolm Sargent, during one of his Australasian concert tours. Although Sir Malcolm became very fond of them, he had nowhere suitable to keep them, so in 1964 he donated the pair to London Zoo, where he visited them on several occasions thereafter, and where they soon became very popular attractions (raising a litter of cubs, containing some dingo blood). I can still readily recall my own first encounter with the London Zoo singing dogs, as it proved to be quite an unforgettable event.

As a child of about six or seven at the time, I had read all about them in various books and magazines with unbounded fascination, and implored my parents to take me to see these wonderful dogs that could sing. When I reached their enclosure, one of them was at that very moment entertaining an enraptured audience with a thrilling rendition in falsetto fortissimo, so I eagerly thrust my way through the throng to obtain a closer view - a little too close for comfort, as it turned out.

I can only assume that its impromptu concert had proven too demanding for its voice, because just as I reached the front of the crowd, the singing dog stopped singing, turned around, and coughed violently and with unerring accuracy directly into my face! Still in a state of shock, I was swiftly dragged away by my mother, who was convinced that I would surely develop some hideous tropical disease. Needless to say, I did nothing of the kind but, not surprisingly, the whole incident remains one of my more vivid if unusual memories of childhood!

Finally, I am greatly indebted to renowned zoologist Dr Desmond Morris, Curator of Mammals at London Zoo during much of the 1960s, for sharing with me the following priceless anecdote concerning these singing dogs. When Spike Milligan visited the zoo one day, Dr Morris showed them to him, and informed him that they belonged to Sir Malcolm Sargent. Spike's opinion, given by way of reply, was, as always, purest Milliganesque: "Their Bach is worse than their Bitehoven!".

New Guinea singing dog at London Zoo

Mount Popa's Mystery Dog, and Australia's *Yokyn*

Another wild dog of controversial scientific status was a mysterious form discovered on Burma's Mount Popa. In 1936 Reginald Pocock stated that no specimens of the Asian wild dog or dhole *Cuon alpinus* had been obtained from Burma, but shortly afterwards he learnt that a Mr Shortridge had secured a specimen on Mount Popa. Naturally Pocock was anxious to examine this unique example, an adult female, especially as Shortridge alleged that it only had five pairs of teats (female dholes have 6-8 pairs), and weighed only 19 lb (unusually light for a dhole).

However, after studying its skull, uncovered at the British Museum, Pocock recognized that it had been nothing more than an old, small domestic dog, with a high crown and short muzzle. But, ironically, genuine Burmese dholes *were* obtained later, and in 1941 Pocock christened their race *C. a. adustus.*

The *yokyn* is a strange dog-like beast reputedly well-known to Australian aboriginals and farmers. Said to have long claws, a stocky build, and a variable (sometimes brindled) coat, a specimen has yet to be formally examined, so its identity remains uncertain *(Fate,* May 1977).

An unknown species, an odd type of feral domestic dog, a dingo, a dog-dingo cross-breed, and even a surviving mainland race of the marsupial Tasmanian wolf *Thylacinus cynocephalus* are among those identities on offer.

Horned Jackals and Reedwolves

One of the most unlikely mystery dogs must surely be the Sri Lankan horned jackal - yet we know that such creatures do exist, because skulls of common jackals *Canis aureus* bearing a small bony horn either at the front or at the rear of the skull have been obtained. A skull with a rear-sited horn was housed in the museum of London's College of Surgeons in the 19th Century, and an engraving of it featured in Sir J. Emerson Tennent's *Sketches of the Natural History of Ceylon* (1861). More recently, this engraving also appeared in an article of mine discussing certain Sri Lankan mystery beasts *(Fate,* January 1989 – reprinted in 1997 within my book *From Flying Toads To Snakes With Wings)*, and is now reproduced here.

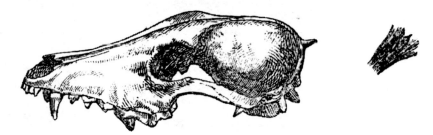

Horned jackal skull, and close-up of horn sheath

According to Sri Lankan lore, only the leader of a jackal pack possesses a horn, re-ferred to as a *narri-comboo* and greatly valued as a lucky charm by the islanders. The mechanism responsible for horn development is currently unknown. A mutant gene could be involved. Alternatively, a physical injury may provide the necessary stimulus (the occasional growth of horn-like structures from the site of former inju-ries has been recorded from a wide range of mammals, including humans). How-ever, it would be extremely difficult to postulate *any* mechanism, genetic or envi-ronmental, that could limit horn growth *solely* to pack-leaders — this aspect is more likely to be folklore than fact.

The Hungarian reedwolf was a small, mysterious form of wild dog existing in Hun-gary and eastern Austria until the early 1900s. In 1856, M. Mojsisovics named it *Canis lupus minor,* treating it as a small wolf, but the precise nature of its identity remained a debated issue long after that. In the late 1950s, this extinct enigma in-spired a series of interchanges in various journals between Hungarian researchers Drs Eugen Nagy and János Szunyoghy. Nagy staunchly supported Mojsisovics's reedwolf classification, but Szunyoghy categorized it as a larger-than-normal ver-sion of the common jackal (in 1938, Dr Gyula Éhik had actually renamed it *C. aureus hungaricus).* However, the detailed studies of Prof. Eduard-Paul Tratz with the handful of museum specimens of reedwolf in existence provided persuasive evi-dence for believing that it had been an unusually diminutive race of wolf after all, an identity that has since won widespread acceptance.

British Mystery Dogs

Great Britain is more famous for its mystery cats (see my first book, *Mystery Cats of the World,* 1989) than for its mystery dogs, but over the years quite a variety have been reported. Most involve extremely large beasts with Baskervillian overtones (comparable to the controversial Beast of Gévaudan that terrorized France during the mid-18th Century), and are often blamed for savage killings of sheep or other livestock. These are surely nothing more unusual than run-wild hounds, or crossbreeds with various of the larger well-established breeds (e.g. mastiff, great dane) in their ancestry. Typical examples reported include an enormous black creature with a howl like a foghorn, hailing from Edale, Derbyshire *(Daily Express,* 14 October 1925); a beast the size of a small pony sighted on Dartmoor by Police Constable John Duckworth in 1969 and again in 1972 *(Sunday Mirror,* 22 October 1972); a sheep-slaughtering marauder stalking the Welsh hamlet of Clyro, Powys *(Sunday Express,* 10 September 1989) - the locality of the real Baskerville Hall (its name was borrowed by Sir Arthur Conan Doyle for his fictional, Dartmoor-sited equivalent); and lupine mystery beasts sighted spasmodically right up to the present day in Staffordshire's wooded Cannock Chase (*Stafford Post,* 30 May 2007).

Some have opined that these mystery dogs are wolves. However, the last verified wolf of mainland Britain died in Scotland in 1743.

Incidentally, long after the last Irish wolf was killed, in County Carlow around 1786, there were rumours that small wolves existed on the Isle of Achill, just off Ireland's western coast. Traditionally, these have been assumed to be wholly mythical, but in a letter to me of 21 February 1998, British zoologist Clinton Keeling provided a fascinating snippet of information on this subject - revealing that as comparatively recently as c.1904, the alleged Achill Island wolves were stated to be "common" by no less a person that okapi discoverer Sir Harry Johnston.

Also of note is that according to Michael Goss *(Fate,* September 1986), when foxes became scarce in a given area, hunters would sometimes release foxes imported from abroad - until as recently as the early 1900s, in fact - and in some cases it seems that these imported 'foxes' were really jackals or young wolves.

A supposed wolf blamed for numerous livestock killings near Monmouthshire's Llanover Park in 1868 was never obtained *(The Field,* 23 May 1868). Conversely, after a long hunt during winter 1904 for an unidentified sheep-killer near Hexham, Northumberland, a wolf *was* finally found - discovered dead, on 29 December 1904, upon a railway line near Carlisle. As John Michell and Robert Rickard discuss in *Living Wonders* (1982), it was initially thought to have been an escapee belonging to a Captain Bains of Shotley Bridge, near Newcastle, which had absconded in October, but his wolf had only been a cub, whereas the dead specimen was fully grown. A visiting American later claimed that the Hexham wolf's head, preserved by a taxidermist, was actually that of a husky-like dog called a malamute, but several experts strenuously denied this.

Wolf – identity of Hexham's canine mystery?

Moreover, when the supposed wolf responsible for several sheep attacks between Sevenoaks and Tonbridge in 1905 was shot by a gamekeeper on 1 March *(Times,* 2 March 1905), it proved to be a jackal. Interestingly, as noted by Alan Richardson of Wiltshire (*The Countryman,* summer 1975), an entry in the Churchwardens' Accounts for the village of Lythe, near Whitby, North Yorkshire, recorded that in 1846 the sum of 8 shillings was paid for "One jackall [sic] head". As this was a high price back in those days, it suggests that whatever the creature was, it was unusual. By comparison, fox heads only commanded the sum of four shillings each at that time.

In May 1883, R. Payze met some men travelling to London, who had caught three very young, supposed fox cubs while passing through Epping Forest. Payze bought one, naming it Charlie, but as he grew older it became clear that Charlie was not a fox. When shown by Payze to A.D. Bartlett, London Zoo's superintendent, Charlie was readily identified by Bartlett as *Canis latrans,* North America's familiar, grey-furred coyote or prairie wolf.

After receiving Charlie for the zoo, Bartlett investigated his origin, and learnt that a few years earlier four coyote cubs had been brought to England in a ship owned by J.R. Fletcher of the Union Docks. They were kept for a few days at the home of a Colonel Howard of Goldings, Loughton, then taken to Mr Arkwright, formerly Master of the Essex Hunt, and released in Ongar Wood, which joins Epping Forest.

Bartlett found that the local people acquainted with this forest well recalled the release of the coyotes, which they termed the 'strange animals from foreign parts' *(The Naturalist's World,* 1884).

Charlie was clearly a first-generation offspring of two of these original four; and those, or their descendants, no doubt explained the periodic reports thereafter from this region regarding grey fox-like beasts, occasionally spied yet never caught by the hunt - but how did this strange saga end? Did Epping's coyotes simply die out, or did they establish a thriving lineage? And, if so, could there *still* be coyotes here today?

Intriguingly, in the *Countryman* (summer 1958), Doris W. Metcalf recalled having seen some very large, grey-furred wolf-like beasts near Jevington prior to World War II; she had assumed that they must be "the last of an ancient line of hill foxes", or perhaps some surviving fox-wolf hybrids (but fox-wolf crossbreeding does not occur, and even it if did, it is highly unlikely that any resulting offspring would be viable). In May 1974, a similar animal, said to be 2ft tall with a distinctly fox-like tail, was spied by Thomas Merrington and others as it slunk around the shores of Hatchmere Lake and the paths in Delamere Forest, Kingsley *(Runcorn Weekly News,* 30 May 1974).

When the Isle of Wight's mystifying lion-headed 'Island Monster', allegedly maned but otherwise virtually hairless, was finally shot in 1940, it proved to be an old fox in an advanced state of mange; almost all of its fur had been lost, except for some still covering its neck, creating the illusion of a mane *(Isle of Wight County Press,* 24 February 1940). During the 1980s, Exmoor naturalist Trevor Beer was shown the carcass of a strange grey fox killed at Muddiford; its pelage consisted almost entirely of grey under-fur (hence the fox's odd colour) - due to disease-induced hair loss, or perhaps a mutant gene?

In January 1990, a peculiar fox-like beast with blue-grey fur was spotted seeking food in a snow-covered field at Cynwyd, Corwen, in North Wales, by farmer Trefor Williams; after capturing it with a lasso, he brought it home. His unexpected find, duly christened Samantha, was an Arctic fox *Alopex lagopus,* once again a species not native to Britain *(Daily Post,* 2 February 1990). Back in March 1983, an Arctic fox had been killed at Saltaire, West Yorkshire, by David Bottomley's collie *(Sunday Express,* 6 March). Their origins are unknown.

In February 1994, an Arctic fox was discovered in the courtyard of Dudley Castle, in whose grounds stands Dudley Zoo, but it had not escaped from there, and yet again its origin remains undetermined *(Wolverhampton Express and Star*, 15 February 1994). So too does that of the female Arctic fox shot in the early hours of 13 May 1998 by a farmer from Alnwick, Northumberland, after he discovered it eating one of his lambs; its body was later preserved and mounted by local taxidermist Ralph Robson *(Fortean Times,* September 1998). Curiously, just three months earlier, a male Arctic fox had been shot less than 30 miles away. Could these have been an absconded pair?

Wonders in White - *Amarok*, *Waheela*, and Medicine Wolf

The Greenland *amarok* is generally believed to be the Eskimo equivalent of the bugbear, a frightening but wholly fictitious beast employed by parents to scare unruly children. However, as noted by Dr Isaac J. Hayes in *The Land of Desolation* (1871), this is not entirely true, because at least one specimen was actually shot. It proved to be a huge white wolf, whose skin was later sent to the Copenhagen Museum.

Enormous white wolves have also been reported from Alaska and the northernmost reaches of Canada, but these may be something very special. As documented fully within my book *In Search of Prehistoric Survivors* (1995), eyewitnesses have commented that they possess unusually wide heads with surprisingly small ears, extremely thick tails, and rather short legs with splayed feet. Their coats are very long, shaggy, and completely white. And unlike typical pack-hunting wolves, these white wonders, known locally as *waheelas*, are solitary, yet are greatly feared locally as being much more ferocious than normal, social wolves. What could such unwolf-like wolves be?

Zoologist Ivan T. Sanderson felt that the above description compared well with that of a taxonomic family of supposedly extinct carnivores called amphicyonids or dog-bears. The last American species officially died out 5 million years ago during the Miocene epoch, but in a *Pursuit* article (October 1974) Sanderson postulated that it may have persisted into modern times within the far north of North America, which is rarely entered by people and hence little changed for thousands of years. (Incidentally, in his article Sanderson referred to the amphicyonids as dire wolves, which is incorrect; dire wolves were very large Pleistocene canid species, hence directly related to the true, modern-day wolves.)

Much more recently, an even more intriguing, and surprising, possibility has come to light. In a *Current Biology* paper (published online on 21 June 2007), geneticist Dr Jennifer Leonard and a team of Smithsonian Institution researchers have revealed that although the wolf *Canis lupus* as a species survived the Pleistocene megafaunal extinctions in North America, one distinctive and hitherto-unknown, undocumented lupine form did not. Brought to scientific attention by the discovery of permafrost-preserved fossil bones in Alaska, this very interesting, unusual wolf ecomorph (a local population or group whose appearance is determined by ecology) is characterised not only by discrete genetic differences from all other North American wolves (including modern-day wolves in Alaska), but also by certain noticeable external features, such as its more robust skull and teeth. The researchers believe that these differences indicate that it was more adapted for making forceful bites and shearing flesh than are other American wolves, i.e. a more savage, carnivorous creature. Yet unlike those latter canids, this newly-revealed but ancient Alaskan wolf did not survive the Pleistocene, dying out around 12,000 years ago - or did it? Could it be that it is one and the same as the morphologically-similar *waheela*, and still persists in small numbers within Alaska's more remote terrain?

On 11 March 2002, American mystery beast investigator Nick Sucik reported on the cz@yahoogroups.com discussion group a most interesting communication that he had received from a correspondent in New Mexico. Late one night during the summer of 1979 or thereabouts, the unnamed trucker in question had been driving in the Oil Fields on the Jicarilla Apache Reservation near Dulce, New Mexico, and was returning to Highway 64 from the old 'Gas Buggy' area, when, as the road entered the short valley ahead, he saw a very large animal come quickly out of the brush and pause briefly in the middle of the road. Lit by the truck's headlights, the creature initially seemed to be a very sizeable husky, but as he drove closer the trucker suddenly realised that it much more closely resembled a wolf – a very large, all-white wolf. Its fur seemed shaggier than that of a husky, its chest much larger, and its snout and body somewhat longer. By the time that he had registered all of this, however, the creature had moved on down the road and into the Wash on the truck's left, disappearing from view. When he subsequently mentioned his sighting to some of the local native Americans, they told him that what he had seen was a medicine wolf, a legendary beast that only very special people can see. They totally believed his sighting, and he maintains to this day that he truly did see the creature – medicine wolf or not.

Don't Shun the *Shunka Warak'in*

Even more extraordinary than the North American canine mystery beasts documented in the previous section is the baffling *shunka warak'in*. Translating as 'carrying-off dogs', this is the name given by the Ioway and other native Americans living along the U.S.A.-Canada border to a strange dark-furred creature likened morphologically to a cross between a wolf and a hyaena, which sports a lupine head and high shoulders, but also a sloping back and short hindlimbs - bestowing upon it a hyaenid outline. As its name suggests, the *shunka warak'in* is said to sneak into the tribes' camps at night and seize any unwary dogs, and it cries like a human if killed.

Sometime during the 1880s, a mystifying creature fitting this description was shot and killed by the grandfather of zoologist Dr Ross E. Hutchins (who documented the incident in his book *Trails to Nature's Mysteries*, 1977) on his ranch in the Madison River Valley north of Ennis, Montana. Unlike so many other cryptozoological corpses, however, this one was actually preserved, becoming a cased taxiderm specimen that was subsequently exhibited for many years by a grocer called Sherwood at his store-cum-museum near Henry Lake, Idaho, Sherwood terming it a 'ringdocus'. Moreover, a good-quality photograph of this unique specimen was taken, revealing its somewhat composite form – and appears in Hutchins's book. This is just as well, because the whereabouts of the specimen itself are currently unknown, as it has apparently been moved in recent years to somewhere in the West Yellowstone area.

After reading Hutchins's account and seeing the photo, veteran American cryptozoologist Loren Coleman keenly pursued this intriguing subject further, and together with fellow cryptozoologist Mark A. Hall he uncovered other accounts and data concerning odd hyaena-like beasts reported in North America over the years, which he duly collated in an article devoted entirely to the *shunka warak'in* (*Fortean Times*, June 1996). One further report dates from as recently as 1991, in Canada, when a peculiar hyaena lookalike beast was observed by several eyewitnesses near to the Alberta Wildlife Park (*Fortean Times*, February-March 1992.

Moreover, an additional report that may well have bearing upon the *shunka warak'in* case but which has not been published until now is one that was brought to my attention by cryptozoological artist William Rebsamen in an email to me of 19 May 1998. In it, Bill recalled meeting up a few days earlier with his high school art teacher, Ron Thomas, and had been very surprised to learn that Ron had a long-standing interest in cryptozoology. Described by Bill as a *very* non-nonsense person with a lifetime's woodsman experience from growing up on a New Jersey horse ranch and moving to the Oklahoma pan-handle working with horses before finally settling down in Fort Smith, Arkansas, to become an art teacher, Ron passed on to Bill some very interesting information:

> *Ron also asked me if I'd ever heard of a strange predator that was not to be mistaken by locals as a bear or dog. Ron said he did not think much after first hearing about this from an old farmer who lived near him until he heard the same description from a totally unrelated second source near the same area. It is described as massively built in the front of its body while having shorter legs in back and travels in an unusual gait. As though Ron read my mind he next told me it sounds to him like some sort of hyena except that it is coal black in color. This reminded me of an article in* Fortean Times *(FT 87, page 42) in Loren's 'On the Trail' of the mysterious (but poorly taxidermed) hyena like creature pictured in a photo from the Southwest.*

I totally agree with Bill that Ron's mystery beast certainly recalls Loren's *Shunka Warak'in* - but if such a beast does indeed exist, what could it be? The most conservative notion is that reports of it feature nothing more than freak/deformed wolves or odd feral mongrel dogs. Even the stuffed specimen, sloping back notwithstanding, appears more canine than hyaenine in overall form as depicted in the photo of it. Additionally, an escaped/released genuine hyaena or two may also have been sighted. However, with the exception of the very dark-furred but also very rare brown hyaena *Hyaena brunnea*, modern-day hyaenas are generally light-coloured with distinctive spots or stripes (depending upon the species).

As for any possibility that it really is a wolf x hyaena hybrid, this is not tenable, because canids and hyaenids belong to two totally separate taxonomic families. Consequently, it is highly unlikely that a wolf-hyaena mating would even produce offspring at all, let alone viable ones.

Three very dramatic identities that have been proposed by Loren and others involve the prospect of prehistoric survival. One of these identities is an undiscovered, modern-day borophagine - a superficially hyaena-like subfamily of canids represented by fossils in North America's Oligocene to Pliocene epochs (34-2.5 million years ago). However, their hypershortened faces differ markedly from the long-snouted profile of the stuffed creature. The second suggestion is a surviving *Chasmaporthetes ossifragus*, America's formidable hunting hyaena, which officially became extinct around 10,000 years ago. And the third is a relict amphicyonid, an identity that has also been applied, as noted earlier, to the *waheela*.

Of course, one of the best possible ways of ascertaining the identity of at least one supposed *shunka warak'in* is to trace the Sherwood-owned taxiderm specimen, and perform DNA analysis on hair samples taken from it. So if you live in or plan to visit the West Yellowstone area, and you happen to spot a strange-looking, stuffed 'hyaena-wolf' ensconced in a large glass case there, don't shun it as a freak or a fake. Take some photos, ask its owners as many questions about it as you can, and please send me whatever images and information concerning it and its new location that you are able to. It may indeed prove to be nothing more startling than a shabbily-preserved wolf or dog - then again, it might prove to be a major cryptozoological find.

Andean Wolves, and Cat-like Dogs (or Dog-like Cats?)

The handsome, flame-furred maned wolf *Chrysocyon brachyurus,* readily distinguished by its long, stilt-like legs, is a denizen of the South American pampas, but in 1947 German zoologist Dr Ingo Krumbiegel proposed that a thicker-furred, shorter-limbed, mountain-dwelling equivalent inhabited the Andes, basing his claim upon what had hitherto been classed as an unusually formed maned wolf skull, and an extremely dense pelt bought some years earlier by Lorenz Hagenbeck at a fur market in Buenos Aires that could not be assigned to any type of canid known to science.

Krumbiegel formally described this seemingly new species, naming it *Dasycyon hagenbecki (Säugetierkundliche Mitteilungen,* 1953). Not long afterwards, however, microscopic examinations of hair samples from this pelt implied that it was merely from some form of domestic sheepdog - but what would today's highly sophisticated DNA hybridization techniques reveal, I wonder?

During his explorations of Bolivia, the lost explorer Lieutenant Colonel Percy Fawcett reported seeing an unidentified dog-like cat called the *mitla*. Jersey Zoo's then assistant director Jeremy Mallinson sought it in the early 1960s, but as he later described in *Travels in Search of Endangered Species* (1989), nothing was found. Dr Roy Mackal suspects it to be the bush-dog *Speothos venaticus,* a strange, short-legged species also implicated as the true identity of another allegedly feline mystery beast, known as the pack-hunting Warracaba jaguar of Guyana.

However, as discussed in my *Mystery Cats of the World* (1989), for the *mitla* identity I support the candidature of an even stranger species, the little-known small-eared dog or zorro *Atelocynus microtis,* of South America's north-eastern portion, whose most striking attribute is its astonishingly feline gait, totally unlike the less graceful, more boisterous movements of other canine species. In short, it is plausible that the *mitla* is not a dog-like cat at all, but rather a cat-like dog!

A Nose (or Two?) for Discovery

Exploration Fawcett (1953), compiled from the field notes of Lieutenant Colonel Fawcett by his son Brian, includes tantalising snippets concerning a variety of seemingly undescribed species, such as the above-mentioned *mitla*, and a giant toothless river shark (possibly a huge catfish?), plus vague mentions of swamp-dwelling relics of the dinosaurian age. One additional mystery beast documented within his book but previously escaping cryptozoological attention, conversely, is a startling oddity encountered by Fawcett in 1913 while visiting Santa Ana, a post on the Marmoré River passing through East Bolivia:

> *Here we saw for the first and only time a breed of dog known as the Double-Nosed Andean Tiger Hound. The two noses are as cleanly divided as though cut with a knife. About the size of a pointer, it is highly valued for its acute sense of smell and ingenuity in hunting jaguars. It is found only on these plains.*

A somewhat droll cartoon of a double-muzzled dog appears on the inside cover of Fawcett's book, after which this twin-snouted canine curiosity was duly forgotten - until almost a century later, when, as reported in London's *Daily Mail* (10 September 2005), modern-day explorer Colonel John Blashford-Snell spied a remarkably similar beast while recently leading an expedition through the very same area.

While staying at a remote village there, he saw a dog whose nostrils were set totally apart from one another, like the barrels of a double-barrelled shotgun.

Making enquiries, he learnt that this dog, called Bella, was not a deformed specimen but one of a distinct, highly-prized, but nowadays rare breed in this area, which was referred to by the same name that Fawcett had recorded - the double-nosed Andean tiger hound.

Photos of Bella brought back by Blashers attracted such interest from Dr Tito Ibson Castro, president of the Bolivian Veterinary Association, that a sequel expedition is now planned, to obtain genetic material and thus determine the origin and relationships to other dog breeds of this dual-nosed wonder.

Interestingly, a few days after newspaper accounts of Bella had appeared in Britain, the *Daily Mail* (17 September 2005) published a follow-up feature containing photos of other, putative Bellas sent in by readers.

The most noteworthy of these was a photo of Henry, a Pachon-Navarro. This rare Iberian breed, related to pointers, is characterised by a very unusual skull, formed into two separate channels with a ridge wide enough for human fingers to be placed inside. Intriguingly, split-nosed Spanish pointers were taken to Latin America by the conquistadors during the 16th Century. So perhaps Henry and Bella have a common ancestor, not just an uncommon nose.

The mystifying 'flying jackal'

Mlularuka – Tanzania's 'Flying Jackal'

No account of canine curiosities could come to a close without mentioning the strange case of Tanzania's *mlularuka* - the 'flying jackal'. As reported by Captain William Hichens *(Discovery,* December 1937), Tanzanian kraalsmen affirmed that this amazing beast, wholly unknown to science at that time, was only too well known to them, as it frequently raided their mango trees and pomegranates during its flights at dusk, and would give voice to loud cries while on the wing. Not surprisingly, their reports were totally disbelieved and dismissed as arrant fantasy - until the 'flying jackal' was discovered!

As I learnt from Dr Maria E. Rutzmoser of Harvard University's Agassiz Museum, in 1926 zoologist Dr Arthur Loveridge was in Tanzania (formerly Tanganyika), collecting specimens for the museum, and at Vituri he succeeded in tracking down the *mlularuka,* but it was not a flying jackal. Instead, it was a large form of gliding rodent.

More specifically, it was a 2.5ft-long scalytail or anomalurid, a peculiar creature with gliding membranes between its limbs so that on first sight it resembles the familiar flying squirrels of Eurasia and North America, but upon closer examination can be readily distinguished via many anatomical differences. Named after the scale-like projections on the underside of the larger species' tails, there are several recognized species of scalytail, but although well-known in West and Central Africa their existence in East Africa had not previously been suspected. Thus the *mlularuka* was believed at first to be a new species, but was later shown to belong to an already wide-ranging species called Fraser's scalytail *Anomalurus derbianus,* and is referred to as *A. d. orientalis* - a mythical flying jackal that was unmasked as an aerial squirrel-impersonator!

Shunka Warak'in - An Extraordinary Animal Revisited

The long-lost stuffed 'ringdocus' (p. 99), which corresponded well with descriptions of the mysterious *shunka warak'in,* has been found! After reading a story about it in late October 2007, Jack Kirby, another grandson of Israel Hutchins, tracked down the elusive exhibit to the Idaho Museum of Natural History in Pocatello. Moreover, the museum agreed to loan it to Kirkby in order for it to be displayed at the Madison Valley History Museum. A new examination of this famous specimen has revealed some previously-undocumented details. It measures 48 inches from the tip of its snout to its rump, not including its tail, and stands 27-28 in high at the shoulder. As portrayed in a photograph accompanying an article concerning its unexpected rediscovery published by the *Bozeman Daily Chronicle* on 15 November 2007, its snout is noticeably narrow, and its coat is dark-brown, almost black, in colour, with lighter tan areas, and includes the faint impression of stripes on its flanks. Despite its age and travels around America, this potentially significant taxiderm specimen is in remarkably good condition, with no signs of wear or tear or even any fading of coat colouration. Could it truly be a *shunka warak'in*? And, if so, what in taxonomic terms is the *shunka warak'in*? Now that the lost has been found, DNA analyses of hair and tissue from the long-preserved exhibit may at last provide some answers.

Chapter Eight

Incongruous Insects and
Stupendous Spiders

There is not space in our museums for the proper display of the prodigious, the unbounded variety of decoration with which Nature has, mother-like, sought to glorify the hymeneal of the insect and to emparadise its nuptials. A distinguished amateur having had the patience to show me in due succession genus after genus, species after species, the whole of his immense collection, I was astounded – in truth, I was stupefied – almost terrified by the inexhaustible energy – I was going to say fury – of invention which Nature displayed. I was overcome – I closed my eyes, and begged for a truce; my brain was dizzied and blinded, and became confused. But she, she would not let me go; she inundated and overwhelmed me with beautiful beings, with fantastic beings, with admirable monsters, with wings of fire, and cuirasses of emerald, clad in a hundred kinds of enamel, armed with singular apparatus – no less brilliant than formidable; some in embrowned steel, shot with yellow – others in silken hoods, embroidered with black velvet; these with fine dashes of tawny silk on a rich mahogany ground; those in pomegranate-coloured velvet lit up with gold; others in luminous, indescribable azures, relieved by jet-black beads; and others, again, bright in metallic streaks alternating with heavy velvet.

It was as if they wished to say:-

"We in ourselves are the whole of Nature. If she perishes, we shall enact a drama, and personate all her creations. For if you look for rich furry garb, behold us here in mantles such as a Russian czarina never wore. Do you wish for feathers? Behold us radiant in plumage which the humming-bird cannot equal; or of you prefer leaves, we can imitate them so as to deceive your eye. Even wood – in fact, all kinds of substances – there is nothing which we cannot imitate. Take, I pray you, this little twig, and hold it in your hand, - it is an insect!"

Then I was fairly conquered. I made a humble reverence to a people so redoubtable; with a burning brain I issued from the magic cave; and for a long time afterwards the sparkling scintillating masks danced and whirled around me, pursuing me, and maintaining on my retina their wild, strange revel.

Jules Michelet – *The Insect*

Insects are the most diverse and numerous of all creatures, so it is little wonder that they are well represented in the chronicles of cryptozoology, as well as in any list of the most astonishing animals alive today. As for spiders, they invariably appear high in any list of phobias as it is, even before considering whether they can attain nightmarish sizes far in excess of anything recognised by science...

Insect Giants - from Daunting Dragonflies to Mighty Mantids

It is well known that the tracheal-based respiratory system of insects, which is only capable of transporting oxygen over tiny distances, precludes their attaining the gargantuan sizes beloved of sci-fi movie makers. However, some reports of larger-than-normal insects have reached me from a number of different sources over the years, of which the following are particularly intriguing.

One of these, forwarded to me in 2001 by *Strange Magazine*'s founding editor, the late Mark Chorvinsky, consists of a report e-mailed to him by correspondent Victor Engel. It reads as follows:

> *You may be interested in an expedition I plan on this summer. In May/June 1974 while driving through Mexico, I saw the largest dragonfly I've ever seen. At the time I estimated its wingspan at 14 inches. Since that time, I've not seriously searched for it again, but I have done some research. I've contacted dragonfly experts and other insect experts. The general consensus in the scientific community is that while there used to be dragonflies of that size, and, in fact, even larger, they don't, and cannot exist today. The reason cited for believing they cannot exist today is that the oxygen content of the atmosphere is too low to support the high metabolism required for the dragonfly to catch its prey. Then I got in touch with Dr Gilbert, of the University of Texas at Austin, who is doing research with imported fire ants and their parasitic phorid flies. He gave me two well thought-out lists. One was a list of all the reasons why such a dragonfly cannot exist. The other was a list of reasons why such an insect could possibly exist. Anyway, I'm so convinced at what I saw in the 70s that now I'm making a special trip just to find one again.*

As Engel correctly mentions, there were once dragonflies that were even bigger than the size estimate offered by him for his Mexican mystery specimen. Indeed, fossil remains of *Meganeura monyi*, a dragonfly that lived approximately 300 million years ago in what is today France, indicate that it sported a spectacular wingspan of up to 29.5in, thereby making it the largest insect species, past or present, currently known to science.

Today, conversely, the largest member of the taxonomic order Odonata - housing dragonflies - is *Megalopropus caeruleata*, a damselfly native to Central and South America, whose wingspan measures up to 7.52in, and whose body length is up to 4.72in. Hence Engel's specimen, if accurately estimated, would have a wingspan twice this. However, due to their rapid aerial movements and continual hawking, the size of these insects is notoriously difficult to gauge accurately.

Maryland University entomologist Dr David Yager has alluded online on the Mantodea listserver to alleged reports of mantids over 1ft long, and noted that people in Washington DC often describe *Tenodera* mantids in their gardens as being "6 in or so" long. He believes that these are over-estimates - or, as he drily refers to them, "variants on the proverbial Fish Story". Having said that, it is certainly true that the world's longest species of insect alive today is a relative of mantids - a species of stick insect (phasmid) from the rainforests of Borneo, called *Pharnacia kirbyi*, with a known body length of up to 12.9in and a total length (including the legs) that can exceed 20in. Currently, the longest known mantid species is a newly discovered, and currently un-named one from the Cameroons, which is known in the pet trade as 'the mega-mantis'. There are rumours of an even longer species from Peru and Bolivia. However, the longest known North American species are not generally longer than 6in. These comprise the afore-mentioned *Tenodera* mantids. Nevertheless, a freak over-sized specimen may occur from time to time, and perhaps, together with exaggerated size estimates, explain some of the 'super-mantis' reports from Washington DC.

Much more disturbing are claimed sightings of giant blackflies said to frequent Dundass Island, in British Columbia, Canada. Reputedly measuring 5-6 inches long, this mysterious species has a red head, but an entirely black body except for a red tip to the abdomen and a yellow band across the thorax. It allegedly sucks blood, eats human flesh, is venomous, and attacks in huge swarms. Apparently, local people often refuse to travel to the island because they are so afraid of these monstrous insects. Could they merely be based upon exaggerated accounts of large horse-flies, known for their aggression and painful bites?

Staying with oversized insects: Housed within the Hope entomological collections at Oxford University Museum is one of the world's most infamous insects, the imperial flea. This is a suitable name for what was once believed to be a spectacularly large species of flea, yet which had somehow been overlooked by science until formally described by Victorian entomologist J.O. Westwood. Tragically, however, the imperial flea's reign as a zoological celebrity was a short one. When its only known specimen was later examined by other scientists, they discovered that it was nothing more than a somewhat squashed nymph (juvenile) of *Blatta orientalis* - a common species of cockroach!

Gooseberry Wife – More Than a Myth?

The quaintly-named gooseberry wife is a giant hairy caterpillar said to lurk amid gooseberry bushes on the Isle of Wight (situated off Hampshire, southern England), lying in wait to devour unruly children hoping to steal the berries. Having said that, you will no doubt be relieved to learn that this daunting creature is no more real than any other imaginary bugbear invented by exasperated parents to deter their errant offspring from doing what they shouldn't. Having said that, I confess to being intrigued as to how such a distinctive bugbear, seemingly confined entirely to the folklore of the Isle of Wight, originated. So if there are any IOW inhabitants who could shed any light on this mystery for me, please let me know – especially as what seems to have been a smaller but real-life version was actually spied elsewhere in southeastern England as recently as the mid-1970s.

In a recent *Fortean Times* letter (*FT* No. 225, 2007), Neil Powney recalled that his girlfriend Lyn, when aged 7-8 and living in the Corringham area of Essex three decades ago, was once startled to see a huge furry caterpillar crawling up a lavender tree less than 5ft away from her in her parents' back garden. She estimates that it was about 1ft long, as thick as a rolling pin, and covered in 4in-long hairs, dark brown-green in colour. As she watched, this extraordinary creature made its way up the tree's trunk, and then across onto a panel of the adjacent fence, which it crawled along until it came to a gap that it squeezed through into the neighbouring garden. When Lyn looked over the fence, she could see the caterpillar making its way across the neighbour's lawn. Lyn then ran inside her own house and fetched her mother, but when they came outside it had vanished. I wonder whether Lyn, as a child, may have mistaken a colony of caterpillars moving together in formation, as a column or procession (as some species do), for a single, giant entity. Yet her view of it was at such close range that this does not seem a very satisfactory explanation.

Life with the Lions

It's official! Britain has a native species of lion, hitherto overlooked by science, living and breeding in its countryside! Lest ABC (alien big cat) enthusiasts become too excited, however, I should point out that this particular lion is only an inch or so long and sports a rather fetching complement of dappled wings, four in total, transporting it in fragile flight through the air. The species in question is, of course, an ant-lion. Although closely related to those pale green filigree-winged insects known as lacewings and belonging to the taxonomic order Neuroptera, with their slender abdomen and long slim wings ant-lions superficially resemble miniature dragonflies or damselflies. However, they are readily distinguished externally by their conspicuous clubbed antennae and the venation of their wings.

Their memorable name derives not from their adults but from their larvae, which are wingless, stout-bodied, voracious predators with huge jaws. Larval ant-lions are famous for digging conical pits in sand and lurking concealed at the bottom, where they seize any ants or other luckless insects that unwittingly fall into their cunning traps.

British entomologists have always viewed these exotic insects with envious eyes, for although ant-lions are common in continental Europe, they were not thought to have any native, breeding representative on mainland Britain (there is a species on Jersey). Nevertheless, a few adult individuals, belonging to the species *Euroleon nostras*, have been recorded from a few localities in East Suffolk over the years.

On 5 September 1931, C.G. Doughty caught one such specimen (erroneously identified at the time as a related species, *Myrmeleon formicarius*) in Gorleston. On 29 August 1988, a specimen that flew into a house in Corton, near Lowestoft, was photographed, and then released, before being identified from the photos by Dr A.G. Irwin. And on 21 July 1994, two ant-lions were found near the toilet block on the road leading to the RSPB reserve at Minsmere by the reserve's warden, Geoff Welch. Their species was identified by Ipswich Museum entomologist Howard Mendel (*Entomologist's Record*, January/February 1996), and a third specimen was found squashed on the floor inside the toilet block on 31 August 1994, by Minsmere's assistant warden, D. Fairhurst.

However, these were all assumed to be vagrants, blown across the Channel by freak winds (or even stowaways whose passage to Britain had presumably been assisted by residing unnoticed on maritime trading vessels travelling here from the continent) - but no more.

Not everyone has been convinced by the above explanations, and several entomologists down through the decades have voiced the exciting opinion that perhaps there could be a native, breeding population of *Euroleon* lurking undetected in Britain. In autumn 1992, Colin W. Plant, Britain's National Recorder for Neuroptera, organised a field meeting to scour the East Anglian coast in search of anonymous ant-lions, but his optimism unfortunately went unrewarded; none was found. Following the discovery of the Minsmere specimens two years later, however, the possibility once more seemed quite promising - but there was one vital missing link that needed to be forged before the promising could become the proven. Only the discovery of larval ant-lions could confirm this insect's existence in Britain as a breeding species, but none had ever been recorded here.

An adult ant-lion

It was now summer 1996, and from 6 to 9 August Richard Cottle, Mike Edwards, and Stuart Roberts were conducting an invertebrate survey of Suffolk Sandlings Heaths. During their survey, they traversed Walberswick National Nature Reserve, and were intrigued to espy at the base of a small cliff, formed by a partially buried root, a number of small conical pits. As they already knew about the recent finding of adult *Euroleon* specimens at Minsmere, they swiftly examined the pits, and in the very first one they unearthed to their delight a living ant-lion larva, but this would only be the first of many - a very great many, as it turned out (*Entomologist's Record*, November/December 1996).

During the four days, the trio spotted about 300 ant-lion pits in this same area, over 1000 at Minsmere, a large population at Dunwich Heath, and a smaller one on Blaxhall Common, just under 10 miles southwest of Minsmere - collectively exceeding 3000 pits in total, mostly on surfaces open to the sun and associated with small cliffs.

They even spied 15 freshly-emerged adult ant-lions, drying their delicate gauzy wings before become airborne in hesitant, virginal flight. There could no longer be any doubt - *Euroleon nostras* was a British lion, in every sense.

It is not every day - not even every century - that a totally new taxonomic family of insects is added to Britain's official faunal checklist, thus confirming the exposure of *Euroleon* as one of the most significant episodes in the U.K.'s modern-day natural history.

Perhaps the most remarkable aspect of this case, however, is how such a distinctive species of insect (in the adult state, at least) as an ant-lion could remain undetected and unsuspected for so long by the entomological community in so zoologically familiar a land as the U.K. Quite evidently, there is more to British cryptozoology than its popular media image of prowling ABCs and periscoping water monsters might have us believe.

All Lit Up in Thailand – Glowing Midge Larvae

In late 2000, English cryptozoological investigator Richard Freeman of the CFZ returned home from his search in northern Thailand's jungles for the naga - a giant snake familiar in Hindu and Buddhist myths, but also said genuinely to exist in Indochina's more remote parts (see my book *The Beasts That Hide From Man*, 2003). Although he did not spy it himself, he amassed a sizeable collection of local eyewitness reports. Moreover, while in Thailand, he also penetrated some remote caves that may not have been explored before by westerners, but where a naga exceeding 54ft long had been reported. Again, he didn't see it himself, but what he did find, as he later mentioned to me, was a small colony of midge larvae (occupying a patch about one square foot in area) living on the cave roof that attracted prey using beads of luminous saliva suspended on 6in-long threads of silk.

A comparable species, *Arachnocampa luminosa*, is a famous sight in New Zealand's Waitomo cave system (though in much larger colonies), where they are popularly, albeit incorrectly, referred to as glow-worms, and which I was delighted to see when visiting these caves in December 2006. However, as far as Richard is aware, there are no such insects recorded from Thailand. Not expecting to find anything like these, he did not take any collecting tubes when exploring the narrow cave passages, so was unable to obtain a specimen for examination. Hence the intriguing question of whether the Thai midges constitute an undiscovered species presently remains unanswered.

Harlequin Beetle – Art Deco on Legs...All Six of Them!

When British geneticist Prof. J.B.S. Haldane was asked what inferences could be drawn about the nature of God from a study of His works, he replied: "An inordinate fondness for beetles". Haldane's response was undoubtedly inspired by the knowledge that, for sheer diversity of form and plenitude of species, the beetles effortlessly surpass all other animal groups. Well over 300,000 species are currently recognized, with many new ones described every year. They include some ostentatiously strange types, but few are any stranger than *Acrocinus longimanus*, the uncommonly unconventional harlequin beetle - an insect of such finely wrought form and elegantly elaborate ornamentation that it could be mistaken for a creation by one of Art Deco's more inspired exponents.

With a wide distribution, stretching southwards from Mexico to the tropical rainforests of southern Brazil, this idiosyncratic wood-boring insect earns its common name from the unique complement of colours and markings borne upon its head, thorax, and long slender wing-cases (elytra). The predominant colours are orange, black, and brick-red, tastefully combined to yield a complicated design more than a little reminiscent of the intricately patterned costume worn by a stage harlequin and overlain by finer tracings in the style of delicate hieroglyphics. So attractive and striking is the sum effect that it is frequently reproduced by Brazilian Indians on their shields.

Even more conspicuous than its decorative markings and coloration, however, are its antennae and first pair of legs - due to their excessive length. Whereas the entire length of its body rarely exceeds 3in, its forelegs are often twice this, and its remarkably slim antennae are even longer (in keeping with its membership of the longhorn beetle family, Cerambycidae).

Precisely engineered for a principally arboreal lifestyle, its immensely long forelegs are used for effectively grasping and retaining hold of wide tree stems and boughs, and are further assisted by sharp, curved spurs at their bases and by hooks on their tibial segments. If the beetle is forced to creep over the ground, conversely, these over-long limbs greatly impede its progress, transforming the adept tree-climber into an awkward, clumsy shuffler. Its elongated forelegs are also used as weapons, the males brandishing them at one another like medieval lances to win the fair tarsus of the lady harlequin.

Its unique, exotic appearance - so bizarre on first sight that it was erroneously classified in 1724 bv J.J. Scheuchzer as an outlandish grasshopper - renders the harlequin instantly identifiable. Nevertheless, its detection is often achieved not by looking, but by listening, for it. Despite its large size and lengthy appendages, the harlequin is capable of sustaining flight - of a loud, rustling nature - but it has yet to master the techniques of directing it, so that it generally blunders into whatever object happens to be in the way, after which it promptly falls to the ground with an undignified and very audible thud. And once on the ground, its attempts at walking are accompanied by a distinctive creaking sound.

The noisy nature of its aerial and terrestrial movements is not alone in betraying this species' presence. Its weakness for the juices secreted by the bagasse tree *Bagassa guianensis* has been capitalised upon by the more canny of coleopterists. The bagasse's thick white secretions exude a peculiarly powerful, penetrating odour when freshly extracted, which can be detected by this beetle at a considerable distance. Consequently, beetle collectors often wound a bagasse and then simply sit back to await the inevitable arrival of harlequins irresistibly attracted by the potent aroma of the tree's sap trickling from the wound. So familiar is the harlequin's fondness for this sap that it is widely known in its native lands as *mouche bagasse*.

A distinctive insect in every sense, the harlequin beetle's strangest of all claims to fame must surely be its role as a mobile home for other animals. As Ewald Reitter described in his magnificent tome *Beetles* (1961), the harlequin is parasitised by

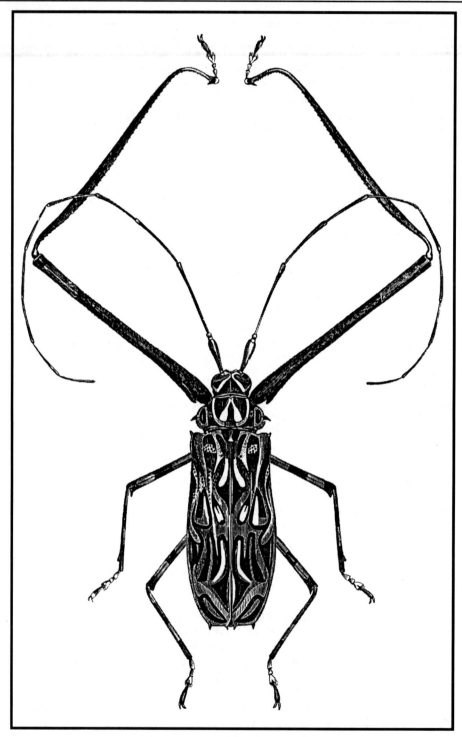

The Harlequin Beetle

tiny acarine mites that live beneath its wings on the upper surface of its abdomen, but alleviating the effects of these unwelcome guests is a small species of superficially scorpion-like arachnid known as a pseudoscorpion, also living under the beetle's wings and preying upon the mites.

Even when the harlequin takes to the air in its somewhat haphazard, blustering flight, its guests merely 'fasten their seatbelts' and come along too - the mites anchor themselves down with strong, sticky secretions, and the pseudoscorpions clasp firmly to any accessible area of soft skin in the joints of the beetle's armour-like external skeleton. The transportation by an animal of other, smaller animals is known as phoresy, and as exhibited here by the harlequin beetle is a singularly novel instance of the dictum 'greater fleas have lesser fleas', but is thoroughly in accord with everything else concerning this most exquisite, and extraordinary, insect.

An Insect from Faerie?

Occasionally, a report so strange and singular comes to light that it defies any serious attempt at explanation. One such example was forwarded to what is now the cz@yahoogroups.com cryptozoology discussion group by its founder and moderator, American cryptozoologist Chad Arment, on 26 May 1998. He received it from a Tennessee correspondent, and it read as follows:

The insect that I saw was humming a song. I was on top of a hill and thought that I was hearing a radio or something like that but I noticed this little bug [and] the closer it got the more like a song it became. This little bug was flying upright like a ...fairy! I was really excited because I thought what I saw was what people in earlier times might have mistaken for real sprites. This bug went from tree to tree and from flower to flower stopping at each one. I didn't see it eat anything but like I said I was excited. It was about 2" long "tall" and white[,] had blue eyes large almond shaped and long antennae that hung like hair. It was really quite intriguing but as I moved to get a better look it saw me and went horizontal and was off like a shot. Also the humming stopped when it saw me and it just buzzed away.

Reading through this extraordinary report, images of hawk moths (notably something along the lines of the famous hummingbird hawk moths) come to mind; but with so little detailed morphological description to hand, there seems little chance of ever obtaining a satisfactory identification for this cryptozoological fairy.

Monstrous Mutants

Giant, hideous mutated insects are popular fodder for the more lurid science fiction novels and films. However, mutant insects, albeit of less threatening demeanour, are sometimes reported in the real world too. Perhaps the most dramatic examples on record are rare instances of lepidopteran individuals whose metamorphosis has malfunctioned, yielding monstrosities with the wings and six-legged body of a butterfly but retaining the vegetation-chomping head of a caterpillar.

Freak insects with additional limbs are much more common, and in most cases their teratological condition merely involves simple limb duplication, so that two limbs emerge from a site that should only bear one. This also occurs with antennae, and is even known with wings – although the extra wing is generally smaller than its twin, as demonstrated, for example, by the small tortoiseshell butterfly *Aglais urticae* illustrated on Plate 47 in T.G. Howarth's *Colour Identification Guide to British Butterflies* (1973). A female specimen, it possessed an extra right hindwing, and had been captured in Epping, Essex, sometime around 1850 by E. Doubleday. It is now housed within the butterfly collection of the British Museum (Natural History).

Far more remarkable, however, are the teratological conditions known respectively as labiopedia (sometimes termed proboscipedia) and antennapedia (also termed aristopedia), because these are responsible for the development of extra limbs via quite extraordinary mechanisms.

The mouthparts of a typical unspecialised insect (such as a cockroach) consist primarily of two pairs of jaws (mandibles and maxillae), which operate from side to side rather than up and down, plus a labrum or upper lip, and a labium or lower lip, which also bears a pair of sensory structures called labial palps. Insect evolutionists believe that these mouthparts are actually modified limbs, i.e. in ancestral insect species millions of years ago they constituted legs rather than feeding organs. This in turn makes labiopedia an especially interesting phenomenon, because in an insect exhibiting it, one or more of the segments comprising the labial palps (and sometimes one or more of the segments comprising the other feeding organs too) have failed to develop. Instead, they have been replaced by leg segments. And in extreme cases, both labial palps are replaced *entirely*, thereby yielding atavistically an eight-legged insect!

Mutations of this type – in which a modern-day structure is replaced by a corresponding ancestral one – are termed homeotic. They have been reported from many different animal types.

A comparable phenomenon to labiopedia is antennapedia, in which some antennal segments, or the whole of one or both antennae, are replaced by leg segments. Once again this is of evolutionary significance, because just like the mouthparts, the antennae of modern-day insects are believed to have evolved from ancestral insect limbs.

The genetics of mutations involving labiopedia and antennapedia have been investigated in detail with a number of species to discover their precise mode of operation. In the parasitoid wasp *Brecon hebetor*, for example, the mutant allele (gene form) responsible for the transformation of antennal segments into leg segments has been shown to be a recessive one. Conversely, the mutant allele responsible for this abnormality in the black-bellied fruit-fly *Drosophila melanogaster* is dominant, and is one of seven genes making up a special 'super-gene' known as ANT-C or the antennapedia complex.

A comparable version of antennapedia can also result from external stimulation. It has been discovered with the common laboratory stick insect *Carausius morosus* that if the tip of one of its antennae is lost, it will regenerate a correct replacement for the missing piece. If, however, an antenna breaks off further down, with the break occurring through one of its two basal segments, instead of regenerating a replacement antenna the stick insect often develops a fully-formed leg, complete right down to the claws at its distal tip.

A third, equally noteworthy homeotic mutation reported from insects is one that, unlike labiopedia and antennapedia, involves wings rather than limbs, but which does not appear to have a formal name.

In advanced modern-day adult insects, the thorax consists of three segments, each of which possesses one pair of legs. In addition, almost all flying insects possess four wings – a pair of forewings borne on the second thoracic segment, and a pair of hindwings borne on the third thoracic segment. There are, however, a few exceptions.

By far the most notable of these is Diptera, the taxonomic order of insects containing the true flies. Typified by species such as the crane-flies or daddy-long-legs, the wasp-mimicking hover-flies, the familiar bluebottles and house-flies, and the all-too-familiar gnats and mosquitoes, the true flies are characterised by possessing only a single pair of proper wings (hence Diptera – 'two-winged'), borne on the second thoracic segment. On the third segment, the hindwings have become modified into a tiny pair of structures termed halteres, each of which resembles a half-dumbbell in shape, serving as organs of balance by acting as gyroscopes when the insect is in flight.

It has been observed, however, that very occasionally the black-bellied fruit-fly gives rise to an adult specimen in which the halteres have been replaced by a second pair of proper wings, thereby hearkening back to the ancestral dipteran condition (as evidenced from fossils and from rare amber-embedded specimens dating back millions of years) in which these insects were still four-winged.

Along Came a Spider

Even in the famously diverse field of cryptozoology, it can sometimes seem as if we've heard it all - and then along comes a truly astonishing report to provide a much-welcomed (albeit highly controversial) breath of fresh air. In the particular instance revealed here, what came along was the *j'ba fofi*, a type of giant Congolese spider - the size of a human!

I first learnt of these nightmarish beasts from veteran Congo explorer-cryptozoologist Bill Gibbons back in 2001, who related an account passed on to him by a Margaret M. Lloyd, formerly living in what was then Rhodesia, but now in England. Back in 1938, her parents Reginald and Margurite Lloyd were exploring the erstwhile Belgian Congo's interior when what looked like a large monkey or small human figure crossed their path a little way ahead. They stopped their car to let the creature pass, and were amazed to discover that it was a huge brown tarantula-like spider, with a leg length close to 3ft!

In November 2003, while exploring Cameroon in search of *mokele-mbembe*-type aquatic cryptids, Bill spoke of the Lloyds' horrific encounter to Timbo, chief of the local Baka pygmy tribe. Unfazed by this report, Timbo replied that his people knew of these mega-spiders (as did the area's Bantu hunters), referring to them as the *j'ba fofi* ('great spider'), and that if Bill had mentioned this to him during his previous expedition here, in 2000, he would have taken him to a location in the forest close by where one of these creatures could have been filmed. Timbo also provided some interesting additional details concerning the *j'ba fofi*.

They were once much more common than they are now, their decreased numbers probably due to deforestation in this area of Central Africa, and would build lairs close to human villages. Their lairs were constructed from leaves, and resembled the huts of the pygmies. Moreover, they would spin a web between two trees, with a trip line stretching across a small game trail, using this to snare prey as sizeable as small forest antelope and birds. The *j'ba fofi* lay white eggs the size of peanuts, from which emerge immature yellow spiders with purple abdomens, but they turn brown as they mature. The Baka claim that these spiders are still met with today, and are able to kill humans, but are themselves killed by the pygmies.

Consequently, before leaving Cameroon in 2003, Bill arranged with his field director, Pierre Sima, for a substantial reward to be made available to whoever succeeded in procuring a *j'ba fofi*, dead or alive, and Timbo promised that he and his hunters would seek one.

Meanwhile, no tangible evidence for the reality of these giant spiders exists. Discussing this on the cryptolist@yahoogroups.com online group during 2004, it was suggested that perhaps the pygmies had misidentified them, mistaking large monkeys for spiders, but Bill refutes this possibility - stating that the Baka are well-acquainted with monkeys and other mammalian fauna, and that they are adamant the *j'ba fofi* are eight-legged spiders, as opposed to four-legged mammals. Nor can he see any advantage to the Baka in inventing such claims, because they would gain nothing from them unless they could produce a body, which they would be unable to do if their claims are false.

However, there is more to consider here than the accuracy or otherwise of native testimony. What about basic anatomy and physiology - surely it is biologically impossible for a spider the size of a human to exist? The largest species of spider known to exist today is the goliath bird-eating spider *Theraphosa leblondi*, inhabiting the rainforests of Surinam, French Guiana, and Guyana, and occasionally collected elsewhere in South America too. The current record-holder is a male captured in April 1965 at Rio Cavro, Venezuela, which sported a body length of 3.5in, and a colossal leg-span of 11.02in - big enough, in other words, to cover a dinner plate! Even so, that is still far short of the Congolese monsters.

Helping to bridge this seemingly irreconcilable difference in size, however, is an equally mysterious spider brought to attention in October 2001 by Peter and Debbie Hynes via the cz@yahoogroups.com discussion group. The mother of one of Debbie's friends claimed that during World War II, while serving in the Australian Army fighting the Japanese forces on the Kokoda Trail in Papua New Guinea's central highlands, her father had encountered an enormous snow-white cotton-like mass of cobweb spread all over the ground and tree trunks for about 10-15ft on either side of him. Then, to his horror, he spotted the web's creator, squatting just 1ft or so from his face - a jet-black spider, as big as a puppy! Its legs were thick and hairy, but not particularly long in comparison with its bulky body. Unsurprisingly, its human observer backed away very slowly and carefully.

Confirming that new species of extremely large spider can still be discovered - and overlooked - in modern times, some massive specimens of a hitherto-undescribed sparassid huntsman spider from Laos were lately uncovered by German zoologist Dr Peter Jaeger in the old collections of the Muséum National d'Histoire Naturelle in Paris. With a leg span of almost 1ft, these remarkable spiders had been collected 70 years earlier, but until rediscovered by Jaeger they had remained incognito at the museum. In 2001, their dramatic species was finally described and named *Heteropoda maxima* (in the museum's journal, *Zoosystema*), and may well be the largest known species of sparassid.

Until recently, prehistory offered a truly spectacular, fully-confirmed super-spider - the aptly dubbed *Megarachne servinei*, formally described in 1980 from a 300-million-year old Upper Carboniferous fossil specimen discovered by Argentine palaeontologist Mario Hünicken in the Bajo de Veliz Formation at San Luis, Argentina.

Its body measured roughly 16in long, and is estimated to have possessed a leg span of some 20in. In 2005, conversely, the identity of *Megarachne* as a mega-spider was challenged in a *Biology Letters of the Royal Society* paper by Manchester University zoologist Dr Paul Selden and Hünicken, who proposed that it had actually been a very different chelicerate creature - not a spider but rather a sea scorpion or eurypterid.

Megarachne notwithstanding, could extra-large spiders truly exist? The respiratory system of permeating tubes (tracheae) limits the upper size attainable by insects, and as the more active, advanced species of spiders also possess tracheae (albeit unbranched ones, in contrast to the highly-branched insect versions), the same restriction must surely apply to them.

More primitive spider species, conversely, respire via two pairs of organs each structured like the pages of a book, and hence known as book-lungs, but these function via passive oxygen diffusion, lacking any active pumping mechanism.

Consequently, this system seems even less likely than the tracheal version to be able to power the upbeat metabolism required for a human-sized spider. In short, the only tenable biological explanation for the *j'ba fofi* would appear to be one that postulated some radical departure in respiratory physiology from either book-lungs or tracheae - which is where the Baka come in.

For if they do succeed in obtaining a *j'ba fofi*, and it does indeed prove to be a spider, its corpse's interior will prove to be of even greater zoological interest than its identity. New species are still being discovered, even dramatically new ones on occasion. But a wholly novel respiratory system having evolved within such a supposedly well-studied zoological group of animals as spiders really would be a wonder - a breath of fresh air in every sense!

Chapter Nine
'Classic' Extinct Birds –
When Did They Really Die Out?

And over them triumphant Death his Dart
Shook, but delaid to strike...

John Milton - *Paradise Lost*

The passenger pigeon, Carolina parakeet, pink-headed duck, the moas, great auk, and huia are all 'classic' extinct birds. Their dates of demise are so familiar to all ornithological students through faithful repetition in successive works dealing with vanished species that any suggestion that they may be other than immutable is generally considered to be little short of scientific heresy. Consequently, it is not widely realised that there are sufficiently convincing and reliable eyewitness reports on record to encourage cautious speculation that all of these species may actually have survived for quite a time *beyond* their official extinction dates (and in some cases may still exist today).

Passenger Pigeon

The most numerous species of wild bird ever known was the phenomenally plentiful passenger pigeon *Ectopistes migratorius,* a dainty, slender-bodied, long-tailed bird with blue-grey head, neck, back, and wings, and cinnamon-pink underparts. It has been estimated that during the 19th Century's early years, its total population contained between five and ten thousand million birds. Or to put it another way, this single species may have accounted for as much as 45% of the entire bird population of America! One of the most evocative descriptions of its immense numbers during its heyday appeared in *The Mirror of Literature, Amusement, and Instruction* for 16 November 1822:

> *The accounts of the enormous flocks in which the passenger, or wild pigeons, fly about in North America, seem to an European like the tales of Baron Munchausen; but the travellers are 'all in a story.' In Upper Canada, says Mr. Howison, in his entertaining 'Sketches,' you may kill 20 or 30 at one shot, out of the masses which darken the air. And in the United States, according to Wilson, the ornithologist, they sometimes desolate and lay waste a tract of country 40 or 50 miles long, and 5 or 6 broad, by making it their breeding-place. While in the state of Ohio, Mr. Wilson saw a flock of these birds which extended, he judged, more than a mile in*

breadth, and continued to pass over his head at the rate of one mile in a minute, during four hours — thus making its whole length about 240 miles. According to his moderate estimate, this flock contained two thousand two hundred and thirty millions, two hundred and seventy-two pigeons.

It seems inconceivable that less than a century after the above report had been published the passenger pigeon had been completely exterminated, but this is precisely what happened. As a result of an unutterably ruthless, relentless programme of persecution (on a scale unparalleled even in man's nefarious history of wildlife destruction), perpetrated by trigger-happy gun-toters attracted by the awesome spectacle of the birds' mass migrations, by 1 September 1914 only one solitary specimen remained alive. This was a 29-year-old hen bird named 'Martha Washington', exhibited at Cincinnati Zoo. And shortly after noon on that fateful September day, this last humble survivor of an ostensibly indomitable, indestructible species died. The unthinkable had happened - the passenger pigeon, whose vast migrating flocks had virtually eclipsed the sun in the time of the great American painter Audubon, was no more.

Passenger pigeon – did it survive beyond 1914?

Officially, that is. For at least another decade, alleged sightings of passenger pigeons were frequently reported, but scientists tended to dismiss these as mistaken observations of the smaller but closely related mourning dove *Zenaida macroura*, still a common species. In September 1929, however, a remarkable report emerged that could not be discarded so readily. This was the month in which Michigan University bacteriologist Prof. Philip Hadley, in the company of a Mr Foard, an old friend familiar with the land, had been hunting in a virtually uninhabited wilderness nestling within Michigan's northern peninsula.

They had been hunting there for some time when Foard drew Hadley's attention to a bird perched close by, and declared that it was a passenger pigeon - which he had observed in enormous numbers when younger. Needless to say, Hadley turned at once to spy this exceedingly unexpected specimen, but just as he caught sight of it the bird took flight. Nevertheless, it did seem to him to be pigeon-like in form, with a pointed tail, and he clearly believed the incident to be of significance, because he sent details to the eminent US journal *Science,* which in turn judged it to be important enough to warrant publication in its issue of 14 February 1930.

Within his letter, Hadley also referred to a couple of other recent sightings, documented a month earlier by Kendrick Kimball in the *Detroit News* (5 January). One of these sightings had been made on 10 June 1929, by Robert H. Wright of Munissing, Michigan. Wright was convinced that the pair of birds that he saw at close range on Highway M-28, about 16 miles from Munissing, were passenger pigeons. In the other sighting, made between Indianapolis and Kokomo while driving from Florida, Dr Samuel R. Landes spotted a flock of approximately 15 birds that he readily identified as passenger pigeons. Both Wright and Landes were familiar with this species' appearance - like so many others, they had shot hundreds of them during the late 1870s.

Nonetheless, the last *confirmed* wild specimen was shot in 1899, at Babcock, Wisconsin, so is it really possible that the birds reported three decades later by the eyewitnesses above were truly passenger pigeons? It seems rather unlikely, at least at first, because after the last major flocks had been slaughtered (in 1878), stragglers did not survive long, and matings became ever fewer. It seemed as if the species could only persist and reproduce when present in huge flocks. At the same time, of course, the familiarity of the eyewitnesses with the species makes their testimony all that more difficult to discount.

Perhaps certain fairly secluded localities did house a last few specimens, which existed undetected beyond the date of Martha's death, and possibly even mated every now and then, and which were encountered only when their flights traversed areas frequented by humans, or when humans occasionally passed by their hideaways. Yet without the immense congregations necessary to provide the stimulus for normal, full-scale reproduction, they could surely do no more than extend their species' survival by a few years. Long before the last individual had died, whether in 1914 or in the 1930s, the passenger pigeon's descent into extinction had already begun, irrevocably and inevitably, with the disappearance of its vast flocks. After that, it could only be a matter of time.

Surely, then, the 'passenger pigeon' spied in March 1965 at Homer, Michigan, by Irene Llewellyn *(Fate,* September 1965) and another spied the same year by Stella Fenell at New Jersey's Park Ridge *(Fate,* January 1966) were only mourning doves ... weren't they?

An Antipodean equivalent of sorts is the flock pigeon *Histriophaps histrionica.* In the 1800s huge flocks, containing millions of birds, lived on the grass plains of New South Wales and Queensland. Today, though, it is a relatively rare species (it was once thought to be extinct). This time the cause is not man himself but his animals: the flock pigeon is a seed-eater, but generations of grazing cattle and sheep have prevented the plains' grass from seeding adequately.

Carolina Parakeet

The Carolina parakeet *Conuropsis carolinensis*, a readily recognizable species with bright green body and striking yellow head, earned its own status as a 'classic' not just by being the only parrot species native to North America, but also because its extinction so closely paralleled the passenger pigeon's. Once very common in North America east of the Great Plains (especially in swampland areas), it acquired notoriety among fruit farmers as a considerable pest, because large flocks would descend upon orchards and devour great quantities of the farmers' valuable produce. This, together with its popularity among woodsmen as a shooting target, and as a pet (responsible for the trapping of great numbers), resulted in its rapid extermination.

The last wild specimen known to have been collected was taken on 18 April 1901 in Florida, and by February 1918 only a single captive specimen remained. By an ironic coincidence, this last living individual, a male called 'Incas', was housed at Cincinnati Zoo - which had already been home to the very last passenger pigeon - where he died later that month. Thus, in less than four years, this same zoo had played host, reluctantly but impotently, to the extinction of two of North America's most distinguished species of bird.

Yet as with the passenger pigeon, reports of Carolina parakeets continued to surface for many years after their species' official extinction date. Some of these may well have been based upon sightings of non-native green parakeets that had escaped from captivity, but other, more compelling accounts are also on record.

For example, in *Extinct and Vanishing Birds of the World* (2nd edn, 1967) James C. Greenway noted that in 1920 a flock of about 30 individuals was reported near Florida's Fort Drum Creek by Henry Redding, a local man. Equally remarkable (but in this case for all the *wrong* reasons) was a sighting made in 1926 by Charles E. Doe - at that time no less a personage than the Curator of Birds at Florida University. The presence in Okeechobee County, Florida, of three pairs of parakeets closely resembling the supposedly extinct Carolina parakeet evidently filled Doe with great excitement. So much so that, according to Errol Fuller *(Extinct Birds,* 1987), he proceeded to rob the poor birds of their eggs!

From carrying out extensive enquiries, esteemed American ornithologist Alexander Sprunt Jr became convinced that before the start of the Second World War in 1939, Carolina parakeets still survived within the Santee swamp area of South Carolina. One account that particularly impressed him had been obtained from a local woodsman named Shokes, who alleged that during the three to four years in which he and his son had been employed in that area as National Audubon Society bird wardens in the 1930s, they had seen green-bodied, yellow-headed parakeets there on three or four separate occasions. During one of these, Shokes had observed two such birds, evidently adults, followed by a smaller, younger individual with wavering flight, as they made their way across Wadmacaun Creek to Wadmacaun Island.

Sprunt himself, conversely, never saw adult specimens but one day sometime between 1936 and 1938, whilst in the company of John Baker (then President of the National Audubon Society) and acclaimed ornithologist/bird painter Roger Tory Peterson, he had seen a bright green bird fly swiftly past about 50 yards away, with a rapid, dove-like flight which convinced him that it was an immature Carolina parakeet. Sprunt sent news of his investigations to his English friend M.S. Curtler *(Animals,* 23 November 1965).

Sadly, even if the Santee Swamp birds were genuine Carolina parakeets, they could not have saved the species from extinction, because the swamp was eventually destroyed by developmental processes for a power plant. Nonetheless, there are many other swamps still existing within this bird's original range that remain aloof and little-explored even today. In 1937, for instance, Oren Stemville shot a colour film of a bird in Georgia's famous Okefenokee Swamp that resembled a Carolina parakeet). So although unlikely, it is not impossible that some Carolina parakeets still linger undetected in such localities, with any occasional sightings of them being discounted as nothing more exciting than non-native escapee species.

Pink-Headed Duck

A similar situation applies relative to claims for the survival of the Indian pink-headed duck *Rhodonessa caryophyllacea,* the only species of duck to have not only a completely pink head but also a predominantly pink neck: cultivation of its swampland habitat and decimation by duckshooters are believed to be responsible for its extinction. The last definite record of a wild specimen is from 1935, with some captive individuals possibly surviving into the 1940s.

In the *Journal of the Bombay Natural History Society* for 1960, however, K.L. Mehta, Deputy Game Warden of Himachal Pradesh, recorded that on 28 and 29 February of that year, along with his friend Shri Grehawal, he spied a drake of this species in a local tank in Kunihar State, about 40 miles south of Simla. They even attempted to take a photograph of this highly significant specimen, but were foiled by the profusion of reeds all around, and the lack of a hide in which to approach close enough.

Six years later, the same journal carried another report, this time by Laliteshwar Prasad Singh, documenting his shooting of a pink-head on 27 January 1947 at Manroopa Lake, in Bihar's Monghyr District. Singh also noted that he saw five to eight individuals there in 1948-9, but did not shoot any during that period. And in February 1974, *Oryx* provided a short report noting a putative pink-head sighting in Nepal.

During the 1980s, explorer Rory Nugent journeyed into the Himalayas and down the Brahmaputra River, becoming the first person to paddle it from Myanmar (formerly Burma) to Bangladesh, in search of this evanescent species. And in a remote marsh along the river, he spotted a bird that just may have been a pink-headed duck, but he could not be certain.

In 1998, after learning of unconfirmed pink-headed duck sightings reported from a remote region 100 miles south of Lhasa, near Tibet's border with Bhutan, by staff from Tibet's Forestry Department, two English explorers, Peter Gladstone and Charles Martell launched an expedition to investigate these claims. They were sponsored in their search by the Wildfowl and Wetlands Trust at Slimbridge, but sadly, they did not spot any specimens.

Even more recently, during a survey of wetlands in northern Myanmar between 29 November and 16 December 2004, members of the survey team - drawn from BirdLife International and a local non-government organisation called the Biodiversity and Nature Conservation Association (BANCA) - made a possible sighting of a pink-headed duck. Although the sighting lasted for no more than 3 minutes, and was in bright light, with the bird in flight, its observers discerned a bright pink head and neck. One of the eyewitnesses, waterfowl veteran Tim Appleton, is 99 per cent convinced that it was indeed a pink-head, and the others too were sufficiently impressed to decide to renew their search here at a later date (BirdLife International press release 20 January 2005), though nothing more has so far emerged.

Sceptics believe such reports as these to be based upon misidentified red-crested pochards *Netta rufina,* or even spotbill ducks *Anas poecilorhyncha.* Yet how likely is it that experienced wildlife observers such as game wardens and hunters could readily mistake a member of one of these very common, familiar species with as renowned a *rara avis* (literally) as the pink-headed duck. Also, there are many potential hideaways for this bird within the borderlands between Nepal and India that cannot be explored due to periodic outbreaks of warfare, so there is still reason for hope that this very striking species of waterfowl will one day be rediscovered.

New Zealand's Moas

In New Zealand, there seems little hope that any of the famous ostrich-like moas of the genus *Dinornis* ('terrible bird') still survive, but it may even now be premature to claim the same for at least one of their less familiar, smaller relatives. Apparently an inhabitant primarily of subalpine shrubland and montane forests, the upland moa *Megalapteryx didinus* is not generally assumed to have survived beyond the 1840s; indeed, some consider that even this extinction date is too recent.

One of the most thought-provoking reports casting doubt upon such claims, however, is contained within the 1952, revised edition of Alice McKenzie's book *Pioneers of Martins Bay* (first published 1947, but lacking this report). In it, she recalled her encounter in 1880 as a 7-year-old child at Martins Bay, South Island, with a strange bird that cannot be conclusively identified with any known species alive today. Able to walk straight up to it, she described it as a large bird at least 3ft high, with navy-blue plumage, dark green legs with large scales, no noticeable tail, and three large claws on each foot. She endeavoured to capture it, and in response it attempted to attack her, so she ran home. When she returned to the spot with her father, the bird was gone, but its three-toed tracks remained. Using a measuring ruler, her father found that the middle toe measured 11in from heel to tip, though the soft sand may have enlarged it a little.

Kiwis and giant moa – is the 'giant kiwi' a miniature moa?

In 1889, she saw the bird again, and her brother spotted it once too. After the rediscovery in December 1948 of another supposedly extinct South Island bird, the famous flightless rail known as the takahe *Porphyrio* (=*Notornis*) *mantelli*, Alice McKenzie examined a preserved specimen, because its dark blue plumage suggested the possibility that the mystery bird she and her brother had seen had been a takahe. Indeed, in 1946 (two years *before* the takahe's rediscovery), she had written to an Otago University professor actually claiming to have seen a takahe. After examining one, however, she then discounted this possibility, stating that the takahe seemed totally different in appearance from the mystery bird that she had seen in 1880 and 1889, noting in particular that the takahe's legs were deep red, not green like her bird's. Could Alice McKenzie's mystery bird have been a living *Megalapteryx?* Some ornithologists are optimistic that it was, but others consider it to have been a takahe after all, or even, as proposed in 1987 by New Zealand author John Hall-Jones, a blue-plumaged white-faced heron.

Alice McKenzie died in 1963, but 44 years later, her granddaughter, Alice Margaret Leaker, convinced of the veracity of her maternal grandmother's testimony, compiled a new edition of her book, in which she delved deeper into this longstanding controversy. Quite apart from the late date of the sighting, however, another problem when attempting to reconcile McKenzie's bird with a moa is that none of the numerous moa remains so far recovered have included any blue-coloured feathers.

During February and March 1978, yet another in a long line of modern-day moa hunts took place. Led by biologist Prof. Shoichi Hollie of Japan's Gunma University and accompanied by Seido Hino (Director of Japan's Nippon Television), a Japanese team of scientists converged upon South Island's Fjordland, armed with a very sophisticated lure — a reconstituted moa cry on tape, created with the aid of computerised analyses of *Megalapteryx* throat structure using fossil remains. Tragically, however, as Prof. Hollie subsequently informed me, it failed to elicit any reply, and he now considers *Megalapteryx* to be extinct. This is also the opinion of Ron Scarlett, the Canterbury Museum osteologist with whom the team consulted upon arrival in New Zealand.

Much of the *Megalapteryx* mystique and the continuing hope that it will eventually be discovered alive stems from another avian mystery. According to Dr Bernard Heuvelmans in *On the Track of Unknown Animals* (1958), the Maoris tell of an unidentified form of 'giant kiwi', termed the *roa-roa,* said to be the size of a turkey, and armed with sharp spurs on its feet. However, as I discovered from Ron Scarlett and from a number of works dealing with New Zealand's avifauna, *roa-roa* is actually the name given to the largest of the *known* kiwis, i.e. the great-spotted kiwi *Apteryx haasti* of South Island.

Even so, *A. haasti* never exceeds 2ft in total length, and does not have spurs - but the well-developed clawed hallux on each foot of the small moas might well be mistaken for a spur by lay observers, and it so happens that *Megalapteryx* was indeed turkey-sized! Moreover, it is very possible that in life, this little moa superficially resembled an extra-large kiwi - its scientific name actually means 'big kiwi'. In short, this suggests that the reclusive 'giant kiwi' is separate from *A. haasti* (the genuine *roa-roa),* but may be one and the same as *Megalapteryx*!

Great Auk

On 19 April 1986, London's *Daily Telegraph* carried the remarkable news that an expedition was to set sail for Papa Westray, a tiny islet in Scotland's Orkneys group, in response to reputed sightings of a living great auk *Alca impennis,* the famous flightless, penguin-like seabird supposedly exterminated in 1844. Unhappily, as documented in a later *ISC Newsletter* (spring 1987), it proved to be more of a canard than an auk! Nothing more, in fact, than an imaginative advertising promotion for a certain brand of whisky.

This is not the first false alarm for this species. Reports of great auks in the Lofoten Islands, off the Norwegian coast, emerged every so often during the 1920s and 1930s; when investigated, the birds proved to be genuine penguins, brought from Antarctica as pets by whalers and released on the Lofotens when no longer wanted.

Great auk – when did it really die out?

Nevertheless there are a number of more promising reports of post-1844 survival too. Many of these are buried in Norwegian journals and newspapers, but a good example from an English publication was contained in Dr Isaac J. Hayes's *The Land of Desolation* (1871), which describes his adventures in Greenland during summer 1869. The auk-related account concerns a conversation that Hayes had with a naturalist called Hansen:

> *The great auk, long since supposed to be entirely extinct, he told me had been recently seen on one of the Whale-fish Islands. Two years before [in 1867] one had been actually captured by a native, who, being very hungry, and wholly ignorant of the great value of the prize he had secured, proceeded at once to eat it, much to the disgust of Mr. Hansen, who did not learn of it until too late to come to the rescue. How little the poor savage thought of the great fortune he had just missed by hastily indulging his appetite!*

A few additional cases of putative post-1844 survival for the great auk can be found within a short chapter entitled 'Late Records, Anomalous Sightings and Cryptozo-ology' in Errol Fuller's definitive book *The Great Auk* (1999).

Huia

Deriving its name from its distinctive melodious call, the huia *Heteralocha acuti-rostris* was a member of a small family of birds found only in New Zealand and referred to as wattlebirds. A crow-sized species whose glossy black plumage dis-closed a deep green sheen when viewed at certain angles in sunlight, it was instantly characterized by its pair of bright orange facial wattles, its elegant tail plumes with broad tips decorated by a wide band of sparkling white (tinged with rufous in young birds), and - above all else - by the truly exceptional, extraordinary nature of its ivory-coloured beak, for unlike all other birds the huia had not one beak but two.

Whereas the male's was short and straight, used for chiselling out grubs (especially those of *Prionoplus reticularis,* a longhorn beetle commonly called the huhu) from decayed wood as a woodpecker does, the female's was long and curved gracefully downward, enabling her to secure grubs from deep woody crevices that her mate's short beak could not reach. Many animal species exhibit some degree of sexual di-morphism, but in birds this usually involves plumage or body size. The huia's dras-tic departure from that tradition, by possessing a sexually dimorphic beak, estab-lished it as a species of immense scientific worth, which made its extinction all the more tragic. (Recently, it has been shown that a second vanished species of bird, the Reunion crested starling *Fregilupus varius*, extinct since 1837, also sported a sexu-ally dimorphic beak, but not to such a pronounced degree as in the huia.)

Never the most common of birds, the huia inhabited beech and podocarp forests, and was apparently confined to North Island's Ruahine, Tararua, Rimutaka, and Kaimanawa mountain ranges, with occasional reports from the Wairarapa Valley too. (Supposed sightings of huias from the woody country near Massacre Bay in South Island's Province of Nelson were never substantiated.) Yet although it had been hunted for generations by the Maoris, who greatly prized its attractive tail feathers for their chiefs' head-dresses, its numbers seemingly did not suffer unduly until the coming of the Europeans.

Their arrival, however, saw the accompanying introduction of Western species that endangered the huia by preying upon it, competing with it for food, and exposing it to various diseases hitherto unknown there; large-scale procurement of huia speci-mens for museums and private collections; destruction of its forest homelands for cultivation and grazing; and ultimately the widespread wearing of huia plumes by *all* Maoris (regardless of status) and by members of European high society. There could be only one outcome. The last fully verified sighting of this species was made on 28 December 1907, when W.W. Smith spotted two males and a female. Since then, the huia has been classed as extinct.

The huia's morphology is unique. No other bird in New Zealand, whether native or introduced, can be readily confused with it - which is why the sizeable number of alleged *post-1907* huia sightings has attracted notable scientific interest. Their most

Huias – male with straight beak, female with curved beak

detailed documentation is presented in William I. Phillipps's *The Book of the Huia* (1963). A noted expert on New Zealand's avifauna, Phillipps listed 23 such sightings, and learnt that as recently as the 1920s eyewitness reports of black birds with orange wattles and white-tipped tails regularly emerged from the huia's former haunts.

Although none were by professional ornithologists, a number of these sightings are sufficiently convincing to give cautious cause for optimism that this unmistakeable species still survived at that time. An official huia search was carried out in 1924, and although no huia were seen, signs of this species' existence were observed. Moreover, a much more recent event, one that greatly impressed Phillipps, occurred on 12 October 1961, featuring Margaret Hutchinson.

As I learnt from Ron Scarlett of South Island's Canterbury Museum, when Hutchinson arrived for a six-month stay in New Zealand in 1961 she visited the museum first of all, before travelling on to North Island; she interviewed at length its then Assistant Director, Graham Turbott, regarding the huia, as she seemed most interested in this species. After reaching North Island, she spent October at the Lake House Hotel, Waikaremoana, in the Urewera State Forest, where she was studying the native bush (forest).

On 12 October, Hutchinson spent the day at a smaller lake called Waikareiti, three miles further on from her hotel, and set amidst New Zealand beech woodland. She had been sitting by the track leading to the lake, watching some large, red-and-green native parrots called kakas pecking dead wood off a tree, when suddenly, as she was looking across a small valley nearby, she saw a bird fly up the middle of it, and disappear into some beeches. It was of similar size to the kaka (17-19 in) but was of slighter build, and its plumage was black, except for the white-banded tip of its tail. In the field-guide that she later consulted, the picture most closely matching her bird was the huia's.

As she noted in an article published in the RSPB's *Birds* magazine (September-October 1970), Hutchinson recounted her sighting not only to William Phillipps but also to Dr R.A. Falla (then Director of Wellington's Dominion Museum), another major authority on New Zealand birds. Both men were sufficiently impressed to deem it likely that she had genuinely seen a huia; in his *The Book of the Huia,* Phillipps goes so far as to conclude: "...there appears to be little doubt she did see a huia".

However, we must also consider the possibility that Hutchinson's evident interest in this species actually conspired against her. Could a combination of excitement and surprise at the bird's brief and unexpected debut have 'transformed' it (albeit unconsciously) in her eyes from its true identity (some still-surviving species, such as a tui) into a huia? In short, could her huia have been an illusion, created unconsciously by an innate desire to see one? The human brain can play some quite extraordinary tricks on our eyes, often 'filling in' details that are not actually there, or modifying the appearance of an object to accord with some subconscious thought or memory - and all without the person concerned even realising what is happening.

More recently, in 1991, Copenhagen University zoologist Lars Thomas, who has a longstanding interest in cryptozoology, also claimed to have seen a huia, while visiting North Island's Pureora Forest.

Yet if the huia really does still survive, why has it not been formally rediscovered by now? In a foreword to Phillipps's book, Falla noted that even at best, New Zealand's bush is not overly conducive to easy birdwatching, requiring such a sustained effort to explore the multitude of potential hideaways for birds that there is rarely enough time to carry out detailed observations at any one given spot, so that all-too-many of its birds are not sighted at all. Having spent quite some time birdwatching in New Zealand during 2006, I can certainly vouch for this.

If the huia *is* alive, it has probably retreated into areas that even by the bush's standards are quite inaccessible, and thus less readily disturbed. Indeed, over the years a number of people have informed Ron Scarlett of possible huia sightings in the remoter regions of the Kaimanawa range, so that he deems it possible that the species still survives here. Moreover, as Hutchinson revealed in her article, careful analysis of the post-1907 reports documented by Phillipps do seem to indicate a movement northwards - away from the huia's most favoured former provenance, the Tarawera Range (now divided up by agricultural cultivation), and into a wilder, mountainous forest region (far less accessible to humans), perhaps as far as the Urewera State

Forest after all.

Equally, Ron Scarlett has identified subfossil huia bones from moa-hunter middens on the Taranaki coast, and from limestone caves in the Mahoenui area, lying on the border of North Taranaki and South Auckland, and much further north than the huia's known modern-day distribution. Could this region's more remote portions be another putative retreat of surviving huias?

Perhaps some huias took refuge in certain northern areas less readily reached by humans during their species' last stand in its favoured territory. In addition, there might be areas that have always housed a resident huia population, wholly unknown to the Europeans, so that this truly unique species - New Zealand's handsome and quite astonishing bird with two beaks - still survives after all.

Chapter Ten

Globsters and Trunko –
When Appearances Can Deceive

Below the thunders of the upper deep;
Far, far beneath in the abysmal sea,
His ancient, dreamless, uninvaded sleep
The Kraken sleepeth: faintest sunlights flee
About his shadowy sides: above him swell
Huge sponges of millennial growth and height;
And far away into the sickly light,
From many a wondrous grot and secret cell
Unnumber'd and enormous polypi
Winnow with giant arms the slumbering green.
There hath he lain for ages and will lie
Battening upon huge seaworms in his sleep,
Until the latter fire shall heat the deep;
Then once by man and angels to be seen,
In roaring he shall rise and on the surface die.

Alfred, Lord Tennyson – *The Kraken*

Down though the ages, the vast seas have spewed forth all manner of bizarre, baffling creatures for laymen and scientists alike to peruse and ponder over. Moreover, like much else in cryptozoology, they are not always what they appear to be - but never more so than with the two classic marine mystery beast cases documented here.

Don't Blub About the Blob – Exposing Pseudo-Plesiosaurs and Quasi-Octopuses

Sometimes, even the most disappointing cryptozoological cases can prove to be of benefit. So it was with the Chilean globster. On 23 June 2003, villagers at Los Muermos, near the city of Puerto Montt, southern Chile, were bewildered by the sight of an astonishing if anomalous object that had been washed ashore on their beach. Later described, rather memorably, in some news reports as resembling a squashed elephant, it was basically an amorphous gelatinous 'blob', grey and pink in colour and of leathery texture, but of stupendous, ultra-elephantine dimensions. For it was roughly 40 ft long, 18 ft wide, 3 ft tall at its highest point, and estimated to weigh over a ton. Members of the Chilean navy examined it, and also revealed the presence nearby of a second object, though this was readily identifiable as a dead humpback whale. As for the 'blob', conversely, the only objects that it in any way

Do unknown giant octopuses exist in the deep oceans?

resembled were the various enigmatic 'globsters' that have been discovered over the years washed ashore on a number of far-flung beaches, in such localities as Tasmania, Newfoundland, New Zealand, Bermuda, and - most famously, in 1896 - Florida.

By the beginning of July, the Chilean globster was attracting headlines worldwide, due in no small way to the optimism of its chief publicist, Chilean marine biologist Dr Elsa Cabrera, director of the Centre for Cetacean Conservation in Santiago. For Dr Cabrera lost no time in dismissing the prospect of the Chilean globster being of cetacean (whale) origin, instead boldly favouring the possibility that it was the earthly remains of a colossal octopus - thereby echoing a popular identity for the Florida globster of 1896 (which had even been assigned the scientific name *Octopus giganteus*) - or even a wholly novel, hitherto unrecorded type of marine organism. And indeed, some reports mentioned the apparent presence of what looked like a tentacle amid the Chilean globster's gelatinous form. She also claimed that it did not have the correct texture or smell to be from a whale.

Not everyone, however, shared Cabrera's views. Dr Steve Webster, senior marine biologist at California's Monterey Bay Aquarium, believed it more likely that the Chilean globster was a greatly decomposed whale skin, noting that much of the length of an octopus (and giant squid) is accounted for by its tentacles, not its body. Dr James Mead, a Smithsonian Institution zoologist also supported a whale identity, as did marine biologist Dr Sidney Pierce from the University of South Florida, and geneticist Dr Steven M. Carr from the Memorial University of Newfoundland. Dr Carr's views were particularly pertinent, as he has become something of an expert at debunking sea monster carcases by virtue of DNA analyses devised by him that have categorically unmasked a number of previous globsters as whale blubber.

Also worthy of note was a statement by Dr Sergio Letelier - a researcher at Santiago's Museum of Natural History - that the globster did not smell like an octopus. This is significant, because rotting octopuses and squids release ammonia, thereby giving off the pungent smell of a cat litter box, whereas a decomposing whale smells like rotting meat.

Accordingly, plans were made by Cabrera's team to send tissue samples from the Chilean globster to at least five different laboratories worldwide for DNA tests to settle the matter of its identity once and for all. As it happened, however, the answer came before any of these tests were even carried out. On 11 July, Dr Letelier and colleague Dr Jose Yanez announced that they had uncovered and conclusively identified within the globster's jelly-like mass the spermaceti organ of a sperm whale *Physeter macrocephalus*. This extraordinary structure is peculiar to sperm whales, occupies much of their greatly-enlarged forehead, and contains a milky fluid.

But how could a decomposed sperm whale be mistaken for a giant octopus? There is a notable precedent for such dramatic misidentification when dealing with beached remains, which is known as the pseudo-plesiosaur effect. When a basking shark *Cetorhinus maximus* dies and its body decomposes, it undergoes a remarkable transformation. The gill apparatus falls away, taking with it the shark's jaws, leaving only its small cranium and exposed backbone, thus resembling a small head and long neck. The end of the shark's backbone only runs into the upper fluke of its tail, so during decomposition the lower fluke falls off, leaving what looks like a long slender tail. And to complete the plesiosaur deception, the shark's pectoral fins, and sometimes its pelvic fins too, remain attached, resembling two pairs of flippers. Little wonder, therefore, why a number of amazingly plesiosaurian carcases have been reported over the years, only for anatomical and biochemical analyses to expose them as sharks.

Now, moreover, we have confirmation that an analogous transformation is responsible for at least some of the hitherto perplexing globsters that have come to light - a transformation that I propose should hereafter be referred to as the quasi-octopus effect. As detailed by Drs Pierce, Carr, and Letelier, after a whale dies its body can float for months, decomposing, until eventually its heavy backbone and skull dissociate from their encompassing skin-sac of rotting blubber, and sink to the sea bottom, leaving behind a thick gelatinous matrix of collagen - the tough protein found in skin and connective tissue. It is this mass of collagen, still encased in its skin-sac, that washes ashore, as a globster. Furthermore, if a few of the whale's ribs remain within the collagen matrix, and any 'fingers' of fibrous flesh are attached to them, these resemble tentacles. And if the whale is a sperm whale, the spermaceti organ gives the resulting globster a bulky shape reminiscent of an octopus. DNA tests that were performed on samples of the Chilean globster's tissue independently confirmed its sperm whale identity (*National Geographic News*, 25 August 2003; *Biological Bulletin*, June 2004).

All of which explains how a rotting whale can metamorphose with ease into a giant octopus - usually, that is. There is still the case of the Florida globster - some tests on samples of its remains having uncovered distinct biochemical similarities with octopus tissue. For its supporters, therefore, the quasi-octopus effect is not an option.

As for other globsters, conversely: no use blubbing over stranded blobs (of blubber). Just pity whoever is given the job of removing the Chilean globster and clearing up the beach afterwards!

A Maritime Mirabilis – The Tantalising Trunko

In his mighty tome, *In the Wake of the Sea-Serpents* (1968), veteran cryptozoologist Dr Bernard Heuvelmans defined and delineated the truly protean 'great sea serpent' to yield no less than nine morphologically-discrete taxa of sea serpent, which included various currently-unrecognised species of pinniped, cetacean, fish, reptile, and possibly an amphibian. However, at least one marine mystery beast included in his book appeared so bizarre that even Heuvelmans – "the Father of Cryptozoology" - was at a loss as how best to categorise it, and so, after briefly describing it, he simply omitted it entirely from his great scheme of sea serpent classification.

Known officially as the Margate sea serpent or more colloquially, in recognition of one of its most distinctive characteristics, as Trunko, this truly anomalous animal made its debut on the morning of 1 November 1922. That was when, according to subsequent local newspaper reports, South African farmer Hugh Balance looked far out to sea from the beach at Margate, Natal, and saw an amazing spectacle. With the aid of glasses, he could perceive what seemed to be two whales fighting with a huge sea monster, resembling a gigantic polar bear on account of the fact that it appeared to sport a dense snow-white pelage. According to Balance, who was joined by an ever-increasing crowd of observers as the formidable battle continued, the creature reared fully 20 ft out of the water and struck repeatedly at the whales with what Balance assumed was its tail - but to no effect, because after three hours the whales moved away and their furry attacker floated lifelessly at the surface.

Later that evening its dead carcase was found washed ashore, and was seen to be of colossal size, roughly 5ft high and measuring 47ft in total length, which included a 10ft tail at one end (said in some later reports to be lobster-like), and, incongru-

Artist Bill Asmussen's superb Trunko reconstruction

ously, an elephantine trunk at the other - in place of a head! This extraordinary structure was approximately 5ft long and 14in across, and its tip resembled the snout of a pig. Even more noticeable, however, was its luxuriant covering of fur or hair, 8in long, and, at least in Balance's view, exactly like a polar bear's, yet with no sign of blood anywhere, despite the ferocity of the earlier sea-battle.

Incredibly, however, despite the huge number of onlookers that it attracted (some of whom brought in a team of 32 oxen to move it seaward, which they failed to do on account of its immense weight), and despite the fact that its corpse remained beached for 10 days, becoming ever more odiferous as decomposition set in, no scientist came to observe or to take samples from it for study. On the evening of the tenth day, the tide took it back out to sea, and the chance to investigate one of the most astonishing zoological secrets of the sea was lost forever.

All that we can do today, therefore, is speculate on what Trunko might (or might not) have been (always assuming, of course, that it was not a newspaper hoax). Certainly, based upon its description taken at face value, this supremely strange 'marine elephant' does not correspond with any known species of animal alive today or known from fossil remains. But perhaps there is more to its description than initially meets the eye, harbouring cryptic clues that may shed light on this otherwise decidedly shadowy mystery – a mystery, moreover, that is generally passed over or totally ignored even in the majority of cryptozoological publications.

However, one detailed and highly intelligent assessment of Trunko that does exist is by cryptid chronicler Lance Bradshaw, and it can be accessed on his Kryptid's Keep website (http://www.angelfire.com/sc2/Trunko/trunko.html). In his discussion, Lance raises several valid, important points worthy of consideration here. Take, for instance, Trunko's unique pelage. It has already been noted in this chapter that dead sharks can acquire, via the pseudo-plesiosaur effect, a covering of 'hair', which in reality is nothing more than connective tissue fibres that become exposed during decomposition of the carcase. However, if Balance's testimony is to be believed, Trunko bore its snowy fur while it was still very much alive, battling the whales. If this is true, then clearly its fur cannot be explained away as exposed connective fibres. Moreover, it also suggests that Trunko was mammalian, albeit wholly unlike any mammal previously recorded by science.

Yet this is not the only mystery associated with its fur. As Lance has pointed out, exclusively marine mammals, such as cetaceans, are not furry, because this would hinder their mobility. Conversely, marine creatures such as pinnipeds and polar bears, which are furry, do not spend their entire lives in the water. Consequently, if Trunko's fur were a genuine feature of its morphology, this suggests that it must venture ashore sometimes. Yet as it was apparently limbless, but stupendous in size, how could it accomplish such a feat without becoming fatally beached, probably suffocating under its own weight, as beached whales so often do, even species much smaller than Trunko?

Then there is the equally odd matter of its trunk and supposed headlessness? Unless the head were so small that it imperceptibly graded into the trunk, how can Trunko's acephalous condition be explained? The most reasonable solution is that the trunk was actually a neck, from which the head had become detached following the creature's death. Yet as with its fur, Trunko was seen to possess a trunk with no head at its distal end while still alive.

Or was it? Trunko's anomalous features are anomalous primarily because they were exhibited by Trunko while still alive, not just when it was dead. But was Trunko ever truly seen alive? The great battle with the whales took place some distance out to sea, not at the shore. Could it be, therefore, as postulated by Lance, that Trunko was not alive at all - that what was actually being seen by Balance and the other observers on the beach was two whales tossing an already-dead carcase back and forth, playing with it just like killer whales, for instance, which are known for frolicking boisterously with their food, often throwing seal victims up and out of the water? During such exuberant activity, Trunko's head may have been ripped off and eaten or lost, and possibly some heavy chafing of its skin might conceivably have yielded a shredded surface of exposed connective tissue fibres.

Perhaps the carcase was that of a decomposed shark, with the pseudo-plesiosaur effect creating its neck-like trunk and fur. Alternatively, it may even have been a globster - a quasi-octopus complete with hairy surface and a false tentacle resembling a trunk, engendered from the remains of some long-dead 'globsterised' whale.

This, incidentally, as Lance has noted, would also explain the otherwise-anomalous lack of blood present when the carcase was washed up. A recently-dead mammal that had battled two whales, in contrast, would have been covered in wounds pouring with blood, or at least stained with it. Instead, Trunko's snowy pelage was apparently immaculate, with (to quote Mack the Knife!) never a trace of red.

Having said that, I am not wholly convinced that even the above-described activity could yield the exceptionally distinctive snow-white pelage described for Trunko both while at sea and while beached, but at least the enigma of this creature's hitherto unclassifiable morphology is now beginning to look a little less impossible than before.

Nevertheless, with no physical remains to examine, the only hope of ever resolving this longstanding cryptozoological case satisfactorily is for another Trunko specimen to turn up one day, and for it this time to be treated with the scientific interest and rigour that it deserves. Interestingly, the prospect of a second Trunko appearing may not be as remote as it may seem. In fact, it may already have happened.

As I noted in *From Flying Toads To Snakes With Wings* (1997), which also contains coverage of Trunko, in November 1936 the carcase of an elephant-headed, white-furred, long-tailed sea serpent measuring 24ft in total length was discovered on Alaska's desolate Glacier Island.

This time, moreover, its remains were examined, by a team led by Chugach National Forest supervisor W.J. McDonald, but no news of their findings has ever been released, and, as with Trunko, the Glacier Island sea serpent's remains were not retained.

How extraordinary if, just like the globsters have now been shown to be, an entity as outwardly astonishing as Trunko ultimately proved to be nothing more than the decomposition-distorted remains of a long-deceased whale. Yet until physical evidence can be procured, it is destined to remain just as controversial as they too once were.

It was the 19th Century English poet Bryan W. Proctor, in *The Return of the Admi-*

ral, who wrote:

> *Strange things come up to look at us,*
> *The masters of the deep:*

The next time that one of these strange things does come up to look, alive or dead, scientists should ensure that they take much more than just a look back at it.

Chapter Eleven
Count Branicki's 'Terrible Mouse', and other Giant Rodents

"Matilda Briggs was not the name of a young woman, Watson," said Holmes, in a reminiscent voice. "It was a ship which is associated with the giant rat of Sumatra, a story for which the world is not yet prepared..."

Sir Arthur Conan Doyle - 'The Adventure of the Sussex Vampire', from *The Case-Book of Sherlock Holmes*

Prof. Constantin Jelski, Curator of Cracow Museum, was certainly not prepared for the creature that he encountered one morning in 1873, wandering through the orchard of a hacienda garden near Vitoc, in the eastern Peruvian Andes. Although it was superficially mouse-like, this animal differed very dramatically from all the mice that Jelski had ever seen before - with a total length of 3ft, it was much the same size as a fox terrier! That extraordinary beast, destined to become one of zoology's greatest enigmas, is just one of the unexpectedly large but little-known rodents in this 'Gnawers of Note' chapter.

Count Branicki's 'Terrible Mouse'

Prof. Jelski's find was unlike any species known to him, so he felt compelled to collect it for identification. The beast proved quite ferocious - at least according to the report received back home in Poland by Jelski's sponsor, nobleman Count Grafen Constantin Branicki. Hence, when formally described later in 1873 by Dr Wilhelm Peters, Berlin Museum's director, this important new species was christened *Dinomys branickii* - 'Branicki's terrible mouse'. However, this turned out to be a complete misnomer.

First and foremost it was not a true mouse. Indeed, the question of just *what* it was proved to be quite problematical, because it seemed to combine the morphological characteristics of several different rodent families. Its black pelage handsomely marked with horizontal rows of white spots, and its limb structure, compared closely with those of another large South American rodent, called the paca - indeed, one of its native names, pacarana, translates as 'false paca', and this is the name by which it is most commonly referred to in English (a less frequently used name is *rukupi*).

In contrast, certain of its cranial and skeletal attributes, plus its long tail (a most *un*-paca-like feature) more closely corresponded with the West Indian hutias (relatives of the coypu); whereas its molar teeth were more reminiscent of a chinchilla's; and various other aspects seemed to ally it with the capybara. Faced with such an ana-tomical anomaly, Peters placed the pacarana in a completely separate taxonomic family, all to itself.

Pacarana – depicted in error as a ferocious creature

Naturally, the scientific world was extremely curious about this highly significant species, the third largest rodent in the world, and became ever more curious as the decades rolled by - because for 31 years no further pacaranas were reported. Then in June 1904, two living specimens of this seemingly lost species were received by Dr Emil Goeldi, Director of Brazil's Para (Belem) Museum. In contrast to the graphic reports concerning the Vitoc individual, these two, an adult female and a subadult male sent in a cage from Brazil's upper Rio Purus, proved to be the most docile, inoffensive animals imaginable, the very antithesis of their 'terrible mouse' title.

Since then, further specimens have been obtained, but the number of live examples recorded is still extremely small - it is perfectly true to say that despite its very no-ticeable size and its taxonomically prestigious status as the only living member of an entire rodent family, the pacarana remains one of the world's least-known mammals. It is generally classed as an endangered species, but whether it really is rare, or simply very elusive, is difficult to say. It has been written off many times as extinct, only to reappear without warning, to the delight and relief of mammalogists everywhere.

Consequently, zoos prize pacaranas almost as much as giant pandas - which is why early 1947 was a singularly memorable time for Philadelphia Zoo. It was then that it received an innocuous-looking crate from animal dealer Warren Buck of Camden, New Jersey, with the remark, "Here's a new one on me. Maybe you know what it is". When the crate was opened, to everyone astonishment it contained a living pacarana! And just like Goeldi's twosome, it proved to be delightfully tame and affectionate, showing no inclination to bite, and liking nothing better than to greet its visitors with a cheerful grunt and to sit upright on its hindlegs crunching a potato or carrot gripped firmly between its forepaws *(Fauna,* March 1947).

Of the handful of captive pacaranas obtained more recently and exhibited at such zoos as Zurich (the first to breed them), Basle, and San Diego (where I was fortunate enough to see my first live pacaranas in 2004), most have been of similarly pacific temperament, actively seeking out their human visitors to nuzzle them and rub themselves against their legs almost like cats, or even to be picked up and carried just like playful puppies - truly a species with no desire whatsoever to live up to its formidable *Dinomys* designation!

Quemi – Forgotten for 300 Years

Not so long ago, a close relative of the pacarana also existed. In his 16th Century account of the West Indian island of Hispaniola (comprising Haiti and the Dominican Republic), explorer Ganzalo Fernández de Oviedo y Valdés mentioned a mysterious rodent that he called the quemi, which was said to be brown in colour like the island's hutias, but larger in size. It was apparently a traditional item of food for the Hispaniolan natives, but after Oviedo's report nothing further was heard of it.

Then in the 1920s, bones of a pacarana-like rodent were discovered in a cave near a plantation at St Michel, Haiti. After studying them, Dr Gerrit Miller of the Smithsonian Institute identified their owner as a representative of Oviedo's obscure quemi, and in 1929, within his formal description of the bones, Miller named their species *Quemisia gravis.* It seems that the quemi died out soon after the arrival on Hispaniola of the Spaniards, and certainly no later than the 16th Century's close.

Awesome *Amblyrhiza,* and Patterson's 'Mouse of Fear'

An additional pacarana relative once inhabiting the West Indies was *Amblyrhiza inundata,* whose remains have been discovered on the Antillean islands of Anguilla and St Martin. This rodent would have been a daunting sight to behold - truly a terrible mouse to end all terrible mice - for it was almost as large as an American black bear! Nowadays, however, the awesome *Amblyrhiza* is no cause for alarm, because it died out some time before the quemi, possibly even before humans first reached its island homes.

Despite this species' impressive nature, its first recorded remains came to light in a distinctly prosaic manner - discovered in a shipment of phosphatic cave earth sent from Anguilla to Philadelphia as a potential fertiliser. These were passed to celebrated palaeontologist Prof. Edward Drinker Cope, who later obtained further remains after requesting Dr H.E. van Rijgersma, colonial physician of neighbouring St Martin, to visit Anguilla and secure whatever *Amblyrhiza* specimens he could obtain. At a meeting of the Philadelphia Academy of Natural Sciences on 1 December 1864, Cope formally named and described this species, but since then few *Amblyrhiza* remains have been found.

However, in 1988 Donald McFarlane and Ross D.E. MacPhee undertook extensive fieldwork in certain Anguillan caves that seemed potential sources of further material; in one, Pitch Apple Hole, they discovered *Amblyrhiza* bones widely distributed in its floor's earth, from a depth of 1in to around 16in (Cave *Science,* April 1989). Their resulting collection of material, donated to the Anguillan Archaeological and Historical Society, is the largest ever made of this extraordinary lost giant among rodents.

Yet there was a South American Pliocene pacarana, *Telicomys,* that was even bigger. Formerly the largest rodent ever known to have existed, and officially described in 1926, it was approximately 6.5ft long. However, its record was torn away in 2003, following the publication of a paper (*Science,* 19 September 2003) describing the unearthing in 1999 within a desert coastal region of northwestern Venezuela of an almost-complete skeleton belonging to an 8-million-year-old late Miocene species first described in 1980 but previously known only from a few fragmentary remains. Now revealed to have been a veritable rodent colossus, measuring just over 9 ft long, its scientific name is nothing if not memorable - *Phoberomys pattersoni* ('Patterson's mouse of fear')!

Estimated to weigh up to 1700 lb (10 times that of the capybara), and rival a buffalo in size, but recall a gargantuan long-tailed guinea-pig in overall outward appearance, *P. pattersoni* is believed to have used its lengthy tail as a balancing organ, enabling it to stand on its hind legs. It inhabited the marshes and lagoons that existed in this region of Venezuela long before they dried out to yield arid desertland here, and, as with *Telicomys*, its closest living relative is believed to be the pacarana. The genus *Phoberomys* presently houses seven species, and one of them, *P. insolita*, is now thought to have been even larger than *P. pattersoni*, but as it is currently known only from very incomplete remains, it is difficult to estimate accurately its full size.

In addition to the quemi and *Amblyrhiza,* the West Indies also once housed some large, long-tailed rodents called giant rice rats or megalomyids ('big mice'). Handsomely coloured species with glossy black or dark-brown upperparts boldly contrasting with their pure-white underparts and chin, at least three – *Megalomys desmarestii* from Martinique, *M. luciae* from St Lucia, and *M. audreyae* from Barbuda - survived into historic times. The extinction of *M. desmarestii* probably occurred as recently as 1902, with the eruption of Martinique's mighty volcano Mount Pelee. This was also the largest species; its head-and-body length was about 14.5in, and its tail around 13in.

Vespucci's Giant Mystery Rodent

Fernando de Noronha is a small, undistinguished volcanic island (albeit the biggest in a small archipelago of the same name) off eastern Brazil's continental shelf. However, it was once the centre of an intriguing if little-known cryptozoological mystery that closely echoes the history of the quemi. The first Westerner to visit this island, which at that time was uninhabited by humans, was none other than the celebrated Florentine explorer Amerigo Vespucci, on 10 August 1503. He later documented his visit within his *Lettera di Amerigo Vespucci delle isole nuovamente in quattro suoi viaggi*, and mentioned that the island was home to what he referred to as "very big rats".

As European rats had not reached Fernando de Noronha at that time, the identity of these animals remained undetermined, with H.N. Ridley proposing in 1888, following his own visit there and finding no such rodents in existence, that they must have belonged to an unknown species. Yet whatever it was, this sizeable rodent had quite evidently become extinct several centuries ago, probably not long after others followed in Vespucci's footsteps and began visiting Fernando de Noronha, because no such creatures have been observed or reported from there in modern times.

In 1973, however, American palaeontologist Dr L. Olson Storrs led a joint United States-Brazilian expedition to this island, where they made a remarkable discovery, which in 1999 Storrs and fellow American palaeontologist Dr Michael D. Carleton formally documented within an *American Museum Novitates* paper. The expedition had uncovered many subfossil bones here belonging to a previously-undescribed species of large, hefty rodent. This 'new' species was quite evidently one and the same as Vespucci's now-vanished "very big rat", but was now exposed as actually having been a huge member of the mouse family, Muridae, and was sufficiently different from all other rodents to warrant the creation of a new genus to accommodate it. In their paper, Carleton and Storr officially named this extraordinary species *Noronhomys vespuccii*, in honour not just of its island home but also of possibly the only notable European ever to have seen it alive.

Giant Beavers, and Rodents with Horns

During the Pleistocene epoch, beginning 2 million years ago and ending 10,000 years ago, the beavers of North America spawned an enormous species, *Castoroides ohioensis,* the aptly-named giant beaver. Known from fossils discovered in the northern USA and Canada, it rivalled *Amblyrhiza* by attaining bear-sized dimensions, measuring up to 8.2ft long, including a hefty 3ft tail (which appears to have been round, rather than flat as in modern-day beavers), and possibly weighing as much as 485lb. If it had been a dam builder like its more modest-sized, present-day counterparts, the resulting edifices would have been truly gargantuan, but despite having proportionately larger teeth than modern beavers it is not generally believed that this Brobdingnagian beaver felled trees. Instead, its extensively webbed feet and short limbs indicate a greater emphasis upon aquatic activity. A second species, *C. leiseyorum*, lived in Florida.

The giant beaver is assumed to have died out shortly after the Pleistocene's close, never to be seen by humans. However, in a fascinating *Ethnohistory* paper, Vermont researcher Jane C. Beck postulated in 1972 that the well-documented giant beaver legend encapsulated within the mythology of several north-eastern Algonkian tribes may be more than just a wholly fictional folktale, instead comprising a prehistoric memory of the extinct *Castoroides ohioensis*.

Even more remarkable, however, is the existence of several modern-day reports of mystery beasts, reviewed in *The Field Guide to Lake Monsters, Sea Serpents, and Other Mystery Denizens of the Deep* (2003) by Loren Coleman and Patrick Huyghe, that some cryptozoologists believe may suggest the current survival of the giant beaver. The focus of most such reports is Bear Lake in Utah, where, for instance, in 1860 the *Deseret News* reported that Marion Thomas and three brothers called Cook had spied at close range a 20ft creature with "light brown fur like that of an otter" and two flippers. As recently as 1946, the Bear Lake monster was still being reported, this time by Preston Pond, a Cache Valley Boy Scout executive. In addition, a Manitoba correspondent of mine (his name and details are on my files) claims to have spied a living giant beaver in 2006, notes that there is a longstanding tradition of such creatures here among the inhabitants of a nearby native American reservation, and is now planning to conduct some extensive investigations concerning this extraordinary prospect.

More bizarre even than bear-sized beavers, however, were the four *Ceratogaulus* species belonging to the now-extinct rodent family Mylagauldae. This *Ceratogaulus* quartet was uniquely distinguished from all other rodents, fossil or modern-day, by possessing a pair of short, pointed nasal horns, which makes them the smallest horned mammals known to science. These extraordinary rodents, otherwise resembling bulky gophers and commonly referred to as horned gophers, existed in Nebraska and Colorado from the Miocene to the early Pliocene. Judging from their other noticeable characteristic - very long and powerful, flattened claws on their forepaws - the ceratogaulids were probably gopher-like in behaviour too, spending their days burrowing (also indicated by their tiny eyes). But why should they require horns?

It was once thought that they performed some function in the excavation of remarkable spiral-shaped burrows nicknamed 'devil's corkscrews', first recorded scientifically in 1891, and often discovered in fossilized form in Nebraska. However, these are now known to have been made by a fossil Oligocene beaver, *Palaeocastor,* so the mystery of the ceratogaulids' horns remains unresolved, although the most popular suggestion is that they were used for defence (*Proceedings of the Royal Society B*, 14 July 2005).

These rodents' nearest modern-day relative, a non-horned species, is the mountain beaver *Aplodontia rufa.* This peculiar, primitive rodent is most famous for being neither a mountain-dweller nor a beaver, and for being host to *Hystrichopsylla schefferi,* the world's largest species of flea.

Maned Rat – Ensures its Safety by Skunk Impersonation

Returning home to Europe in 1866 after spending some time on the Mascarene island of Reunion, traveller M. Imhaus stopped off at Aden for a few hours. While there he met a man with a most interesting pet - a large rodent of very distinctive appearance, belonging to a species completely unknown to science. Of stout build with small head and short limbs but long bushy tail, it was principally blackish-brown in colour, but its forehead and the tip of its tail were white, and its flanks each bore a lengthy horizontal strip of pale brown, edged with white and with a white stripe running along its centre. This strip was separated by a type of furrow from the notably long dark hairs borne upon the middle of the animal's back, and also upon its tail, which were erectile, capable of yielding a very odd-looking mane or crest.

Imhaus bought the man's pet, and took it to France's Garden of Acclimatisation in the Bois de Boulogne, where it thrived for about 18 months upon a diet of maize, vegetables, and bread, and slept during the day. After its death, its body attracted the attention of acclaimed zoologist Prof. Alphonse Milne-Edwards, whose studies of it uncovered sufficient anatomical idiosyncrasies to warrant the creation for its species of a brand new taxonomic family.

In his description of this radically new rodent, published in 1867, Milne-Edwards

Maned rat — an accomplished skunk impersonator

Zorilla — Africa's 'Father of the Stenches'

named it *Lophiomys imhausi* - 'Imhaus's maned rat'. Distributed from Kenya in eastern Africa northwards as far as Ethiopia's border with Sudan, and measuring up to 21 in long (females are larger than males), its closest relatives appear to be the cricetines (voles, hamsters, etc), with which it is nowadays classed by some authorities.

A sluggish, generally slow-moving animal, undoubtedly the most distinctive feature of this species is its erectile mane of hair, which has a very important function. The maned rat has few enemies - and little wonder. When challenged by a would-be predator, it raises its mane, and instantly 'transforms' into a surprisingly convincing replica of one of the most feared medium-sized mammals of Africa - a long-furred relative of the weasels known as the zorilla *Ictonyx striatus.*

Although only distantly related to the New World skunks, the zorilla is extraordinarily similar to them, due not only to its vivid black and white fur, but also to its deadly propensity for ejecting streams of unutterably foul-smelling liquid from its anal glands at anything foolish enough to approach it too closely. So dreaded and dreadful is its malodorous arsenal that if a zorilla approaches a lion kill, the lions will back away and wait impatiently but impotently at a safe distance until the little zorilla has eaten its fill and departed. Not for nothing is it referred to by many tribes as 'Father of the Stenches'!

Thus, by impersonating this Dark Continent untouchable, the relatively harmless maned rat (it does have a strong bite) is assured of similar immunity from most would-be assailants. If, however, it does fail to convince, it can actually exude a very toxic glandular secretion that is sufficiently potent to kill a dog if swallowed.

The Giant Rat of Sumatra, and the Cloud Rats of Luzon

Contrary to the assumption by many aficionados of the Sherlock Holmes stories that it was wholly fictional, there really *is* a giant rat of Sumatra, although until quite recently it *had* remained largely a mystery, even to zoologists. In 1983, however, following an in-depth study of this mighty 2ft-long rodent, Dr Guy G. Musser (Curator of Mammals at the American Museum of Natural History) and museum research student Cameron Newcomb attempted to disperse the veil of obscurity surrounding it by publishing its very first full scientific description, in the museum's *Bulletin.*

A very large, forest-dwelling species with dense, woolly, dark-brown fur and powerful jaws, the Sumatran giant rat had traditionally been categorized as a typical, *Rattus* rat. After a meticulous investigation of its anatomy, however, one that surely would have met with Holmes's own approval, Musser and Newcomb recognized that its aural, nasal, and dental characteristics fully justified separation of this legendary form from the *Rattus* horde, so that it was officially rehoused (along with two other species) in a new genus, *Sundamys.*

Despite its name and size, the giant rat of Sumatra is not the largest species of rat in the world. This title is claimed by another little-known Asian rodent, the slender-tailed cloud rat *Phloeomys cumingi* - a denizen of the cloud-forests on the northwestern mountains of Luzon, one of the Philippines. Sometimes attaining a total length little short of 3ft and of robust build, this species is characterized by its harsh, dense pelage - interspersed with long hair and predominantly yellow-brown in colour but offset by a very striking black triangle extending backwards from its neck and shoulders. Its tail is also thickly furred, but with short, dark brown hair.

Of particular note, anatomically, is its unexpectedly short-muzzled, broad head, and its molar teeth are more similar to those of gerbils than to those of other rats. All in

Slender-tailed cloud rats – world's biggest rats

all, a very distinctive mammal, on account of which it has become quite an attraction as a zoo exhibit; it seems to thrive well in captivity - one specimen born in Washington Zoo lived for more than 13 years. Yet, very surprisingly, its biology remains almost as much a mystery today as it was when this species was first described, by Backhouse in 1839.

Sharing its habitat and distribution range is the pallid cloud rat *P. pallida,* a little smaller in size but ostensibly similar in overall morphology, except for its somewhat longer, softer fur. This species is also prized as a zoo exhibit - indeed, when London Zoo received its first specimen in 1948, which was the first cloud rat of any species to be seen alive in Europe, it commanded a full-page photograph and coverage on 23 October 1948 in the prestigious *Illustrated London News.* A third species, *P. elegans,* is known only from a single specimen, from an unknown Philippines location.

Finally, the slender-tailed cloud rat is the world's largest species of rat, but the world's most elegant must surely be one of its relatives and neighbours - *Crateromys schadenbergi.* This is the great rat of Schadenberg, also known as the bushy-tailed cloud rat. Just an inch or so shorter than *P. cumingi,* and again endemic to Luzon's mountainous cloud-forests, this quite spectacular species is everything that a rat is not supposed to be.

In overt defiance of the unwritten edict that rats should be scrawny-looking creatures with short, greasy fur and naked tails, the bushy-tailed cloud rat is clothed in a most luxuriant woolly coat of extremely soft, silky texture, which is exceptionally long on its profusely furred tail, so that the resulting rodent looks more like one of

Madagascar's more exotic lemurs than a mere rat. Usually dark brown or black dorsally, with slightly paler underparts, its sumptuous fur is occasionally further adorned by vividly contrasting bands of white - enhancing the already highly attractive appearance of what must assuredly be the most delightful and least rat-like rat of all.

Chapter Twelve

Gliding Frogs, Parachuting Palm Civets, Flying Gurnards, and Volplaning Frilled Lizards

Volare qui potest, ne serpat. [He who can fly, let him not creep.]

Pontanus - *Collectio Proverbiorum*

Sine pennis volare hau facilest; meae alea pennas non habent.
[Flying without feathers is not easy; my wings have no feathers.]

Plautus - *Poenulus*

Among modern-day animals, the birds, the bats, and the winged insects are capable of true flight. In addition, there are many species capable of gliding, using specialized membranes or other modifications for short-term aerial activity. Almost invariably (albeit inappropriately) labelled in popular parlance with the adjective 'flying' rather than 'gliding', these latter include such creatures as the flying scalytails (see Chapter 7), flying 'lemurs', flying squirrels and flying phalangers, flying snakes, flying geckos and flying 'dragons', flying fishes, flying crustaceans (various *Pontellina* copepods), and flying squids. Furthermore, there are certain others whose airborne abilities have attracted appreciable controversy over the years, as now revealed.

Gliding Frogs

These extraordinary little amphibians were first brought to widespread Western attention by Alfred Russell Wallace, the great traveller and co-proponent (with Darwin) of the theory of evolution, during his detailed explorations and researches in south-east Asia. In his book *The Malay Archipelago* (1869), he described his first encounter with one of these fascinating frogs (destined to be named *Rhacophorus nigropalmatus)* as follows:

> *One of the most curious and interesting reptiles [in those days, amphibians were classed as reptiles] which I met with in Borneo was a large tree-frog, which was brought me by one of the Chinese workmen. He assured me that he had seen it come down, in a slanting direction, from a high tree, as if it*

flew. On examining it, I found the toes very long and fully webbed to their very extremity, so that when expanded they offered a surface much larger than that of the body. The forelegs were also bordered by a membrane, and the body was capable of considerable inflation. The back and limbs were of a very deep shining green colour, the under surface and the inner toes yellow, while the webs were black, rayed with yellow. The body was about four inches long, while the webs of each hind foot, when fully expanded, covered a surface of four square inches, and the webs of all the feet together about twelve square inches. As the extremities of the toes have dilated discs for adhesion, showing the creature to be a true tree-frog, it is difficult to imagine that this immense membrane of the toes can be for the purpose of swimming only, and the account of the Chinaman, that it flew down from the tree, becomes more credible.

This is, I believe, the first instance known of a 'flying frog' and it is very interesting to Darwinians as showing that the variability of the toes which have been already modified for purposes of swimming and adhesive climbing, have been taken advantage of to enable an allied species to pass through the air like the flying lizard [Draco]. It would appear to be a new species of the genus Rhacophorus, which consists of several frogs of a much smaller size than this, and having the webs of the toes less developed.

Gliding frog - an aerial amphibian

Clearly, there was no doubt in Wallace's mind that this 'flying frog' was able to become airborne, and his description was initially received by the scientific world with great interest. Unfortunately, Wallace's enthusiasm concerning his remarkable herpetological discovery got the better of him. In attempting to demonstrate, by calculations based upon the total area of the frog's membranes when fully expanded, that these membranes collectively afforded a sufficient surface area for the frog to succeed in gliding, Wallace made a mistake in his arithmetic. By now, some authorities had already begun to disbelieve that such frogs genuinely exhibited any aerial ability, and these eagerly seized upon Wallace's mathematical faux pas to reinforce their case - rather than choosing to carry out the necessary calculations for themselves (which, when computed correctly, *still* gave a surface area capable of sustaining short-term gliding).

Accordingly, the gliding frog's aeronautical claim to fame was unceremoniously discredited, and as little attempt was made to re-examine its case in the field, *R. nigropalmatus* remained grounded (at least in the scientific texts) for many years thereafter. Its first vindication came in 1926, when H.B. Cott showed that even a certain Brazilian tree frog called *Hyla venulosa,* which has far less webbing between its toes than *R. nigropalmatus,* still dropped to the ground only very slowly, and at a gradient of about 60°, thus landing at quite a distance away from its descent's starting point. This is because its limbs were outstretched laterally during its descent, thereby preventing it from turning somersaults; this would be improved upon by *R. nigropalmatus,* whose toe webs would act as miniature parachutes.

From that important discovery, it was only a matter of time before the case of *R. nigropalmatus* itself was reassessed. And in the late 1950s, this species was studied and filmed in Borneo by Prof. John Hendrickson, who was able to show that, just as Cott had predicted, *R. nigropalmatus* is a competent parachutist, descending in a stable manner at a gradient of approximately 60° - observations that fully confirmed Wallace's expectations, with some individuals sustaining glides of up to 40 ft from their original tree-trunk launching pads.

Although it is still the most famous, Wallace's *R. nigropalmatus* is no longer the only species of gliding frog known to science. Southern China's Mount Omei is home to *R. omeimontis,* Japan has *R. schlegelii,* and others include *R. reticulatis* in Sri Lanka, *R. prominanus* in Thailand, and Malaysia's *R. reinwardtii.* A particularly notable species is *R. dennysi* of Malaysia and southern China, said to be capable of gliding up to three times as far as Wallace's *R. nigropalmatus,* and reverently worshipped as a god by some of its human neighbours, who carry it in a regal procession upon its own sacred chair on certain holy days, the chair deftly bound with flowers in a manner designed to secure the frog in place so that it cannot leap or glide away, but without harming it.

In view of this frog's important standing in the religion of these people, it is a great pity that the gliding frog sceptics of the past did not think to consult them regarding the question of whether such amphibians were truly able to glide through the air; the dispute could have been conclusively resolved in this way long ago. Sadly, however, some scientists seem to ignore, almost as a matter of course, anything that 'uneducated' native people tell them - smugly preferring to believe that these people have never acquired even the tiniest amount of knowledge concerning any of the animals whose world they have shared intimately for countless generations.

Parachuting Palm Civets

Resembling a portly, round-headed genet with very dense, woolly brown fur dappled with small black spots, and an extremely long, barred tail, but without any form of gliding membrane or other device for achieving aeronautical success, the arboreal, 3-to-4-ft-long nandinia or African palm civet *Nandinia binotata* is the most unexpected and least known of all mammals with gliding prowess. Indeed, I learnt of its surprising abilities quite by accident myself. While flipping through some *African Wild Life* issues from 1958 in search of an account on a totally different subject, serendipity brought to my attention a fascinating letter by G.V. Thorneycroft.

In it, Thorneycroft recalled seeing two nandinias high up in a tree one morning on his farm at Zomba, Nyasaland (now Malawi). One became frightened by his dogs, standing at the foot of the tree barking loudly, and as a result it chose to exit the tree in a quite astonishing manner. As noted by Thorneycroft, the nandinia:

...made a leap from a high branch and volplaned to the ground with legs and tail outstretched. It made a perfect landing on the bare ground, ran to another tree from which it again volplaned and repeated the action.

Nandinia – a parachuting palm civet

The mechanism responsible for this highly unexpected capability from as bulky and unlikely a gliding animal as a palm civet is a somewhat familiar one.

What struck me was the graceful way it planed or almost floated to the ground at an angle greater than half a right-angle so that it landed at a considerable distance from the tree it was in. Its tail was extended straight behind, the long hair at the base seeming to be 'on end' and its legs stretched out as far as possible. On each occasion it made a perfect four-point landing.

In short, the nandinia provided a surprising but nonetheless wholly corresponding verification of Cott's findings with gliding frogs back in 1926, unequivocally underlining the importance of a fully outstretched body and limbs (with or without the possession of a gliding membrane) for successful aerial accomplishment.

Flying Gurnards

Flying gurnards are extremely distinctive in appearance, and exceptionally difficult to classify. The 1ft-long Atlantic *Dactylopterus volitans* and the comparably sized Indo-Pacific *Daicocus peterseni* are among the most familiar representatives of these curious fishes - variously categorized with the true gurnards, the sea-robins, and the sea-horses, but nowadays generally assigned a taxonomic order of their own. Superficially similar to true gurnards but distinguished anatomically by subtle differences in the arrangement of their head bones and the spines of their pectoral fins, the bottom-dwelling (benthic) flying gurnards are characterised by their large, bulky heads encased in hard bone; their brightly-coloured, box-shaped bodies, dappled with multi-hued spots; and, above all else, by the enormously enlarged pectoral fins of the adults, expanded like giant, heavily ribbed fans, and responsible for the age-old dispute regarding their out-of-water activity.

Records dating back as far as Greek and Roman times tell of how these attractive fishes are able to launch themselves out of the water and glide over the surface for a notable distance, just like the better known 'flying fishes' *(Exocoetus* spp.), before plunging back down into the sea again, and even compared their gliding with that of swallows. According to early authorities such as Salvianus, Belon, and Rondelet, the reason for this behaviour was to escape predators in the water (even though by leaping out of it they surely exposed themselves to the danger of being swooped upon by gulls and other seabirds).

Yet whatever the *reason* for gliding, for a long time there seemed no reason to doubt that they *did* glide. There are numerous reports on record from schooners and other ocean-going vessels, recounting the impressive sight of whole schools of these colourful sea creatures suddenly breaking through the surface of the sea and gliding for up to 300 ft or more on their varicoloured outstretched pectorals, before sinking back beneath the waves, only to be replaced by a second school, and then by a third, and so on, in a breathtaking display of piscean aerobatics.

One of the chief reasons for subsequent scepticism arose from a grave error by naturalist H.N. Moseley and fellow researchers aboard the late 19th Century research vessel *Challenger*. Their reports testified to the frequent occurrence of schools of flying gurnards rising up out of the water and gliding past on wing-like pectorals; tragically, however, it was later shown that they had misidentified these fishes. Instead of flying gurnards, they had been the true *Exocoetus* flying fishes! Naturally, this did not help the flying gurnard's case, having much the same damaging effect upon the credibility of its gliding prowess as Wallace's arithmetical error

Flying gurnards – can they really glide through the air?

had had upon that of his gliding frog. Since then, the general consensus has been that flying gurnards are too heavy and cumbersome even to lift themselves up out of the water, much less to soar above it. Not everyone, however, is convinced by this.

During communications with distinguished ichthyologist Dr Humphrey Greenwood, I learnt that he once saw a single flying gurnard (probably a *Dactyloptena orientalis)* glide up out of the disturbed waters at the bows of a small tug moving slowly in shallow water (about 10ft deep) off the Indo-Pacific island of Inhaca, in Maputo Bay. Dr Greenwood stressed that when the fish emerged, it did become airborne, and that its passage through the air seemed to be supported by its spread pectoral fins (spanning roughly 8in). The movement genuinely appeared to be a controlled glide, tracing more of a gentle parabola than the sharp, uncontrolled, haphazard leap out of and back into the water that many authorities consider to be the very most that could be expected of such fishes, especially benthic types like the flying gurnards. Greenwood believes that the reason for his fish's uncharacteristic occurrence in shallow water was most likely disturbance by the noisy, water-displacing passage of the tug, the fish ascending to the sea's surface as an escape response.

By coincidence, Dr Greenwood has also provided some support for the alleged aerial abilities of another controversial fish *Pantodon buchholzi,* the strange, freshwater butterfly fish of tropical West Africa, first discovered in 1876 and seemingly related most closely to the bonytongues (see Chapter 5). Its pectoral fins have some thin, stilt-like rays, which enable it to 'stand' on the sea bottom, but in overall shape they are very large and wing-like, just like those of the flying gurnards. However, there are reports that *Pantodon* can not only achieve controlled gliding but also undertake true flight - powered by deliberate flapping of its pectoral fins. Although science was willing to accept (in this instance) that it could glide, flapping flight was disbelieved - even though it is well-documented for the tiny freshwater hatchetfishes or gasteropelecids of South America.

Then Drs Greenwood and K.S. Thomson carried out a detailed anatomical study of *Pantodon,* and discovered to their great surprise that its shoulder girdle's structure, and the arrangement of muscles linking it with the pectorals, closely compared to the corresponding anatomy of flying birds.

Moreover, unlike those of other fishes, the pectorals of *Pantodon* could not be flattened against its body, but remained permanently extended at right angles, and could indeed be flapped up and down *(PZSL,* 1960). Thus, although there is still no conclusive evidence that it *does* fly (as well as glide), its anatomy implies that it *could,* if the need to do so ever arose.

Correspondingly, it seems reasonable to assume that although the flying gurnards' lifestyle is one that does not normally involve gliding, their pectoral fins can sustain it if some exceptional circumstance should arise to warrant such activity. Yet until precisely monitored (preferably filmed) observations of flying gurnards engaged in purposeful gliding are (if ever) obtained, it is likely that their aerial capability will continue to be dismissed as (in every sense of the expression) a pure flight of fancy.

Volplaning Frilled Lizard

Not long after the publication of this book's original edition, I learnt of an additional, equally controversial glider - none other than Australia's famous frilled lizard *Chlamydosaurus kingii*. As already described and depicted in Chapter 2 of this present book, it is renowned for the extraordinary crenated frill around its head and neck, which it expands if threatened, in order to startle and ward off any would-be attacker. However, some writers contend that it also utilizes its frill for volplaning, enabling it to glide from tree to tree.

In his book *Bunyips and Billabongs* (1933), Australian scientist Dr Charles Fenner included a remarkable statement made by Queensland naturalist Mrs Adam Black concerning this distinctive reptile:

> *...a pair lived outside our garden fence for years. They would run up a tree if one approached, and I've often seen my husband put his hand round the tree (they always climb up the opposite side to where you are) and catch one's tail; he would then hold it and go round and stroke the lizard's back and frill. If really alarmed when up a tree they extend their gaily-coloured frill and glide down to the root of another tree.*

Sadly, Black gave no description of the volpaning itself. I can only assume that if it does occur, the frill must act like a parachute, opening out, thence enabling the lizard to drift passively downwards.

Summing up, Fenner stated:

> *I believe that Mrs Black and other observers have produced convincing evidence that we have an Australian "flying lizard". It is to be hoped that some zoologist will take steps to observe these volplane flights of* Chlamydosaurus.

Unfortunately, this does not seem to have happened, so for now, this intriguing subject is very much up in the air. Whether the same can be said of the frilled lizard itself, therefore, remains to be seen - literally!

Chapter Thirteen
Legends and Lore of the Peacock

I am not going to be so impertinent as to describe in detail the plumage of a bird so well known as the Peacock. Who does not know his empurpled neck so elegantly bridled, his ai-grette of four and twenty battledore-feathers, his pencilled body-clothing, and, above all, his grand erectile train with its rows of eyelets? Who has not admired the lustre and beauty of those eyelets,- the kidney-like nucleus of deepest purple, the surrounding band of green, wid-ening in front and filling the notch of the pupil, the broad circle of brown, and the narrow black ring edged with chestnut, and then the decomposed barbs of the feather, gilded green, all presenting the effulgence of burnished metal, or rather the glitter and glow of precious gems, flashing in the varying light?

Philip H. Gosse – *The Romance of Natural History, Second Series*

It is odd to think that the peacock - one of the world's most spectacular yet familiar birds - was once exceedingly rare in the West. Known formally as *Pavo cristatus*, its correct name is the blue or Indian peafowl; in its strictest sense, 'peacock' refers specifically to the male. However, it is so widely applied to the entire species that for the purpose of convention I shall do the same in this chapter. Similarly, what most people think of as the peacock's glorious tail is technically a train or fan (composed of greatly enlarged tail-covert feathers supported by its inconspicuous true tail), but for simplicity's sake I shall refer to it here as the tail.

From Solomon the Wise to Charles the Bald

Originating from India, where it is sacred to the Hindus, the peacock appears in Western records dating back as far as early Bible days; the First Book of Kings (10:22) documents that every three years King Solomon received gold, silver, ivory, apes, and peacocks from his navy of Tarshish. This implies that the Phoenicians were undertaking voyages to India as long ago as 1000 BC. By the time of Pericles (499-429 BC), the peacock was known in Greece, but not until the return of Alex-ander the Great's Indian expedition did it became established there.

In Greek times, it was dedicated to Hera, the goddess of Heaven, so that sacred pea-cocks resided thereafter at her temple on the island of Samos, and this is probably the source of the specimens arriving in Athens around 450 BC. Nevertheless, it re-mained very rare here, fetching high prices and attracting large crowds from neighbouring towns to see for themselves this resplendent, near-legendary bird.

The peacock was cherished by the Romans too (and became associated with Juno – Roman mythology's counterpart to Hera) - although not only for its decorative beauty, but also for its gastronomic value, so that it was bred in great quantities for the banquets of the emperors and other eminent personages. Some of these feasts promoted monumental wastefulness - those of Vitellius and Heliogabalus, for example, regularly featured dishes consisting solely of the heads or brains of peacocks, with the bodies simply discarded. In medieval Europe, profligate gluttony was manifest. At the celebration of his marriage to Isabella of Bourbon, Charles the Bald of Burgundy (1433-1477) ordered the slaughter and serving of 100 roast peacocks (including young birds) each day for a week!

The peacock's great popularity as a table bird during Roman times and the Middle Ages is actually rather surprising, for its flesh is not particularly tasty. After the 16th Century, it was increasingly supplanted by the more palatable pheasant, and also by the turkey - introduced to Europe from America. Nevertheless, its strident, piercing cry - uttered at the approach of strangers or threats from would-be predators (and said by some to be the loudest cry of any bird) - made the peacock a popular sentinel (except in densely-populated areas!), so that it still provided a useful service even when its days as an epicurean delight had passed. Today, however, it is maintained almost exclusively for ornamental purposes.

Unfortunate Argus, Unlucky Feathers, and Ugly Feet

As I have noted in Chapter 6 of this book, the peacock and the birds of paradise are major contenders for the identity of the Egyptian phoenix as well as for that of the Chinese *feng-huang*. Moreover, one fabulous bird unequivocally inspired by the peacock is the golden peacock of Sri Lankan legend, which differs from the genuine article not only in the uniformly shimmering, luteous splendour of its plumage, but also in its pure, dulcet voice singing a glorious paean of praise to the sun.

Engraving by Conrad Gesner of the blue (Indian) peacock

The peacock features in one of Greek mythology's most famous legends too. Argus was the myriad-eyed guardian of Io - a priestess of the goddess Hera, and desired by Hera's husband, Zeus, king of the gods, who had transformed her into a heifer during an unsuccessful attempt to hide her from Hera. Argus had thus been appointed guardian of Io by Hera, in order to prevent Zeus from approaching her unseen; for as only two of Argus's numerous eyes ever closed at any one time, Hera was satisfied that Zeus would never be able to steal her away.

Zeus, however, sent the messenger god, Hermes, to lull Argus to sleep with the melodious music of his lyre - and as soon as Argus's last pair of eyes closed, Zeus appeared and slew him, rescuing Io. Argus was dead - but in recognition of his loyal service to her, Hera placed his multitude of eyes in the tail of the peacock.

A little-known sequel to this incident featured in *Prometheus Bound*, written by the Greek playwright Aeschylus (525-456 BC), often called the originator of tragedy, in which Io is later pursued by the ghost of Argus, and cries out:

> *"Spectre of Argus, thou, the earth-born one –*
> *Ah, keep him off, O Earth!*
> *I fear to look upon that herdsman dread,*
> *Him with ten thousand eyes.*
> *Ah, lo! he cometh with his crafty look,*
> *Whom Earth refuses even dead to hold."*

Clearly, Argus did not let so trivial an inconvenience as death dissuade him from continuing with his appointed task!

Another myth provides a very different origin for the eyes in the peacock's tail. As recalled by Venetia Newall in her fascinating book *Discovering the Folklore of Birds and Beasts* (1971), peacock feathers are supposed to be unlucky because they contain the colours of the Seven Deadly Sins. Following the creation of the peacock by God, the Sins were very jealous of this magnificent species' beauty; and so to punish them for that, God took away Envy's yellow eye, Wrath's red eye, and the coloured eyes of the other five Sins too, and placed them all in the tail of their jealousy's focus - the peacock. From that day onwards, the peacock has been continually pursued by the Sins, seeking to recapture their eyes - giving rise to the belief that wherever there are peacock feathers, the Seven Deadly Sins cannot be far away, and hence to the superstition that these plumes are unlucky.

The eyes in its tail have also become the symbol of foresight - it was said that a man can lose foresight just as the peacock loses its tail feathers (temporarily) when it moults.

In the Christian church, the peacock symbolises immortality and the resurrection of the flesh, due to the enigmatic (albeit erroneous) belief in earlier days that the peacock's flesh never decayed after death, but remained incorruptible forever. Described somewhat less romantically in Bartholomeus's *de Proprietatibus Rerum* (translated into English by J. Trevisa in 1535), the peacock's flesh is said to be ". . . so hard that unneath [with difficulty] it rotteth, and is full hard to seething".

On account of its resplendent appearance, the peacock also came to symbolise the glories of Heaven, so that many medieval paintings depicted angels with wings containing peacock plumes; and during the Age of Chivalry, a knight would often raise one arm above a peacock when uttering a solemn vow, pledging himself before it – as described fully by R.P Audras (*Découvrir les Animaux*, 19 March 1973). This is the origin of the once widely-uttered oath "By the peacock!".

A very different use of the peacock's name stems from the tragic deterioration of

King George III's mental state during his reign as Britain's monarch (1760-1820). To quote from Rev. E. Cobham Brewer's classic *Dictionary of Phrase and Fable* (1894):

> *When George III. had partly recovered from one of his attacks, his Ministers got him to read the King's Speech, but he ended every sentence with the word "peacock." The Minister who drilled him said that peacock was an excellent word for ending a sentence, only kings should not let subjects hear it, but should whisper it softly. The result was a perfect success: the pause at the close of each sentence had an excellent effect.*

Thus arose the saying "Let him keep peacock to himself" - meaning "Let him keep his eccentricities to himself".

One might assume that a bird as splendid in appearance as the peacock would have no reason to despise any aspect of itself. Yet according to folklore, this species does have a deep-rooted loathing for one particular part of its body - its feet! According to Bartholomeus's *de Proprietatibus Rerum* once again:

> *And the peacock hath foulest feet and rivelled (wrinkled]. And he wondereth at the fairness of his feathers, and reareth them up, as it were a circle about his head, and then he looketh to his feet, and seeth the foulness of his feet, and, like as he were ashamed, he letteth his feathers fall suddenly, and all the tail downward, as though he took no heed of the fairness of his feathers. And hath a voice of a fiend, head of a serpent, pace of a thief.*

The peacock's extremely loud, raucous voice has attracted its fair share of legends too. One of the most widespread of these is the belief that its cry predicts the coming of rain: "When the peacock loudly calls, then look out for rain and squalls". And in an edition of the 16th Century work *Hortus Sanitatis* quoted by H.W. Seager in his *Natural History in Shakespeare's Time* (1896), Section 93 of Book 3 reads:

> *By his voice he frightens serpents, and drives away all venomous animals, so that they dare not stay where his voice is often heard. The Peacock when he ascends on high betokens rain.*

That explains the origin of one of this bird's less familiar soubriquets - 'rain-bird'.

Multicoloured Mutants, and a Congolese Enigma

So far, this chapter has been devoted solely to the blue peacock *Pavo cristatus* - but this is not the only species in existence. Equally (if not even more) stunning is the green peacock *Pavo muticus*, split into three subspecies and native to much of southeast Asia, in which, true to its name, the shimmering blue colouration of its Indian relative is replaced by a dazzling selection of vivid greens and turquoise. Its neck is somewhat longer, as are its legs, and its crest is composed of fully-vaned feathers, in contrast to those of the blue peacock, in which only the tips are clothed, the stems remaining totally bare.

These two species will sometimes interbreed, yielding an incomparably handsome fertile hybrid called the Spalding peacock. As described by Josef Bergmann in *The Peafowl of the World* (1980), this gorgeous crossbreed's neck and breast are bright, iridescent emerald green, its back is golden and green with v-shaped green-bronze central patches, and it appears to have longer legs than domestic blue peacocks, thus giving it the green peacock's proud and slender appearance. Its facial skin has the same form as the latter species too, but is white instead of blue around the eye, whereas its crown is similar to that of the blue peacock, but is more compressed and brighter blue. Specimens with at least 75% green peacock blood are termed emerald Spaldings.

The blue peacock has given rise to 10 colour mutant forms (blue, white, cameo, purple, peach, opal, charcoal, midnight, jade, and bronze) and five pattern mutants (barred-wing, black-shouldered, pied, silver pied, and white-eye). These colour mutants can be combined with the pattern mutants (and with the hybrid Spalding) to yield 185 different varieties (as recognised in 2005 by the United Peafowl Association). The most familiar mutant forms are the pied, the black-shouldered, and - most ethereal of all - the white peacock, an albino form wholly lacking in plumage pigmentation (but its eyes are blue, not pink as in full albinos). When a white peacock's tail is spread open in display, it resembles a huge white fan of gauzy lace, hung with gleaming opalescent discs of mother-of-pearl. These discs are the familiar 'eyes' (ocelli) of the peacock's tail, rendered colourless through albinism but still visible because their form is structural, i.e. a consequence of the feathers' structure.

The cameo peacock, with dark neck but pale coffee-milk wings and (slightly darker) tail, lacks feather iridescence. It arose in Maine during the 1960s, and was first bred by Oscar Malloy. Similar but darker is the opal peacock, originating during the early 1990s. Another dark brown mutant is the bronze peacock, appearing during the 1980s.

One of the newest colour mutants is the purple peacock, a blue peacock mutant in which the latter's plumage shades of blue and bluish-green are replaced by purple and bluish-purple. The first known specimen of purple peacock was hatched in 1987 by a black-shouldered peahen on the farm of Jack Siepel in Arizona. It was later sold to Roughwood Aviaries, where the purple mutation was developed, officially introducing it to the avicultural world in 1994. It now breeds true, but the mutant allele responsible is sex-linked, yielding more females than males. For a detailed survey of all peacock colour and pattern mutants, see http://database. amyspeacockparadise.com/

In addition to the blue and green peacocks, a third, much more enigmatic and aberrant species is also known, with a singularly unusual history, heavily shrouded in mystery. During 1913, while seeking okapis in what is now the Democratic Congo (formerly Zaire, and, before that, the Belgian Congo), American zoologist Dr James Chapin noticed a very strange feather, rufous with black bands, in a native's headdress. Although well-acquainted with the Congolese avifauna, Chapin was unable to identify this feather, and all that he could learn from the local people was that it had come from a reclusive fowl-like jungle bird called the *mbulu*, whose zoological identity he could not ascertain. Moreover, his diligent attempts back home in America met with equal failure.

Then in 1936, while spending time at the Congo Museum at Tervueren, Belgium, Chapin accidentally came upon two old, dusty, taxiderm specimens labelled as young Indian peacocks. He could see at once, however, that these birds were nothing like young peacocks. Conversely, and to his great excitement, he perceived that one of them had rufous, black-banded plumes identical to the mystifying feather that had puzzled him for so long!

Further investigations and visits by Chapin to the Congo soon resulted in the formal description of a large, distinctive species of forest-dwelling bird hitherto wholly unknown to science, but represented (albeit unknowingly until then) by the dusty pair of mounted specimens at Tervueren, which proved to be a male and female (the male sported the banded feathers).

This remarkable 'new' bird was shown to be a very primitive species of peacock, the only species native to Africa, and was accordingly named *Afropavo congensis*, the Congo peacock (unlike the two *Pavo* species, it is never referred to as a peafowl). Lacking the ornamental train of its Asian relatives, the Congo peacock resembles a dark, glossy-plumaged guineafowl, with a red throat and a large white crest immediately in front of a smaller black one, and it remains one of the most sensational ornithological discoveries of the 20th Century.

A Tale Without Tails

Of considerable curiosity value is the Burmese belief that some peacocks never develop their characteristic fan-shaped tail. These freakish, tail-less individuals, also said to utter a very peculiar cry quite unlike that of normal peacocks, are referred to as *pago-daung*, or as *haing* (this latter name is also given to freakish male elephants that do not develop tusks). There would appear to be some truth behind this claim - because on 12 January 1930, H.C. Smith, a Mayamo game warden and Deputy Conservator of Forests, shot one of six seemingly tail-less peacocks sighted by him in a covey at Mônnyin, on Mon River, in Burma's Minbu Forest Division, and he noted that their call was indeed very odd, quite distinct from that of typical specimens (*Journal of the Bombay Natural History Society*, 15 July 1930).

Such specimens could of course simply be young birds - but if so, surely the Burmese locals would recognise this, and hence would not deem them to be something special?

Detailed ornithological studies have demonstrated that even a structure as wantonly ostentatious as a peacock's tail has a resoundingly sober, serious purpose - attracting the attention of a mate. Happily, however, this does not detract from its wholly incidental but incomparably compelling beauty - as much a source of delight and wonder today as in the days of Solomon, awaiting the arrival of his latest seaborne consignment of peacocks from their far-off Indian homeland.

Chapter Fourteen
A Furry Woodpecker and a Marsupial Hummingbird

In the case of an island, or of a country into which new forms could not freely enter, places in the economy of nature would assuredly be better filled up if some of the original inhabitants were in some manner modified.

Charles Darwin - *The Origin of Species*

On long-isolated islands, evolution can pursue bizarre courses in its endeavours to ensure that all major ecological niches are satisfactorily occupied, as the examples presented in this chapter succinctly demonstrate. Madagascar has no woodpeckers, so evolution has moulded a squirrel-like lemur, the aye-aye, into a furry equivalent. Similarly, with no hummingbirds in Australia a tiny marsupial called the honey possum has evolved to fulfil their function. Not surprisingly, these two very odd and highly specialised mammals have engendered all manner of scientific controversies, and remain as intriguing today as they were when first discovered.

The Aye-Aye – A Furry Woodpecker

Madagascar is renowned as an island mini-continent of strange, extraordinary creatures found nowhere else on Earth; the most famous of these are, of course, its numerous species of lemur. However, few animals, even here, were any stranger than the pair of remarkable little mammals captured on its western coast in 1780 by the French explorer Pierre Sonnerat.

Each was roughly the size of a domestic cat, measuring just over 3ft in length, almost half of which was accounted for by its long, bushy tail. Clothed in a rather shaggy and loose outer coat of dark-brown fur, supplemented by woolly under-fur, in overall appearance it superficially resembled a large but unusually thin, unkempt squirrel, and was equipped with a single pair of upper and lower chisel-shaped incisor teeth that were undeniably rodentian in form. Nevertheless, it also exhibited some decidedly un-squirrel-like features.

For example, its head was broad and rounded like that of various lemurs, its face was short, and its ears very noticeably large, naked, membranous in appearance, and highly mobile. Its fore-paws were also very large, and its fingers were remarkably long and slender - especially the quite extraordinary middle digit, which was so thin that it seemed virtually skeletal. Moreover, unlike that of any rodent, the hallux (big toe) on each of its feet was opposable (another lemur characteristic), and in contrast to the claws on the creature's other toes (and fingers) it bore a flat nail. Clearly, this was a species that would not be readily classified.

Indeed, even its native name proved to be a controversial issue. When Sonnerat showed his two captives to the local natives, they immediately exclaimed "Aye! Aye!". According to some authorities, this means 'Amazing! Amazing!', a reply elicited because the natives had not seen anything like these animals before. Sonnerat, however, assumed that this was their native name, leading in turn to the adoption of 'aye-aye' as the species' common name in French (and also in English and Italian) ever since.

Although widely documented, the validity of that derivation of the aye-aye's common name has been challenged by a number of researchers, some of whom state that its native name is genuinely 'Aiay Aiay' or 'Hai Hai'. Various other researchers have attempted to explain its name as a rendition of the call that it makes when startled or frightened; but according to lemur expert Dr Jean-Jacques Petter, a scraping, hissing cry is emitted under such circumstances.

Irrespective of the veracity of any of these theories, however, the natives would certainly have been surprised to see the two aye-ayes, because it is now known that this species has always been confined largely to Madagascar's *eastern* region. So the inhabitants of western Madagascar would naturally be unfamiliar with it.

The aye-aye of Madagascar

The question of the aye-aye's official scientific name incited comparable confusion - it has received at least eight of these, beginning in 1788 with Prof. Johann Friedrich Gmelin's contribution, but is nowadays known by worldwide agreement as *Daubentonia madagascariensis* (commemorating French zoologist Louis J.M. Daubenton). The reason for this nomenclatural fluctuation lay with the aye-aye's baffling anatomy and morphology, which was so exceptional that for the next 80 years (and sometimes involving the most heated and histrionic of altercations), zoologists throughout the Western world would be discussing (and discounting) one another's theories concerning the precise taxonomic affinities of this most bemusing of beasts. Just what *was* the aye-aye?

Basing his opinion solely upon an examination of the preserved skins of Sonnerat's two specimens, Count George-Louis de Buffon considered that the aye-aye was most closely related to the squirrels, but noted that its opposable, nail-bearing big toes (differing greatly from squirrels' non-opposable claw-bearing counterparts) were more similar to those of another rodent - a southeast Asian relative of the hopping jerboas, known as the tarsier. This, of course, only added to the confusion regarding the aye-aye's identity, because it was eventually shown that the tarsier, a small arboreal creature with enormous orb-like eyes, was not a rodent at all, but a primate, distantly related to the lemurs and lorises.

In 1801, the eminent zoologist Baron Georges Cuvier, while fully recognising the taxonomic inconvenience of the aye-aye's big toes, nonetheless preferred to support a squirrel identity for it - although he readily conceded that it was assuredly a very anomalous squirrel! At around the same time, however, a German researcher called Schreiber examined the limb bones of Sonnerat's two preserved specimens, and discovered that they were fundamentally lemur-like.

Following this up, Cuvier examined their skulls, and similarly discovered several unequivocally lemuroid features present. Yet in direct contradiction, their incisors were unquestionably rodent-like - large, flattened, and curved in shape, with persistent pulps that enable the teeth to grow throughout the animal's life, and enamel present only upon the fronts. These were evidently teeth used for gnawing wood. Moreover, the dental parallel between rodents and the aye-aye was continued by the latter creature's lack of canine teeth, thereby yielding a distinct gap (diastema) between its incisors and premolars.

The aye-aye seemed to be an incongruous composite of lemur and squirrel; and so, thoroughly bewildered, Cuvier passed no further opinion concerning its classification, electing to refer to it thereafter merely as a 'doubtful animal' (whatever that meant!). Other researchers were no less confused, some even seeking to ally it with certain marsupials of the phalanger family, or, in an almost defeatist gesture; assigning it to an entire taxonomic order of its own, thereby delineating it from all other mammalian species known to science. There were still some who maintained, despite the associated paradoxes, that it was best categorised as an aberrant rodent, but this was widely recognised to be a classification of convenience rather than a conclusion based upon certainty.

What made matters even worse for aye-aye researchers was the lack of specimens available for study - because, quite remarkably, not a single aye-aye had been procured since the original couple brought back to Europe in preserved form by Sonnerat. In short, the aye-aye was not only unclassifiable, it was also unobtainable. Could it have become extinct? Happily, this was not the case - the aye-aye was simply an extremely elusive, nocturnal species, spending the daylight hours ensconced in a large nest constructed from leafy branches in the higher reaches of trees, and (as will be discussed a little later) was additionally protected from would-be trappers by a formidable barrier of native superstitions and taboos. Consequently, it was not until 1860 that a third specimen found its way to the West, but once it did arrive it precipitated the solution of not just one mystery concerning its species, but two.

The specimen in question was a male aye-aye captured in 1859 by a Dr Sandwith (appointed Colonial Secretary of nearby Mauritius in 1858), who sent its preserved body to that most famous of British zoologists, Prof. Richard Owen, together with a detailed letter describing its behaviour as observed during its period of captivity following capture. Equipped with this invaluable specimen and data (and eventually with additional specimens too), Owen announced that in spite of its squirrel-like appearance the aye-aye was truly a lemur after all (albeit an exceedingly specialised one), as revealed by Owen's painstaking studies of its anatomy and soft parts (*Transactions of the Zoological Society of London*, 1852).

Of particular interest was Owen's discovery that the incisors of young aye-ayes are completely lemuroid in form and structure; their deceptively rodentian counterparts are restricted to the adults, and can be seen to be an evolutionary consequence of the aye-aye's adoption of a gnawing, rodent-like style of feeding. Owen's conclusions concerning the aye-aye's identity were fully confirmed and supplemented three years later by the corresponding researches of Dr Wilhelm Peters, Director of the Berlin Museum (*Abhandlungen der Konigl.-preussischen der Wissenschaften zu Berlin*, 1865).

Not only did Owen succeed in bringing to an end the decades of dispute regarding the precise nature of the aye-aye, however, he was also able to disclose (by virtue of Sandwith's observations) the extraordinary function of one of the aye-aye's most bizarre characteristics. As noted earlier, the middle digit on each of its fore-paws is exceptionally slim, very like a long piece of bent wire with a pointed claw at its tip. Its extremely odd appearance had even contributed to one of the aye-aye's several obsolete generic names, *Cheiromys* ('handed mouse'), but what could this most delicate appendage be used for?

Ever since the species' discovery, this had been a major mystery; but in his letter to Owen, Sandwith supplied the answer. Each night during its confinement in a cage following capture, the aye-aye had vigorously attempted to gnaw through the cage's wooden walls. As described by Sandwith:

> *I bethought myself of tying some sticks over the woodwork, so that he might gnaw these instead. I had previously put in some large branches for him to climb upon; but the others were straight sticks to come over the*

woodwork of his cage, which alone he attacked. It so happened that the thick sticks I now put into his cage were bored in all directions by a large and destructive grub called here the Montorek. Just at sunset the Aye-Aye crept from under his blanket, yawned, stretched, and betook himself to his tree, where his movements were lively and graceful, though by no means as quick as those of a Squirrel. Presently he came to one of the worm-eaten branches, which he began to examine most attentively; and bending forward his ears and applying his nose to the bark, he rapidly tapped the surface with the curious second digit [actually the second of the four fingers, counting along from, but not including, the thumb], as a Woodpecker taps a tree, though with much less noise, from time to time inserting the end of the slender finger into the worm-holes as a surgeon would a probe. At length he came to a part of the branch which evidently gave out an interesting sound, for he began to tear it with his strong teeth. He rapidly stripped off the bark, cut into the wood, and exposed the nest of a grub, which he daintily picked out of its bed with the slender tapping finger, and conveyed the luscious morsel to his mouth. I watched these proceedings with intense interest, and was much struck with the marvellous adaptation of the creature to its habits, shown by his acute hearing, which enables him aptly to distinguish the different tones emitted from the wood by this gentle tapping, his evidently acute sense of smell aiding him in his search; his secure footsteps on the slender branches to which he firmly clings by his Quadrumanous members [opposable big toes]; his strong Rodent teeth enabling him to tear through the wood; and, lastly, by the curious slender finger, unlike that of any other animal [but see later in this chapter], and which he used alternately as a pleximeter [or, more accurately, a plexor], a probe, and a scoop.

No longer was the aye-aye merely a much-modified lemur of uncertain lifestyle. It could now be categorised in all sincerity as a bona fide mammalian woodpecker. Furthermore, as meticulously documented within a paper in *Prosimian Anatomy, Biology and Evolution* (1977), analysis of the aye-aye's skull by Dr M. Cartmill has revealed that the aye-aye not only parallels the woodpeckers behaviourally but also structurally - its cranium exhibits a conspicuous number of specialised features also possessed by the cranium of woodpeckers. They include a foreshortened and rounded braincase, an extensive presence of bone between the eye-sockets, a short face, and a moderate degree of klinorhynchy (i.e. downward sloping of the facial skeleton).

As all of these features enhance the performance of a creature attempting to bite or chisel through wood, it should come as no surprise to learn that species as dissimilar taxonomically, but as comparable behaviourally, as aye-ayes and woodpeckers share them. It is simply an example of evolutionary convergence, i.e. the transformation via evolution of taxonomically-unrelated species occupying the same ecological niche into morphologically-similar ones.

The accuracy of Sandwith's detailed observations of the aye-aye's wood-tapping behaviour in search of hidden cavities that may contain grubs has been verified on numerous occasions since, but the precise mechanism behind its success is still being debated today. Back in spring 1991, what remains a very enlightening, key study of this mystery was published in the journal *Animal Behaviour*, stemming from the investigations by primatologist Dr Carl J. Erickson of four captive aye-ayes' grub-seeking prowess, at North Carolina's Duke University. Erickson's researches disclosed that in their repeatedly successful detection of cavities hidden beneath the bark of trees, the aye-ayes were not dependent upon visual clues; nor did they rely upon sensing the smell or the sounds made by the grubs themselves.

Instead, the significant factor in each of the four aye-ayes' searches appeared to be the echoes reverberating back from the wood into the animal's large, poised ears following its gentle tapping with its special wire-like middle digit (Erickson referred to this tapping process as percussive foraging). It seems that the aye-aye is actually able to discriminate between echoes bouncing back from solid wood and those bouncing back from cavity-containing wood (thus substantiating Sandwith's speculations, voiced more than a century earlier). In short, the aye-aye would appear to be employing a system of echolocation, comparable to the version utilised by bats when flying in very dark or wholly lightless caves, and is therefore much more advanced in its modus operandi than are any of its avian equivalents, the woodpeckers. Erickson published further findings on this subject in 1998 within *Folia Primatologia* and *International Journal of Primatology* papers.

In his letter, Sandwith also included an observation that suggested a second, less familiar cavity-related application for the aye-aye's slender fingers - though in this instance an application apparently not exclusive to its highly-modified middle digit:

> *I gave him water to drink in a saucer, on which he stretched out a hand, dipped a finger into it, and drew it obliquely through his open mouth; and this he repeated so rapidly that the water seemed to flow into his mouth. After a while he lapped like a Cat; but his first mode of drinking appeared to me to be his way of reaching water in the deep clefts of trees.*

The specialised nature of its grub-detecting and grub-extracting capabilities has attracted so much attention over the years that many people do not realise that the aye-aye's middle digit has a number of other uses too, and also that the aye-aye itself is by no means restricted in diet to insect grubs (these, incidentally, are generally the wood-bearing larvae of beetles and moths). For example, the middle digit is also employed with equal success for scratching, coat-preening, and parasite removal - clearly a very versatile instrument.

The aye-aye's diet is varied as well, and includes such items as birds' eggs, the pith of bamboo shoots, and a wide selection of fruits, such as mangos, litchis, and coconuts. Indeed, after gnawing a hole through the shell of a coconut, the aye-aye makes use once again of its indispensable middle digit, using it to scoop out the nut's succulent flesh. It follows a similar procedure when obtaining the pulp of sugar cane too.

Giant Aye-Ayes, and Strange Superstitions

Although the aye-aye's identity as a lemur is no longer questioned, it is sufficiently distinct from all others to be housed within a taxonomic family all to itself. Not so very long ago, however, there was a second species of aye-aye. In 1934 it was formally described by C. Lamberton, who based his description upon a skull-less skeleton and a single incisor tooth discovered at Tsiravé in western Madagascar. Judging from the dimensions of its bones, the complete animal would have been approximately one third larger and much sturdier than *D. madagascariensis*, so Lamberton christened its species *D. robusta*, the giant aye-aye. In fact, as far back as 1905 Guillaume Grandidier had unearthed some chisel-like incisors of an unusually large aye-aye from fossil deposits at Lamboharano, roughly 25 miles south of Morombe on Madagascar's southwestern coast, but scientists had not realised at that time that the specimen from which they had originated actually belonged to a separate, second species of aye-aye.

Nevertheless, once Lamberton had demonstrated the existence of *D. robusta*, the incisors found by Grandidier acquired particular significance, because in 1928 Grandidier had announced that close examination of these teeth had revealed that they had been cut, and pierced, to be worn as ornaments by men contemporary with their original aye-aye owner. This meant that the giant aye-aye had persisted on Madagascar beyond the arrival of the first humans onto this island, and the fact that it no longer existed suggested that it may have been exterminated by humans. Certainly, there is very good evidence to indicate that humans annihilated a number of other large species of lemur. What was unclear, however, was the date of its extinction. Did it die out a few millennia ago, or only a few centuries ago, or perhaps even more recently than that?

There is a tantalising piece of evidence to suggest that the giant aye-aye may still have been alive very recently indeed. Within his description of this species in 1934, Lamberton recorded that just a few years earlier, a Madagascan government official called Hourcq had encountered a native near the village of Andranomavo in the Soalala District who was holding the skin of an exceptionally large aye-aye - so large, in fact, that Lamberton and various other researchers consider that it may truly have been from a modern-day specimen of giant aye-aye.

Sadly, there is no further indication of this intriguing species' continuing survival on record. Moreover, for quite a time not all that long ago zoologists were expressing grave doubts as to whether *D. madagascariensis* itself was still alive! Just over a century ago, aye-ayes were still relatively common in forests throughout much of eastern Madagascar and also within a small area in the island's northwestern portion, stretching from Ambilobe to Analalura, but extensive deforestation for agricultural purposes in all of these regions rapidly depleted their numbers. By 1957, the aye-aye was thought to be extinct, because there had been no conclusive records of its survival since 1935, but later that same year it was rediscovered on the island's eastern coast by Dr Jean-Jacques Petter.

Nonetheless, it was clear that this species was in imminent danger of disappearing, so plans were drawn up to safeguard it, by establishing it within its very own sanctuary - in the shape of a small island called Nossi Mangabé, held to be sacred by the natives and sited just off Madagascar's northeastern coast. In 1957, nine aye-ayes were released onto Nossi Mangabé, in the hope that they would breed and perpetuate their species. As the aye-aye is still thriving there, the experiment appears to be succeeding. The existence of this species on the Madagascan mainland, conversely, remains far from secure, due primarily to the traitorous turnabout of a very powerful force that once operated very much in its favour - native superstition.

Untold centuries of deep-rooted native belief have warned that anyone who kills an aye-aye will certainly die within a year, and some natives were once convinced that even to touch an aye-aye was to risk death. Such beliefs were still prevalent at the end of the 19th Century. In his detailed account of the aye-aye (*Proceedings of the Zoological Society of London*, 1882), Madagascan missionary Rev. L. Baron reported the following:

> *It does not flee at the sight of man, showing that for generations it has not been molested by him; which is indeed true, as the following will show. The natives have a superstitious fear of the creature, believing that it possesses some supernatural power by which it can destroy those who seek to capture it or to do it harm. The consequence of this is that it is with the greatest difficulty one can obtain a specimen. With most of the people no amount of money would be a sufficient inducement to go in pursuit of the creature, 'because,' say they, 'we value our own lives more than money.' It is only a few of the more daring spirits among them, who knowing the odiny, that is the secret by which they can disarm it of its dreaded power, have the courage to attempt its capture. Occasionally it is brought to Tamatave for sale, where it realises a good sum. Now and then it is accidentally caught in the traps which the natives set for lemurs; but the owner of the trap, unless one of those versed in the aye-aye mysteries, who know the charm by which to counteract its evil power, smears fat over it, thus securing its forgiveness and goodwill, and sets it free.*

According to another traditional conviction documented by Baron, if an aye-aye spies a person asleep in the forest it will weave a cushion for him, from strands of soft grass. Should the aye-aye then place the cushion under the sleeper's head, when he wakes he will soon become very rich. If, however, it places the cushion at his feet, he will very shortly afterwards become bewitched, ensnared by the enchantments of a powerful sorcerer (the aye-aye itself, according to some versions of this myth). As for its skeletal middle digit: many natives believe that the aye-aye has only to point this at someone, and that person will assuredly die. All in all, the overriding impression among Madagascans was that this was a beast to be avoided at all cost - and never, under any circumstance, to be harmed or killed.

Although the aye-aye is, in truth, very inoffensive and quite harmless, to be held in such superstitious awe is really no bad thing - especially when, as in this particular case, the outcome is absolute protection from human persecution. Accordingly, the aye-aye survived - until the arrival of the Europeans.

With the coming of Western explorers and settlers, the Madagascan natives found their entire way of life - fundamentally unaltered for generations - swiftly and irrevocably changed. Ancient customs and traditions were ultimately abandoned as Western cultural influences superseded them, variously modifying or erasing every facet of human life on Madagascar - including the superstitions and myths previously surrounding and often safeguarding the island's indigenous wildlife.

One creature for which these changes were quite disastrous was the aye-aye. Emboldened by the Westerners' fearless attitude towards this species, and readily perceiving that they did not appear to suffer untowardly on account of it, by the early part of the 20th Century native tribes in many parts of the aye-aye's distribution range were assuming a notably aggressive, belligerent stance against this supposed harbinger of doom. Instead of avoiding aye-ayes, they began actively seeking and killing them, to free themselves and their villages of these animals' allegedly malevolent influence. Suddenly, the persecutor had become the persecuted, the oppressor the oppressed. Little wonder, then, that the unfairly-maligned aye-aye became ever rarer - and with the concomitant loss of its habitat too, it seemed only a matter of time before this extraordinary species would be completely wiped out.

Happily, due to the Nossi Mangabé sanctuary (whose sacred status has provided an additional safeguard against native persecution), the aye-aye's rediscovery on the mainland, the passing of many wildlife preservation laws, and a successful, continuing policy pursued by schools and other on-site establishments to educate the native peoples concerning their island's unique irreplaceable wildlife, this superstition-fuelled massacre is being countered, and the aye-aye still survives here. It is also being bred in captivity, notably at Jersey Zoo, founded by Gerald Durrell, and at Duke University's Duke Lemur Centre, which, with over 20 individuals at present, boasts the world's largest and most successful aye-aye captive breeding programme.

Undeniably, the aye-aye remains gravely endangered, but there is hope for its future now - and for the perpetuation in its island homeland of Madagascar's thoroughly remarkable furry woodpecker.

Antipodean Aye-Ayes and Ancient Apatemyids

One could certainly be forgiven for assuming that anything as morphologically and behaviourally bizarre as the aye-aye must surely be a unique, never-repeated experiment in evolution. Remarkably, however, this is not true, because at least two other mammalian lineages have also given rise to species surprisingly similar to this peculiar primate.

Once, the marsupials or pouched mammals were distributed widely throughout the world. Today, with the exceptions of the opossums and various other rat-like species (caenolestids and microbiotheriid) inhabiting the New World, they are confined solely to Australasia. Even so, millions of years of diversification have yielded a wide variety of marsupial species, which have evolved Down Under to fulfil many ecological roles carried out elsewhere by more familiar mammalian forms. Indeed,

Australasia's marsupials have adapted so effectively to this end that many even look like their counterparts in the rest of the world. The thylacine or Tasmanian wolf, for example, greatly resembles the true wolf of Eurasia and North America; the marsupial mole is extraordinarily similar in appearance to genuine moles; the insectivorous marsupial 'mice' mirror the familiar shrews; the flying phalangers parallel the flying squirrels; and so on. Most surprising of all, however, is that their marsupialian membership even includes a convincing aye-aye equivalent.

Hailing from eastern New Guinea, and known scientifically as *Dactylopsila palpator* ('naked-fingered touch-examiner'), the long-fingered striped possum is somewhat smaller than the aye-aye, measuring no more than 20in long. Also, in stark contrast to the aye-aye's subdued, blackish-brown pelage, this New Guinea marsupial sports a very handsome tawny-grey coat boldly patterned with dark brown stripes, and its lengthy tail has a most striking white tip. Nonetheless, in general shape it is very reminiscent of the aye-aye - with slender body; relatively large, mobile ears; broad, rodent-like incisors (though these are rootless, unlike the aye-aye's); and bare, slender fingers.

Equally, it shares the latter species' nocturnal, arboreal lifestyle, but by far the most impressive correspondence with its Madagascan counterpart is the feature that has earned this marsupial its expressive scientific name. In a remarkably faithful *Daubentonia* duplication, one of the digits on each fore-paw is not only very long but also inordinately thin, which is used by the possum to tap wood in search of internal cavities that may harbour wood-boring insect larvae, and then (once such insects have been located and subsequently exposed by gnawing away the intervening wood) to scoop them out.

There is, in fact, only one major deviation from the aye-aye condition. Whereas the latter species' wire-like tapping finger is the middle (third) digit on each fore-paw, in the case of the long-fingered striped possum it is the fourth digit (i.e. the fourth when counting from, and including within that count, the thumb).

The explanation for this conspicuous morphological and behavioural convergence between mammals as unrelated as a marsupial and a primitive primate is that New Guinea, just like Madagascar, does not contain any species of woodpecker, and so a mammal has once again evolved to occupy this vacant ecological niche. Indeed, in the case of the striped possum, more than one species has evolved, for New Guinea also houses two related species - the large-tailed striped possum *D. megalura* of western New Guinea, and the Fergusson Island striped possum *D. tatei* (Fergusson Island is sited just east of New Guinea). Moreover, there is yet another species, the common striped possum *D. trivirgata*, found not only in New Guinea but also in northeastern Queensland, because Australia does not contain any woodpeckers either. Worth noting, however, is that in all of these latter three species the fourth digit is not as lengthy as in *D. palpator*; accordingly, this species is sometimes separated from the others, and referred to as *Dactylonax palpator*.

In his comparison of cranial structure between woodpeckers and the aye-aye, Cartmill also examined the cranium of *D. palpator*. As expected, it too shares those earlier-listed specialised features enhancing the efficiency of a creature that habitually bites through wood.

In contrast to the aye-aye and its Antipodean counterparts, the third type of mammalian woodpecker belongs to a wholly extinct taxonomic family, whose members are known as apatemyids, and are believed to have been insectivores, related to the shrews, moles, and hedgehogs. Their aye-aye equivalent is called *Heterohyus*, and lived approximately 35 million years ago, during the late Eocene and early Oligocene epochs, in what is now Germany. Until very recently, only skulls and teeth of this early mammal had been unearthed, but then in May 1987 German researchers Drs W. von Koenigswald and H.P. Schierning documented three almost-complete skeletons, each measuring just under 1ft long, recovered from the Messel oil shale near Darmstadt.

At last, the morphology of this long-extinct form was known, and among the anatomical surprises unveiled by the skeletons was the discovery that *Heterohyus* came equipped with some exceedingly slender, elongated fingers very comparable to the tapping digits of the aye-aye and the striped possums. Furthermore, as it also had remarkably rodent-like, chisel-edged incisors, scientists now believe that *Heterohyus* exhibited a parallel lifestyle to that of these unrelated modern-day mammals, tapping for grubs and then ripping away bark to reveal them.

However, there is one significant difference between *Heterohyus*'s tools of the trade and those of *Daubentonia* and *Dactylopsila* – for whereas each of the modern-day species has only a single digit modified for percussive foraging on each fore-paw, *Heterohyus* had two. Both the third and the second digits were long and wire-like (*Nature*, May 1987). The reason why *Heterohyus* had two pairs of tapping digits has yet to be ascertained; but in view of the fact that its entire lineage died out many millions of years ago, perhaps its performance was in some way diminished rather than enhanced by its double supply?

The Honey Possum – A Marsupial Hummingbird

The final mammal to be considered here is one that bears no resemblance in any way to aye-ayes, striped possums, or apatemyids. Nevertheless, it does share one fundamental feature with them - because it too occupies a specialised niche in Nature commonly filled not by mammals but by birds.

In spite of the marsupials' success at morphologically and ecologically mirroring many of the more familiar mammals found elsewhere in the world, there are certain species that do seem to be unique experiments in marsupial evolution, which have no direct counterparts outside Australasia. The koala is one such example. We could also cite a miniscule marsupial known scientifically as *Tarsipes*, but this would not really be fair. True, it lacks a mammalian equivalent elsewhere. However, even though it has no wings, there is good reason for considering this intriguing little creature to be the marsupial answer to a hummingbird!

A tiny animal, with a head-and-body length not usually exceeding 3in, and a slen-

The honey possum

der whip-like tail that is virtually hairless, prehensile at its tip, and not more than 4 in long, *Tarsipes* is generally referred to as the honey possum (even though it does not eat honey and is not a true possum!), or noolbenger (its Aboriginal name). Its grey brown fur is handsomely marked with three longitudinal stripes of dark brown - one running along its spine, and one on either side of this.

The honey possum was first brought to scientific attention on 11 January 1842, at a meeting of London's Zoological Society, when P. Gervais exhibited a drawing of one of the specimens then housed in the Paris Museum, and originally obtained from the Swan River area of south Western Australia. He also read a paper, written jointly with Jules Verreaux, in which this species was formally described, and christened *Tarsipes rostratus*. This paper was published on 3 March 1842

Just five days later, a description based upon honey possum specimens sent from Western Australia's King George Sound by Captain George Grey, Governor of South Australia, to the British Museum was also published. In this paper, Grey's specimens were classed by zoologist J.E. Gray as a separate, second species, which was dubbed *Tarsipes spenserae*. Nowadays, however, only a single species of honey possum is recognised, so *T. spenserae* is merely a junior objective synonym of *T. rostratus*.

The paper by Gervais and Verreaux revealed that despite its diminutive proportions, the newly-described honey possum posed a giant-sized problem for mammalian classification. Although unquestionably a marsupial, it did not seem to be closely related to any other species known.

The chief problem lay with its diet, because the honey possum exhibits an inordinately marked degree of anatomical specialisation for an almost exclusive subsistence on nectar and pollen. To begin with, its muzzle is extraordinarily elongate, little more than a drinking straw, which is thrust into flower blossoms in search of nectar. This is then sucked up through its jaws' 'straw' into the possum's mouth, thus comparing closely with the feeding mechanism employed by hummingbirds with their long slim beaks. Also, the honey possum has a very lengthy, slender, brush-tipped tongue, once again remarkably similar in basic structure and function to those of nectar-feeding birds, especially hummingbirds. It uses this to pick up sticky particles of pollen that cannot be readily sucked up through its 'straw'.

The honey possum's morphological modifications for this unique lifestyle among mammals are so pronounced that they have effectively obliterated many of the anatomical indicators that would have readily revealed its ancestry and affinities with regard to other marsupials, and there are no early fossil predecessors to expose its line of origin either. Its dentition, a major clue to origin and taxonomic affinities with most mammals, is of little help with this particular species, as it is exceedingly degenerate - a nectar-sipper has little need for teeth.

Accordingly, the honey possum has been classed variously as an extremely modified possum, as a close relative of the koala, and as a highly distinctive, discrete species that branched off from the main lines of Australian marsupials millions of years ago to follow its own, independent course of evolution ever since. At present, some researchers still house it within the possum family, but many prefer to allocate it a family of its own, placed near the possums and the koala.

Yet despite its specialisations for a nectar- and pollen-sustained existence, the honey possum will also feed upon insects and other tiny creatures encountered within or near to flowers. Zoologists have postulated from this that it probably descended from an ancient insectivorous form that gradually supplemented its diet with pollen and nectar, until it eventually moved over almost entirely to these latter food sources.

Also worth noting is that the honey possum's limited distribution, confined almost completely to the coastal areas of Western Australia's southern section, corresponds with Australia's greatest concentration of nectar-producing flowers. Twenty million years ago, there were much greater floral expanses across the continent, and this is most likely when the honey possum first evolved. Although typically solitary or living in pairs, honey possums, just like hummingbirds, will congregate in large numbers on nectar-producing plants during their blossom season - a charming, unexpected sight for observers not familiar with these delicate, diminutive mammals.

Also, as shown by Australian workers Drs K. Richardson, R. Wooller, and B. Collins (*Journal of Zoology*, February 1986), when nectar is plentiful the honey possum imbibes as much as possible, storing it within a side-chamber of its stomach for digestion in later periods when there is less nectar available. Despite the seemingly sparse content of its diet, the honey possum obtains all the vital ingredients for a healthy existence - pollen contains essential protein, fat, and vitamins, whereas nectar is rich in energy-yielding carbohydrate. Nectar can be absorbed into its body directly, but with pollen grains digestion probably occurs through tiny pores in their shells - a process taking place during their passage through the intestine.

At one time, the honey possum was considered rare, but its tiny size has apparently caused it to be overlooked, because it is currently known to be rather more common than traditionally supposed. Of course, its own existence depends entirely upon the plentiful existence of the flowers and trees sustaining its specialised diet. If these expanses of flora were cut back or destroyed, the honey possum would also be lost - attempts to maintain it in captivity have not met with long-term success.

Let us hope, therefore, that responsible conservation-based approaches prevail here, safeguarding for all time Australia's delightful and engagingly unique marsupial hummingbird.

Chapter Fifteen

The Bird With Four Wings,
and Other
Nightjar Novelties

They are birds of omen and reverential dread. Jumbo, the demon of Africa, has them under his command, and they equally obey the Yabahou, or Demeraran Indian Devil. They are receptacles for departed souls who come back again to earth, unable to rest for crimes done in their days of nature; or they are expressly sent by Jumbo or Yabahou to haunt cruel or hardhearted monsters, and retaliate injuries received from them.

Charles Waterton - *Wanderings of a Naturalist in South America*

The birds to which Waterton was referring were nightjars, those long-winged, short-legged birds of woodland habitat and of nocturnal but harmless, inoffensive nature, whose intrinsic elusiveness has engendered all manner of completely unfounded myths and superstitions throughout their distribution (even in the West there is a bizarre but baseless country belief that they suck milk from the nipples of nanny goats). Most are drab, nondescript species, but there are some very notable - and noticeable - exceptions.

Standards and Pennants on the Wing

Senegal's Mandinka tribe speak of a strange entity that they refer to as 'the bird with four wings', and Europeans visiting Senegal and other West or Central African countries have sometimes encountered a peculiar bird that seems, when seen in flight, to be perpetually pursued by a pair of small bats. In fact, it is neither four-winged nor bat-pursued - for this is the extraordinary standard-winged nightjar *Macrodipteryx longipennis*. Formally described in 1796 from Sierra Leone by George Shaw, it looks much like any other mottle-plumaged nightjar, except for one diagnostically dramatic difference.

On each wing, the second primary feather is enormously elongated, attaining a length of up to 2in (i.e. three times as long as the entire wing). For most of its length, each of these feathers is completely bare, lacking a vane, but at the tip it is vaned, taking the form of a dark-brown racquet-shaped standard, roughly 6in long. When the bird is in flight, these spectacular standards trail above and behind it like kites on strings, an extra pair of wings, or even a couple of small birds or bats, thus explaining the Mandinkas' name for it, and the bat-pursuit illusion - enhanced by its preference for flying at twilight, when viewing conditions are poor.

Standard-winged nightjar — Senegal's 'bird with four wings'

But what is the purpose of the standards? For a long time this remained unanswered, due to the rarity of sightings by ornithologists. Even preserved specimens in museums were scarce, which makes a London *Daily Mail* report for 11 April 1896 of great worth, recounting the rediscovery of a taxiderm specimen by a Mr Coburn of Holloway Head.

Thirty years ago a Dublin friend gave it to Mr. Coburn, but he was unable to stuff it, as the skin was so tender that it crumbled under the finger. Mr. Coburn threw the fragments aside. Not long ago he remembered the prize, and finding that it was an almost unique specimen hunted for it, and luckily found it among his stores. After three days' work he put it together, and now it looks lifelike. He knows of no other stuffed specimen, for so far as he can ascertain, not even the Kensington Museum possesses one of these rare creatures.

A lucky find indeed. At the time of that report, it appeared that only a single European had ever seen a living standard-wing in its native homeland. This sighting had been made by Joseph Gedge, while accompanying Sir Samuel Baker's Sudan expedition. Gedge had observed a specimen squatting on the ground, and noticed that its standards were held upright, so that they resembled a pair of grass stems, each stem bearing a feathery head waving back and forth in the breeze. From this observation, it was suggested that the standards serve as lures, enticing moths and other night-flying insects to settle on them while the bird sits concealed in long grass. Once the unwary insect has alighted, the standards are drawn down into the grass, to the mouth of the hidden nightjar. Although this is a very ingenious theory, it was later shown to be totally incorrect.

In fact, like so many extreme plumage modifications exhibited by birds, the standards are used in mating displays. They are only possessed by the male, which displays in groups of one to four before an audience of about four females, perched separately on open ground. Within this arena, the males perform slow, aerial figure-of-eight dances, with bowing wings to elevate their standards, which glide above them like feathery pom-poms as the females sit and watch. Each display lasts no longer than 10 seconds or so, but they are repeated every 1-3 minutes for at least 15 minutes, according to Fry, Keith, and Urban in their *The Birds of Africa, Vol. 3* (1988). It is believed that once the mating season is over, the males deliberately break off their standards, leaving the vaneless stems behind; if true, this presumably prevents them from impeding normal flight.

Pennant-winged nightjar

Whereas West Africa has the standard-winged nightjar, southern Africa is home to the pennant-winged nightjar *Semeiophorus vexillarius,* first described in 1838 by renowned bird painter John Gould, and a species with equally extraordinary plumes. As with the standard-wing, the feathers in question are the second pair of wing primaries, which are immensely long, measuring up to 31in (once again three times as long as the total wing length). In the case of the pennant-winged nightjar, however, these feathers are fully-vaned throughout their length, and are white in colour, continuing a white stripe that runs across the otherwise dark shading of the wings to yield a striking pair of pennants.

Present only in the male, and in pristine condition only during the breeding season (afterwards they generally break off or fray), these pennants are used for courtship displays, the male flying at treetop height with pennants trailing during the early evening in autumn, and sometimes accompanied by the female. The males must appear quite uncanny, even spectral, to the unacquainted observer - and especially so in the case of the freak albino specimen reported in 1966 by A.J. Tree in the journal *Ostrich*.

Strange Tales of Strange Tails

No less spectacular than the standard-wing and pennant-wing is *Uropsalis lyra,* the exquisite, almost unreal, lyre-tailed nightjar of Colombia. First described in 1850 by Bonaparte, the lyre-tail is one of several New World nightjars with incredibly lengthy tails. In sharp contrast to its modest-sized, 11in-long body, its outermost tail feathers measure around 3ft in length, and are curved outwards towards their tips to create the elegant lyrate outline that has earned this species its name. Closely related is its comparably long-tailed and fittingly named neighbour, the swallow-tailed nightjar U. *segmentata,* and the tail feathers are just as lengthy in the long-trained nightjar *Macropsalis creagra,* an inhabitant of south-eastern Brazil.

In the shear-tailed nightjar *Hydropsalis climacocerca* ('ladder-tailed water-shearer'), the two outer and the two centremost pairs of tail feathers are equally elongated. Inhabiting the Amazon Basin and extending northwards as far as Guyana and French Guiana, this striking species, first described in 1844 by Tschudi, earns its unusual scientific name from the rung-like bars across its long tail feathers, and from its habit of opening and shutting those pairs of feathers like shears or scissors when flying over pools within its forest domain. A near relative is *H. braziliana,* the scissor-tailed nightjar, of comparable appearance and habit. The sight of such exceptional birds flitting through a shadowy forest or skimming over the surface of a still jungle pool could well be sufficiently strange to ex-

Lyre-tailed nightjar

plain their unearthly identity in native myths.

The Mystifying Devil-Bird – Rarely Seen, Often Heard

None, however, has engendered the degree of speculation and terror inspired by the notorious devil-bird of Sri Lanka - a bird which, unlike the others described here, is more noted for its ability to *avoid* being seen than for its visual distinction. It earns its sinister name from its truly hideous cry, described by one 'ear-witness' (see Mitford below) as sounding like "a boy in torture, whose screams are being stopped by being strangled". Reports of this macabre creature have been documented for centuries, but its identity is still unresolved, as I have discussed in a detailed article on this subject *(Fate,* January 1989, republished and expanded in my book *From Flying Toad To Snakes With Wings,* 1997).

The most popular identity is that of Sri Lanka's common brown owl *Strix leptogrammica ochrogenys,* but if the devil-bird is really as common and widespread a

species as the brown owl, why should its identity have ever been mysterious to begin with? Some, like George M. Henry in his *Guide to the Birds of Ceylon* (1955), prefer to believe that its eldritch cries are the mating calls of the Sri Lankan eagle owl *Bubo nipalensis blighi.* Certain others, such as Dr R.L. Spittel, favour one or more of the island's species of eagle *(Loris,* 1968), and there is also the possibility that a species of water rail or crake may be involved - birds famous for their vociferous screams and powers of concealment. Yet one of the few people ever to have seen (rather than merely heard) a devil-bird offered a wholly different identity.

Sri Lankan wood owl - the eerie devil-bird?

In his *Sketches of the Natural History of Ceylon* (1861), Sir J. Emerson Tennent recorded the eye-witness account of a Mr Mitford of the Ceylon Civil Service, to whom the island's avifauna was well known. According to him, the devil-bird is not an owl, eagle, or rail, but a pigeon-sized, long-tailed bird that he believed to be some form of nightjar. Moreover, in his *A History of the Birds of Ceylon* (1880), William Vincent Legge specifically suggested Sri Lanka's jungle nightjar *Caprimulgus indicus kelaarti* as a possible devil-bird identity.

Conversely, whereas the shape of Mitford's bird is compatible with a nightjar, none of Sri Lanka's recognized forms is known to produce the horrific shrieks that are the devil-bird's terrifying trademark. However, much of the island's forests, especially the denser ones reputedly inhabited by this eerie entity, have yet to be fully explored - does an unknown species of nightjar survive here, safeguarded by the superstitious horror that its bloodcurdling cry engenders?

Charles Waterton collected material concerning the fears and fancies inspired by nightjars among the natives of many parts of the world; a great pity, therefore, that he never encountered the Sri Lankan devil-bird, which may one day be unmasked as the most successful myth-generating nightjar of all!

Chapter Sixteen
Courting the Cobra

'Who is Nag?' said he. 'I am Nag. The great god Brahm put his mark upon all our people when the first cobra spread his hood to keep the sun off Brahm as he slept. Look, and be afraid!'

Rudyard Kipling - 'Rikki-Tikki-Tavi', from *The Jungle Book*

Since time immemorial, humans have been irresistibly fascinated by snakes - but most especially by cobras, nurturing an innate, inexplicable desire for close interaction, and even intimacy, with these large, highly venomous, and ostensibly imperious entities. This arcane aspiration has attained expression by all manner of different means - including fear-infiltrated veneration and handling by acolytes of Indian snake cults that perceived cobras as reincarnations of bygone leaders and referred to them as nagas; the fragile balance of respect and control achieved in authentic cobra charming; and even highly-emotive displays of devoted, unreserved love for the regal reptiles that are fervently believed by many to bestow blessings upon their homes and lives.

Yet for many Westerners, cobra cults and other manifestations of humankind's mystical inter-relationship with these serpents are totally alien concepts - exhibiting facets of human and reptilian behaviour that seemingly transcend traditional explanation or rationalisation.

The Serpent-God and the Snake-Priestess

One particularly dramatic case, recorded in his book *On Safari* (1963), was witnessed by no less an authority than Armand Denis, the pioneering wildlife filmmaker and author. In 1939, during a filming expedition to the Far East, Denis was in northern Burma (now Myanmar), investigating whether ophiolatreia (snake-worship) was still practised there, when he met an old Buddhist priest who told him to travel to a remote mountainous village, where he would be shown all that he hoped to see - and more! Two days later, Denis had arrived, and the next morning he found himself sitting in a flower-decorated oxcart alongside the village's snake-priestess, a beautiful young woman in her early 30s, at the head of a procession containing most of the other villagers, who were bearing gifts for the serpent-god and providing enthusiastic musical accompaniment with an ample supply of bells and gongs.

After a sedate journey along a winding mountain path, Denis and company finally neared a small cave, the journey's destination. Quite a while later, during which time the villagers had busied themselves strewing assorted offerings to the serpent-god on either side of the path leading to the cave, the snake-priestess walked steadily towards the cave's opening, accompanied for part of the way by Denis. At the opening the priestess paused, and called into it. A few minutes later an enormous snake emerged, and coiled itself at her feet. It was a cobra - but no ordinary one, for this was nothing less than *Ophiophagus hannah*, the king cobra. As thick as a man's arm and sheathed in olive-green scales imparting a deep, velvet-like sheen, with a total length of up to 16ft the king cobra is the world's largest venomous snake - it is also one of its most deadly, and most aggressive.

Even as the priestess stood there, absolutely motionless, the huge snake rose up with hood outstretched, standing erect and poised to strike. Able to hold itself 3ft or more above the ground, and positioned less than 4ft away from her, it was well within range. Yet in answer to the cobra's challenge, the priestess merely bowed her head towards it, slowly, deferentially, and seemingly without fear. Responding immediately, the snake lunged forward, striking at the level of her knees, but in the same instant the woman had moved slightly to one side, so that the cobra's deadly fangs made harmless contact with the fabric of her pure-white skirt. This macabre dance of would-be death between snake and woman, or deity and priestess, was repeated many times, and on each occasion the woman succeeded in avoiding the powerful reptile's fatal fangs - recalling a skilful matador deflecting the terrible horns of a charging bull, but equipped with a skirt of snow rather than a cloak of crimson.

Suddenly, however, the snake-priestess's performance reached its particular climax in a manner never mirrored by that of any matador. With her hands placed behind her back, she moved a little closer to her lethal god, and during a moment when it remained erect but immobile she leaned forward and lightly kissed the king cobra on top of its head! Drawing back instantaneously, she countered the inevitable strike that ensued, after which she promptly kissed the cobra again, and, after deflecting its consequent lunge, kissed it a third time too. The ceremony thus concluded, she simply turned her back on the cobra, and walked away, slowly but apparently untroubled, towards Denis and the waiting villagers. Nor was her confidence betrayed by the cobra - instead of striking her from behind, it merely turned aside and slid swiftly from sight into its cave.

If, during the journey back to the village, Denis had suspected that he had been hallucinating, and that this astonishing ritual had never happened, one could surely have forgiven him, for it certainly seems almost beyond belief that such a performance could ever take place. However, he had conclusive evidence for its reality right before his eyes. Clearly visible on the woman's white skirt were many damp, amber-hued stains - the potent venom of a king cobra, the legacy of her audience with her ophidian deity.

This astonishing performance has been witnessed over the years by other Western observers too, and Dr Desmond Morris's book *Men and Snakes* (1965) includes photos of an even more incredible variation on its macabre theme - in which the snake-goddess is shown kissing the king cobra not on top of its head but directly on its mouth!

Spitting in the Face of Danger – Literally!

Narrating a selection of his varied wildlife experiences on an LP record (again entitled *On Safari* - see bibliography), Armand Denis recalled a second, no less extraordinary encounter that he had witnessed between king cobra and human. Just before World War II, Denis was in Singapore on a filming assignment, and in order to complete the wildlife film that he had been working upon he advertised locally for a number of king cobras, a common species in that area. Eventually, he received about a dozen, all adult and extremely belligerent, which he maintained in a securely-fastened crate with a fine wire-netting top, whose mesh they profusely drenched with their potent venom as they struck at it repeatedly in their fury at finding themselves held captive in this manner.

One day, a young Chinese boy, dressed in a strange white garb with deep sleeves, arrived at Denis's hotel, and gravely volunteered his services to Denis as a snake-handler, provided that Denis would give him one of the king cobras at the end of the filming sessions. Although he naturally doubted the boy's capability to handle such dangerous snakes as these in safety, Denis was sufficiently intrigued by his serious demeanour and outlandish offer to allow him to take a look at the cobras, while they writhed irritably but impotently within the confines of their locked crate. The boy soon focused his attention upon one especially large and aggressive specimen, which he considered to be very beautiful, and which, he assured Denis, he would have no problem in handling. Needless to say, Denis swiftly reminded him

A captive king cobra

that this was a lethal creature that no-one would dare to handle in its current, highly emotional state; not until it had quietened down during several days of captivity could it be considered in any way safe to deal with, and only then for filming purposes.

The boy merely smiled, however, and asserted confidently that it would be very easy for him to handle it now - straight away - and in complete safety. He then began to prise up one corner of the crate, and Denis, very much alarmed, implored him to leave the snake alone. In response, the boy paused, and withdrew from the folds of one of his long sleeves a small vial of strange green liquid, which, when uncorked, released a fragrance vaguely reminiscent of freshly-cut grass. He poured some of this into his mouth, and then leaned down to the crate, until his face was well within the cobra's striking range. Hardly daring to look, Denis could only stand and await the inevitable, instantaneous strike that would swiftly bring death to this foolish child. Instead, it was the boy who acted first, and in a very unexpected manner.

Leaning even closer to the crate, he suddenly spat the liquid out of his mouth, spraying it liberally all over the face, head, and body of his chosen cobra! The boy waited for about a minute, and then - to Denis's even greater surprise, and absolute horror! - he casually reached into the crate and lifted the cobra out, his hands around the middle of its body's great length, holding this huge deadly serpent with no more concern than any other child might display when holding a length of cord or a skipping rope. By some uncanny means, the green liquid appeared to have rendered the cobra almost totally passive; true, it reared its ebony-scaled, fist-sized head upwards to gaze evenly at its young captor, but it made no attempt to strike at him.

After a time, the boy placed the cobra back into the crate, bowed solemnly to a still-stupefied Denis, and walked out of his room, promising to come back the following morning, and handle all of the cobras in the crate - but he did not return, and Denis never saw his mysterious visitor again.

Repelling Rattlesnakes

Science has yet to offer a satisfactory explanation for the phenomenal spectacle that Denis witnessed that day, but it is known that there are certain substances that successfully repel various snakes, including some of the most venomous species. For example, there is a longstanding belief in parts of Ohio that rattlesnakes are effectively repelled by the leaves of the white ash *Fraxinus americanus*. As he reported in the *American Journal of Science* in 1823, Samuel Woodruff once had the opportunity to test this belief, when he unexpectedly encountered a large *Crotalus* rattlesnake near northeastern Ohio's Mahoning River.

Searching for a white ash to assess its effects upon this snake, Woodruff soon found one nearby, and cut a wand from it, bearing a quantity of its leaves. He then returned to the snake, and, when it coiled and made ready to strike him as he approached, Woodruff leaned forward and placed the leaves on its body. The snake immediately threw its body into violent contortions, writhing and twisting upon its back as if in great agony. Not until Woodruff lifted the wand off its body did the snake assume its former pose, ready to attack.

When obtaining his wand of white ash, Woodruff had also cut a wand from another species of tree, the sugar maple *Acer saccharum*, to serve as a control. He now placed this wand on the snake, but it had no effect at all - instead, the snake struck fiercely at it, its head momentarily becoming obscured among the wand's leaves.

Woodruff repeated this ploy with the sugar maple wand several times, always with the same outcome, but when he subsequently applied the white ash wand once more, the snake again threw itself into anguished contortions upon its back, which only ceased when the wand was removed. At around this same time, the renowned American zoologist Prof. Benjamin Silliman tested this response of rattlesnakes to the leaves of the white ash, and he obtained comparable results.

Nulla Pambu – The Good Snake

During the late 1960s, naturalist Harry Miller was privileged to witness one of the most mystical, and mystifying, of all cobra rituals - the festival of Naga Panchami, held at Shirala, a village in Maharashtra, India (*National Geographic*, September 1970). Taking place each July (on the fifth day of the moon in Sawan, according to snake symbolism researcher J.H. Rivett-Carnac, quoted in Tutor Press's *Serpent Worship*, 1980), it celebrates *Naja naja*, the familiar spectacled cobra - which the Shirala villagers call *Nulla Pambu*, the Good Snake, and deem to be a manifestation of the god Shiva.

For days before the festival, cobras were assiduously collected from the surrounding countryside and placed inside earthenware pots, which were then sealed to restrain their occupants from emerging prematurely. On the morning of the festival, the pots were carried in a joyful if noisy procession through the village, and onwards to a small temple, into which the reptiles were released - but the ceremony was far from over.

On the contrary, the cobras were frequently handled devotedly by their former captors, displayed to the deity, worshipped by throngs of villagers, sprinkled deferentially with confetti-like showers of rice, exhibited in brightly-bedecked mobile carts, crowned with coronets of single flowers, and then returned to their pots overnight, awaiting release into the countryside the following morning.

Yet never once, through all of this, and with hundreds of cobras at large and freely handled by the villagers, was a single person bitten! Moreover, when Miller's assistant examined many of the participating cobras prior to their release, he discovered to his great surprise that they all possessed their poison fangs intact - none had been removed or tampered with in any way.

The cobras were therefore fully able to bite, and to kill - yet they did neither. True, the spectacled cobra can often be essentially docile and rather reluctant to bite; also, from a very early age the Shirala villagers are taught how to handle snakes correctly, beginning with harmless species and eventually graduating to the cobras and other venomous species. Even so, can these factors really be enough to explain such astonishingly intimate yet apparently wholly safe interaction with these potentially lethal reptiles?

The Temple Vipers of Penang

A comparably close association between human and snake is the standard feature at one of the most unusual yet popular tourist attractions in the Far East - the Snake Temple of Penang, Malaysia. Here, amidst the sultry half-light and heady fumes of burning incense, countless numbers of lethargic serpents repose languorously upon branches planted in ceremonial urns, placed reverentially before the altar of this extraordinary Buddhist shrine.

Bright emerald green with encircling bands of gold, and belonging to the highly venomous species known as Wagler's pit viper *Tropidolaemus wagleri*, these sacred snakes never leave their temple abode. Instead, they spend their days feeding upon eggs conveyed to them in baskets by obeisant human attendants, and gazing inscrutably with ever-open eyes upon the congregation of Eastern worshippers and Western sightseers visiting the shrine every year - compelled by an intrinsic, inexplicable desire to experience the mystical union of fear and fascination that snakes have so effortlessly aroused in humankind from the earliest times.

Aztec Adoration

Of course, snake-worship and snake-handling are by no means limited to cobras, but few other examples involve such feats of raw courage and hair-trigger emotional control upon the part of the worshipper as those exhibited by the Burmese *Ophiophagus* priestesses and by the villagers participating in Naga Panchami. Perhaps the most comparable, paradoxically, is one that involves a non-venomous species - the boa constrictor *Boa constrictor*, native to Mexico, the Caribbean, and South America.

Numerous snake temples existed during the great Aztec civilisation, and their priests traditionally carried living boas, often of great size, wreathed around their bodies, in order to inspire fear, wonder, and obedience among the general populace.

Needless to say, however, if the boas were not treated with great care during such performances their innate instincts for constriction would instantly be triggered, and their hapless servitors would suffer the dreadful consequences of their remiss conduct. Notwithstanding this, it is possible that on occasion the priests derived some very positive benefits from their hazardous profession - the inspiration for an electrifying segment of Robert Southey's famous poem *Madoc: The Curse of Kehama*, in which Neolin, the snake-god's priest, is a prisoner of Madoc and his party...when suddenly:

Forth from the dark recesses of the cave
The serpent came; the Hoamen at the sight
Shouted; and they who held the priest, appall'd,
Relaxed their hold. On came the mighty snake,
And twined in many a wreath round Neolin,
Darting aright, aleft, his sinuous neck,
With searching eye and lifted jaw, and tongue
Quivering; and hiss as of a heavy shower
Upon the summer woods. The Britons stood
Astounded at the powerful reptile's bulk,
And that strange sight. His girth was as of man,
But easily could he have overtopp'd
Goliath's helmed head; or that huge king
Of Basan, hugest of the Anakim.
What then was human strength if once involv'd
Within those dreadful coils! The multitude
Fell prone and worshipp'd.

As well they might, since heretics were generally sacrificed!

The Aztecs are not the only constrictor snake worshippers. Danh-gbi, the serpent god worshipped by tribes in the West African country of Benin (formerly Dahomey), is represented in corporeal form by the African rock python *Python sebae*. It was the arrival of this creed in the West Indies (especially Haiti) with the transportation of Benin natives during the terrible years of the slave trade that gave rise to the mysterious religion nowadays referred to as voodoo. This initially involved the continuing worship of Danh-gbi, but under the new name of Damballah-wèdo; and featured living specimens of boa (these specimens were the actual Voodoo), the New World counterpart of pythons.

Macabre Playmates

There are many cases on record of interactions between cobras and people in which the human participants had no experience whatsoever in snake-handling, yet have nonetheless survived their close encounters of the serpentine kind wholly unharmed.

One of the most outstanding of these was reported by the Sri Lankan wildlife journal *Loris* (December 1967). After leaving her baby alone in a room for a short time one morning, its mother returned just before noon to feed it - and discovered that it was no longer alone. Her child now had a playmate, with whom it was enjoying a happy game - the playmate was stroking the baby's face with its head, and the baby was pushing the playmate's head away, a simple game that was being repeated over and over. Indeed, the game was so innocuous that the mother would not have been in any way concerned - had it not been for the terrifying fact that the baby's playmate was an adult cobra!

The cobra was coiled around the child's body, and its hood was fully expanded, yet it seemed totally disinclined to strike the child. If anything, and at the risk of sounding anthropomorphic, it actually appeared to be enjoying the game! In contrast, the mother was almost demented with fear, but wisely decided to remain perfectly still and hope that the snake would leave of its own accord, without biting the baby. Happily, the cobra did indeed depart eventually, and when the frightened mother examined her child she found it to be completely unharmed and no worse for its extraordinary encounter.

That same issue of *Loris* also contained another startling example of an apparently benign child-serpent inter-relationship. Taking place in Port Elizabeth, South Africa, it featured a two-year-old boy called Allan Jonker, who went off to play in his parents' garden each morning with what his parents innocently assumed to be an imaginary friend - a friend that Allan always referred to as his baby. One day, out of sheer curiosity, Allan's older brother went along too - to see what type of game Allan played, and to find out whether there really was someone, or something, that he played with. To his horror, the brother discovered that Allan's 'baby' was not imaginary but was very real - only too real, in fact, for it proved to be a fully-grown adult *Bitis arietans*, Africa's notoriously deadly puff adder!

As soon as Allan's father learnt of this, he raced up to the infant, diverted his attention using a bouncing ball, and, once the child was out of harm's way, dispatched the snake with a spade. He later discovered that his young son had been affectionately squeezing the puff adder between his hands; yet, incredibly, the snake - belonging to a species noted for its belligerent temperament - had never attempted to bite him. Indeed, the boy had become so attached to his bizarre 'baby' that he cried all through the night after learning of its death.

Snake Charming and Cobra Cooling

In the dim half-light she sits, a motionless statue veiled in shadow - but all is not entirely still. Out of the shadows a sibilant hissing pervades the silence, and her long dark hair writhes and coils, just like living serpents - which is not at all surprising, because this is precisely what they are. Recalling a latter-day Medusa, this exotic, mesmerising figure is Aasha, daughter and accomplished protégé of Yogi Raj Bengali - one of the world's most celebrated modern-day snake charmers. Festooning her hair with animate cobras as other young women might decorate theirs with flowers, and adorning her fingers with living scorpions in the way that her peers wear rings, is all part of her extraordinary vocation in life, to emulate her esteemed father in their sensational shows held in Rajasthan, and are all facets of her extraordinary talent for handling these potentially deadly beasts.

Although he hails from Rajasthan, Yogi Raj Bengali has performed at all of the major Indian festivals, and at the special request of many eminent dignitaries, in Asia and overseas, during a lifetime of snake charming - thereby maintaining an extraordinary traditional spectacle whose origins are shrouded in the mists of far-distant ages.

Just like snake worship, snake charming has been taking place for thousands of

Snake charming with cobras

years and has featured the cobra very prominently - for good reason. No other type of serpent can engender the tangible aura of menace personified by the erect cobra, swaying before the pipe-playing snake charmer with its hood expanded and its slender tongue flickering.

The two principal species used are the Asian spectacled cobra *Naja naja* and the Egyptian cobra *N. haje* in North Africa - though Bengali and Aasha also regularly defy death by incorporating a king cobra in their spectacular act. Most Asian snake charmers are Indian, who travel as far afield as Nepal and Sri Lanka to perform. The most famous and accomplished of these are ones who, like Bengali, use 'hot' cobras in their act, i.e. specimens that have not been tampered with to render them harmless. Hence their very lives depend entirely upon the consummate skill and detailed knowledge regarding the safe handling of such snakes that these performers acquire during their hazardous careers. Moreover, the importance of acquiring such skills extends beyond the requirements of their specified performances. Once a snake charmer has become well known for his prowess in handling dangerous serpents, he will also be regularly called upon to rid houses and villages of snakes - i.e. wholly wild specimens that have never been tampered with and thus are able to inflict potentially lethal bites.

Indeed, as I learnt during a conversation with Mark O'Shea, an internationally-renowned herpetologist and snake-handler based at the West Midlands Safari Park in England, there are certain tribes in India, most notably the Jogi, whose entire lives are focused exclusively upon the capture and exhibition of snakes. In fact, as Mark pointed out to me, it is very likely that in many instances snake charming began as a flamboyant advertisement by snake-catchers seeking to attract customers and to reveal their skills in serpent subjugation.

Yet for every snake charmer who uses hot cobras, there are any number of fraudsters and tricksters who prefer to employ 'cold' versions in their acts, particularly in North Africa. More concerned with cajoling coins from the pockets of gullible tourists than with enticing serpents from their baskets, the charlatan charmers use cobras that have been 'cooled'. Also known as venomoids, cooled cobras are ones that have been rendered harmless by any one of several different means, which include removing or destroying the poison fangs and reserve fangs, sometimes the poison sacs too, and cauterising the sockets. Tragically, however, the snakes do not always survive such ill-treatment (unless the fangs have been removed via skilful surgical techniques and replaced by specially-manufactured harmless counterparts - an expensive procedure beyond the finances of many snake charmers). Some charmers will even resort to sewing up the snake's mouth - a barbarous practice inevitably resulting in the snake's death from starvation, but the callous attitude prevailing among such unscrupulous showmen is that as cobras are common in Africa, dead specimens can easily be replaced.

Sometimes a snake charmer does not tamper with his cobra's mouth, but secures its tail inside its basket instead, so that the cobra cannot reach the charmer if he sits beyond its striking range. Once again, however, this can be lethal for the cobra, because infections arising from such treatment can readily set in - particularly gangrene, if the blood supply to the tail is restricted or cut off by the tightness of the rope tying the tail to the basket.

As for the charming process itself, there is more to this than meets the eye - or ear, bearing in mind that as snakes neither possess eardrums nor external ears, they cannot detect many airborne noises and are therefore virtually deaf (but see also Chapter 2 for some notable exceptions). Consequently, it is not the music played by the snake charmer on his familiar bheen (snake-pipe) that stimulates the cobra to dance. Instead, it is the charmer's actions, such as the tapping of his knee or toe, and the overt swaying movements of his pipe (often bearing a light-reflecting mirror at its tip), that serve this function - inducing the cobra to sway in synchrony with hood erect as it strives to keep the pipe in view, and sometimes even strikes at its tip if feeling threatened.

Cataleptic Cobras?

A truly astonishing feat can be achieved by some of the more accomplished Egyptian cobra handlers, as described in *The World of Wonders* (1881):

> *The Egyptian conjurers know how to render this serpent stiff and immovable by pressing the nape of the neck with the finger, and thus throwing it into a sort of catalepsy. The serpent is thus apparently converted into a rod or stick. Traces of this trick occur in Scripture, and it affords a striking illustration of the passage where Pharaoh's wise men cast down their rods,*

which were turned into serpents, but were devoured by the serpent of Aaron.

In my files, I have many well-attested records of animals being rendered prone by human hypnotists, including a wide range of mammals, birds, reptiles, and even arthropod invertebrates - to place a lobster in a trance, for instance, simply balance it vertically on its head, i.e. stand it upside-down on its claws with its rostrum ('beak') touching the ground, to yield a tripod. Hence the above-claimed technique with snakes is not as improbable as it might otherwise seem.

Favoured by the Gods?

The ancient legend encapsulated in this chapter's opening quote from Kipling's 'Rikki-Tikki-Tavi', of how the cobra deity Muchilinda used its hood to shade the god Brahm from the sun's hot rays, has given rise to the long-lasting Indian belief that if a cobra should raise its hood over someone without displaying aggression, that person is destined for great fortune and success. This prophecy has been dramatically verified on more than one occasion.

During the mid-1870s, a tyrannical maharajah had been deposed by the British in the Indian state of Baroda, but as he had no sons to continue the royal line, a search was instigated for a suitable youngster to become his official heir. Time passed, yet no-one could be found anywhere in the land, until the searchers began to despair of ever succeeding in their quest - and then they saw him, surely the unlikeliest future ruler of all time.

There, in a clearing alongside a dusty road, lay a scruffy beggar boy, fast asleep, but across his prone body a tall shadow had fallen - the shadow of a huge cobra. The snake had raised itself erect, and was swaying slowly back and forth over the sleeping child, its outstretched hood shielding his face from the sun, but it did not try to strike him.

To the searchers, this mesmerising scene was unequivocal proof that their quest was finally at an end - in spite of his humble appearance, the boy had clearly been revealed by divine intervention as their land's true future maharajah. Eventually, the cobra sank to the ground, and glided away - and as soon as it had done so the searchers awoke the boy, informed him of his new, exalted status, and took him with them, back to the royal palace.

The cobra-mediated prophecy had transformed fairytale into fact, turning a ragged pauper into a regal prince. Moreover, when he was of age, he did indeed become the ruler of Baroda and, as such, one of the world's richest men - but he was also a very benevolent, enlightened monarch, under whom the country flourished and his people prospered.

As Jacqueline Mudie revealed in *Early Years: The Childhood of Famous People* (1966), a similar case history began one day in 1916 when, while lying on the grass outside the house where she was staying during a visit to Kashmir, a 16-year-old girl found herself face to face with a cobra. The cobra reared upwards, extended its hood, and swayed backwards and forwards over her head for a moment, but did not try to harm her, then lowered its head to the ground again and slipped away through the grass. When an Indian soothsayer learnt of this, she informed the girl's family that it signified the gods' special favour.

Her prophecy was certainly fulfilled - for the girl, born as Swarup Kumari Nehru (and sister to future Indian prime minister Pandit Nehru), but changing to Mrs Vijayalakshmi upon her marriage, ultimately became Ambassador to the USA and to the then USSR, Indian High Commissioner in London, and President of the 8th General Assembly of the United Nations in an illustrious career, retiring in 1961.

When asked during an interview with a British newspaper some years ago to disclose the secret of successful snake training, Yogi Raj Bengali merely smiled, and stated that although some do become accustomed to a certain touch and are quite placid, for the most part snakes cannot be trained; they simply do whatever they want to do.

Bearing in mind that these are the words of an expert in the handling of potentially lethal snakes, it seems safe to assume that the mystical links between cobras and their contemporary human courtiers have far from vanished, and that there is much still to be comprehended in this most perilous but potent of partnerships.

Chapter Seventeen
Rhino Riddles

Words can convey but a very confused idea of this animal's shape: and yet there are few so remarkably formed.

Richard Cope - 'The Rhinoceros', in *Natural History*

It is well known that the alleged aphrodisiac properties of their horns are responsible for the relentless and continuing persecution that has brought most rhinoceros species to the very brink of extinction in modern times. Less well known, however, is that these much sought-after structures have also generated all manner of mysteries and controversies for rhino researchers over the years.

Science currently recognizes five present-day species of rhino. These are: the African black or round-lipped *Diceros* (originally *Rhinoceros*) *bicornis* (2-horned); African white or square-lipped *Ceratotherium* (originally *R.*) *simum* (2-horned); great Indian *R. unicornis* (1-horned); Javan *R. sondaicus* (1-horned); and Sumatran or hairy *Dicerorhinus sumatrensis* (2-horned). However, little more than a century ago a number of additional species were also recognized, because of their various horn-related characteristics. Furthermore, it has been suggested that certain mysterious rhino forms - with unexpected horn complements or other strange features, and whose existence is currently based only upon anecdotal evidence - may actually represent unknown species, still awaiting formal scientific acceptance and description.

Holmwood's Rhinoceros and Oswell's Rhinoceros

One of the principal reasons for the taxonomic tribulations caused by rhino horns is their wide variation in size - especially with regard to the black rhinoceros. The average length for this species' anterior horn (borne upon its skull's nasal bones) is generally 20-32 in, whereas that of its posterior horn (borne upon its skull's frontal bones) is usually 14-16in. Nevertheless, much longer examples have also been recorded, particularly from female specimens.

During the 19th Century, F. Holmwood purchased two rhino horns from a Zanzibar dealer that were so long that some authorities believed them to be from a totally new species, duly christened Holmwood's rhinoceros, whereas various others considered them to be from a white rhinoceros. After a detailed study, however, Dr Richard Lydekker identified them as black rhino horns (*The Field,* 24 July 1909).

Another very odd African form, described at much the same time, was named *R. oswelli*, Oswell's rhinoceros. Characterized by an anterior horn that pointed forward (and occasionally even downward), it was finally recognized to be nothing more than an accidental or local variety of the southern white rhinoceros *C. simum simum*; the first horns attributed to 'Oswell's rhinoceros' had been obtained near Lake Ngami, Botswana.

More recently, two black rhino equivalents to Oswell's rhinoceros enjoyed long-standing celebrity status. Affectionately known as Gladys and Gertie, these remarkable animals lived in Kenya's Amboseli Game Park, and Gertie in particular gained international fame from featuring in wildlife films made by pioneering television naturalists Armand and Michaela Denis. For much of its length, Gertie's anterior horn pointed horizontally rather than upwards, and had attained a length of roughly 55 in before its tip (and eventually the entire horn) broke off.

The Blue Rhinoceros

Yet another mysterious African rhino mentioned in most natural history tomes during the 1800s was the exotic-sounding blue rhinoceros (also referred to, more mundanely, as Sloan's rhinoceros or the keitloa). Known scientifically as *R. keitloa,* this was a relatively rare form, distributed sparingly south of the Zambezi, and not usually gregarious. In his *Illustrated Natural History* (1859-63), Rev J.G. Wood noted:

> *The keitloa can readily be recognised by the horns, which are of considerable length, and nearly equal to each other in measurement. This is always a morose and ill-tempered animal, and is even more to be dreaded than the borele [black rhino], on account of its greater size, strength, and length of horn. The upper lip of the Keitloa overlaps the lower even more than that of the borele; the neck is longer in proportion, and the head is not so thickly covered with wrinkles.*

Formidably belligerent it may be, but some naturalists considered its credentials as a distinct species to be rather less impressive. W.B. Dawkins and H.W. Oakley, for example, within Prof. P. Martin Duncan's *Cassell's Natural History, Vol. 2* (1883-9), commented that the blue rhinoceros or keitloa differed little from the black rhino, except for the shape of the head:

> *...which is somewhat shorter and broader, and it has a less prehensile lip. Its chief characteristic is the posterior horn, which is flattened at the sides, being of almost equal length to the anterior, and even occasionally longer, twenty inches and twenty-two inches being about the average.*

A short-lived controversy ensued during the second half of the 1800s, which was finally ended by the famous explorer Captain Frederick Selous. In a comprehensive paper published in the Zoological Society of London's *Proceedings* for 1881, and referring to an extensive collection of horns, Selous demonstrated that blue and black rhinos belong to the same species. As noted in *Rhinos: Endangered Species* (1987) by Malcolm Penny, the difference in horn lengths was most probably due to

Blue rhinoceros – not a separate species after all

environmental conditions: black rhinos inhabiting relatively dry localities are smaller and tend to possess shorter horns than those frequenting wetter terrain. Exit the blue rhinoceros!

Rhinos with Extra Horns

Intraspecific differences in *size* are not the only sources of variation and mystery with rhino horns. Many records exist of specimens of two-horned species that actually possessed *extra* (supernumerary) horns. It is well known, for example, that three-horned black rhinos were once relatively common around Zambia's Lake Young, and Botswanan examples are noted in C.J. Anderssons's *Lake Ngami* (1851). In the past, Sumatran natives asserted that three-horned specimens of the Sumatran rhinoceros were occasionally met with too. Even Linnaeus mentioned three-horned rhinos - to his description of the black rhinoceros in Gmelin's edition (1788) of *Systema Naturae* is added: "Rarior est Rhinoceros tricornis, tertia cum cornu ex alterato priorem excrescente".

In most cases, the extra horn is usually nothing more than a small, rounded knob - a rudimentary third horn positioned behind the two normal ones. Similarly, towards the end of the 19th Century, London Zoo exhibited a female great Indian rhino that bore a rudimentary second horn upon her forehead. Alternatively, a pseudo-third horn can develop via the splitting into two of one of the normal, pre-existing horns, as seen in the following photo of a zoo specimen.

Captive rhino with pseudo-third horn

Occasionally, even more extreme cases are recorded. One such individual was the abnormal black rhino shot during August 1904 in a dense covert west of Kenya's Jambeni Mountains, and reported by Colonel W.H. Broun in the Zoological Society of London's *Proceedings* during 1905. In addition to the two normal representatives, this rhino had a third, rudimentary horn between its ears, and a *fourth,* equally diminutive example located about 4 in further back.

During his extensive black rhino researches, renowned German zoologist Dr Bernard Grzimek encountered reports of a five-horned specimen, and even of rhinos with horns growing out of their bodies. He also suggested that the famous illustration by Albrecht Dürer (later copied by Conrad Gesner in his *Historiae Animalium, Liber I,* 1551) of a great Indian rhino bearing an incongruously sited horn on its shoulder may have been truly based upon an abnormally horned specimen.

At one time, this idea was discounted in favour of the theory that the horn was either an error on the part of Dürer, or, if genuine, merely an excrescence developed by the rhino in question during its long confinement in the ship bringing it from India to Portugal's King Manuel the Great, at Lisbon. Moreover, as discussed in an

Dürer's famous shoulder-horned rhinoceros

entire paper on the subject by Dr K.C.A. Schulz *(African Wild Life,* 1961), rough sores of a horny nature have been observed for some time among black rhinos too.

However, Grzimek's view was reinforced in spring 1968, when Prof. Heini Hediger photographed a white rhino living in San Francisco Zoo that bore a bona fide, un-equivocal shoulder horn, measuring some 4 in high (*Zoologische Garten,* Leipzig, 1970).

At present the precise reasons for the development of extra horns by rhinos remain relatively unclear. In some cases, a genetic origin is indicated, especially when they involve several multi-horned specimens inhabiting one specific locality, as with the Lake Young individuals. Injury-induced development (echoing the 'excrescence theory' for Dürer's specimen) may also occur - as documented from various ante-lopes and deer possessing supernumerary (and often oddly located) horns, some-times emerging from the forehead, face, or even sites on the body (see also the horned jackal, Chapter 7).

Rhinos with Fewer Horns than Normal

At the opposite extreme, records also exist of hornless rhinos (indeed, hornless fe-males of the Javan rhinoceros were quite common prior to the species' modern-day decline), and of specimens of two-horned rhino species that only have a single horn.

For example, Charles Knight in his *Pictorial Museum of Animated Nature* (1856-8) stated:

*...there is some reason to believe in the existence of a single-horned spe-
cies in that region [Ethiopia]. Bruce states that a one-horned rhinoceros is
found towards Cape Gardafui, according to the account of the natives in
the kingdom of Adel. Accounts of such an animal were received by Dr
Smith from the natives in the interior of South Africa, who represented it as
living far up the country; moreover Burckhardt alludes to a one-horned
species in the territory above Sennaar, and states that the inhabitants there
give it the name of the 'mother of the one horn'. According to this traveller, its northern boundary, like that of the elephant, is the range of mountains to the north of Abou Huaze, two days' journey from Sennaar. The
hide of this animal is manufactured into shields, which have an extensive
sale; the material of the horn is also sold, and at a high price. Burckhardt
having seen four or five Spanish dollars paid for a piece four inches long
and one inch thick...it may be added that Dr Smith adduces the testimony
of Mr Freeman respecting an animal by no means rare in Makooa, north
of the Mosambique Channel, which, overlooking the absurdities and exag-
geration of the description, he suspects to be a one-horned rhinoceros, and
probably that of which he heard, and which may extend to the countries
mentioned by Bruce and Burckhardt.*

'Dr Smith' was Sir Andrew Smith, whose investigations are documented fully in
his *Illustrations of the Zoology of South Africa, Vol. 1* (1838). Ten years later, similar reports, but this time emanating from the Lake Chad district and the White Nile,
were presented by F. Fresnel (*Comptes Rendus,* 1848).

Much more recently, in her book *Mapungubwe: An Archaeological Interpretation
of an Iron Age Community* (1983), Elizabeth Voigt documented a 12th-Century
gold-plated carving depicting a single-horned rhinoceros, excavated at the
Mapungubwe archaeological site in South Africa's Northern Province. What could
these one-horned rhinos be?

In some cases, they may have been based upon sightings of black or white rhino
specimens in which one horn had been lost through injury. However, as pointed out
by Lydekker (*The Field,* 28 December 1907), records exist of white rhinos that have
never developed a true posterior horn, bearing nothing more than an inconspicuous
tubercle behind the front horn, so that to all intent and purposes these individuals
really are one-horned. There is a further, if rather more remote, explanation of one-
horned rhino sightings in Africa - that they represent a distinct species still undescribed by science. If true, it will probably remain undescribed indefinitely, as rhinos no longer exist in most of the northern regions noted in the above narratives.

The *Badak Tanggiling* – A Sumatran Surprise

In 1941, Willy Ley noted in *The Lungfish and the Unicorn* that at some stage during
the middle portion of the 1920s, a Dr Vageler - regularly contacted by zoos wishing
to replenish their animal collections - was seeking some specimens of the Asian rhinos when he met up with J.C. Hazewinkel, a noted big game hunter. After learning
that Vageler required new rhinoceroses, Hazewinkel showed him some photos of

eight that he had shot in Sumatra, and which appeared to be new in every sense of the word. For the type that they represented — although familiar to the natives, who called it *badak tanggiling* - seemed to differ greatly from the form familiar to Vageler on Sumatra.

Unlike the known, two-horned Sumatran rhinoceros *Dicerorhinus sumatrensis,* the *badak tanggiling* bore just a single horn. If this had been the only difference, it could have been explained as a mere freak of nature. However, Hazewinkel stated that the female *badak tanggiling* was often totally hornless, and that the form as a whole attained a length of 10 ft. In contrast, the female Sumatran rhinoceros is rarely if ever hornless, and the species as a whole only attains a length of 8—9 ft.

As Dr Vageler readily recognized, the Sumatran rhino thus became an unlikely candidate for the *badak tanggiling's* identity. In his coverage of this episode, Willy Ley stated that Hazewinkel's photos convinced Vageler that a second species of rhinoceros existed on Sumatra, and that in reply to his requests Vageler was promised living specimens of it to send on to various zoos worldwide, but they never arrived. Ley concluded his account by stating that the *badak tanggiling* therefore remains a shadow in our zoological encyclopedias, but: "...it may, however, be rediscovered almost any day".

From all of this it would seem that Ley considered the *badak tanggiling* to be a wholly unknown, undescribed species. In fact, its identity is surely no mystery, for this enigmatic creature is clearly *Rhinoceros sondaicus,* the Javan rhinoceros. Not only is it of comparable size to the *badak tanggiling,* and a one-horned species whose females are indeed sometimes hornless, but at the time of Vageler and Hazewinkel it did exist on Sumatra (but this was not widely known outside scientific circles). Indeed, the last known Sumatran specimens of the Javan rhino did not die out until World War II.

There is a further, more specific, piece of evidence confirming this identification. On 23 December 1933, the *Illustrated London News* published an article by Hazewinkel, in which he described his pursuit and shooting of the first of eight specimens of large, one-horned rhinoceros on Sumatra during the mid-1920s. The photos of the animal dispel any doubt as to its identity - one that Hazewinkel, moreover, freely announced. It was a Javan rhinoceros. Indeed, echoing the general unawareness concerning the existence of this species on Sumatra at that time, Hazewinkel had entitled his article 'A One-Horned Javanese Rhinoceros Shot in Sumatra, Where It Was Not Thought to Exist'.

Clearly, there can be no question that those eight Javan rhinos shot by Hazewinkel on Sumatra in the mid-1920s are one and the same as the eight Sumatran *badak tanggiling* shot by him and mentioned to Vageler by him during that same period.

According to Joseph Belmont, another animal collector for zoos, a mysterious beast known as the scaled rhinoceros allegedly existed amidst the inhospitable, fever-ridden swamps of Java. Writing in *Catching Wild Beasts Alive* (1931), Delmont reported that this cryptic creature, supposedly distinct from the known species of

Javan rhinoceros, had only been shot twice, with no living specimen ever having been obtained. However, as the 'armour' of the known Javan rhino is noticeably scale-like, quite different from that of its closest relative the great Indian rhinoceros, it would once again seem that the creature in question is *Rhinoceros sondaicus* after all.

Rhinoceroses in New Guinea and New Caledonia?

As far as science is concerned, the fauna of New Guinea does not include any species of rhinoceros, but that has not prevented the documentation of some interesting reports supporting the existence of supposed rhinos on this island. For example, on 28 January 1875, the journal *Nature* published an intriguing account from Alfred 0. Walker:

> *Lieut. Sidney Smith, late of HMS Basilisk, reports that while engaged in surveying on the north coast of Papua, between Huon Bay and Cape Basilisk, being on shore with a party cutting firewood, he observed in the forest the 'droppings' (excrement) of a rhinoceros in more than one place, the bushes in the neighbourhood being also broken and trampled as if by a large animal. The presence of so large an animal belonging to the Asiatic fauna in Papua is an important fact.*

It is indeed - if true. However, the *Nature* editors were not so readily convinced, adding in a footnote that they were "... inclined to doubt very seriously the occurrence of any rhinoceros in New Guinea". Notwithstanding this, the very next issue of *Nature* (4 February 1875) featured a thought-provoking report by zoologist Dr Adolf Bernhard Meyer, which included the following details:

> *I am quite of your opinion that the occurrence of a rhinoceros in New Guinea is very seriously to be doubted ... but I beg leave to mention a report of a very large quadruped in New Guinea, which I got from the Papuans of the south coast of the Geelvinks Bay...when hunting wild pigs along with the Papuans, they told me, without my questioning them, of a very large pig, as they called it, fixing its height on the stem of a tree at more than six feet. I could not get any other information from them, except that the beast was very rare, but they were quite precise in their assertion. I promised heaps of glass pearls and knives to him who would bring me something of that large animal, but none did. I cannot suppose, so far as my experience goes, that the Papuans are remarkably prone to lies; notwithstanding I seriously doubted the existence of such a large 'pig' It is true this statement does not strongly support Lieut. Smith's aperçu, but the one gains a grain by the other; I mean, the probability of the existence of a large quadruped in New Guinea increases a shadow.*

It was increased a further shadow in the same *Nature* issue, courtesy of a second, longer letter from Alfred Walker, containing extra details supplied by Lieut. Smith:

> *The heap of dung first seen, which was quite fresh (not having apparently*

been dropped more than half an hour), was so large that it excited Mr Smith's curiosity, and he called Captain Moresby to see it. Neither of them knew to what animal to assign it. Quantities of dry dung were afterwards seen. Shortly afterwards, the Basilisk *being at or near Singapore, Capt. Moresby and Mr Smith paid a visit to the Rajah of Johore, who had a rhinoceros in confinement. Mr Smith at once observed and pointed out to Capt. Moresby (who agreed with him) the strong resemblance between the dung of this animal and that they had seen in Papua.*

It hardly need be said that heaps of animal droppings rarely arouse such interest unless there really is something very strange about them! And what of Meyer's 'very large pig'? Feral domestic pigs in New Guinea rarely exceed 2.5ft at the shoulder.

Meyer's report recalls a comparable one from Papua pioneer Charles A.W. Monckton's *Last Days in New Guinea* (1922), repeated in Edmond Demaitre's *L'Enfer du Pacifique* (1935). During an expedition led by Monckton in 1906 through the jungle near New Guinea's Mount Albert Edward, two of the team's native members, Private Ogi and Village Constable Oina, were sent on ahead to find out whether a newly discovered trail was negotiable. When they did not come back, the team became anxious and fired a number of shots to signal them to return to camp immediately, but no-one appeared.

Eventually, however, sounds of gunfire reverberated from the jungle depths, so a party set off in their direction and brought the two men back, with Ogi in a very agitated state. Apparently, Ogi and Oina had become separated from one another while investigating the trail, and during his subsequent wanderings Ogi had come face to face with a pair of very large and extremely unusual animals - animals that he referred to as 'devil-pigs'!

They were allegedly 5 ft long and 3.5 ft high, with cloven feet but a horse-like tail, a black or very dark-coloured hide, and, strangest of all, a very long nose. Ogi tried to shoot at one, but was so cold and afraid that his hands shook, causing him to misfire. What happened after that is not clear - whether Ogi chased the beasts or whether they chased him is not known - but he was finally located in an exhausted state by Oina.

Dubbed 'Monckton's gazeka' by some writers, the devil-pig was also alluded to briefly in Sir William MacGregor's Mount Scratchley Expedition report. It does not seem to be a rhino; its cloven feet, tail, and long nose recall the large, distinctly odd wild pig of Sulawesi (Celebes), the babirusa *Babyrousa babyrussa* - famed for its extraordinary tusks.

Except for its feet, the devil-pig also has similarities to the Malayan tapir *Tapirus indicus,* one of those strange relatives of horses with slender trunks and usually very dark, virtually black hides. True, this particular tapir species has a 'saddle' of white, but some all-black Malayan specimens have also been recorded (and even kept in zoos), as documented in my book *Mysteries of Planet Earth* (2001). No tapirs, how-

The bizarre babirusa of Sulawesi

ever, have ever been discovered in New Guinea.

Demaitre succinctly differentiated the devil-pig from any putative New Guinea rhino by noting that although zoologist Luigi d'Albertis and former Papua governor Sir William MacGregor were willing to acknowledge the existence in New Guinea of *some* form of unidentified herbivorous creature, they were *not* willing to believe that it was a rhino. Similarly, when Dr H.J.V. Sody mentioned Lieut. Smith's observations, and requested news of any further data alluding to the possible existence of such a beast (*Zeitschrift für Säugetierkunde,* 1959), Moscow zoologist Prof. W.G. Heptner responded in 1960 by stating that not a single mention of rhinoceroses was contained within the authoritative six-volume work on New Guinea compiled by eminent researcher Dr M.N. Miklukho-Maklai, who had spent an appreciable amount of time in several different areas of New Guinea at much the same time as Smith was there. Surely, Heptner argued, if such a beast did exist, Miklukho-Maklai would have learned of it from the Papuans. Heptner also noted that the latter's magnum opus did not contain any mention of Meyer's 'very large pig' either.

Overall, there seems to be little support for the occurrence of a rhino species in New Guinea but, Heptner's comments notwithstanding, rather more in favour of a sizeable pig-like or tapir-like beast. Unfortunately, there is one major problem even with these identities. New Guinea's known mammalian fauna is of a predominantly Australian nature, i.e. it is dominated by marsupials. Hence if a large herbivorous mammal does exist in New Guinea, it is most likely to be a marsupial (which pigs and tapirs are not).

This is assuredly why Dr Bernard Heuvelmans suggested that the *gazeka* may actually be a surviving species of diprotodont - a family of huge marsupial herbivores that 'officially' died out at least 6000 years ago (though there are rumours of similar beasts still existing in Central Australia's inhospitable deserts). Some did have elongate noses. Moreover, certain early stone carvings, discovered in New Guinea's Ambun Valley and traditionally believed to portray this island's long-nosed spiny anteater *Zaglossus,* have subsequently been likened by renowned palaeontologist Dr James I. Menzies to a long-nosed diprotodont called *Palorchestes (Science in New Guinea,* 1987).

Diprotodonts are generally believed to have been contemporary with early humans in Australia - there is even a putative painting of one in a remote northern Queensland cave (*New Scientist,* 2 October 1986). If Menzies's tentative identification of the Ambun stones' creature is correct, then this was also true in New Guinea, adding weight to the possibility that some diprotodonts here have even persisted into historic times, as further discussed within my book *In Search of Prehistoric Survivors* (1995).

Also of note is that one type of diprotodont, called *Nototherium,* even bore a nasal horn and is actually referred to as a marsupial rhinoceros. Given the persistence of rhino reports from New Guinea, it is odd that references to the possession of *horns* by such beasts are conspicuous by their absence. In view of *Nototherium,* however, even if horns *are* present a diprotodont identity may still apply.

Lastly, the finding of a Pleistocene-dated rhinoceros-like tooth in New Caledonia's Diahot Valley by some gold miners during the 1800s has also inspired longstanding scientific debate. If it really is a rhino's tooth (and not that of a diprotodont, as some researchers suggested in 1981, naming its species *Zygomaturus diahotensis),* it must surely have been brought here from elsewhere by a human agency, because there is no other evidence (so far) to imply the former existence of a rhinoceros species on this island.

Undiscovered Rhinos in the Dark Continent?

There is anecdotal evidence for the presence of several mystery rhinos in Africa. Even before their modern-day persecution, neither of the two accepted species of African rhinoceros was known to occur further to the west than Cameroon. Yet, as noted in Knight's *Pictorial Museum of Animated Nature* (1856-8), clubs made from rhinoceros horns and measuring about 3ft in length have been obtained by travellers in Dahomey (since renamed Benin). Had the horns been imported from elsewhere? Or were they from some type of rhino native to Dahomey, whose existence has never been formally recorded?

Equally enigmatic is the pygmy rhinoceros allegedly inhabiting the forests of Liberia, a creature which the locals readily differentiated from the giant forest hog and the pygmy hippopotamus according to Hans Schomburgk (rediscoverer of the latter species in 1912). Furthermore, chief game inspector Lucien Blancou collected several reports (*Mammalia,* 1954) of an even more mysterious, much larger form reputedly dwelling in the dense forests of Cameroon and around the Middle Congo River. Rather surprisingly, it appears to be somewhat amphibious.

Similarly, in the Likouala region of the People's Republic of the Congo (formerly the French Congo), an unidentified semi-aquatic one-horned beast of elephantine proportions known as the *emela-ntouka* is accredited with a heavy tail (very unlike that of any known rhino), and an unexpected propensity for disembowelling elephants entering its swampy domain. Moreover, whereas the horns of all known species of modern-day rhino are composed of matted hair, the *emela-ntouka*'s horn is said to resemble the ivory tusks of elephants.

Alleged appearance of the emela-ntouka

All of this suggests something very different from the rhinos currently recognized by science - so much so, in fact, that, albeit with notable reservations, cryptozoologist Dr Roy P. Mackal suggested in his book *A Living Dinosaur? In Search of Mokele-Mbembe* (1987) that the *emela-ntouka* might not be a rhino at all, but instead a surviving ceratopsian dinosaur! As discussed in my own book, *In Search of Prehistoric Survivors* (1995), similar cryptids have been reported elsewhere in tropical Africa too, under a variety of different local names - including the *chipekwe*, reported from Zambia's Lake Bangweulu, and the *irizima*, reported from the Democratic Congo (formerly Zaire).

Elasmotherium and the Black Unicorn of Russia

Once native to the steppes of southern Russia and Siberia, one of the most extraordinary fossil rhinos on record is *Elasmotherium sibiricum* – a monstrous creature roughly 20ft long, standing over 6 ft high, and weighing up to 5 tons, i.e. almost as big as a modern-day elephant. However, its most striking feature was its horn, a colossal structure up to 7ft long, and whose extremely broad base was not borne upon the creature's nose as with the sole or principal horn in all living rhino species, but arose instead from the centre of its brow. Little wonder, therefore, that *Elasmotherium* is sometimes known as the giant unicorn – but this may not be its only link to the unicorn of fable.

The traditional legends of the Evenk or Tungus people, inhabiting the vast taiga forest of Siberia, tell of the erstwhile existence there of a gigantic black bull, distinguished from all normal cattle not merely by its size but also by possessing just a single, median horn, of mighty form, arising from the centre of its brow. According to a detailed account by the 10th-Century Muslim writer-traveller Ahmad ibn Fadlan, a comparable single-horned beast also roamed the southern Russian steppes.

Claimed to be smaller than a camel but taller than a bull, with a mule-like body, ram-like head, and cow-like hooves and tail, this daunting creature sported a huge pointed brow-horn, round in cross-section, that it employed in deadly fashion if it encountered any local rider - for it would pursue him, hook him from his steed's saddle with its horn, and then toss the hapless rider repeatedly into the air until he was dead. In revenge, other riders would seek to kill their lethal foe by concealing themselves in trees and shooting poisoned arrows at it when it passed by underneath. Three large bowls shaped like seashells that Ibn Fadlan saw while staying in Russia were claimed by his hosts to be made from the horn of one such beast – but what could it and its Siberian taiga counterpart have been?

Recalled by veteran cryptozoological writer Willy Ley in his books *The Lungfish and the Unicorn* (1941) and *Exotic Zoology* (1959), as far back as 1895 the famous Viennese geologist Melchior Neumayr had been struck by the outward similarity in description between the Russian black unicorn and *Elasmotherium* – so much so that in Volume II of his great work *Erdgeschichte* ('*History of the Earth*') he suggested that perhaps this mighty rhinoceros did not die out, as officially believed, during the Pleistocene epoch (2 million to 10 thousand years ago). Instead, Neumayr speculated that it may have lingered into historical times within Siberia's more remote, inhospitable regions, where its awe-inspiring, brow-horned form would doubtlessly have made a great impact upon any humans encountering it, ultimately giving rise to the still-recalled legends of a great black unicorn.

Katch Me a *Kilopilopitsofy*!

For me, possibly the most fascinating section in Dr Bernard Heuvelmans's classic cryptozoological tome, *On the Track of Unknown Animals* (1958), was the final one - 'The Lesson of the Malagasy Ghosts'. It dealt with early reports of bizarre mystery beasts in Madagascar that may have alluded to this vast island's extraordinary megafauna, including giant lemurs, elephant birds, and dwarf hippopotamuses.

However, as Heuvelmans concluded, by the time that European naturalists finally decided to take notice of such reports, these extraordinary beasts had become extinct, some just a few hundred years before the 20th Century: "In Madagascar fortunate circumstances have almost enabled us to watch the extinction of the giant fauna of the past, but we have missed our opportunity". Nevertheless, judging at least from the findings of a quite recent and thoroughly remarkable scientific paper, all may not be lost after all.

Authored by Fordham University biologist Dr David A. Burney and Madagascan archaeologist Ramilisonina, this research report was published in December 1998, by the journal *American Anthropologist* Documenting ethnographic data collected by the authors during late July-early August 1995 at Belo-sur-Mer, a remote coastal fishing village in southwestern Madagascar, it contained a number of local eyewitnesses reports describing what they claimed were fairly recent sightings of two scientifically unrecognised creatures. These are known respectively as the *kidoky* (possibly a late-surviving giant lemur, which I have discussed elsewhere – see my book *The Beasts That Hide From Man*, 2003), and the *kilopilopitsofy* ('floppy ears' - also termed the *tsomgomby* in Heuvelmans's book). (Their paper also documents a third mysterious creature, the *bokyboky*, but this merely seems to be an exaggerated version of one of Madagascar's modern-day viverrids.)

In the past, the tortuously-named *kilopilopitsofy* or *tsomgomby* had been variously compared to a giant lemur, a wild ass, a wild sheep, and even a rhinoceros – the last-mentioned identity having been suggested because some reports claimed that it bore a horn, either on its snout or in the middle of its brow. Evidently, a great deal of confusion had infiltrated this cryptid's file over the years, with characteristics of other, totally separate mystery beasts having been wrongly attributed to it (as also seems to have occurred with certain other cryptids elsewhere, such as the Congo's horned *emela-ntouka* and hornless sauropod-resembling *mokele-mbembe*, for instance). Now, however, thanks to the careful study by Burney and Ramilisonina, a clearer picture of what the *kilopilopitsofy* looked like – and what it may actually be - would finally be revealed.

Each eyewitness was questioned independently of the others, and prompting for specific answers was avoided wherever possible. In order to ascertain how zoologically accurate and trustworthy were the knowledge and testimony of each eyewitness, the two authors asked each one to identify local faunal species from unlabelled colour plates. The results obtained generally satisfied them that the eyewitnesses were indeed knowledgeable and trustworthy regarding their region's fauna.

In their paper, the authors recorded details from seven major interviewees, the most informative and authoritative of which was Jean Noelson Pascou, an elderly villager who was literate and had very good eyesight. He claimed to have seen a *kilopilopitsofy* several times, most recently in 1976. According to his description, this creature is nocturnal and cow-sized but hornless (as noted above, some early reports had claimed that it bore a rhino-like horn, but these seem to have been confusing it with a very different Madagascan mystery beast), with very dark skin, pink colouration around its eyes and mouth, and fairly large, floppy ears.

When shown pictures of elephants (in case reports of the *kilopilopitsofy* were merely derived from stories of African elephants narrated by sailors visiting Madagascar from the mainland), Pascou readily identified them as elephants. He also claimed that the *kilopilopitsofy* was smaller, with no trunk, but a larger mouth and big teeth, produced a loud grunting sound, and escaped pursuit by fleeing into water (swamps). He selected a hippopotamus picture as closest to the *kilopilopitsofy*. Corresponding descriptions were given by all of the other *kilopilopitsofy* eyewitnesses too.

As Burney and Ramilisonina noted, the *kilopilopitsofy* does recall the officially extinct Madagascan dwarf hippo *Hippopotamus lemerlei* (or possibly the even smaller but equally demised Madagascan pygmy hippo *Hexaprotodon madagascariensis*). Moreover, as Pascou was skilled at imitating local animal noises, the authors asked him if he could give a rendition of the *kilopilopitsofy*'s vocalisation. In reply, he uttered "a series of deep, drawn-out grunts, very similar to *H. amphibius* [the common mainland African hippo] (and quite different from the bush pig) [a species of wild pig native to Madagascar]". As there seems not to have ever been a captive mainland hippo exhibited on Madagascar, and as Pascou denied ever visiting the mainland, the authors freely admitted that they could "offer no explanation as to how his imitation of the call of the *kilopilopitsofy* happened to match so well the sound of *H. amphibius*".

Yet even if this mystery beast really is a surviving representative of the Madagascan dwarf hippo, how can its decidedly unhippo-like ears be explained? The authors suggest that these may in reality be loose cheeks and jowls, misidentified as ears when seen fleetingly at night. Alternatively, if, as some researchers believe, Madagascar's dwarf hippo already possessed certain terrestrial modifications, large ears may simply be another example, assisting it in dispelling excess heat.

At present, therefore, the riddles posed by the *kilopilopitsofy* (and the *kidoky*) remain unanswered. As concluded by Burney and Ramilisonina: "For the time being, at least, neither paleontology nor oral tradition can fully resolve the mystery, but both are clearly relevant to the discussion". Too often in the past - and still today, regrettably - some cryptozoological sceptics have loftily discounted the worth of oral traditions in helping to elucidate the identities of mystery beasts. Happily, however, this myopic attitude has been discredited on many notable occasions, and in many localities - perhaps the next one will be Madagascar?

Rhino Rediscoveries

Judging from some of this chapter's cryptids, it seems possible that even after beasts such as the blue rhino, Holmwood's rhino, and Oswell's rhino have been denied the rank of valid species, several other mysterious forms still await recognition. Naturally, opponents of such a prospect will reply that it is inconceivable that creatures as large and conspicuous as rhinoceroses could still exist unknown, anywhere in this, the 21st Century. Perhaps they should be reminded that as recently as 1983, an entire herd of Sumatran rhinos was discovered in Sarawak (*Oryx,* April 1987); until that remarkable find, this species was believed to have died out here almost 40 years earlier. Even more astounding was the rediscovery in 1988 on the Asian mainland, in Vietnam, of the Javan rhino - reputedly extinct there since the early 1940s (*Oryx,* April 1990).

From events such as these, it is evident that the existence of rhinos and rhino-like beasts still to be recorded by modern science is by no means impossible - especially when, in terms of exploration potential, their habitats include some of the world's most impenetrable, inhospitable, and inaccessible areas.

Chapter Eighteen
A Little Local Cryptozoology

And above all, watch with glittering eyes the world around you, because the greatest secrets are always hidden in the most unlikely places. Those who don't believe in magic will never find it.

Roald Dahl – *The Minpins*

The West Midlands is my home county, but traditionally it is one of England's industrial heartlands, and is therefore not the most likely location for creatures of cryptozoology. Nevertheless, it has revealed some unexpected mystery beasts over the years, including the trio of cases documented here.

It's the Sandwell Valleygator!

It may be my home town, but West Bromwich in the West Midlands is more readily associated with football, courtesy of West Bromwich Albion FC, than cryptozoology - until the Sandwell Valleygator came on the scene, that is. Also nicknamed the Sandwell Snapper in early media accounts, it first reared its snouted head on 30 March 1999, when fisherman Mike Sinnatt saw what he initially thought to be "a marvellously shaped piece of wood", measuring over 2 ft long, suddenly come alive and attempt to seize an unsuspecting Canada goose on Swan Pool.

Situated in an RSPB reserve within the Sandwell Valley Country Park - a verdant oasis for nature right in the heart of urbanised West Brom - Swan Pool measures more than a mile in circumference, and is not only inhabited by a rich variety of waterbirds but is also popular for angling, yachting, and wind-surfing. Or at least it was until, within a short time of Sinnatt's sighting, a dozen other similar reports had surfaced, all describing a fairly sizeable four-legged aquatic beast with a notable snout, long tail, and a penchant for snapping at anything avian or piscean that came too near. Eyewitnesses included local angler Tony Price and pool lifeguard Ricky Downes, who spied its two "very chunky" hind legs and tail.

Occurring so close to 1 April, the Sandwell Valleygator was originally dismissed by sceptics as an April Fool's hoax, but this was strenuously denied by Sandwell Council, who were so concerned about the potential danger posed to the general public by the creature that they closed the pool to all watersports throughout the Easter Bank Holiday (3-6 April). Needless to say, however, the considerable media publicity generated not only locally but also nationally and even internationally by Swan Pool's stealthy snapper resulted in a massive influx of visitors here (estimated at more than 9000) during the Bank Holiday, all eagerly scanning the reed beds and shallows in search of its cryptic interloper.

As I deemed it highly unlikely that the creature would appear when confronted by such a barrage of human activity, however, I waited until the holiday period was over before visiting Swan Pool myself. Walking around this sizeable lake, peering at the large island at its centre, at the smaller pools and marshes fringing its border, and down into its murky depths, it swiftly became evident that an aquatic creature of the proportions described by the Valleygator's eyewitnesses could live out a secluded, rarely-spied existence here indefinitely.

Author Karl Shuker keeps a sharp lookout for the Sandwell Valleygator

Yet although neither the Valleygator itself nor any convincing reports of it surfaced during the Bank Holiday or my own subsequent visit, official opinion as to its identity had by now veered away from the scenario of a vicious snap-happy crocodile, caiman, or suchlike to the rather more placid scenario of a giant salamander. Specifically, the North American hellbender *Cryptobranchus alleganiensis*, which measures up to 30in long, subsists upon small animal life such as frogs, fishes, snails, crustaceans, and insect larvae, and is native to the eastern United States.

Such a beast could certainly survive, therefore, in the prey-filled, temperate waters of Swan Pool. However, the fatal flaw in this otherwise promising proposal is that the hellbender is hardly ever maintained in captivity by private individuals. So the chance of one having escaped and taken up residence in Swan Pool is extremely remote.

On 7 April, Swan Pool was formally re-opened, with the Sandwellmander, as it had by now been redubbed in media accounts, no longer deemed to pose a risk to watersport enthusiasts. Or, to quote the optimistic words of Sandwell's senior countryside ranger Roy Croucher: "We have decided to re-open the pool on the basis that this thing is not going to leap out of the water and grab someone around the throat".

North American snapping turtle

Less than a week later, however, an unexpected water beast did make an appearance - a North American snapping turtle *Chelydra serpentina*, discovered sunbathing on a marsh close to Swan Pool. As its name suggests, this belligerent, sturdy species of freshwater tortoise is famous for snapping viciously, possesses a prominent snout, a long tail, and can grow up to 2 ft long (its close relative the alligator turtle can reach lengths of almost 3 ft). Hence it exhibits the very same features consistently described by eyewitnesses of the Swan Pool mystery beast. Moreover, in sharp contrast to the hellbender, the snapping turtle is commonly kept by amateur herpetologists, so an escapee (or even a deliberately released) specimen of this species turning up here is by no means implausible.

All of which only adds, therefore, to the mystery of why, or how, an unnamed Sandwell Council spokesman could confidently state in subsequent media accounts that this captured snapping turtle was not the elusive Swan Pool cryptid. How did he, or anyone else, know? Snapping turtles are readily able to walk on land, so one could easily have made its way back and forth between Swan Pool and any of the neighbouring marshes.

In late July 2001, moreover, a notable sequel occurred - the netting in Swan Pool of an 18-in-long American snapping turtle, weighing in at a hefty 4 lb. Captured alive but in a distinctly irate state by teenager Harry Billingham, assisted by his stepdad Mark, Harry's brother Jack, and friend Dean Cooke, the aggressive reptile was swiftly brought to the attention of the local RSPCA office by its astonished captors.

As this species is not native to Britain or anywhere else in Europe, the Swan Pool specimen must have been abandoned there by someone, no doubt when it was much smaller - hence quite some time ago, and possibly far back enough for it to have been responsible for the 1999 Sandwell Valleygator flap? Perhaps, when some initial media accounts nicknamed it the Sandwell Snapper, they were closer to the truth than anyone realised. And as further support for this identity as a plausible solution to the Valleygator mystery, on 18 July 2003 a second sizeable adult American snapping turtle, sporting a shell diameter of 14 inches and believed to be up to

20 years old, was snared in another West Midlands pool, this time one just north of Slacky Lane in Walsall.

Is the Brum Beast Just a Gas?

In August 1997, the Gas Street canal basin of Birmingham in the West Midlands briefly acquired a degree of cryptozoological fame, courtesy of the mysterious Gas Street monster. On August 5 and 6, Wolverhampton's *Express and Star* carried claims that this stretch of waterway harbours a spectacular if secretive 20ft eel, "black, with little beady eyes" according to one angler eyewitness, but nothing measuring up this description materialised on the end of any of the local fishermen's lines. Eels of a more traditional, modest size, conversely, measuring up to 3ft or so in length, are often seen in Birmingham and Black Country canals.

Making Monsters Out Of Mole-Hills

It's always good to stumble upon the history of a mystery beast not previously documented in the cryptozoological literature, especially when it happens to be a local one. Yet although the case of the Peel Street Monster began in high drama, the outcome was distinctly underwhelming.

During winter 1933-34, rumours began circulating in the area of Brickkiln Street and Peel Street in Wolverhampton, West Midlands, of a bizarre creature that was attacking children. One bold lad who tried to pursue this beast, which became known as the Peel Street Monster, presumably angered it, because it allegedly leapt at his throat, attempting to bite him.

One day in January 1934, however, this vicious creature made one onslaught too many. A crowd of boys and youths, who included among their number a 17-year-old called Georgie Goodhead, were playing on the corner of St Mark's Street and Raglan Street, when another boy, Jackie Franklin, raced out of Peel Street and up towards them in a state of great alarm. Shouting for help, he told them that a youngster called Billy Wright was being attacked by the monster on some waste ground. Georgie and his mates raced back to Peel Street at once with Jackie, where they observed a peculiar-looking animal threatening a small boy. In a later *Wolverhampton Express and Star* report, Georgie recalled:

> I went and saw a queer animal, far too big for a rat, leaping towards a child about five-year[s]-old. I shouted and the thing turned on me. It crouched, its eyes bulging, then it leaped like lightning.

According to the newspaper report, as the creature neared his throat Georgie picked up a brick and hit it with this as hard as he could. The animal collapsed, falling into a pool of water, but was swiftly kicked to death by the crowd that had gathered to watch the boys confronting it. Happily, little Billy was unhurt, and was taken by some of the boys to his parent's sweetshop in Peel Street, while Georgie and Jackie gave a statement at the Red Lion police station and received half a crown each for their bravery.

As for the Peel Street Monster: apart from noting that it was a male, no-one had any idea what this mystifying beast was. According to media reports, naturalists, taxidermists, and vets were all called in to identify it, but to no avail. One unnamed 'expert' did suggest that it may be an anteater - in Wolverhampton? Another one considered it possible that the creature (despite being dead!) might become a serious rival to the Loch Ness monster.

Events took an even more surprising turn the following day, when a second mystery beast was found in the Brickkiln region. This one, a female, was already dead, but it closely resembled the Peel Street Monster. Moreover, a photo of it published in the *Express and Star* helped to identify its species. It was a South American coati (coatimundi) - a long-tailed relative of the raccoon, with a head-and-body length of up to 2ft, a thin tail of much the same length, and distinguished by its very elongate snout (responsible for the 'anteater' identity proffered for the Peel Street Monster?). But where had it, and the Peel Street specimen, come from? And if there had been a pair on the loose, could there be more?

South American coati

The prospect of a plague of coatis terrorising the good residents of Wolverhampton may seem decidedly slim (not least because the favoured diet of coatis consists of invertebrates and small lizards - as opposed to small children!). Nevertheless, the council was clearly taking no chances, for as the *Express and Star* duly reported:

> And fresh fears arose in Wolverhampton as rumours spread that there may be a colony of the creatures hiding in partly closed cellars. Hundreds of people gathered in Salop Street to watch council workers trying to ascertain if a colony of the creatures were hiding there. The crowds were so great they hampered the efforts of the official rat-catcher. In the search, weapons brought in to confront any coatimundis found included poison gas, traps, sulphur, terriers and ferrets. It was uncertain whether the ferrets were to be used following a suggestion that they might form part of the coatimundi diet [I don't think so!].

Ferrets or no ferrets, the search did not find any other errant coatis. Police investigations did reputedly reveal that the female coati had been in a travelling menagerie that had parked here earlier (circuses and fairs would sometimes set up on this waste ground at that time), and had discarded the creature's body after it had died. However, the Peel Street Monster's origin remains a mystery to this day - as do various other aspects of this curious case.

Can we even be sure that the Peel Street Monster was a coati? For if the accounts of it are true, it must have been an exceptionally belligerent specimen. The *Express and Star* published a photo of this creature lying dead with a crowd of onlookers surrounding it, but its form cannot be discerned. And what happened to the two carcases? Some correspondences reminiscing about this incident appeared 50 years later in the *Express and Star* during March 1994, but conflicting recollections only served to muddy these already murky waters even further. All in all, after also allowing for the likelihood of embellished descriptions with such an odd episode, the only thing that can be said with certainty regarding the Peel Street Monster is that something unexpected was seen and killed in Wolverhampton - a most unsatisfactory end to one of the most intriguing OOP animal cases on file from the West Midlands.

Chapter Nineteen
Megapode Mysteries

[In Australia] great numbers of high and large mounds of earth exist, which were formerly thought to be the tombs of departed natives, and indeed, have been more than once figured as such. The natives, however, disclaimed the sepulchral character, saying that they were origins of life rather than emblems of death; for that they were the artificial ovens in which the eggs of the Jungle Fowl were laid, and which, by the heat that is always disengaged from decaying vegetable substances, preserved sufficient warmth to hatch the eggs.

Rev. J.G. Wood – *Illustrated Natural History, Vol. 2*

Whereas most birds incubate their eggs simply by sitting on them, thereby directly harnessing their own body heat, those fowl-like species known as the megapodes are renowned for eschewing this tried and trusted method in favour of much more remarkable and ingenious versions. Some megapodes, for example, erect huge mounds composed of dead plant material, inside which they deposit their eggs and allow the heat generated internally by the rotting vegetation to incubate them. Others excavate pits in the ground, within which they then bury their eggs in order for them to be hatched by whatever external sources of heat are present - including the sun's rays, subterranean steam, and even volcanic activity!

Today, therefore, the megapodes are notable avian celebrities, with their extraordinary modes of incubation faithfully documented in ornithological publications worldwide. Yet these same publications invariably neglect to mention that for over three centuries, all reports of this most famous facet of megapode lifestyle were vigorously discounted by scientists as fanciful travellers' tales with no basis in reality. Accordingly, the history behind the formal scientific verification of these birds' idiosyncratic incubation is a classic, compelling, yet nowadays all-but-forgotten example of a long-running zoological controversy.

Hatching Up a Mound of Controversy

Of the 21 recognised species, whose collective distribution includes southeast Asia, Australia, New Guinea, Vanuatu, Tonga, and Samoa, the megapode responsible for unveiling their egg-rearing secrets was *Megapodius freycinet* - a crested, hen-like species commonly called the dusky scrubfowl or jungle fowl (but not to be confused with the true, *Gallus* jungle fowl - the domestic chicken's wild ancestor). In April 1521, following Magellan's famous but ill-fated global circumnavigation, survivor Antonio Pigafetta recorded in his journal that the Philippines housed a chicken-sized bird that laid eggs as large as a duck's, but instead of hatching them itself it chose to bury them in the sand, leaving them to be hatched by the sun's heat.

It is nothing if not ironic that in an age when mermaids, unicorns, and other wholly imaginary creatures were still widely accepted by naturalists as factual fauna, Pigatetta's egg-burying bird was dismissed in no uncertain terms by those selfsame authorities as arrant poppycock. Conversely, on p. 207 of his *Historia Naturae Maxime Peregrinae* (1635), Juan Eusebio Nieremberg, a Jesuit, alluded to a dove-sized bird variously referred to as the *daie* and the *tapun*, which made good use of its feet to gouge a hollow in the sand, into which it would then lay a clutch of large eggs. Unfortunately, Nieremberg did not record this curious creature's provenance, but that omission was remedied in 1651 via the publication of Francisco Hernandez's *Historia Avium Novae Hispaniae*. Offering a more detailed, accurate account, Hernandez corrected Nieremberg's 'daie' to *daic*, and his 'tapun' to *tapum*, as well as revealing that this bird inhabited the Philippines.

During 1673, the Dominican missionary Navarrete returned to Europe after spending a considerable time in the Philippines. In a lengthy account entitled *A Collection of Voyages and Travels*, he recorded that many of the Malay Archipelago islands boasted a very unusual bird known locally as the *tabon*. After excavating great holes in the sand into which it deposited its eggs, it filled the holes up again, in order for the hot sand and sun to hatch the buried eggs. In 1699, veteran globe-trotter Gemelli Careri provided comparable details regarding the Philippine jungle fowl, which he termed the *tavon*; and additional data, drawn from his avifaunal observations on Luzon, was presented in 1703 by Camelli within the *Philosophical Transactions of the Royal Society of London*.

In view of such close correspondence between reports originating for the most part from wholly independent eyewitnesses and spanning two centuries, one might have expected that the jungle fowl's internment of its eggs for hatching purposes would thereafter have been accepted as a fully verified ornithological fact. Instead, Buffon and many other leading naturalists continued to disparage and reject totally all claims that birds could behave in such an overtly reptilian manner. After all, the burial of eggs in warm sand for incubation was a trait of turtles and various oviparous lizards - but surely not of birds? And so the matter remained unresolved for another century, until attention switched from the jungle fowl's Philippine representatives to those inhabiting Australia (nowadays separated as *M. reinwardt*, the orange-footed scrubfowl or jungle fowl).

Here, however, the subject was even more controversial. Whereas the Philippine jungle fowl stood accused merely of interring its eggs beneath the sand, in Australia the aboriginals insisted that this diminutive form was actually the architect responsible for all manner of immense mound-like structures widely distributed across much of northern Queensland and the Northern Territory - and that deep, concealed holes hewn into the mounds' sides by the bird contained its eggs, with the mounds serving as giant incubators.

In contrast, when the first Western settlers in Australia had encountered these incongruous edifices, some measuring up to 30ft long and 5ft high, they had taken them to be ancient burial mounds (tumuli), erected long ago by the aboriginals' ancestors. Other, smaller mounds were deemed by them to be mud-castles built by

The Australian jungle fowl and its incubation mounds

native mothers to amuse their children. The fact that the aboriginals themselves vehemently denied all of this was ignored not only by the settlers but by Western scientists too - thereby rejecting the claims of a people whose knowledge of this island continent stretched back many millennia.

When English naturalist John Gilbert (assistant to famed ornithological painter John Gould) arrived in autumn 1839 at Port Essington, Northern Territory, however, he resolved to bring to an end this heated conflict once and for all - by accompanying a knowledgeable aboriginal to a little-known area of Port Essington called Knocker's Bay, undisturbed by Westerners and where the native people asserted that a number of jungle fowl could be found. Here, if anywhere, he might succeed in solving the mystery of the mounds.

Reaching the bay in November 1839, almost immediately they came upon a mound of sand and shells, incorporating a slight mixture of black soil too, and resting on a sandy beach just a few feet above the high-water mark. Standing roughly 5ft tall, with a circumference of 25ft, and conical in shape, the mound was profusely festooned with large yellow hibiscus blooms. Gilbert at once asked his native companion to identify this structure, to which the aboriginal replied "Oregoorga Rambal" - 'jungle fowl's nest'.

Encouraged by this, Gilbert duly scrambled up the mound's sides to seek its alleged hidden holes and any eggs that they may contain, but he failed to do so. However, his companion was unconcerned, pointing out that there were no signs to suggest that any adult birds had been there for quite some while. Nevertheless, Gilbert's searches were not entirely in vain - on one side of the mound he spotted a tunnel-like shaft about 2ft deep, which proved to contain a jungle fowl chick, lying on some dry, withered leaves. As it was only a few days old, presumably it had indeed hatched inside the tunnel, but Gilbert could not be absolutely sure of this. After all, it was possible that the chick had somehow made its way into the tunnel from outside the mound, especially as in comparison to similarly-aged domestic chickens it exhibited a remarkably advanced degree of development - with a well-formed, extensively-feathered body, plus the ability to run and even fly.

Due to other commitments, Gilbert was unable to stay any longer at Knocker's Bay, but by February 1840 he had returned - and this time his quest met with success. After selecting a likely-looking mound inside which to find eggs, his native companion dug down six times in succession to a depth of at least 6-7ft without finding any eggs, but on the seventh attempt he successfully retrieved one egg, followed after two or three more attempts by a second egg. We now know that an average clutch contains about 15 eggs, and one egg is laid and buried each day, within its own separate hole, until the entire clutch has been deposited.

Gilbert also discovered that whereas mounds primarily created from sand and shells are usually erected in the most exposed localities available, presumably to ensure that the necessary heat required for egg-incubation will be met by the sun, mounds constructed in darker, cooler localities, protected from the sun's rays, are largely composed of plant material and hence rely principally upon the heat released by its decomposition for egg incubation. Yet even today, mystery still surrounds the mound-building megapodes, as some scientists, such as Cambridge University's Dr Geoff Bailey, have opined that certain of the sand-and-shell mounds existing at Weipa, on Queensland's Cape York Peninsula, are not bird-built (as deemed by Australian researcher Dr Tim Stone among others) but rather are of aboriginal origin.

It is said that history never repeats itself, but in the case of the Australian jungle fowl it currently seems to be running backwards - from tumulus to incubator to tumulus again. Yet perhaps we should not be too surprised. After all, what else but mystery and controversy can we expect from birds whose name, megapode, is Greek for...bigfoot!

Nor is that the only controversy surrounding these intriguing birds. As already noted, 21 different species of megapode are currently recognised by science, of which 13 (including the previously-discussed mound-building jungle fowl of Australia) belong to the genus *Megapodius*. However, there are some tantalising clues suggesting that until very recently there may well have been several additional *Megapodius* species, now lost forever.

Enigmatic Eggs of Lost Megapodes?

The case for the erstwhile existence of certain examples of missing megapodes appears to rest upon the fact that *Megapodius*-like eggs have been collected in earlier ages from localities that do not contain any such birds today. During the 19th Century, supposed *Megapodius* eggs were brought back from one of the minuscule islets comprising the Ha'apai group of Tongan Islands. Similar eggs were also obtained from Tikopia.

A few of the supposedly distinct if uncaptured species represented by such specimens as these have even been assigned official scientific names. One is the alleged species based upon eggs from India's Andaman Islands, just north of the Nicobars; this example was accordingly dubbed *Megapodius andamanensis*. Others include *M. burnabyi* and *M. stairi*.

Killed Off in the Kermadecs - By a Volcano

There is somewhat better evidence for the onetime existence of a megapode native to the Kermadecs. This is because a number of different travellers claimed to have seen the birds themselves, rather than merely their eggs, while visiting this very isolated trio of islands (situated about 550 miles northeast of New Zealand, their nearest neighbour).

Even so, the species no longer exists, on account of an unavoidable natural catastrophe. It was apparently confined to Sunday Island (also known as Raoul), an island volcano with a forest-covered peak and a total surface area of just over 11 square miles. The megapodes lived on the floor of the volcano's crater, until 1876 - when, even before their species had been formally named, let alone described and documented, the volcano erupted. No megapodes have ever been reported from the Kermadecs since.

The *Sasa* of Fiji

Perhaps the best documented case of a missing megapode is that of the Fijian *sasa*. The most detailed coverage of this ornithological enigma is that of Dr Casey A. Wood, contained within a comprehensive paper dealing with Fijian avifauna, jointly written with fellow ornithologist Dr Alexander Wetmore, and published by the journal *Ibis* in 1926.

According to the information that Wood had collected from several different sources and earlier investigators, the bird in question was referred to locally as the *sasa*. It incubated its eggs in specially-created mounds like a number of other megapodes elsewhere in the world, and was similar in general form to Pritchard's megapode *Megapodius pritchardii* of Niuafo'ou in the Tongan Islands. However, it seemed unable (or at least unwilling) to fly - preferring to evade any would-be predators by scurrying swiftly on its short legs through the reeds and undergrowth constituting its habitat on Viti Levu, one of the principal Fijian islands.

Tragically, although that seemed to be a successful enough ploy for avoiding this island's native aggressors, it apparently proved wholly ineffective against the much greater threat posed by the Indian mongoose - introduced by man onto Viti Levu during the late 1800s - because by the time that Wood had learnt about it, the *sasa* had already vanished. The native inhabitants of Viti Levu were convinced that the mongoose was to blame, for although they conceded that the *sasa* had never been common (even in the island's mountainous interior), they were adamant that it was still alive at the time of the mongoose's introduction here.

Only one slender hope remained for the *sasa*'s continuing survival. Some Fijians thought that a few may have lingered on the smaller island of Kandavu, just south of Viti Levu. Encouraged by this, one of the *sasa*'s seekers, an Englishman named W.A.W. Moggridge who resided on Kandavu, announced that he would give a size-able reward to anyone who succeeded in capturing a specimen. The reward was never claimed.

Intriguingly, what may have been a mystery megapode was briefly referred to by H. Wilfrid Walker in his book *Wanderings Among South Sea Savages* (1909). While visiting the Fijian island of Taviuna:

> *I also obtained some good duck shooting on a lake high up in the moun-*
> *tains, and Ratu Lala described to me what must be a species of apteryx, or*
> *wingless bird (like the Kiwi of New Zealand), which he said was found in*
> *the mountains and lived in holes in the ground, but I never came across it,*
> *though I had many a weary search.*

A flightless megapode might well be confused with a kiwi.

Still Living on Levuka?

Intriguingly, the native people inhabiting the small island of Levuka (Ovalau), just to the east of Viti Levu, also have a tradition regarding the former existence here of a megapode. So perhaps the *sasa*'s Fijian distribution was wider than Wood supposed. Moreover, in view of the megapodes' very appreciable known penetration of many of the South Pacific's major islands, it is not impossible that out of the myriad of minute islets in this region still to be explored scientifically, some may actually harbour types of megapode unknown to science. In short, the case of the missing megapodes may not be closed after all.

The Dynamic *Du*

No chapter on mystery megapodes could end without considering the most spec-tacular mound-builder ever known to have existed on our planet. The following ac-count is excerpted (and slightly expanded) from my book *In Search of Prehistoric Survivors* (1995), the most detailed cryptozoological coverage published on this fascinating species:

The modern-day megapodes are little more than dwarfs in comparison with certain fossil species. If, as currently believed, the ancestors of today's aboriginals reached Australia no later than 45,000-55,000 years ago, they would have been familiar with the Australian giant megapode *Progura gallinacea*. Although generally similar in overall shape, this very robust species was approximately half as large again as today's biggest megapodes. These are Australia's 2ft-long mallee fowl *Leipoa ocellata* and brush turkey *Alectura lathami* - this latter vulture-headed species creates mounds up to 9ft in height. Leg bones of an even larger, hitherto-unknown form of megapode have been discovered in a Polynesian midden on one of Fiji's tiniest islands, demonstrating that it too was clearly contemporary with early humans. Yet even these sizeable species pale into insignificance in comparison with a truly spectacular relative, recently exposed as a bona fide prehistoric survivor.

To the east of Australia is the island of New Caledonia, a former French territory whose southernmost tip looks out towards a very much smaller isle nearby, the Isle of Pines. In 1976, the *Bulletin de la Société d'Études Historiques de Nouvelle Calédonie* published an extremely interesting paper by historian Dr Paul Griscelli, who revealed that, according to oral traditions of the Houailou people (one of the isle's native Melanesian tribes), this minuscule speck of land once harboured an enormous and extraordinary bird.

Their ancestors called it the *du*, and described it as a huge, aggressive bird with red plumage and a star-shaped bony casque on its head. Although unable to fly, it could run very swiftly, usually with its wings outstretched. It laid a single egg, which took four months to hatch (from November's close to April's onset), but it did not incubate the egg itself.

As expected with any item of mythology, there were certain aspects that were unquestionably fictional. In particular, it was asserted that the *du* practised a most unlikely cuckoo-like deception to avoid brooding its egg - by laying it in a hollow banyan tree used as a lair by some form of giant lizard, in order for the lizard to incubate it instead!

In stark contrast to such tall tales as this, however, the fundamental, mainstream details regarding the *du* are precise and sober, indicating that these may have stemmed from sightings long ago of some real creature. Even so, bearing in mind that many fabulous birds of monstrous form with no claim whatsoever to a basis in truth do occur in numerous myths and folktales around the world, it is nonetheless very possible that the *du* would have been dismissed as nothing more than just another example of such a fantasy animal, especially as there appeared to be no way of pursuing the matter further. Fortunately, the *du*'s seemingly imminent descent into obscurity was not to be.

While preparing the final draft of his paper, Griscelli received some staggering news. Excavating fossils at Kanumera, on the Isle of Pines in 1974, Paris lecturer Dr J. Dubois had disinterred some bones that had since been identified by Professor François Poplin of Paris's Natural History Museum as limb portions from a gigantic bird! Relics of the *du*? In addition, when the bones were dated by radiocarbon techniques, they were found to be no older than 3,500 years, and as humans were known to have reached the Isle of Pines prior to this period they would have been well acquainted with the birds.

The dimensions of this vanished bird's remains have shown that it was as large as the modern-day emu (5-6ft tall), and flightless. Indeed, after studying the bones, in 1980 Poplin published a scientific description of this dramatic species (*Comptes Rendus*), named by him *Sylviornis neocaledoniae*, in which he announced that, like the emu, it too may have been a ratite – i.e. one of those widely-dispersed species of giant flightless bird that also include the ostrich, rheas, and cassowaries, as well as the extinct moas, and elephant birds.

New Caledonia postage stamp depicting Sylviornis neocaledoniae

Three years later, however, following further researches, Poplin changed his mind and announced that *Sylviornis* was actually an immense megapode (*Comptes Rendus*). Moreover, as he and co-worker Cécile Mourer-Chauviré discussed in another paper (*Geobios*, February 1985), there is an intriguing supplementary source of evidence favouring this identity, contained within the Houailou's mythology - for, according to their oral traditions, the *du* did not incubate its egg. Unfortunately, however, if we exclude from serious consideration their lizard-hatching legend, their folklore offers no clue as to the egg's resulting fate.

Nevertheless, as Mourer-Chauviré and Poplin pointed out just a few months later (*La Recherche*, September 1985), researchers seeking the answer to this riddle on the Isle of Pines might not have to look very far for it, because if Poplin's later hypothesis is correct, the riddle's answer is readily visible in many parts of the isle, and also on New Caledonia.

Both of these islands bear a great number of very large mound-like structures, measuring up to 150ft in diameter and as much as 15ft in height. Constructed from materials present in their immediate surroundings (soil, particles of iron oxide, coral debris, sometimes black silicon as well), their precise nature has never been conclusively ascertained - despite a century of archaeological investigations.

In the meantime, it has simply been assumed that they are ancient tumuli (burial mounds) erected by the islands' early human occupants. However, no human remains have been found within them. Hence Mourer-Chauviré and Poplin postulated that they may really be egg-incubator mounds of *Sylviornis*, the last visible evidence of this mighty species' former existence. If ultimately verified, this identification would not only solve a long-standing topographical mystery but also demonstrate that *Sylviornis* existed on New Caledonia itself, not just on the Isle of Pines.

Speaking of New Caledonia, it is possible that a much smaller megapode once hailed from this island too. When Captain James Cook's second voyage reached New Caledonia in 1774, one of its members recorded seeing a small, bare-legged form of gallinaceous bird that could well have been a megapode. Certainly, fossil bones of a comparably-sized megapode of relatively recent date (geologically speaking) have been unearthed here; their species has been named *Megapodius molestructor*.

Returning to the *du*/*Sylviornis* issue, there is no doubt that a mound-erecting megapode the size of an emu would have been a stunning sight, and it is one that may have persisted for much longer than originally believed. According to Dr Jean-Christophe Balouet in his *Extinct Species of the World* (1990), this species is now thought to have survived into early historical times - until at least the 3rd Century AD.

Even so, it had vanished long before its island domain was reached by Europeans - but why? After all, during his researches into Houailou mythology, Griscelli found that for at least a time the *du* had been deemed by their ancestors to be little less than an avian deity - a sacred creature of reverence. The punishment for killing a *du* was death, and an insignia in the shape of its stellate casque was a symbol of great esteem, worn only by the most powerful of tribal chiefs. But, like all things, customs change, especially when eroded by changing priorities.

On as tiny an island as the Isle of Pines, food was scarcely plentiful, particularly for entire human tribes, and, not surprisingly, cannibalism was prevalent in those early days of human occupation. It could only be a matter of time, therefore, before the awe-inspired taboos protecting the *du* would be weakened and violated by the more practical realisation that these enormous, robust birds were actually an abundant, readily accessible source of top-quality meat. And so it was that this colossal bird's once-exalted status plummeted precipitously, and prosaically - from the *du* as demigod, to the *du* as dinner!

There could only be one outcome. Long before Westerners could ever receive the opportunity of witnessing this magnificent bird, *Sylviornis* had been exterminated. For many centuries it would survive merely as a curious native legend, its morphology and lifestyle preserved only by verbal transmission through successive generations of its annihilators' descendants - until the day when its bones would finally be disinterred, and the reality of the Isle of Pines' bygone feathered deity at last be confirmed beyond any shadow of doubt.

From mythical *du* to extinct *Sylviornis* - clearly not a resurrection . . . or is it? Tantalisingly, while visiting New Caledonia in 1991, Danish zoologist Lars Thomas discovered that the native people speak of the *du* as if it were still alive today, and describe it accurately. Racial memories - or *Sylviornis* survival?

Update: In 2005, i.e. 10 years after the publication of my book *In Search of Prehis-*

toric Survivors (containing the above account), Mourer-Chauviré and Balouet published a detailed *Sylviornis neocaledoniae* paper in which they reclassified this enigmatic mound-building species, deciding that it was sufficiently distinct from all other megapodes to warrant the creation of an entirely new taxonomic family to accommodate it – Sylviornithidae.

Chapter Twenty
Solifugids – Fleet of Foot, Strong of Jaw

Though I have always viewed with horror the bird-eating tarantulas of South America, they shrank into insignificance when compared with the loathsome creature that faced us now across that lamplit room. It was bigger in its spread than a large dinner-plate, with a hard, smooth, yellow body surrounded by legs that, rising high above it, conveyed a fearful impression that the thing was crouching for its spring. It was absolutely hairless save for tufts of stiff bristles around the leg-joints, and above the glint of its great poison mandibles clusters of beady eyes shone in the light with a baleful red irridescence [sic]...

'They were nightmare creatures, Holmes,' I exclaimed, as we retraced our steps towards the house, 'and of some unknown species.'

'I think not, Watson,' said he. 'It was the Galeodes...'

Adrian Conan Doyle - 'The Adventure of the Deptford Horror', from *The Exploits of Sherlock Holmes*

Some of the most celebrated Sherlock Holmes novels and short stories written by his creator Sir Arthur Conan Doyle featured compulsively gruesome creatures - an Indian swamp adder in 'The Speckled Band', a huge jellyfish in 'The Adventure of the Lion's Mane', and a monstrous dog in *The Hound of the Baskervilles*. This tradition was continued by Sir Arthur's son, Adrian Conan Doyle, who wrote the Sherlock Holmes tale quoted from above, which occupies a unique position in English literature as the first (and only?) detective story to feature as its principal antagonists a pair of markedly macabre but *bona fide* beasts most commonly referred to as solifugids.

During the Victorian era in which the Sherlock Holmes stories were set, solifugids were sometimes classed with spiders, but they are nowadays separated into a taxonomic order of their own, of equal rank to that of the spiders, within the class Arachnida (also housing such creatures as scorpions, ticks and mites, harvestmen, and certain more obscure forms). On first sight, solifugids do look rather like large-bodied, long-legged spiders (they are sometimes called false, sun, or camel spiders) and are often confused with them. (Worth noting is that Sherlock Holmes's adversary actually exhibited certain unexpectedly spider-like characteristics, such as its clusters of eyes and almost hairless body; in contrast, genuine solifugids possess only a single pair of direct eyes, and are usually very hairy.)

Closer observation, however, exposes several basic differences between them.

Whereas the head and thorax of spiders comprise a single, undivided unit, they are well-delineated in solifugids, yielding a large head region and a short thorax. Also, the abdomen of solifugids is visibly divided into segments, whereas such segmentation in spiders is much rarer. Probably the most striking feature of any solifugid is its head, not only because of its notable bulk but also because of the exceptional size of its poison fangs (chelicerae). Actually, there is no evidence to suggest that these are actually armed with poison (another feature distinguishing solifugids from spiders), but what they lack in toxicity they more than compensate for in sheer power. To quote H.M. Bernard, from his *Science Progress* solifugid paper of April 1897:

> *It is well...that they are measured in millimetres and not in feet or even inches, for anything more terrible than the jaws of these creatures could hardly be imagined ...One writer speaks of them as the most horrible jaws in the whole animal kingdom, eclipsing even those of the tiger, the crocodile and the shark.*

Indeed, these formidable fangs, shaped like a pair of sturdy lobster pincers, are probably stronger, proportionately, than the jaws of any other type of animal alive today, and can seize and dispatch creatures as large as rats and songbirds - even though the total body length of a solifugid does not usually exceed 3in. Solifugids

Solifugid (right) battling with scorpion (left)

will even use these 'pincers' against an unwary human, snapping like tiny dogs at fingers or toes.

In contrast, smaller victims and food particles are captured by a much slimmer pair of mouthparts, sited just in front of the chelicerae, equipped with adhesive tips, and known as the pedipalps. Also used as organs of touch and assisting in climbing, they look sufficiently leg-like to deceive casual observers into thinking that solifugids have five pairs of legs (instead of four, like spiders and all other arachnids).

Once a prey victim has been caught and killed, it is swiftly macerated into a thick soup that the solifugid can then suck up into its mouth, thereby obtaining all of the fluids that it requires for survival. Thus it need never seek out water to drink - which is just as well, because the principal habitat of most solifugids is the arid desertlands of Africa, the Middle East, and North America (though there are also species in certain coastal regions of tropical America, Florida, and even southern Spain).

During World War I, the pugnacity of the desert-dwelling *Galeodes* solifugids attracted much attention from the soldiers stationed in Egypt and the Near East, who referred to them as jerrymanders, and sometimes kept them as pets. Indeed, as noted by eminent British zoologist Prof. John L. Cloudsley-Thompson in his *Spiders, Scorpions, Centipedes, and Mites* (2nd edn, 1968), the troops based at Aboukir used to stage battles between their solifugids, matching them as in cock-fighting contests.

Apart from their sparring prowess, however, little is known about the lifestyle of solifugids, as they have rarely been studied in detail, but they have a longstanding reputation as fearless, ferocious predators, as revealed in many eyewitness accounts. One of the most descriptive was published more than a century ago, in Rev. J.G. Wood's *Illustrated Natural History* (1859-63), featuring observations by Lieutenant-General Sir J. Hearsey, KCB, involving an Old World *Galeodes*. In one incident, it attacked a small bat (wingspan 3-4in) fluttering under a glass shade. As recounted by Wood, the solifugid leaped onto it and then:

> *...proceeded to drive its fangs into the neck, and clung so tightly that it could not be shaken off. In vain did the bat try to beat off the enemy with its wings, or to rid itself of the foe by flying in the air. Nothing could shake off the Galeodes; the long legs clung tightly to the victim, the cruel fangs were buried deeper and deeper in its flesh, the struggles gradually became weaker, until the point of a fang touched a vital spot, and the poor bat fell lifeless from the grasp of its destroyer.*

Later, this same solifugid found itself pitted against a 4in-long scorpion. The fact, however, that this opponent was not only sizeable but also, zoologically speaking, a close relative, did little to staunch the solifugid's bloodlust:

> *The Galeodes seemed nothing daunted, seized the scorpion by the root of the tail, just where it could not be touched by the sting, sawed its way*

through the tail, severed that deadly weapon from the body, and then killed and ate the scorpion together with its tail.

Attacks upon scorpions are not uncommon when these two awesome arachnids encounter one another in the desert, but in such cases the solifugid aggressor is generally a female, larger and more belligerent than the male, which will usually flee from this type of confrontation. This leads to another notable characteristic of solifugids. They are extremely fleet-footed. Indeed, *Solpuga* solifugids inhabiting the arid regions of Africa and the Middle East hold the *Guinness World Records* title as the world's fastest land-living invertebrates, with a burst sprint capability estimated at 10 miles/hour. To enable them to attain such speeds, and to sustain a highly active existence, their respiratory system is more advanced than that of true spiders; whereas the latter breathe by means of leaf-like structures termed book-lungs, a solifugid's body is permeated by a ramifying series of tiny tubes called tracheae, resembling the respiratory system of insects.

Although a few solifugids are abroad during the day (hence the name 'sun spider'), most species are predominantly nocturnal ('solifugid' translates as 'fleeing from the sun'). During the course of history their night-time activities have given rise to a variety of strange and often lurid legends, together with certain comparably curious hypotheses, as summarized in various publications by Prof. Cloudsley-Thompson (after whom the solifugid *Rhagodessa cloudsley-thompsoni* was named in 1964 by P.L.G. Benoit).

For example, A.A.H. Lichtenstein, writing in 1797, was not satisfied with the traditional translation from Hebrew into English of the Old Testament's First Book of Samuel; instead, he considered that the creatures plaguing the Philistines when they captured the Ark of the Covenant were not mice, as generally accepted, but solifugids! Moreover, he postulated that the sores or 'emerods' suffered by the Philistines were really caused by solifugid bites. Not surprisingly, this distinctly odd interpretation failed to gain much support. However, it is true that the body and legs of some species of solifugid are hairy enough to suggest, when coupled with their scurrying activity, the appearance of furry mice.

Also, it has been verified that on occasion solifugids will assault travellers sleeping on the desert sands. Such incidents are responsible no doubt for the highly exaggerated terror that these creatures inspire in some Egyptians who believe that solifugids will crawl into a person's bed at night and bore into the unfortunate sleeper's groin, in order to deposit their eggs there. Another equally bizarre but unfounded belief is that if a solifugid should somehow become entangled in a woman's hair, it cannot be removed until its chelicerae have sheared through the entangling locks (hence its Afrikaans name, *haarskeerder* - 'hair-cutter').

Perhaps the most astonishing legend of all concerning solifugids is of very recent date and is of the urban variety. In spring 2004, the following anonymous email circulated widely around the world, and had purportedly been written by a soldier who had been bitten by a 'giant spider' inside his sleeping bag while stationed in the desert near Baghdad, Iraq:

Subject: Fw: Iraqi Spiders

Here are some pets for you...... but Read this before looking at the picture. They run 10 mph, jump three feet, are a nocturnal spider, so only come out at night unless they are in shade. When they bite you, you are injected with Novocaine so you go numb instantly. You don't even know you are bitten when you are sleeping, so you wake up with part of your leg or arm missing because it has been gnawing on it all night long. If you are walking around and you bump something that is casting a shadow over it, and the sun makes contact with it, you better run. It will instantly run for your shadow, and scream the whole time it is chasing you.

PS. The one on the bottom is eating the one on the top. These are Spiders found daily in IRAQ by troops. Imagine waking up and seeing one of these in your tent!!

If all of that sounded astonishing, the photo (again of unknown source) referred to in the email and reproduced below was truly astounding...at least on first sight.

As can be seen, this dramatic picture depicts two creatures that, far from being spiders, giant or otherwise, are very clearly solifugids, albeit of seemingly immense, monstrous size. A closer inspection of the photo, however, reveals that the only monster present in it is one of misleading perspective.

Anonymous photo of two 'giant spiders' in Iraq

The photo was taken with a wide-angle lens, which has exaggerated the size of objects in the foreground in relation to the background, thus making the solifugids appear much larger than they truly are - indeed, they look as large as the leg of the soldier behind them. If, however, you look at the sleeve of the soldier in the foreground, directly alongside the solifugids rather than behind them, they are then seen to be far smaller than originally thought, because the soldier's sleeve appears quite vast in comparison with them. In reality, solifugids native to the Iraqi deserts are no bigger than an adult human's hand.

Equally misleading are the 'facts' provided by the unknown serviceman. Quite apart from the fundamental error in calling them spiders, unlike spiders solifugids do not possess any glands injecting poison, Novocaine, or anything else into their victims. Nor do they bite chunks out of unsuspecting humans. Moreover, they are totally silent, so they do not scream when pursuing prey. Exit the giant, screaming, Novocaine-injecting, flesh-munching spider of Iraq!

They may be relatively small in size, but the stature of their fear-generating prowess is more than sufficient to explain why Adrian Conan Doyle chose a pair of solifugids as the Deptford Horror; certainly they are among the most novel adversaries ever faced by his father's famous if fictitious detective.

Chapter Twenty-One
Snake-Stones and
Serpent Kings

A very curious subject...is the power of extracting venom from a wound inflicted by reptiles, attributed to the 'snake-stone,' which the Hindoos and Cingalese usually carry with them.

Philip H. Gosse - *The Romance of Natural History, Second Series*

Snake-Stones, Scorpion-Stones... and Catfish-Stones?

Snake-stones and their alleged powers of extracting venom from seemingly fatal snakebites have generated substantial debate for centuries. Many adamantly deny that there is any substance to the numerous accounts on record, but there are others who believe just as firmly that the prompt application of one of these strange objects has saved them from certain death. Nowadays, they scarcely rate a mention in wildlife books, but many pre-20th-Century works contained detailed accounts, including the following selection. Read them now, and consider for yourself the extraordinary case of the snake-stones.

The use of snake-stones and their reputed properties have been reported from many parts of the world harbouring highly venomous snakes, but in particular from those frequented by the most famous venomous snake of all - *Naja naja*, the Asian spectacled cobra or *cobra de capello* ('hooded cobra'), a name commonly applied to it prior to the 1900s but not so widely used today. Some of the most familiar accounts of snake-stone use in relation to cobra bites are those included in Sir J. Emerson Tennent's *Sketches of the Natural History of Ceylon* (1861), where the snake-stone is referred to as the *pamboo-kaloo*. These incidents featured some impeccable eye-witnesses. For example:

On one occasion, in March, 1854, a friend of mine was riding, with some other civil officers of the Government, along a jungle path in the vicinity of Bintenne, when he saw one of two Tamils, who were approaching the party, suddenly dart into the forest and return, holding in both hands a cobra de capello which he had seized by the head and tail. He called to his companion for assistance to place it in their covered basket, but, in doing this, he handled it so inexpertly that it seized him by the finger, and retained its hold for a few seconds, as if unable to retract its fangs. The blood flowed, and intense pain appeared to follow almost immediately but, with all expedition, the friend of the sufferer undid his waistcloth, and took from it two snake-stones, each of the size of a small almond, intensely black and highly polished, though of an extremely light substance. These he applied, one to each wound inflicted by the teeth of the serpent, to which they attached themselves closely; the blood that oozed from the bites being rapidly imbibed by the porous texture of the article applied. The stones adhered tenaciously for three or four minutes, the wounded man's companion in the meanwhile rubbing his arm downwards from the shoulder towards the fingers. At length, the snake-stones dropped off of their own accord; the suffering of the man appeared to subside; he twisted his fingers till the joints cracked, and went on his way without concern.

The second incident related by Tennent is no less astonishing:

In another instance, in 1853, Mr. Lavalliere, then District Judge of Kandy, informed me that he saw a snake-charmer in the jungle, close by the town, search for a cobra de capello, *and, after disturbing one in its retreat, the man tried to secure it, but, in the attempt, he was bitten in the thigh till blood trickled from the wound. He instantly applied the* Pamboo-Kaloo, *which adhered closely for about ten minutes, during which time he passed the root which he held in his hand backwards and forwards above the stone, till the latter dropped to the ground. He assured M. Lavalliere that all danger was then past. That gentleman obtained from him the snake-stone he had relied on, and saw him repeatedly afterwards in perfect health.*

The root used by the snake-charmer seems to have been either the stem of an *Aristolochia* or that of some form of jungle vine. As for the snake-stone's composition, Tennent later submitted one to the famous research chemist Prof. Michael Faraday for analysis. In reply, Faraday stated that in his belief it was:

...a piece of charred bone which has been filled with blood perhaps several times, and then carefully charred again. Evidence of this is afforded, as well by the apertures of cells or tubes on its surface as by the fact that it yields and breaks under pressure, and exhibits an organic structure within. When heated slightly, water rises from it, and also a little ammonia; and, if heated still more highly in the air, carbon burns away, and a bulky white ash is left, retaining the shape and size of the stone.

Predictably, the ash proved to be largely calcium phosphate in composition. Continuing with Faraday's comments:

...if the piece of matter has ever been employed as a spongy absorbent, it seems hardly fit for that purpose in its present state; but who can say to what treatment it has been subjected since it was fit for use, or to what treatment the natives may submit it when expecting to have occasion to use it?

Summing up the case, Tennent concluded, quite reasonably:

The probability is, that the animal charcoal, when instantaneously applied, may be sufficiently porous and absorbent to extract the venom from the recent wound, together with a portion of the blood, before it has had time to be carried into the system; and that the blood which Mr. Faraday detected in the specimen submitted to him was that of the Indian on whose person the effect was exhibited on the occasion to which my informant was an eye-witness.

Many snake-stones used in Sri Lanka apparently originate from India, brought to the island by travelling snake-charmers from India's Coromandel coast. Moreover, according to Dr John Davy's *An Account of the Interior of Ceylon, and of Its Inhabitants* (1821), they also reach Sri Lanka via Indian merchants who purchase them from the monks of Manilla. Davy described three main types: one composed of partially burnt bone and slightly absorptive, a second manufactured from chalk, and a third made from plant material and resembling bezoar; the latter two are not absorptive.

Can venomous snake bites be alleviated with snake-stones?

In view of the plenitude of venomous snakes inhabiting tropical Africa, it should come as no surprise to learn that the use of snake-stones is prevalent here too. As far back as 1772, Carl Peter Thunberg described seeing snake-stones used by the Boers in South Africa's Cape Province. Once again these were mostly imported from India, particularly from Malabar, though at such extortionate prices that few of the South African farmers could afford to purchase them. Examining one of these stones, Thunberg described it as being black in colour (hence its alternative name, black-stone), convex on one side, and so porous that bubbles rose out of it when it was plunged into water.

Moreover, a modern-day Kenyan teaching leaflet produced by the organisation REAP (Rural Extension with Africa's Poor), commending the efficiency of black-stones in treating snake bites and scorpion stings, and even providing a 'recipe' for creating such stones from sections of cattle thigh bones, is available online, at http://www.reap-eastafrica.org/reap/pdf/blackstone.pdf - thus confirming that belief in their powers is still prevalent in Africa.

Snake-stones are also known widely in Latin America. In Peru, they are called the *piedra negra*, which once again translates as 'black-stone', and are still popularly utilised. Mexican snake-stones had been brought to popular attention in 1829, by Lieutenant R.W.H. Hardy's book *Travels in the Interior of Mexico...* Then, on 30 January 1860, he communicated some further details, received by Tennent, regarding their preparation. In Mexico, the snake-stone is called the *piedra ponsona,* and according to Hardy is prepared as follows:

> *Take a piece of hart's horn [stag antler] of any convenient size and shape; cover it well round with grass or hay, enclose both in a thin piece of sheet copper well wrapped round them, and place the parcel in a charcoal fire till the bone is sufficiently charred. When cold, remove the calcined horn from its envelope, when it will be ready for immediate use. In this state it will resemble a solid black fibrous substance, of the same shape and size as before it was subjected to this treatment. USE - The wound being slightly punctured, apply the bone to the opening, to which it will adhere firmly for the space of two minutes; and when it falls, it should be received into a basin of water. It should then be dried in a cloth, and again applied to the wound. But it will not adhere longer than about one minute. In like manner it may be applied a third time; but now it will fall almost immediately, and nothing will cause it to adhere any more. These effects I witnessed in the case of a bite of a rattle-snake at Oposura, a town in the province of Sonora, in Mexico, from whence I obtained my recipe.*

This detailed but wholly unsensationalised account aroused the curiosity of Rev. J. G. Wood. He decided to follow Hardy's recipe to see if he could indeed manufacture a snake-stone in this manner, and recounted his experience in his *Illustrated Natural History* (1859-63):

> *Being desirous of testing the truth of this recipe, I procured a piece of stag's-horn, cut it into proper shape, and exposed it to the heat of a fierce charcoal fire for an hour and a half. On removing it from the copper, the hay had been fused into a black mass, easily broken, and forming a complete cast of the inclosed horn, which fell out like an almond from its shell. On comparing the charred horn with the veritable Snake-stones, I find them to be identical except in the polish. The fracture of both is the same, and when exposed to a white heat in the air, my own specimen burned away, leaving a white ash precisely as related of the real specimen [analysed by Faraday], and the ashes of both are exactly alike, saving that my own is of a purer white than that specimen calcined by Mr Faraday, which has a slight tinge of pink, possibly from the absorbed blood. On*

throwing it into water, it gave out a vast amount of air from its pores, making the water look for a few seconds as if it were newly opened champagne, a peculiarity which agrees with Thunberg's description of the Snake-stone used at the Cape The rather high polish of the Cingalese Snake-stone I could not rightly impart to my own specimen, probably for want of patience. I found, however, that by rendering the surface very smooth with a file, and afterwards with emery paper, before exposing it to the fire, it could be burnished afterwards by rubbing it with polished steel. Even in the original objects, the polish is not universal, the plane side being much rougher than the convex.

So far, only the application of snake-stones to snake-bites has been mentioned, but in some localities they have wider uses. In Sri Lanka and India, for instance, they are also said to be highly efficacious in the is extraction of poison from scorpion stings, as demonstrated by the following incident, reported by Major-General Edward Napier in his *Scenes and Sports in Foreign Lands, Vol. 2* (1840):

These people generally have for sale numbers of snake-stones, *which are said to be equally an antidote against the bite of the serpent and the sting of the scorpion. For the former I have never seen it tried; and to prove its efficacy with the latter, the samp-wallah generally carries about in small earthen vessels a number of these animals, one of which he allows to wound him with his sting. The snake-stone, which is a dark, shining, smooth pebble, about the size and shape of a French bean, on being applied to the wound, instantly adheres to it, and by a power of suction appears to draw out the poison, which is supposed to be contained in the small bubbles which, on the immersion of the stone into a glass of water, are seen in great numbers to rise to the surface.*

My first idea on beholding the samp-wallah allow himself to be stung by the scorpion was, that the latter had by some means been rendered harmless. However, not wishing voluntarily to put this to the test by personal experience, I purchased some of the stones, resolved on the very first opportunity to try their efficacy. Shortly after this, happening to be marching up the country with a detachment, we pitched our camp on some very stony ground, in clearing which one of the English soldiers happened to be bit [stung] in the hand by a large scorpion. As soon as I heard of this circumstance, I sent for the sufferer, who appeared to be in great pain, which he described as a burning sensation running all the way up his arm to the very shoulder.

I applied one of the snake-stones to the puncture; it adhered immediately, and during about eight minutes that it remained on the patient, he by degrees became easier; the pain diminished, gradually coming down from the shoulder, until it appeared entirely confined to the immediate vicinity of the wound. I now removed the stone: on putting it into a cup of water, numbers of the small air-bubbles rose to the surface, and in a short time the man ceased to suffer any inconvenience from the accident.

In 1927, black, porous 'scorpion-stones' were shown to Dr Graham Netting by the monks of Trinidad's Mount St Benedict. When analysed, they were found to be composed of animal bone charcoal, and when placed upon moistened skin they remained attached until they had absorbed some moisture, after which they dropped off, suggesting that they may indeed be of use in drawing out poison from a freshly inflicted scorpion sting wound. And in rural areas of the USA, 'madstones', created from a variety of substances (including bone, deer antlers, certain porous minerals, and sometimes even semi-precious stones), have been used against scorpion stings, as well as bites from rabid dogs.

One of the most unusual incidents in which a snake-stone was employed was described by D. Hervey (*Nature*, 24 May 1900):

> *A good many years ago, when sea-bathing in the Old Straits of Singapore (i.e. those separating the island from the Malay Peninsula), I put my foot in a slight muddy hollow in the sandy sea-bed; the moment I did so, I received an agonising stab near the ankle (from some red-hot poisoned blade, it seemed) which drove me in hot haste ashore, where a Malay constable on hearing what had happened, and on examining the wound, pronounced my assailant to be the 'ikan sembilang' (sembilang fish),* Plotosus canius, *one of the siluroids [catfishes], I am informed by Mr Boulenger of the British Museum. The fish is armed with three powerful spines on the head, one projecting perpendicularly from the top, and one projecting horizontally from each side. The Malay lost no time in running to the barracks near by, whence he shortly returned with a little round charcoal-like stone about the size of a small marble. This he pressed on to the wound, to which it adhered, and remained there by itself, without any continuation of pressure, for a minute or more. Then it fell off, and black blood began to flow, which, after a little, was succeeded by blood of normal colour. The pain, which had been excessively acute, began to diminish soon after this, and in an hour had practically disappeared. The wound gave me no further trouble, but a fortnight afterwards I noticed a hole about the size of a pea where the wound had been...The black stone applied by the Malay to the wound came, he alleged, from the head of a snake, and claimed, therefore, to be a bezoar stone. It was, no doubt, a snake-stone, probably made of charred bone, and therefore porous in character, which would account for the adhesive and absorptive powers it displayed in my case.*

Leaving aside momentarily the curious Malay belief that such objects originate from the heads of snakes, is there still room for doubt that at least those snake-stones composed of charred bone or horn (and which are almost exclusively termed black-stones nowadays) can really alleviate the effect of venomous bites and stings? In fact, very appreciable doubt continues to be expressed in scientific circles.

Modern-day sceptics find it difficult to believe that such an object can generate sufficient powers of suction quickly enough to draw the venom out of the wound before the victim's blood circulatory system begins to transport it further into the body. Moreover, a recent Bolivian study by Dr J.P. Chippaux and two co-workers

(*Toxicon*, April 2007), testing the effectiveness of black-stone application upon mice following intra-muscular injection of venom from the puff adder *Bitis arietans*, West African carpet viper *Echis ocellatus*, and black-necked spitting cobra *Naja nigricollis*, failed to demonstrate any positive envenomation effect. Comparable criticism had been voiced over a century earlier, by Sir Joseph Fayrer in his book *The Thanatophidia of India* (1872), and also by other snake-stone sceptics of the late 19th Century, when interest in snake-stones had reached its zenith.

However, in defence of the snake-stone's abilities, it must be pointed out that accounts describing its actions generally state specifically that it was (or should be) applied *straight after* the bite or sting had occurred (if it were to exert its full effect), i.e. well *before* the venom had begun to pervade the victim's system. Hence the Bolivian study, featuring direct intramuscular injection of venom, is hardly relevant after all.

In addition, we must consider the educated, reliable nature of many of the eyewitnesses whose testimonies have been presented here. Indeed, in some cases they had even admitted to scepticism concerning the natives' claims regarding snake-stones prior to witnessing with their own eyes the startlingly effective results obtained with them. Can we really justify choosing to discount all of this testimony as fraudulent or mistaken, as we must do if we are to deny the capability of snake-stones? Furthermore, if snake-stones *are* impotent, is it not a quite extraordinary coincidence how similar are all of the cases reported here, despite having occurred independently of one another and in totally different parts of the world and involving very dissimilar forms of animal? Unless there is at least some degree of truth to the snake-stone belief, it is highly unlikely that localities so distant from one another as those cited in this chapter could yield such similar accounts, corresponding with one another not just in general features but also in much more specific, ostensibly insignificant ones.

Elephant-Pearls and the Elephant-Stone

Occasionally, an elephant is reported in the wild with only a single tusk instead of two. The missing one may have been lost through injury, may simply never have developed – or, more rarely still, may have developed, but grown internally instead of externally. The outcome of the latter occurrence is an internal block of solid ivory, sometimes spherical in shape, buried within the elephant's jawbone. This aberrant object is traditionally known as an elephant-pearl, and was highly-prized by ivory poachers.

Even more sought-after, however, was the legendary elephant-stone, which according to East African native belief was said to be concealed at the very core of any elephant-pearl produced by a tuskless bull elephant, and was claimed to possess magical powers. To quote the famous elephant hunter John Albert Jordan, the elephant-stone is: "larger than the Koh-i-noor [diamond] and glitters more wondrously".

Once, while out hunting with the Wanderobo tribe, Jordan shot a tuskless African bull elephant, and, as he later recounted in his book *Elephants and Ivory*, once it had expired, his Wanderobo companions:

> ...*cut into the skull with their axes and there, at the right side of the skull, where the tusk should start, was a large ball of ivory about the size and shape of a cocoanut [sic]. I hacked at it with a hatchet, believing it to be the shell of the Stone, and in the end I had nothing but splinters and shavings of ivory, for there was no Stone. But it is my fancy to believe that it exists.*

Indeed, such was his belief in this mythical treasure that Jordan spent much time searching vainly for such a stone, documenting his quest in another of his books, *The Elephant Stone*. As discussed by A.H.E. Molamure in a detailed *Loris* article from 1970, elephant-pearls are treasured by Sri Lankan natives too. Referred to locally as *gaja mutu* or *gaja mukta*, these are truer (albeit less spectacular) pearls than the African variety noted earlier here. For whereas those are actually freak, inward-growing tusks, Sri Lankan elephant-pearls are simply the result of excessive, concentric layers of dentine deposited around foreign bodies entering an elephant tusk's pulp cavity, and thus are much smaller and less valuable in terms of ivory content. One such elephant-pearl's discovery was documented by P.D. Stracey in his fascinating book *Elephant Gold* (1963):

> *The myth that a certain super-race of elephants possessed pearls in their skulls may also have had its origin in very ancient times. At least one case of something which primitive fancy might well have regarded as a 'pearl' has been reported in the present century. During the 1928 khedda operations in the Chittagong Hill Tracts, a Forest Officer who had destroyed a wild tusker found a small oval object, about as big as a man's little finger-nail, in the fleshy pith of one of the tusks. It had the appearance and consistency of ivory, but was slightly rough and striated. The elephant men were very excited and claimed that it was a gaja mukta or elephant-pearl and extremely valuable.*

Interestingly, in his *Loris* article Molamure notes that in the Brihat Samhita of Varahamihira, an ancient Sanskrit treatise, wild boars are also believed to yield pearls – valuable, lustrous, and borne at the roots of their tusks. So too, it claims, are certain cobras, concealing blue tinted pearls inside their hoods. Indeed, cobra-jewels and other serpent-derived gems have such an extensive tradition that they deserve a discussion all to themselves, as now follows.

Cobra-Jewels and Adder-Stones

The curious Malay belief recalled by Hervey, that snake-stones were derived from the heads of snakes, is immediately reminiscent of the toad-stone (bufonite) myth – "...the toad, ugly and venomous, wears yet a precious jewel in his head", as Shakespeare wrote in *As You Like It*. The snake-stone equivalent to this is not confined to Malaysia - in a short *Nature* report (26 July 1900) responding to Hervey's, and based upon information received from a Mr E.H.L. Schwarz of Cape Town, it was disclosed that South African farmers also hold this belief. However, as the report commented, it may have reached there via the Malay slaves obtained from Batavia by the early Dutch. In *Venomous Reptiles* (1971), Sherman and Madge Minton report that in India it is believed that some cobras bear in their hood a dark brown, luminous stone termed a *mun*, which heals snake-bites instantaneously. Those that the Mintons examined proved to be bezoar stones, or enteroliths (stones swallowed by various animals to aid digestion), or, in most cases, samples of heat-treated agate.

A similar myth was documented by Tennent from Sri Lanka:

> *One curious tradition in Ceylon embodies the popular legend, that the stomach of the cobra de capello occasionally contains a precious stone of such unapproachable brilliancy as to surpass all known jewels. This inestimable stone is called the* nāga-mănik-kya; *but not one snake in thousands is supposed to possess such a treasure. The cobra, before eating, is believed to cast it up and conceal it for the moment; else its splendour, like a flambeau, would attract all beholders. The tales of the peasantry, in relation to it, all turn upon the devices of those in search of the gem, and the vigilance and cunning of the cobra by which they are baffled; the reptile itself being more enamoured of the priceless jewel than even its most ardent pursuers.*

One of the oddest of such myths, which links this chapter's snake-stone section with the serpent king section to come, is that of the adder-stone, also known as the *ovum anguinum* ('snake-egg'). This is a stone-like object that originates as a ball of froth exuded by entwined masses of snakes (often common adders *Vipera berus)* at midsummer – or at least according to an ancient Celtic belief reported by the Druids of Gaul and documented by Roman philosopher Pliny the Elder. This was the inspiration for the druid song included by English poet William Mason within his epic poem *Caractacus* (1759):

> *From the grot of charms and spells,*
> *Where our matron sister dwells,*
> *Brennus, has thy holy hand*
> *Safely brought the Druid wand,*
> *And the potent Adder-stone,*
> *Gender'd 'fore the autumnal moon?*
> *When in undulating twine*
> *The foaming snakes prolific join,*
> *When they hiss, and when they bear*
> *Their wondrous egg aloft in air;*
> *Thence, before to earth it fall,*
> *The Druid in his hallowed pall*
> *Receives the prize,*
> *And instant flies*
> *Followed by the invenom'd brood,*
> *Till he cross the crystal flood.*

The last lines record the belief that the adder-stone could protect anyone who captured it (within a cloth, and before it hits the ground) from poison and all manner of other undesirable substances, provided that he could successfully escape the pursuing adders - by crossing a river. According to 18th-Century naturalist Thomas Pennant:

> *Our modern Druidesses give much the same account of the ovum an-*
> *guinum (Glein Neidr, as the Welsh call it; or the adder-gem) as the Roman*
> *philosopher [Pliny] does; but seem not to have so exalted an opinion of its*
> *powers, using it only to assist children in cutting their teeth, or to cure the*
> *hooping-cough, or drive away an ague.*

In reality, it is unlikely even to have achieved these feats, for although adder-stones, ova anguina, and the like did exist, they were merely fossil sea urchins, also known from Cornwall and referred to there as *milprev* or *milpref* - as reported by geologist Dr Michael Bassett in his booklet *'Formed Stones', Folklore and Fossils* (1982).

Serpent Kings

Occasionally, a group of rats is discovered whose members (sometimes as many as 20) are closely huddled together and found to be inextricably bound to one another by their hopelessly entangled tails. Such a congregation is known as a rat king, of which there are many records (some dating back centuries) and a few highly prized,

A small serpent king of adders

painstakingly preserved specimens in museums. However, the phenomenon remains a source of mystery to zoologists, who still cannot explain satisfactorily how the tails of the rats managed to become inseparably intertwined in this Gordian manner.

A smaller number of cases involving squirrels - squirrel kings - are also known, plus at least one fieldmouse king. And if a cat gives birth to a litter of kittens whose umbilical cords are similarly tangled, the litter is termed a cat king.

There are certain cases of extraordinary intertwined snake masses on record too. Hence for the sake of nomenclatural uniformity, it would seem appropriate to refer to these as serpent kings. Such throngs have been spasmodically reported for a long time, with a number of different species, and because of their grotesque appearance have generally attracted appreciable if cautious attention from their eyewitnesses.

During his expeditions through Guyana during the late 18th Century, explorer, Alexander von Humboldt recorded seeing some piles of entwined serpents, which since then has served as an inspiration to others to make a point of documenting comparable sights. In 1848, for example, an anonymous *Scientific American* account of its author's travels across the Izacubos savannahs in Guyana contained a vivid description of what he called "the most wonderful, and most terrible spectacle that can be seen". He continued:

We were ten men on horseback, two of whom took the lead, in order to sound the passages, whilst I preferred to skirt the great forests. One of the blacks who formed the vanguard, returned at full gallop, and called to me - 'Here, sir, come and see the serpents in a pile'. He pointed out to me something elevated in the middle of the Savannah or swamp, which appeared like a bundle of arms. One of my company then said, 'this is certainly one of the assemblages of serpents, which heap themselves on each other after a violent tempest; I have heard of these but have never seen any; let us proceed cautiously and not go too near'. When we were within twenty paces of it, the terror of our horses prevented nearer approach, to which none of us were inclined. On a sudden the pyramid mass became agitated; horrible hissing issued from it, thousands of serpents rolled spirally on each other shot forth out of their circle their hideous heads, presenting their envenomed darts and fiery eyes to us. I own I was one of the first to draw back, but when I saw this formidable phalanx remained at its post, and appeared to be more disposed to defend itself than attack us, I rode around it in order to view its order of battle, which faced the enemy on every side. I then thought what could be the design of this numerous assemblage, and I concluded that this species of serpents dread some collosean enemy, which might be the great serpent or cayman [actually a type of crocodile], and that they re-unite themselves after having seen this enemy, in order to resist him in a mass.

Reading this graphic account, it occurred to me that an unexpected encounter with such a horde in olden days may well have helped to foster the famous Greek myth of the multi-headed hydra. Assuredly, it would be an almost supernatural spectacle to witness, and one likely to remain in the onlooker's memory for many a long day afterwards. As for the above author's record that these serpent kings were presumed to be formed following a violent storm, and his own notion that they amass as a means of defending themselves against a very much larger enemy, neither of these is really very plausible. Rather, it is much more likely that what he encountered was a frenzied mating *en masse.*

After emerging in spring from a winter's hibernation, some snake species congregate in enormous numbers for mating. In the case of the North American garter snake *Thamnophis* (formerly *Eutoenia*) *sirtalis,* for instance, a harmless, handsomely striped species related to Britain's grass snake and smooth snake, several hundred males will all seek to copulate with a comparatively small number of females. In one closely monitored incident, a pre-copulating serpent king comprised a solid ball of 15-20 garter snakes, observed by J.B. Gardner on 18 April 1954 at Seymour, Connecticut (*Copeia,* 1955); in April 1955 he saw a second example, again at Seymour (*Copeia,* 1957).

Equally, an early account of a garter snake mass mating was one of two serpent king reports penned by the quasi-anonymous 'E.L.' *(American Naturalist,* 1880). Both encounters had taken place during the early spring, in expanses of Maryland wilderness:

> *I first saw such a bundle of snakes in the neighbourhood of Ilchester, Howard Co., Md., on the stony bank of the Patapsco river, heaped together on a rock and between big stones. It was a very warm and sunny location, where a human being would scarcely disturb them. I reasoned that the warmth and silence of that secluded place brought them together. Some hundreds of them could be counted, and all of them I found in a lively state of humor, hissing at me with threatening glances, with combined forces and with such a persistency that stones thrown upon them could not stop them or alter the position of a single animal. They would make the proper movements and the stone would roll off. All the snakes in this lump were common snakes* (Eutoenia sirtalis L.). *The second time I noticed a ball of black snakes* (Bascanion [now Coluber] constrictor L.) *rolling slowly down a steep and stony hillside on the bank of the same river, but about two miles above Union Factory, Baltimore county, Md. Some of the snakes were of considerable length and thickness, and, as I noticed clearly, kept together by procreative impulses.*

In Britain, adder aggregations are sometimes met with, newly emerged from hibernation (often communal). Encounters with serpent kings of this type no doubt contributed to the adder-stone legend.

Incidentally, a piscean parallel to serpent kings is the occurrence of eel kings - see Christopher Moriarty's *Eels: A Natural and Unnatural History,* 1978 - comprising tightly entwined balls of pre-migrating eels, occasionally spied floating along streams.

Staying with aquatic creature kings but returning to serpents: as Sherman Minton and Harold Heatwole reported in *Oceans* (April 1978), the yellow-bellied sea-snake *Pelamis platurus* is well-known for congregating in immense numbers, often several thousand at a time, passively drifting at the Pacific Ocean's surface, and carried by wind and wave for great distances. The sea-snake serpent king *par excellence,* however, was witnessed sometime before 1932 by Willoughby P. Lowe, a collector of natural history specimens for the British Museum. As recorded in *The Trail That is Always New* (1932), Lowe was aboard a steamer travelling in the Malacca Strait between the Malay Peninsula and the Indonesian island of Sumatra, when:

> *After luncheon on 4 May I came on deck and was talking to some passengers, when, looking landward, I saw a long line running parallel with our course. None of us could imagine what it could be. It must have been four or five miles off. We smoked and chatted, had a siesta, and went down to tea. On returning to the deck we still saw the curious line along which we had been steaming for four hours, but now it lay across our course, and we were still very curious as to what it was. As we drew nearer we were amazed to find that it was composed of a solid mass of sea snakes, twisted thickly together. They were orange-red and black, a very poisonous and rare variety known as* Astrotia stokesii *[heaviest of all sea-snakes and measuring up to 6 ft long]...Along this line there must have been millions; when I say millions I consider it no exaggeration, for the line was quite ten feet wide and we followed its course for some sixty miles. I can only presume it was either a migration or the breeding season...it certainly was a wonderful sight.*

The spectacle of millions of extremely venomous serpents heaving and writhing in a solid, 60-mile-long mass at the ocean's surface may not be everyone's idea of a wonderful sight, but it definitely merits inclusion in any book dealing with extraordinary animals!

Chapter Twenty-Two
In Pursuit of Fraudulent Fauna and other Ambiguous Animals

Her shabby skill lies in disguise. And even that knack would be beyond her, if it weren't for the eagerness of these gulls, those marks, to believe whatever comes easiest. She can't turn cream into butter, but she can give a lion the semblance of a manticore to eyes that want to see a manticore there – eyes that would take a real manticore for a lion, a dragon for a lizard, and the Midgard Serpent for an earthquake. And a unicorn for a white mare.

Peter Beagle – *The Last Unicorn*

Things are rarely what they seem in cryptozoology. Or, to put it another way: if, as is said, the road to Hell is paved with good intentions, then the road to Crypto-Hell must surely be strewn with good identities. Sadly, however, these may turn out to be nothing more than hoaxes and spoofs, some decidedly tongue-in-cheek, others rather more mystifying, as illustrated by the following eclectic assortment.

In a Tizzy over Tizzie-Wizzie

In May 1994, the British media were greeted with news of a creature guaranteed to perplex even the most liberal-minded of cryptozoologists, for this was the month that introduced us all to the wonder of Tizzie-Wizzie - the bushy-tailed, winged hedgehog endemic to the shores of Cumbria's Lake Windermere!

According to news reports emanating from the Lake District National Park Authority, a boatman had recently spied one of these noteworthy animals scuttling from the Brockhole jetty into some nearby undergrowth - supposedly the latest in a long line of sightings dating back to the beginning of the 20th Century. Yet if this were true, why were books of English fauna and folklore singularly lacking in literature devoted to this aerial anomaly, and, even more remarkably, why hadn't its mating habits been filmed in voyeuristically close-up detail for a TV documentary?

In my quest for answers to such fundamental questions as these, I followed the only logical course open to the dedicated investigator - and contacted the World of Beatrix Potter Attraction, sited not a million miles from Lake Windermere. As I'm sure you'd agree, an institution devoted to a lady whose fictional characters included the hedgehog heroine Mrs Tiggy-Winkle is where any self-respecting cryptozoologist would immediately turn for advice when confronted with a problem as prickly as Tizzie-Wizzie. And sure enough, after receiving some gentle prodding of an inquisitorial inclination, the enigma that became known to me as *Erinaceus volans* ('flying hedgehog') obligingly uncurled itself to reveal a fascinating history.

It seems that in or around 1900, a Bowness boatman with an ear for a good yarn and a taste for even better beer recounted to some visitors at the Stag's Head Hotel a thrilling tale of how he had just encountered an extraordinary beastie resembling a cross between a hedgehog and a squirrel sporting the additional novelty of a pair of distinctive wings. Searches were duly made, and the boatman and colleagues were liberally plied with liquid refreshment by tourists whenever their strength seemed likely to flag from the pursuit. Strangely, their strength appeared to flag rather more frequently than one might have expected in relation to a hedgehog hunt, but that is neither here nor there - unlike Tizzie-Wizzie, which was apparently sighted all over the place with inexplicable regularity, invariably coinciding with opening time at the local public houses.

Even so, for a long period this mystifying mammal remained unremittingly elusive, but in 1906 a specimen was eventually acquired, and was taken to the studio of local photographer Louis Herbert, whose unique Tizzie-Wizzie portrait was later reproduced in postcard form and also in Irvine Hunt's book *Fenty's Album*. Lucidly depicting its bushy tail, its translucent wings, and its slender antennae, the photo provided sufficient evidence for me to feel secure in naming as this exotic species' nearest relatives the American jackalope and the fur-bearing trout.

As the years went by, Tizzie-Wizzie fervour died down, but although the hunt for flying hedgehogs passed into local oral tradition, what in all seriousness must surely be one of the most charming and hilarious of all wildlife hoaxes never received much in the way of formal documentation - an omission finally rectified by the present account.

As for Tizzie-Wizzie's belated comeback in May 1994, this stemmed from a delightful, well-publicised idea jointly conceived by the World of Beatrix Potter Attraction, the Brockhole Visitor Centre, and the Bowness Bay Boating Company to feature the Beast of Bowness as the star attraction of a treasure-hunt style of competition - 'The Tizzie-Wizzie Trail', which led its tourist detectives on a pleasant quest along the shores and across the waters of Windermere, answering questions related to local sites and sights, with a limited edition sculpture of the fabled T-W as a monthly prize.

All that remains to be said, in response to the many bemused callers who bombarded me with queries regarding Tizzie-Wizzie when the story broke, is that their hopes of locating a flying hedgehog were doomed to disaster from the very beginning. After all, another name for the hedgehog is the hedge-pig - and I hardly need give odds on the probability of tracking down any type of pig with wings!

...and Deeply Dippy over *Diplocaulus*

In September 2004, *Fortean Times* forwarded to me a short note from reader Stuart Pike enquiring about an attached photograph (reproduced below) of a bizarre-looking mystery beast, labelled as a hammerhead lizard. Not long afterwards, Maltese journalist Tonio Galea independently contacted me, requesting details about this same photo (of unknown origin), whose creature, according to local Maltese rumour, had lately been discovered alive on a rocky beach at Il-Maghluq, Marsascala, in the south of the island. Since then, I have received several more enquiries from other correspondents, and so too, it transpires, have various other scientists, including Malta University biologist Prof. Patrick J. Schembri (*Times of Malta*, 23 November 2004).

The supposed Maltese hammerhead lizard

In reality, what this intriguing photo depicts is an apparently plastic or resin model of an ancient prehistoric American amphibian called *Diplocaulus*, whose fossils date back to the lower Permian Period (roughly 270 million years ago). Belonging to an extinct group of salamander-like amphibians termed nectridians, *Diplocaulus* was characterised by its head's two enormous lateral horns, out of all proportion to its body. In short, if, as seems to be so, this photo is being put forward as a picture of a real, living beast, then it is a hoax, but *Diplocaulus* itself is a genuine albeit long-extinct animal.

You Don't Fool Me...?

What do you call a newly-found hairless mole-like creature from the Antarctic, with a heat-emitting bony plate on its brow for melting tunnels in the ice beneath unsuspecting penguins, which the creature can then seize and devour? A successful April Fool joke, that's what!

The story of the hot-headed naked ice borer, a 6inch-long subterranean surprise revealed in the frozen southern continent, was featured in the April 1995 issue of the
American science magazine *Discover*, and even included an impressive photo. Such
a distinctive new species naturally attracted a lot of interest, and reports subsequently appeared in several other publications - until June 1995, that is, when *Discover*'s editors triumphantly exposed the ice-borer as a spoof. In the true spirit of
the event, however, the original *Discover* article had contained a quite obvious clue
as to the ice-borer's real identity. The name of the wildlife biologist who had supposedly found it was given as Aprile Pazzo - Italian for 'April Fool'!

Cryptozoology is perpetually on the lookout for frauds and hoaxes when assessing
reports of mysterious animals. It must always be especially vigilant near the onset
of the fourth month, however, because the unveiling of sensational new species is a
perennially popular choice for an April Fool spoof. Some of them, moreover, have
become classics in their field, like the following example.

In spring 1984, London Zoo received a wonderful new animal, which immediately
became a popular star - and for good reason. How many animals can you think of
that can perfectly mimic their human observers? Yet this remarkable creature,
standing upright on its back legs, would wave when the crowd waved, and even
clapped its front paws together when the crowd applauded. It resembled a shaggy
bear, dark on top with a white chest, white toes, and a long white mandarin-like
moustache that drooped down over its cheeks. According to the label on its enclosure, it was from an eastern Himalayan locality a few hundred miles north of Bangladesh, and the local people there called it a *lir-pa loof*. Zoologically, it was the
only known member of a new mammalian family, and had been dubbed *Eccevita
mimicus*.

The *lir-pa loof* generated an incredible amount of public interest. During the first
week after its arrival, London Zoo received around 1000 telephone calls from people requesting further information about it, and the Natural History Museum and the
BBC were similarly bombarded. When you're as famous as this, there is only one
thing to do - make your television debut. And that is precisely what the *lir-pa loof*
did - appearing with its keeper, George Callard, on the popular BBC show *That's
Life*, hosted by Esther Rantzen.

By now, there were ample clues for exposing the secret of this creature (whose
loose-fitting skin could so easily conceal a child or kneeling adult!). Spelled backwards, 'lir-pa loof' becomes 'april fool'. The date of its debut on *That's Life* was 1
April. And for the more classically-minded, the *lir-pa loof*'s scientific name, *Eccevita*, is Latin for 'that's life'.

Yet, amazingly, there were still a surprising number of people who believed in the
lir-pa loof's authenticity - until the very next *That's Life* show. That featured the
second (and final) appearance of this marvellous mammal and its keeper, singing
"We apologise".

Animal April Fools come in many forms. Some are simple, slapstick fun, like Charlie the 'chickpanzee'. This genetically-engineered miracle combined the DNAs of a chicken and a tamarin monkey, and appeared in London's *Daily Mirror* newspaper on 1 April 1991. More deceptive was George - a vicious crossbreed between a gold-fish and a piranha but outwardly resembling true goldfishes. Photographed in the *Daily Mail* on 1 April 1987, George appeared alongside his 12-year-old owner, Amanda Baker - nursing a bandaged finger. People who were not experienced fish fanciers probably didn't realise that piranhas and goldfish are far too distantly re-lated to yield hybrid offspring, but the *Daily Mail* owned up on 2 April - enabling goldfish owners everywhere to breathe a sigh of relief again at feeding time.

Another of the *Daiy Mail*'s priceless piscean April Fools appeared on 1 April 1998, when it announced the discovery off Dorset of a long-vanished fish species not pre-viously seen for 500 years. And the name of this extraordinary Lazarus fish? None other than the red herring!

On 1 April 1989, London's *Today* newspaper included an amusing spoof concerning the arrival at London Zoo of a living brontosaur-like dinosaur from Guinea. This was clearly inspired by reports of a bona fide dinosaurian mystery beast, the Congo-lese *mokele-mbembe*.

Also in 1989, the 1 April issue of *Garden News* featured a front-page special on the astounding germination of a prehistoric plant from fossilised dinosaur droppings. Aptly dubbed the dinosaur vine, it was being studied by Professor Adge Ufult - just say his name outloud!

Appropriately, however, the most famous cryptozoological April Fool involved the most famous cryptozoological creature - the Loch Ness monster. On April 1 1972, newspapers worldwide reported the astonishing discovery of a 9-ft-long seal-like beast, weighing over half a ton, that had been found dead at the side of the loch. Soon afterwards, police intercepted a van transporting the body south to Flamingo Zoo Park in Yorkshire.

When examined, it was found to be the carcase of a dead bull elephant seal, which had been deep-frozen for several days, giving it a peculiar greenish hue. Its whisk-ers had been shaved off too, and its cheeks had been stuffed with rocks.

On 2 April, Flamingo Zoo Park's public relations officer, John Shields, confessed that it was an April Fool hoax, which he had secretly set up as a joke directed at the managing director of the company owning the zoo. Shields had used the body of an elephant seal that had died a week earlier at Dudley Zoo, owned by the same com-pany.

So whenever in the future you see any reports describing a spectacular new animal that seems excessively amazing even for a cryptozoological creature, remember to check the date of the paper or programme before becoming too excited!

It's Dino-Bird!...or is it?

In late January 2002, rumours were circulating on the Net to the effect that the palaeontological community was 'abuzz' with news of the discovery of some incredible 'dinosaur-birds' living in seclusion atop a Venezuelan tepui (high isolated plateau) called Aqueputa. According to their alleged discoverer, a Dr José Ramos-Pajaron of Caracas University, who claimed to have observed them with his students, these extraordinary creatures travel in small cooperative family groups, walk upright, stand roughly 6ft tall, are three-toed, and superficially avian, but with a tooth-bearing beak, long stiff bony tail, primitive hair-like feathers, a horny violet crest in the males, long flexible neck, and claw-bearing wings.

Yet no such researcher can be traced via Internet searches; and as noted by Fortean investigator Scott Corrales, the name 'Pajaron' actually translates as 'big bird'. Corrales feels sure that this whole story is nothing more than an Internet-based hoax, as does palaeontologist Dr Darren Naish - who has pointed out that the palaeontological community is certainly not 'abuzz' with news of this case, and that the creatures themselves seem to be based directly upon modern reconstruction proposals for Cretaceous coelurosaur dinosaurs.

The (Un)usual Suspects

Two other equally suspect claims came to my notice at much the same time as the dino-birds. One was the briefest of mentions: a colleague stated in passing that during the 1980s a small pterodactyl was reputedly killed and displayed in a store front in Queensland, Australia, until the decomposing carcase was discarded. No further details are available, but if such a specimen did exist, it may well have been a variation upon the modified 'Jenny Haniver' or composite 'Fijian mermaid' theme of fake fauna.

The same surely applies to the supposed stuffed 'skunk ape' head with fearsome tusks that was for sale on eBay during mid-February 2002. Commenting upon this specimen in various cz@yahoogroups.com postings at that time, American crypto-zoologist Chad Arment noted that he had previously seen pictures of a similar taxiderm creation labelled as an 'Ozark mountain monkey', with the same kind of red and white hair colouration but without tusks.

Close Encounters of the Leafy Kind

One of my many correspondents is Juan Cabana, who skilfully constructs and sells as curiosities amazing stuffed/preserved fake monsters, especially mermaids - some of which (including a wonderful baby Nessie) can be seen on his website at http://www.borderschess.org/mermaid.htm.

During one e-mail conversation on 31 May 2004, however, he informed me of a truly extraordinary kind of entity that I had never previously heard of. Juan mentioned that he had once seen a couple of examples of so-called plant people - small mummified humanoids, each about 12 inches tall and originating from southeast Asia, that were made from plant tissue and, according to local tradition, grew upon a plant, just like a fruit!

Juan examined them very closely and was astonished at the degree of detail - such that they did not appear to have been hand-crafted. He now believes that they had been made by growing some type of fruit or vegetable inside a human-shaped glass vessel until the plant tissue had totally filled and thus acquired the container's shape, whereupon the vessel was broken, and the resulting humanoid plant tissue dried out to resemble a leafy corpse.

A Missing Lake Monster - and a Missing Lake!

On October 5 1998, Chad Arment, webmaster of the cz@onelist.com (now cz@yahoogroups.com) cryptozoology discussion group, posted to the group a fascinating piece of information that he had lately encountered on an Internet web page entitled 'Unpublished Stories of Ogopogo', found at http://sunnyokanagan.com/ogopogo/index.html and comprising a page within the 'Sunny Okanagan' website. It consisted of a paragraph that reads as follows:

> It is a known fact that a plesiorsaur [sic] like animal exists in Africa. Taxonomists are struggling to classify an animal which washed up dead on the shores of Lake Mankalla, Zimbabwe in March, 1995. Results of preliminary studies of the animal were published in the January 1996 issue of the South African Journal of Science. The creature in question is described as a "Quadruped, whose feet have evolved to form flipper like appendages which evidently propelled the animal through the water as they would be almost useless on land." The article goes on to state that the animal's skeleton, "though smaller than that of a prehistoric plesiosaur, bears a striking resemblance to fossilized specimens of those animals." The remains of the creature are currently housed at Witwatersrand University. Specialists from several universities and scientific institutions are currently at Lake Mankalla, searching for living specimens.

After reading this astonishing account, my first thought (echoing the immortal words of tennis superstar John McEnroe) was: "You cannot be serious!". It had to be too good to be true - otherwise I would surely have learnt about it much earlier than this. Nevertheless, there was only one way to find out - pursue the leads that it offered.

Consequently, I duly e-mailed a query to the *South African Journal of Science*, requesting whether it could send me any information concerning the identity proposed for the Lake Mankalla carcase by its researchers, and possibly even a copy of the paper itself.

On 6 October, I received a reply from the journal's editor, Dr Graham Baker. Sadly, however, he was unable to respond to my requests, for the simple reason that no such paper had appeared in the January 1996 issue - nor, indeed, in any other issue!

However, Dr Baker very kindly promised to make enquiries at Witwatersrand University the next day, beginning with the zoology department.

In the meantime, I posted a summary of the situation so far to the cz@onelist group. This elicited a response from fellow member Chris Orrick, who had seen this same story about a year ago, and had tried to track it down but without success. Nor could he find any mention of a Zimbabwean Lake Mankalla in any atlas or through any Internet search engine, leading him to suspect that it may be just another hoax. I too had been seeking Lake Mankalla in atlases, and had been equally unsuccessful. Not even the weighty *Times Atlas of the World, Comprehensive Edition* includes a lake of this name, in any country.

On 8 October, Dr Baker e-mailed me with the depressing news that he had likewise drawn a blank. Two senior zoologists whom he had contacted at Witwatersrand University knew nothing about any such carcase from Zimbabwe, and although Dr Baker now planned to contact the university's palaeontology department and medical school, he quite rightly felt that these did not seem very likely depositories for such a specimen.

Dr Baker also provided me with e-mail addresses for two zoologists based in Zimbabwe who may be able to shed some light on this mystery - university biologist Professor Brian Marshall, and Dr David Cumming of the WWF office in Harare. Accordingly, I e-mailed both of them with details from the original Internet report, and requests for any information that they may have concerning it. To date, however, their replies have not been forthcoming. Needless to say, I also e-mailed requests for information to two different e-mail contact addresses given by the 'Sunny Okanagan' website that provided the information regarding the Lake Mankalla carcase in the first place. Frustratingly, however, on each occasion my e-mail was returned, with the standard 'User Unknown' response obtained in such situations.

In addition, Dr Baker revealed that he too had been unable to locate Lake Mankalla on any map - not even in any of the local African atlases readily accessible to him. Nonetheless, he promised to pursue the matter further, including enquiring from his wife, who was raised in Zimbabwe, whether she was aware of this elusive lake, and would let me know if he succeeded in uncovering any details. So far, however, neither he nor I have done so - leading me to concur with Chris Orrick that the whole subject must surely be a hoax, perpetuated unsuspectingly by the 'Sunny Okanagan' website.

Strictly for Goons - The Gunni, and Other Mixed-Up Marsupials

Many of Australia's marsupial mammals have evolved by convergence to resemble ecological counterparts elsewhere in the world, e.g. marsupial mole, marsupial wolf (thylacine), marsupial mice (albeit more like shrews), flying phalangers (closely paralleling flying squirrels). Now, however, it seems that Down Under can even boast a marsupial counterpart to that most infamous of fraudulent fauna, the jackalope.

Known as the gunni (and pronounced 'goon-eye'), this horned wombat-like beast is proudly represented by an ingenious taxiderm specimen on display in the visitors' information centre at the tourist town of Marysville, Victoria. Its wombat body is additionally adorned with stripes on its back and hindquarters, plus a tail, and it bears deer antlers on its head. It was recently presented to the centre by local ranger Miles Stewart-Howie as a private project, along with a detailed account of the gunni's fictitious history, which is now also displayed by the centre alongside their newest and certainly most entertaining wildlife exhibit.

Certain other mysterious marsupials brought to my attention over the years have featured hilarious misidentifications rather than outright hoaxes, but are no less memorable. During the mid-1990s, for example, one of my colleagues, zoology curator Dr Ralph Molnar of the Queensland Museum, recalled a priceless instance that would have perplexed the most Sherlockian of crypto-sleuths, and which Watson might well have entitled 'The Curious Case of the Web-Footed Mouse'. Several years ago, Ralph received a telephone call from an excited Brisbane resident who had just found in his swimming pool a creature that sounded decidedly strange - judging, that is, from the description that he gave over the phone. According to the man, it resembled a short-tailed mouse, but its forefeet were very distinctly webbed.

Australia has many species of shrew-like marsupial 'mice', plus several introduced and native species of true mice - but none has a short tail and webbed feet. Having said that, many totally new species of small mammal have been discovered Down Under during the past three decades, so could this short-tailed web-footed mouse be another one?

Very intrigued, Ralph decided to pay the Brisbane man a visit, and see for himself the nature of his pool's uninvited visitor - which he did, only to discover that the mystery mammal in question was...a bat! When a thoroughly bemused Ralph asked the pool owner whether he had actually noticed the animal's wings, the man replied: "Well, I did think the forefeet were just a bit large". Quite.

Ralph's own assistant had a similar experience not long afterwards, when he received a phone call alleging that a thylacine *Thylacinus cynocephalus* had been captured near Brisbane. Also known as the Tasmanian wolf, although this striped canine marsupial officially became extinct on the Australian mainland more than 2000 years ago many modern-day sightings have been claimed - but none has ever been conclusively verified. The capture of a mainland thylacine would therefore be a major cryptozoological triumph, and as his phone caller had described the beast that he had caught as being "large, dog-like, with stripes", Ralph's assistant naturally followed up the report straight away. After all, what else but a thylacine could it be? In fact, it could be just about anything, as he was soon to find out.

When he arrived at the home of the caller and his family, and was proudly shown their newly-captured animal, he was stunned to discover that it was nothing more startling than a quoll *Dasyurus maculatus* - a zoologically-familiar, cat-sized marsupial handsomely marked with white spots.

"But it's not large," he protested.

"Well, more or less large," they replied.

It was less.

"It has white spots, not black stripes," he exclaimed.

"Well," they said, "spots and stripes are both much the same thing, aren't they?"

No.

Not surprisingly, he was too taken aback to comment any further, but he no longer bothers to check out thylacine reports...

During the late 1990s, I received an interesting letter from a correspondent describing the head of a strange animal mounted as a trophy on a shield, and seen in a Portobello Road antique shop. My correspondent likened the head to that of a gigantic guinea pig with greyish rabbit-like colouring, mentioned that the shield was engraved "Kintail 1894", and stated that Kintail is one of the wilder areas of Inverness-shire. What could this creature possibly be?

The wombat - native to Australia, not Scotland!

Needless to say, the prospect of an unknown species of gargantuan guinea pig scampering over the heather on the hills of northern Scotland seemed about as likely as an undiscovered species of okapi browsing in the New Forest. However, I did concede the possibility that it was an absconded inmate from the type of travelling menagerie-cum-circus that was still common in Victorian times, and which often exhibited many unusual non-native animals.

Perhaps the Kintail mystery beast was a South American capybara, which not only resembles a gigantic guinea pig but is also closely related to guinea pigs. In 1990, an errant capybara named Bert went awol from Porfell Animal Land, near Lanreath, Cornwall, and thrived for 17 months in a man-made fishery close by before being recaptured alive. Bearing in mind, conversely, that its head was a mounted trophy, one can only assume that the Kintail specimen's period of freedom had been curtailed in a rather more terminal manner.

Resolving to unmask this cryptic creature, I tracked down the shop in question, and learnt that the animal was - of all things - a wombat! True, a wombat's head does look a little like that of an outsized guinea pig - but who would ever have imagined that a specimen of so exotic a species as this had been brought to Scotland more than a century ago (especially when even in modern times wombats have rarely been exhibited in British zoos)?

In fact, as I was soon to learn from the shop's owner, this particular wombat had died long before it had ever reached our shores - because it had been killed not in Kintail, Scotland, but in Kintail, Australia, where this marsupial mammal is of course a native species.

Many years ago, a cartoon in *Life Magazine* featured a New Jersey farmer visiting a circus where he sees a dromedary for the first time. "There ain't no such animal," exclaims the astonished farmer. Sometimes, I know just how he feels.

Chapter Twenty-Three
At the Sign of the Deathshead

On the 4th of September [1883] one of these insects flew into a house near the Brunswick Brewery, Leeds. There was a sick child in the house at the time, and the mother, terrified at what she thought an evil omen, could not be pacified for some time. The insect was secured and taken to Wardman's, the bird-stuffer's.

John Grassham - *The Naturalist's World* (January 1884)

*A*cherontia atropos, the insect referred to above, is nothing if not distinctive in appearance. A rare migrant to the UK, with a wingspan that can exceed 5.5in and a weight that can fall little short of 0.1oz, it is incontestably Britain's largest species of moth. Its plum-coloured, wavy-lined forewings and rich golden-yellow hindwings, not to mention its bulky body striped boldly underneath in dark brown and primrose bands, also render it one of this country's most attractive moths. Nevertheless, all of these features are eclipsed by a single, but very singular, additional characteristic - one which instantly identities this species and distinguishes it from all others in Britain, which has woven around it a near-indestructible web of folklore and fear, and which has earned it its extremely sinister-sounding English name.

This feature is a strange marking on top of its thorax's front portion, which, by a grotesque quirk of nature, forms a surprisingly realistic image of a human skull, ghostly white in colour with black, empty eyesockets. Enhancing this macabre image, the thoracic hairs bearing it are erectile, so that when they are raised up and down while the moth is resting, the 'skull' appears to be nodding!

To many superstition-ridden people in the past (and even to some today) this bizarre insignia is considered to be nothing less than the symbol of Death itself, so that *A. atropos* is commonly referred to as the deathshead, or deathshead hawk moth in full.

As can be imagined, its uncanny skull simulacrum has burdened this perfectly innocent insect with a fearful but wholly undeserved reputation as a harbinger of death, doom, and disaster, and has spawned a rich if ridiculous wealth of fanciful rural beliefs and old wives' tales. For example, on occasions when specimens have been observed in a given region just prior to an outbreak of an epidemic disease, the moths have been automatically blamed, and labelled as the messengers of impending mourning. Indeed, many people blamed the entire French Revolution upon the appearance of an unusual number of deathshead moths shortly before its com-

The Deathshead Hawk Moth

mencement. Moreover, this insect is said in some localities to be in league with witches and to murmur into their ears the names of persons soon to be visited by Death. In central France, it is widely believed that blindness will result if dust particles falling from the wings of a deathshead in flight happen to land in the eyes of anyone watching it...and so on, and so forth.

If these tales were treated lightly, with the humour and contempt that their imaginative but baseless claims deserve, they would constitute nothing more than intriguing yet harmless additions to the annals of modern-day folklore. Tragically, however, for a very long time they have been accepted as truth so wholeheartedly by the credulous and ingenuous that this magnificent moth has been subjected to extensive, barbaric persecution - as illustrated graphically by Rev. J.G. Wood's account in his *Illustrated Natural History* of an all too typical incident that he witnessed during the mid-19th Century:

> *I once saw a whole congregation checked while coming out of church, and assembled in a wide and terrified circle around a poor Death's-head Moth that was quietly making its way across the churchyard-walk. No one dared to approach the terrible being, until at last the village blacksmith took heart of grace, and with a long jump, leaped upon the moth, and crushed it*

beneath his hobnailed feet. I keep the flattened insect in my cabinet, as an example of popular ignorance, and the destructive nature with which such ignorance is always accompanied.

Yet ironically, and despite its eerie thoracic emblem, this much-maligned species was not always so intimately associated in the human mind with death and ill-fortune. Its first English name, apparently given to it in 1773 by nature writer Wilkes, was much more pleasant-sounding - the jasmine hawk moth, after a favoured food-plant of its caterpillar. In 1775, Moses Harris renamed it the bee tyger hawk moth, because of its brown and yellow stripes. If only he had been content with this. Sadly, however, in 1778 he changed its name again, this time to the deathshead, which, to its great cost, it has retained ever since. Its scientific name is no less ominous either. *Acherontia* is derived from Acheron, a river in the underworld of Greek mythology; and Atropos, eldest of the Fates or Moirae, was the black-veiled goddess responsible for cutting every mortal's Thread of Life.

Acherontia atropos has two close relatives that share its deathhead motif and also have equally doomladen names. *Acherontia lachesis* (inhabiting the Orient and also the Hawaiian Islands) is named after another of the three Fates, this time Lachesis, who measures out every's mortal's Thread of Life, thereby allotting the length of their life. And *Acherontia styx* (native to the Middle East and eastern Asia) is named after the river of death encircling the Greek underworld.

The tenacity of the deathshead's fallacious notoriety as a winged memento mori has even attracted the attention of the entertainment world. In 1967, Tigon Productions released a UK horror movie entitled *The Blood Beast Terror*, which starred Peter Cushing among others, and concerned a Frankensteinian entomologist of the Victorian era who constructs two humans with the ability to transform themselves into giant deathshead moths! This species is also associated with Salvador Dali's macabre surrealist film *Un Chien Andalou* (1929). And it appears on the cover of Thomas Harris's chilling novel *The Silence of the Lambs* (1988), as well as in the official theatrical release posters for the 1991 film adaptation starring Jodie Foster and Anthony Hopkins.

Only a fairly rare spring and summer visitor to Britain, the deathshead *A. atropos* occurs as a breeding species throughout North Africa and the Middle East and northwards to the Mediterranean. It is resident in parts of southern Europe, and migrates throughout Europe - but cases of breeding have been reported on occasion from Britain, with discoveries of caterpillars in several southern counties. Up to 5 in long, and of robust girth, the impressive-looking deathshead caterpillar varies from several shades of green to lemon, dark brown, or even purple, and is embellished on each flank by seven mauve or azure chevrons, edged decorously with bright yellow or cream. This bold but beautiful colour scheme is topped off with a hazy sprinkling of deep violet or sparkling white dots, and as a final flourish its body's rear end bears a striking curved horn.

Pupation takes place underground, the caterpillar digging its way 2-4 in beneath the soil surface and transforming after about a fortnight into a hard, brown, somewhat shiny chrysalis, surrounded by its cocoon of soil, whose function seems to be to maintain the correct degree of humidity around the chrysalis for its successful metamorphosis. By late September or early October, metamorphosis is generally complete and the adult moth emerges. Sometimes two generations occur in the same year; the second emerges during November.

Whereas the caterpillar thrives upon leaves (especially from the potato), the moth is a fruit-eater primarily - but not exclusively, as beekeepers will verify. Unlike the long slender proboscis ('tongue') of so many other hawk moths, perfectly designed for probing flowers in search of nectar, the deathshead's is much shorter and stouter, adapted instead for piercing the tough outer skin of fruit to obtain their succulent juices. However, it is also well-suited for puncturing the honey-containing cells in beehives, which has enabled the deathshead to expand its dietary scope, and explains why this attractive species is frequently discovered inside hives (as are *A. lachesis* and *A. styx*). This is exemplified by a startling discovery made in 1901 by the curator of a marine biology station's museum at Rovigno, Istria. As documented by Alfred Bunbury (*The Field*, 7 December 1901):

> *On the second floor of a house next to this zoological museum is a window whose wooden persienne have for a long time been closed. Though the shutters have been shut, the old wood was full of chinks, and Dr Hermes, the curator of the museum, noticed that a swarm of bees had utilised the space between the window and the shutters for a hive. Curious to see the work of the bees, on Oct. 1 he climbed up to the window, and was astonished to find it covered with death's head moths* (Acherontia atropos). *The moths, which are extremely fond of honey, had either failed to find their way out of the chinks through which they had entered, or, having fed too heavily on the food, had become dazed in the semi-dark light of the window. Dr Hermes and an assistant made their way into the room by another entrance, and removed a lower pane of the window. Quantities of moths were found hanging on the walls and others on the floor. Many that were dead had evidently been killed by the bees, which had got in under their wings, and those that were still alive were badly mutilated. More than one hundred large specimens were taken that day, and though every day five or six more were found in the same way, by Oct. 13, on which day Dr Hermes was summoned to Berlin, he thought that he had freed the last prisoner. But a few days ago a telegram informed him that 154 moths had again fallen a prey to the bees.*

Its liking for honey also appears to explain a characteristic of the deathshead that is every bit as uncanny and superficially unnatural as its thoracic skull sign - namely, it has the highly unexpected and singularly unmoth-like ability to squeak!

Records of this odd behavioural trait date back at least as far as the 1700s, and its physiological basis has incited much speculation. Some researchers assumed that the squeak was created by friction of the moth's abdomen against its thorax at the junction of these two body portions. Certain others suggested that it occurred if the moth's palps (accessory mouthparts) grated upon its proboscis. It is now known to result from the moth's inhalation of air into its pharynx, causing a stiffened flap (the epipharynx) to vibrate very rapidly.

In their *Illustrated Encyclopedia of Beekeeping* (1985), Roger Morse and Ted Hooper report that the epipharynx's oscillation yields a pulsed sound of approximately 280 pulses per second for a period of about 80 milliseconds (80 thousandths of one second), followed by a brief pause of 20 milliseconds before the epipharynx is held upwards, enabling the air to be blown out - creating the moth's famous squeak. Lasting a mere 40 milliseconds, it is a very high-pitched sound of about 6 kHz - above the audible range of many humans, though children and acute-eared adults can usually hear it. The moth will perform up to six of these 'squeak-cycles' in as little as one second, but the squeak shortens as the moth tires.

Naturally, there has been much debate about the precise purpose of the deathshead's squeaking. It is certainly a deliberate action, as the moth raises its body when doing so, which enables the sound to be carried to the bees through the air. And as the bees often react by permitting it to enter the hive unmolested (though its tough cuticle is sufficient to withstand occasional stings imparted by any less trusting hive workers, and it is in any case resistant to the venom imparted by such stings), it would seem that its squeaking serves as an effective password. Indeed, some researchers even assert that the moth's squeak is sufficiently similar to the sound made by the hive's queen bee to fool the workers into believing that their queen is instructing them to remain passive. According to this idea, therefore, the deathshead's squeaking is not so much a password as an inspired voice impression!

Moreover, as revealed by R.F.A. Moritz and colleagues, this extraordinary moth is even able to mimic the scent of the honey bees' cutaneous fatty acids, thus rendering it chemically invisible to them, and so further enabling it to move about freely inside their hives (*Naturwissenschaften*, vol. 78, 1991).

Intriguingly, writer and photographer Des Bartlett has discovered that in Kenya the presence of deathshead moths inside the beehives comes as a great shock to many of the native Kikuyu people, who seem convinced that they must be some form of wonderful queen bee (*Animals*, 30 July 1963). Also, their unexpected squeaking has been looked upon by all too many Westerners as something ominous or even preternatural - no doubt inspiring the earlier-mentioned myth that this species whispers into the ears of witches.

All of which brings us back to the subject of superstition, whose anachronistic, irrational utterings of ignorance and fear are still inciting mindless acts of vengeance and violence against this very elegant, showy, and thoroughly harmless insect. Even though we have entered the ultra-scientific 21st Century, there are still people who will not hesitate to kill any deathshead hawk moth that they encounter, atavistically recalling foolish fancies from the centuries of the past.

What can we say to such people? Ironically, the best reply is one that was published almost 150 years ago, but which is still as appropriate today as it was then. To quote from Louis Figuier's *The Insect World* (1872):

In spite of its ominous livery, the Atropos does not come from Hades; it is no envoy of death, bringing sadness and mourning. It does not bring us news of another world; it tells us, on the contrary, that Nature can people every hour; that it was her will to console them for their sadness, to grant to the twilight and to the night the same winged wanderers which are at once the delight and ornament of the hours of light and of day. This is the mission of science, to dissipate the thousands of prejudices and dangerous superstitions which mislead ignorant people.

I pray that its mission will succeed, to ensure the survival of the deathshead hawk moth and every other animal currently endangered by the baneful influence of fatuous notions that should have been buried by rationality and compassion a very long time ago.

Chapter Twenty-Four
The Unmentionables

Even though their existence is hotly disputed by science, most mystery creatures on record can be provisionally assigned with a measurable degree of certainty to at least one already established zoological group. The yeti, for example, is surely either a large anthropoid ape or a primitive species of human. The Congolese mokele-mbembe seems most likely to be a surviving sauropod dinosaur or a very sizeable species of monitor lizard, and so on. These are beasts that the cryptozoologist can feel secure with; they may disturb traditional scientists, but their eventual discovery would not require the creation of completely new categories within the zoological catalogue. In contrast, there are certain other mystery creatures that do not seem to resemble anything known on earth, either in the present or in the past...such animals defy every attempt made to classify them. Indeed, in some cases they are so bizarre that even the most open-minded of cryptozoologists finds it difficult to suppress a shudder of disbelief and discomfiture when casting his eyes warily through their files. For these seem to be creatures beyond cryptozoology, too peculiar and too perplexing for even the science of hidden life to feel comfortable with.

Karl P.N. Shuker – *From Flying Toads To Snakes With Wings*

When writing those lines just over a decade ago to introduce the final chapter in my book *From Flying Toads To Snakes With Wings* (1997), I had no idea just how popular that chapter – dealing with a wide range of truly weirder-than-weird mystery beasts, or 'creatures beyond cryptozoology' - would prove to be with readers. In fact, it has probably elicited more correspondence and additional information than any other chapter in the book. Consequently, it seemed appropriate to end this book with a new selection of 'ultra mystery beasts', creatures that refute comparison or categorisation even within the flexible boundaries of cryptozoology. Who knows, if Oscar Wilde's companion, Lord Alfred 'Bosie' Douglas, had been a cryptozoologist, he may well have termed such entities "the beasts that dare not speak their name". Or, as I prefer to call them, The Unmentionables.

Return of the Walking Fir Cone!

Speaking of *From Flying Toads To Snakes With Wings*: One of the strangest mystery animal reports emanating from my native British Isles appeared in that book of mine's Creatures Beyond Cryptozoology chapter:

Equally as incongruous...is a scaly anteater (pangolin) abounding in England, but how else can we explain the baroque beast encountered in Dumpton Park, Ramsgate, Kent, on April 16, 1954, by Police Constable S. Bishop, and described by him as a "walking fir-cone"? This is an excellent description of a pangolin, those insectivorous mammals covered in huge scales remarkably similar to those of a fir cone or pine cone. Pangolins, however, are wholly restricted to the tropics of Africa and Asia. Also, they are so difficult to maintain in captivity that they are seldom exhibited in zoos, and hardly ever kept as pets. So even if we do identify PC Bishop's beast as a pangolin, how can we explain its presence in a Kent park? We have simply exchanged one mystery for another, and emerged none the wiser.

On June 3 1999, however, I received a very interesting e-mail from reader John Mitchell of San Francisco, who had enjoyed reading about PC Bishop's 'walking fir-cone' in my book and wished to nominate what may indeed be another candidate for this odd beast's identity:

In March, I had the opportunity to visit a friend I had hitherto known only through email and telephone conversations...He is an insatiable collector, and his house is full of rare and wondrous contraptions many a museum would love to have. At one point, he asked if I'd like to meet his beloved pet of 15 years - an Australian shingleback skink. When he brought the lizard out and set it on the floor, my exact words were, "It looks like a walking pinecone!". Not the least surprised at this observation, my friend revealed that these skinks are commonly known in Australia as "pinecone lizards". In fact, "walking fir cone" would be a more apt name for this strange beastie, as the lizard's brown coloration, tight cone-like scales and elongated shape make it a dead ringer for a balsam fir cone...Given England's close ties with Australia, it is not hard to imagine that a visitor from Down Under might have transported a shingleback skink or two to England. If one were to escape or be released, it might well favor a park as its new residence, since these lizards love to hide under logs (further enhancing the fir cone appearance?) and can eat just about anything. I don't know how big the beast in question was supposed to be [no details appear to be recorded regarding its size], but shinglebacks are reported to come in a wide range of sizes. The one I saw was about a foot long. One more thing:

The shingleback or pine-cone skink

*having seen the peculiar head-shaped tail of this lizard (I nearly petted the
wrong end!) I no longer consider the possibility of the tatzelworm a mere
flight of Teutonic fancy.*

John's e-mail is an accurate description of the shingleback or pine-cone skink
Trachydosaurus rugosus, also called the bobtail or stumpy-tail. Probably the best-
known reptile in Australia due to its abundance, harmless vegetarian lifestyle, general sluggishness, and occurrence in patches of bush in and around a number of
Aussie city suburbs, the shingleback usually measures roughly 14in when adult, and
is indeed uncannily reminiscent of an animate fir or pine cone.

Its placid temperament and rugged survival ability make it an easy reptile to maintain as a pet, favouring John's suggestion that an escapee specimen in Kent might
explain PC Bishop's curious encounter in Dumpton Park. Certainly, the scenario of
a shingleback on the loose here is in my view a much more plausible prospect than
an absconded pangolin, and I am most grateful to John for bringing this thought-
provoking identity to my notice.

The Cryptic Case of the Colorado Platypus

Online cryptozoologists everywhere owe a great debt of thanks to longstanding
cryptozoological and herpetological enthusiast Chad Arment, author of *The Search
For Hidden Animals* (1995), for establishing a highly successful Internet cryptozoological discussion group - cz@onelist.com (now cz@yahoogroups.com). As its
webmaster, Chad has overseen discussions concerning all manner of fascinating
mystery beasts, including numerous examples not aired outside of cyberspace. One
of the most remarkable, however, is one that Chad himself brought to the group's
attention - the exceedingly curious case of the giant platypus from San Luis Valley,
in Colorado.

In a short cz@onelist posting of 18 June 1999, Chad referred to Christopher
O'Brien's book *The Mysterious Valley* (1996), in which O'Brien had briefly mentioned that strange animals have been seen for many years in San Luis Valley and
that during the 1960s some individuals claimed to have found a supposed platypus
in a high mountain lake within the Blanca Peaks area. Not surprisingly, Chad was
curious to learn whether anyone else knew anything further. On 7 August 1999,
Colorado-based cz@onelist contributor Bobbie Short posted an e-mail received by
her that same day from a correspondent, Rob Alley, concerning this same subject. It
read as follows:

*Several years ago Mike F., a successful Ketchikan businessman, contractor
and retired fisherman asked me following a chat about Sasquatches
whether I had ever studied or read anything about platypuses in North
America, specifically whether I knew of any prehistoric giant forms. When
I got back to him on this and replied that there may have been a slightly
larger earlier form known but not in N.A., but nothing really big, he looked
puzzled. I asked him why and after a moment's hesitation he answered that
as a young man forty or so years ago he had stood on shore near Mountain*

Point south of Ketchikan and spent a minute watching an animal in the water at very close range that simply resembled a giant platypus. He described the creature as dark with a bill and feet like a platypus only the overall size was six feet or possibly greater. He gave no mention of the tail if there was one. The sighting was in shallow water on a rocky shoreline and the creature was close to the surface. I could probably get a few more details such as season and so on. This man is an experienced commercial fisherman and stated categorically that it was not a known species of seal. Ocean temp here doesn't vary much from 50 degrees. All I have right now.

The platypus is an egg-laying, monotreme mammal, and as noted by Rob Alley there are indeed larger species of monotreme on record, but these are fossil forms, from Australasia (one such species, originally thought to have been a giant platypus, has since been reclassified as a zaglossid spiny anteater). In more recent years, fossil remains of monotremes have also been uncovered in the New World, but currently only in South America. However, only one living platypus species, *Ornithorhynchus anatinus*, is known, and that is of course exclusively Australian and freshwater. So if it was definitely not a seal, just what did Michael F. see near Mountain Point (which is in Alaska)? An otter is the most likely non-cryptozoological possibility, yet if his sighting was as good as it appears to have been, such an identity can hardly reconcile his description of a platypus-like bill and feet.

As for the Colorado mountain lake, unnamed by O'Brien: in an e-mail to me of 26 September 1999, Bobbie stated that Blanca Peak is in Colorado's Sangre de Cristo mountains and the only lake up that high (approximately 14,300 ft) is Lake Como, so this is presumably the body of water in which that creature was sighted. Nevertheless, these two mystery platypus-lookalike beasts - one freshwater in Colorado, the other marine in Alaska - remain among the most tenuous, but also most tantalising, to have emerged from the Crypto-Web, and are definitely Unmentionables!

Incidentally, the fossil monotreme remains lately discovered in South America mentioned earlier comprise a single upper and two lower teeth, which were found in Patagonia, Argentina, and date from the lower Palaeocene epoch (61 million years ago). In 1992, the species from which they originated was formally christened *Monotrematum sudamericanum* (but more recently some researchers have reclassified it within the existing Australian fossil genus *Obdurodon* as *O sudamericanum*). Its teeth are approximately twice as large as those of any other species of platypus, living or fossil, and it is currently the only platypus known from outside Australia.

Doubts About the Devil's Horse?

Imagine, if you will, a grey-plumaged hawk that for some unexplained reason has been invested with the long slender legs and neck of a stork, bestowing upon it a total height of 3.5-4ft when standing upright. Combined with these is a pair of extremely lengthy, black-pinioned wings attaining a span of 7ft when fully extended, plus an elegant, elongated tail. Lastly, added almost as an absurd afterthought (judging from its somewhat disorderly appearance), is a crest of drooping, black-tipped feathers that conjure up the incongruous image of a office scribe with an un-

The secretary bird

tidy sheaf of quill pens protruding from behind his ear!

The product of this exercise in creature composition will probably be a surprisingly accurate reconstruction of a truly singular species of African bird. Referred to in some Arab countries as 'the devil's horse' on account of its remarkable turn of running speed when called for, it is known scientifically as *Sagittarius serpentarius* - the secretary bird.

Named after its manner of stalking on foot in long, measured strides like an archer preparing to shoot his arrows, and also after its passion for attacking and devouring serpents great and small, only one modern-day species of secretary bird is currently recognised. Back in 1835, however, English zoologist William Ogilby attempted to distinguish three - and, in so doing, created a very curious if little-known cryptozoological enigma.

One of his three species comprised the secretary bird populations of eastern, central, and southern Africa; and another constituted those from western Africa's Senegambia region. The third, and by far the most unexpected, conversely, was based upon an illustrated description by French naturalist Pierre Sonnerat within his *Voyage dans la Nouvelle-Guinée* (1776) of an alleged variety of secretary bird existing very much further afield - in the Philippines!

As there are certainly no secretary birds indigenous to these (or any other) southeast Asian islands, the least contentious answer to this zoogeographical riddle is that

Sonnerat's description must have been founded upon specimens brought there by man, probably as exotic exhibits. To my mind, however, there is another possible explanation - rather more remote, but much more interesting from the standpoint of ornithological discovery.

The largest bird of prey known to be native to the Philippines is a magnificent crested species called *Pithecophaga jefferyi*, the monkey-eating or Philippine eagle, which is closely related to the Amazonian harpy. Sonnerat's description (and inaccurate depiction) of his supposed Philippine secretary bird contained certain morphological characters that set it well apart from the bona fide African version, yet which recalled this very impressive eagle.

For example, Sonnerat recorded that the feathers comprising the lower portion of the Philippine secretary bird's crest were longer than those of its upper portion. This is the exact converse of the crest structure in Africa's *Sagittarius*, but is suggestive of *Pithecophaga*. Similarly, whereas the central feathers are the longest ones in the tail of *Sagittarius*, Sonnerat claimed that the outermost feathers were the longest ones in the tail of its Philippine counterpart - a condition agreeing once again with that of *Pithecophaga*.

From these and other correspondences, it is possible that Sonnerat's description of what we now know to be a non-existent Philippine secretary bird was inspired at least in part by vague, second-hand accounts of *Pithecophaga*, the Philippine eagle.

If this is so, it is an especially interesting and cryptozoologically significant case (albeit until now a long-forgotten one), because at the time of Sonnerat's report *Pithecophaga* was still undiscovered by science. Not until it was formally described and named just over a century later by W.R. Ogilvie-Grant in 1896 did the existence of this spectacular species finally become known to the ornithological world. And certainly, if the so-called Philippine secretary bird is indeed one and the same as the Philippine eagle, it would not be the first time that accounts of a creature have actually appeared in the literature long before that creature's reality has been recognised, and its true identity unveiled, by science.

Speaking of out-of-place secretary birds: it is fully confirmed that in 1832 this snake-eating species was introduced onto the West Indian island of Martinique, in order to eliminate the highly-venomous yellow fer-de-lance *Bothrops* (=*Trigonocephalus*) *lanceolatus*. However, it failed to establish itself here - but this failure is probably no bad thing. After all, as the secretary bird is partial not only to snakes but also to small birds, especially ground-dwelling types, its permanent presence on Martinique may well have endangered this island's native avifauna - in turn affording another example of the disastrous events that can be set in motion when humankind attempts to meddle with an ecosystem's natural balance.

Making a Fuss About Fossas

The fossa *Cryptoprocta ferox* is a large superficially cat-like yet civet-related carnivore indigenous to Madagascar. There was formerly a much bigger version here too, the cave fossa *C. spelia*, measuring 6 ft (excluding its lengthy tail), weighing 200 lb, and as strong as a lion. However, this formidable beast is supposed to have died out many centuries ago - but did it? There have long been rumours and uncon-

Madagascar's fossa

firmed native reports of a giant-sized fossa existing in the more remote regions of Madagascar.

Consequently, in November 1999, biologist Luke Dollar trekked to one such region, the so-called Impenetrable Forest in the northeast of this island, officially known as Zahamena National Park, in the hope of espying one of these cryptic mammals (*Discover*, April 2000). Sadly, he did not do so. Nevertheless, in view of the fact that this locality is indeed virtually impenetrable, with no detailed maps of its interior ever having been made and much of its forest expanse still unexplored, hope must surely remain that this uninviting area may yet unveil a major surprise or two for cryptozoologists.

Setting the Seal on the Coelacanth Goblet

In 1996, French crypto-correspondent Michel Raynal sent me details of a remarkable Spanish goblet described to him (and also sketched) by one of his own contacts. The goblet in question is supposed to date from the 17th Century and depicts a strange fish that greatly resembles the modern-day African coelacanth *Latimeria chalumnae*, which remained undiscovered by science until December 1938, and has never been caught off European waters - only off South Africa, Mozambique, various neighbouring islands (including Madagascar), and (mostly) the Comoro Islands, plus a closely-related second species, *L. menadoensis*, discovered alive off Indonesia during the late 1990s.

Does the goblet provide evidence, therefore, for an unknown *Latimeria* population existing in the seas around Spain, or even Mexico - if the goblet was of Mexican origin but was brought back to Spain at a later date? As noted in my books *The Lost Ark* (1993) and *In Search of Prehistoric Survivors* (1995), some enigmatic silver figurines of fishes strikingly similar to *Latimeria* have already been found in Spain. (Originally, they were thought to have significantly pre-dated the discovery of *Latimeria* and possibly to have arrived in Spain from Mexico, but coelacanth seeker Prof. Hans Fricke has lately cast doubt upon these claims – *Environmental Biology of Fishes*, August 2001).

Michel's correspondent stated that the mystifying goblet was on display in the Carnegie Museum of Natural History at Pittsburgh, and that, emphasising the similarity of its portrayed fish to *Latimeria*, a specimen of *Latimeria* preserved in formaldehyde was exhibited alongside the goblet, with a caption asking whether there could indeed be coelacanths in the Atlantic still undiscovered by science. Greatly intrigued by this, on 30 April 1996 I wrote to the museum to request further details concerning the goblet - its origin, previous ownership, opinions from the museum's zoologists, whether any photos of it could be made available to me - and on 9 May 1996 I received a kind but very unexpected reply from Elizabeth A. Hill, Collection Manager of the museum's Section of Vertebrate Paleontology.

According to Ms Hill, the goblet was not on display there, and she could find no information that the museum had ever possessed such an item! Moreover, its Recent (i.e. modern-day) fish collection was disposed of many years ago to another museum, which meant that it does not exhibit *any* fish in formaldehyde. As a further check, Hill contacted the museum's Anthropology Division, which holds a collection of glassware, just in case the goblet was here instead, but it was not - nor did its records list anything fitting its description that had arrived there on long-term loan from another museum.

Indeed, the only remotely similar item on display in the Carnegie Museum of Natural History proved to be a small blue and white Wedgwood plate with *Latimeria* itself in the centre - according to its label, this plate was presented to the museum by the Buten Museum of Wedgwood in Merion, Pennsylvania.

I can only assume that if the story of the goblet is genuine, Michel's correspondent was mistaken as to which museum was displaying it - which is where you, gentle readers, come in! If anyone out there has seen this goblet while visiting a museum in the U.S.A. (or anywhere else, for that matter), I would greatly welcome details. Who knows - we may even have another 'quest for the thunderbird/ *Ameranthropoides* photo' in the makings here!

A Relic from the Garden of Eden's Serpent?

One of the most enigmatic yet hitherto-obscure zoological relics held in any scientific establishment must surely be the 8in by 4in piece of scaly rusty-red leathery skin contained inside Archive Box #1920.1714 within the very sizeable collection of the Chicago Historical Society. For according to its yellowing French label, this is supposedly a genuine piece of skin from the very serpent that tempted Eve in the Garden of Eden!

Indeed, the label goes on to say that the serpent was killed by Adam on the day after its treachery to Eve, using a stake whose traces can be seen on this skin sample, which was preserved by his family in Asia. Affixed to the skin is a document written on velum or similar hide in an Asian script. The society purchased this mystifying exhibit, along with many other items, in 1920 from the eclectic collection of Chicago confectioner Charles F. Gunther - a grand collector of curios.

Although the society's chief curator, Olivia Mahoney, has no doubt that it is a fraud (as opposed to a bona fide piece of snakeskin dating back to the dawn of time), no research has ever been conducted on it to ascertain what it really is. Moreover, Mahoney is very reluctant to permit any, in case the skin is damaged, and also because in her view it is so evidently a fake. That may well be, but it still doesn't answer what - if not a sample of skin from the Eden serpent - this anomalous object is.

As noted by the *Chicago Sun-Times*'s religion writer, Cathleen Falsani - who personally viewed this biblical(?) relic and then wrote about it in the newspaper on 10 October 2003 - after watching it being carried back in its box to the society's archives: "I couldn't help thinking about that scene from *Raiders of the Lost Ark*, where the Ark of the Covenant, and all of its power, is crated up and wheeled into a military warehouse among thousands of other generic crates. I wonder what else might be hiding anonymously in a quiet corner of a museum archive somewhere else, waiting to shock us with its mystery". What else indeed?

A Giant Owl and a Giant Hyrax...?

While carrying out Marine Corps training at a Californian bootcamp during the first half of 1999, cryptozoological investigator Nick Sucik put to good use the opportunity to question his fellow recruits, many of whom were hunters and from a variety of different U.S. states, concerning mystery animals. On 3 July 1999, Nick posted an extremely interesting account to cz@onelist.com, in which he detailed some of his findings. Two of the most intriguing sections concerned reports of a giant owl and a giant mystery herbivore, which I have quoted below with Nick's kind permission. Nick had this to say regarding the giant owl:

One thing I did hear about though, came from southern Texas. I was told of a huge white owl claimed to be about 4 feet tall. The local Mexican population was extremely superstitious of this animal and I was told that the one time this kid actually DID see the creature, everyone around him ran away in fear, their belief was that the owl was actually a witch and if it landed it would transform into just that, and if it looked at you, you'd receive a curse. Of course he didn't believe any of that, but it goes to show this creature was viewed in awe by the locals. The significance he stressed was the size of the owl and it being the color white made it an eerie spectacle. What I couldn't determine from him was if this bird was known scientifically, could it be found in bird books so to speak, or was it only known locally. He never gave a very confident answer, I think he only assumed it was known scientifically.

Needless to say, however, such an owl, of that size and colour, in that location, is certainly not known scientifically. Morphologically, probably the closest correspondence can be obtained with the snowy owl *Nyctea scandiaca*. However, this only stands 12-14in tall, and although of circumpolar distribution it is restricted to the arctic tundra - which is a far cry indeed from the environs of southern Texas and Mexico! The largest of all known species of living owl are the biggest eagle owls, notably the European eagle owl *Bubo bubo* and Blakiston's eagle owl *B. blakistoni* from the Far East (only recently reclassified as an eagle owl after traditionally being categorised as a fish owl), but these rarely if ever stand 2ft tall, let alone 4ft. Much larger owls are known from the fossil record, including *Ornimegalonyx oteroi*, formally described in 1976 from Cuba's Pleistocene, whose height exceeded 3ft, but none is believed to have survived into modern historical times.

Of course, giant owls are not new to cryptozoology. In his writings, veteran American cryptozoologist Mark A. Hall has promoted the possibility that the mysterious entity known as mothman, reported spasmodically from West Virginia during the 1960s, was actually a species of giant owl. Although still undescribed by science, such a bird was reputedly known to the native American people and also the early Western settlers in neighbouring Pennsylvania's Allegheny Plateau and Missouri's Ozark Mountains, who referred to it variously as the great owl, booger owl, or big-hoot. Could the white version reported by Nick be one and the same, thus extending this reclusive species' distribution southwards?

The second mystery beast that was brought to Nick's attention during his period of training at boot camp is even more fascinating:

> Another one that may very well be a familiar animal but sounded unique I heard by [i.e. from] one recruit we had from Ethiopia. I asked him if they had anything unusual or mysterious where he was from. He said no, but told me about an animal called in their language a 'deep', described as being "like a bear" except herbivore, they're about 2ft high and 4ft long found in the deserts of Ethiopia, light furred and very rare. He claimed it was considered dangerous even though it was herbivore. It's said to be incredibly strong and known to flip over vehicles by ramming them with its head! Unfortunately, he was unfamiliar with the English name with [i.e. for] this creature but brought it up because "there is nothing else like it in the world".

This posting elicited a reply from British cryptozoological researcher Allan Edward Munro, who voiced my own thoughts when he noted that Ethiopia's mystifying *deep* sounded like a very large hyrax - i.e. those famous elephant-related but diminutive and deceptively rabbit-like ungulate mammals from Africa and the Middle East, also known as dassies or conies, with hoof-like nails instead of claws. Nevertheless, no known species alive today is anywhere near as big or as powerful as the deep; the largest, Johnston's rock cavy *Procavia johnstoni* from Central Africa, is no more than 2ft in total length.

However, as Allan also noted, and as I have documented within my book *In Search*

Hyrax - could the deep *be an unknown giant version?*

of Prehistoric Survivors (1995), enigmatic bronze statuettes dating from the War-
ring States period of Chinese history (480-222 BC) have been likened by Brown
University ungulate expert Professor Christine Janis to an officially extinct giant
hyrax-like ungulate from the late Pliocene/early Pleistocene epoch known as *Pliohyrax* - thus implying that perhaps this pig-sized creature persisted into much more
recent times than suggested solely by the fossil record. (Incidentally, as its name
indicates, *Pliohyrax* has traditionally been classed as a gigantic form of hyrax;
lately, however, some palaeontologists have opined that it belongs to a distinct lineage of ungulates.) Certain early northern African geniohyids (fossil hyrax relatives)
were as big as tapirs or small horses, but these vanished millions of years ago.

Eager to learn more about the *deep*, I contacted Nick to request any additional information that he could supply to me, and on 5 July 1999 I received the following detailed reply:

> *I'm not sure that's a cryptid at all. According to Deems (the recruit), it was
> a known animal. I wondered though, was it known to his people or region-
> ally known or is it an actual scientific animal so to speak. I believe it may
> be the latter though he was unsure [of] the English name given to it...
> Demesa 21, migrated from Ethiopia when he was 14 and had been living in
> Las Vegas. Since he was originally from Africa I asked if he was familiar
> with Ethiopia having any mysterious animals. He didn't grasp what I
> meant by there being 'mysterious' or 'hidden animals'. I used Mokele-
> Mbembe as an example. He then understood but their philosophy of nature*

and the animals within tends to vary against ours. According to Demesa, whether an animal was unknown to science was irrelevant. Nature needed to be respected and exist unharmed by man. He told me that there was once a time in Africa when the animals lived harmoniously amongst men and that you could actually walk right past a lion without harm. After he was done with the Green Peace speech he did bring up a unique animal called in their language a "Deep". He described it as resembling a bear but smaller and herbivorous found in the desert part of the country. About 2.5 ft tall and 4 ft long and it didn't have [as] much hair as a bear he claimed. The strength of this animal was incredible, allegedly able to flip over a jeep ramming it with its head. Nowadays they're rare due to hunting. Demesa admired it because it was "one of a kind" like the lion, he said. That was about it. I think he did say he'd seen one once but at a distance. Allan Munro suggested this could be a "hyrax". I have no idea what that is.

If Demesa's description of the *deep*, as relayed by him to Nick, is accurate, it does not appear to be a species presently known to science (at least in the living state). In any case, it would certainly warrant investigation by any future zoological visitors to Ethiopia - especially in view of Demesa's claim that this creature is nowadays rare, due to hunting. How wonderful it would be if a chance comment by Demesa ultimately led to the scientific unveiling and accompanying protection of a significant new mammal in his native Ethiopia.

Indeed, it may not even be confined to Ethiopia. Chad Arment recently received an e-mail from a correspondent whose wife is Somalian. He informed Chad that his wife apparently knows of the *deep* (or at least of a creature resembling it). She claims that in Somalia it is referred to as the *dewacco* (in Somali, the 'c' in its name is pronounced like a deep 'h'). *Deep* or *dewacco*, there is clearly a notable mammalian mystery awaiting a satisfactory resolution in parts of eastern Africa's more remote terrain.

Something in the Air...?

There has been a revival of interest lately in the concept of atmospheric life-forms (see my book *The Unexplained*, 1996, for a survey of critters and other alleged sky beasts), due at least in part to considerable online discussion of certain mysterious fast-moving aerial objects referred as rods, which some researchers claim may be a type of living airborne entity. Consequently, I offer, albeit without comment, the following two accounts that I have received lately and which may be relevant to this subject.

The first of these was given to me in early March 2001 by a exceedingly knowledgeable, well-respected, but thoroughly mystified British naturalist who, while willing for me to publish an account of his sighting, was understandably reluctant to be publicly identified in relation to it, or to permit the precise location of his sighting to be publicly revealed until he has investigated it further himself. (I have full details on file.) However, he averred that he did indeed see what he described to me, and that he was stone-cold sober at the time.

His sighting had occurred a week before he contacted me, and had taken place while he and two colleagues were visiting a certain locality in the county of Powys, Wales. The reason why they were there is that the naturalist had been contacted by an inhabitant of that locality, asking him to come and see "something", but declining to say what that "something" was. Consequently, to avoid any chance of becoming the victims of a hoax, the naturalist and his two colleagues did visit this locality, spending three days there, but in secret - not having told the naturalist's informant that they were coming.

Their sighting occurred on the evening of Day 2. Standing at the edge of some woods by a quarry at around 6.00 pm, they suddenly spied an extraordinary entity. Measuring 2.5ft or so in length, it resembled a serpentine dragon with four short limbs, but its head was shaped very like that of a sea horse, and it was airborne - undulating and wriggling as it flew about 10ft above the surface of the quarry in a wide circle. They were unable to recall seeing any wings, but it had a long tail that terminated in a pair of horizontal, whale-like flukes. The entity was green in colour and shimmered somewhat, but appeared solid, not translucent or ethereal, and they watched it for 3-4 minutes, at a distance of roughly 50ft, before it finally vanished into one of the numerous caves and large crevices pitting the quarry.

The naturalist had the distinct impression while watching it that this creature, or whatever it may be, was deliberately seeking to keep them at bay, warning them off from approaching further into its territory. Attempts by him to photograph it proved unsuccessful, as the early evening light was not bright enough for the camera's automatic system to function satisfactorily. He is convinced that it was neither an optical illusion nor a model, but was truly alive, although its appearance was so uncanny that he felt chilled by the encounter.

After their sighting, they then visited the naturalist's informant, who duly confirmed that this is what he had hoped they would see, as he had seen it several times himself and was totally perplexed as to what it could be.

The second account, which I also received in early March 2001, was from a Californian correspondent (whose name I again have on file but am not releasing publicly, to preserve this person's privacy):

Just wanted to let someone know. Me and some of my family members were helping my brother put up a new roof. I took a break and was lying on my back on the roof. As I was looking up I saw the most fantastic thing. How can I say this. It was something like a bird but it was transparent. Like when you see one celled animals through a microscope. You can see the outline and the insides like a jelly fish. That's why I don't tell anybody, it sounds crazy. I want to say the shape of it was like a Pterodactyl. No I don't take drugs and I don't drink. The location is Hacienda Hgts, California.

Early reports of skyborne dragonesque entities have traditionally been explained away as meteorological phenomena such as aurorae, or even comets, but neither of these is plausible with regard to the Powys case recorded here. More recent reports of supposed sky serpents have emerged from several locations in the States, Brazil, and elsewhere, but these remain enigmatic. If any readers have had similar sightings, please feel free to email me with details at karlshuker@aol.com

Cureloms and Cumoms

Cryptozoologically, the Holy Bible is famous for mentioning two very mystifying creatures - the leviathan and the behemoth. Less well-known, however, is that another sacred work also contains a pair of highly mysterious animals. The following quote is from Ether 9:19 in the Book of Mormon: "And they also had horses, and asses, and there were elephants and cureloms and cumoms; all of which were useful unto man, and more especially the elephants and cureloms and cumoms". But what exactly are, or were, these latter two beasts?

Surfing the internet in search of answers, the best that I could find was the curelom entry in Wikipedia, which notes that Mormons have suggested various possibilities. These include: late-surviving mastodons or mammoths - Orson Pratt, an early Mormon apostle, identified cureloms as mammoths in the *Journal of Discourses,* 12:339-340; a yet-undiscovered but probably now-extinct species; or some South or Central American species with which Joseph Smith was unfamiliar, such as the tapir, llama, alpaca, or jaguar.

So unless any readers out there can shed some additional light on this matter, the curelom and cumom seem doomed to remain sequestered away in cryptozoology's most shadowy, unexplored backwaters.

An Unexpected Tail?

I am greatly indebted to correspondent Larry Tribula for sharing the following intriguing discovery with me, in a communication of 21 June 2002. While dining a little earlier that same year at a rustic restaurant called 'Antlers' in the Upper Peninsula of Michigan, which was filled with taxiderm exhibits, Larry noticed one very unusual specimen. He describes it as being a bear on all fours, displayed near to some black bears. However, this particular individual, roughly the size of a juvenile black bear, was golden brown in colour and, departing significantly from the typical ursine form, sported a long bushy tail, resembling that of anteaters but not quite as large.

Larry felt that this odd creature looked like a giant wolverine, noting that a true wolverine *Gulo gulo* was mounted close to it but was much smaller, only a third or a quarter the size of this strange 'tailed bear'. Larry did not consider it to be a hoax, and hopes to take a picture of it, should he ever return there. If, meanwhile, any of this book's readers happen to pay 'Antlers' a visit, I'd be very interested to see a photo of its enigmatic exhibit.

Look Out for the Invisible Fish!

On 1 July 1990, Gerald L. Wood, author of all three editions of the exhaustively-researched, definitive book on zoological superlatives, *The Guinness Book of Animal Facts and Feats*, wrote a letter to me concerning a range of different mystery animals, and which included the following brief but fascinating enquiry:

> *Do you know anything about a new species of fish that can make itself invisible? Discovered near coral reefs off the Seychelles in the Indian Ocean this mysterious creature turns from black to grey before 'vanishing'! Apparently a pair sell for £15,000.*

Knowing Gerald well, I was fully aware that this could not be a joke on his part. If he was seeking information from me concerning an invisible fish, then as far as he was concerned, such a fish really did exist. Consequently, although I had not encountered any information regarding it elsewhere, I vowed to investigate the case and get back to him with any news that I may uncover.

Tragically, however, this was not to be, as only a short time later Gerald died suddenly. And despite my best efforts, I never have succeeded in adding any details to those supplied by him. So if there are any aquarists or fish fanciers out there who know anything about this very baffling ichthyological mystery, I'd very greatly welcome any data that you could supply.

And finally: this last item, even though it is a genuine case, may not find favour with the more po-faced members of the cryptozoological and anomalozoological fraternity, and certainly it is not the most serious piece that I have ever written. Nevertheless, ever since it first appeared in the *CFZ Yearbook 1997*, edited by Jonathan Downes, it has remained a favourite of mine and also of the many correspondents who have told me how much they enjoyed it. So what better way to end a chapter on unmentionable creatures than with a lighthearted look at a truly iconoclastic curiosity, who just happened to be called Molly:

Pearl's a Singer (as Recorded by Whelkie Brooks?)

After our esteemed editor [Jonathan Downes]'s tour de force in *Fortean Studies* dealing with those musical murids of mellifluous melody (or singing mice, to thee and me), I felt compelled to share with you the wondrous saga of Molly, the singing oyster.

T'was a dark and stormy night - possibly - in 1840 when Mr Pearkes was first captivated by Molly's bewitching siren song, resonating from the dank depths of a cask of shellfish newly-delivered to his store in Vinegar Yard, Drury Lane. In reality, it sounded more like a high-pitched whistle, but if you should ever find yourself being serenaded by an oyster, you will no doubt appreciate why Pearkes did not worry himself unduly about such phonic technicalities. Here was a star in the making, a veritable diva from the sea depths!

And so it was that Molly was proudly displayed by Pearkes in Vinegar Yard for all to see, and hear. During the next few weeks, regally ensconced within a tub of oatmeal and brine, this shrill soprano of the shellfish world delighted an ever-present audience with her reedy repertoire - enchanting the acting company from the nearby Theatre Royal, and featuring in several contemporary newspaper stories. Indeed, as befitting this molluscan megastar, she even inspired a song, penned by a popular music-hall artiste called Sam Cowell; and her lamellibranchian likeness was faithfully committed to paper and ink within the pages of *Punch*, which dubbed her "a phenomenal bivalve".

Not surprisingly, Pearkes received several sizeable offers of money from circus owners and theatre managers to purchase Molly, but he declined to relinquish his protégé, thereby ensuring that this nacreous nightingale sang on in Vinegar Yard.

Tragically, however, in the unfathomable workings of the universe, dragons and shellfish sellers may well live forever (or seem to, at least), but not so little boys or singing oysters. And so it was that the sad day finally came when Molly whistled no more, having departed this mortal maelstrom for a bright celestial sea transcending her humble oatmeal abode.

But why - and how - did she acquire her unique vocal talent? Popular opinion was sharply divided, between the satirical and the scientific. On one hand, in the words of Douglas Jerrold, perhaps our fair Molly "had been crossed in love and only whistled to keep up appearances". On the other hand, her musical attributes most probably owed their origin to a simple structural quirk in her shell's architecture - water passing across her gills creating a whistling sound through a small hole that had somehow formed in her shell.

Whatever the answer, however, Molly's place in the chronicles of contemporary music must surely be assured. As to her favourite arias: whether or not they included such treasures as "Shell be coming round the mountain when she comes" or "Thank Heaven for little pearls" is not recorded. (And neither, as far as I am aware, are they. Such is life.)

Lest this harmless little history should indeed offend the sensitive mind of anyone scandalised by the abhorrent concept that science can be entertaining as well as educational, permit me now to bring this book to a close by recalling the following lines for future reflection:

> *At the height of laughter the universe is flung into a kaleidoscope of new possibilities. High comedy, and the laughter that ensues, is an evolutionary event. Together they evoke a biological response that drives the organism to higher levels of organization and integration. Laughter is the loaded latency given us by nature as part of our native equipment to break up the stalemates of our lives and urge us on to deeper and more complex forms of knowing.*

> Jean Houston – *The Possible Human*

Selected Bibliography
and Further Reading

JBNHS = *Journal of the Bombay Natural History Society*
PZSL Proceedings of the Zoological Society of London

-, 'Serpents in a Pile in South America' (*Scientific American*, vol. 3, 1848), p.147
-, 'Prairie Wolves in Epping Forest' (*The Naturalist's World*, vol. 1, 1884), pp.150-2
-, 'A Supposed Jackal Shot' (*The Times*, 2 March 1905)
-, 'New "Hound of the Baskervilles"' (*Daily Express*, 14 October 1925)
-, 'The Great Coati Hunt' (*Wolverhampton Express and Star*, 18 January 1934)
    [reprinted in *Wolverhampton Express and Star*, 13 January 2000), p.13]
-, 'Island Monster Shot' (*Daily Mirror*, 17 February 1940)
-, 'The Island "Monster" a Fox' (*Isle of Wight County Press*, 24 February 1940)
-, 'Zoological Jackpot' [Philadelphia pacarana] (*Fauna*, vol. 9, March 1947), p.31
-, 'Seen Alive in Europe for the First Time: A Pallid Cloud Rat' (*Illustrated London News*, vol. 213, 23 October 1948), p.469
-, 'Hunting the Aardvark: An Animal That Can Dig Faster Than a Gang of Men' (*Illustrated London News*, vol. 216, 14 January 1950), pp.54-5
-, [Cobra playmate] (*Loris*, vol. 11, December 1967), pp.123-4.
-, 'Adder For a Playmate' (ibid., vol. 11, December 1967), p.124.
-, 'The Mystery Hound is Back' (*Sunday Mirror*, 22 October 1972)
-, 'Enter the Thing of Delamere' (*Runcorn Weekly News*, 30 May 1974)
-, *Serpent Worship* (Reprinted by Tutor [not Tudor] Press: Toronto, 1980).
-, 'Yowling Sid' [miaowing cave racer] (*BBC Wildlife*, vol. 2, April 1984), p.173
-, 'Search for the Great Auk' (*Daily Telegraph*, 19 April 1986)
-, 'Sumatran Rhino Rediscovery' (*Oryx*, vol. 21, April 1987), p.120
-, 'Sly Cub Who Came in From the Cold' (*Daily Post*, 2 February 1990)
-, 'The Alberta Hyena' (*Fortean Times*, no. 61, February-March 1992), p.9
-, 'Totally Foxed' (*Wolverhampton Express and Star*, 15 February 1994)
-, 'Slither of Doubt Over Monster' [Gas Street monster] (*Wolverhampton Express and Star*, 5 and 6 August 1997)
-, 'Foxy Lady' (*Fortean Times*, no. 114, September 1998), p.18
-, 'Crowds Flock For Glimpse of 'Valleygator'' (*Sandwell Express and Star*, 3 April 1999), p.1
-, 'Valley Croc May Be Water Lizard' (ibid., 5 April 1999)
-, 'Eel Trap Plan to Catch 'Croc'' (ibid., 6 April 1999)
-, 'Pool of Mystery Reopens' (ibid., 7 April 1999)
-, 'Croc Ice Man' [Sandwell Valleygator] (ibid., 8 April 1999)
-, '9,000 Flock to See 'Valleygator'' (*Sandwell Chronicle*, 9 April 1999), p.3
-, 'Turtle Terror Time at Valley' (*Sandwell Express and Star*, 14 April 1999), p.1
-, 'Time Up For Beast of Pool' (ibid., 19 April 1999), p.11
-, 'Butcher's Tale Sounds a Croc' (ibid., 30 August 1999)
-, 'Fossil Bonanza in a Brazilian Cave' (*National Geographic Magazine*, vol. 197, January 2000)

-, 'Beached "Blob" Mystery Solved' (Reuters, 11 July 2003)

-, 'Wolves May Live On Chase – Expert' (*Stafford Post*, 30 May 2007)

, 'Ice Age Extinction Claimed Highly Carnivorous Alaskan Wolves' (*ScienceDaily*, 21 June 2007)

Alexander, A., 'Visitors Snap Up the Chance to Spot Croc' (*Sandwell Express and Star*, 2 April 1999)

Allen, G.M., *Extinct and Vanishing Mammals of the Western Hemisphere* (American Committee for International Wild Life Protection, Washington DC, 1942)

Anderson, A., *Prodigious Birds: Moas and Moa-Hunting in Prehistoric New Zealand* (Cambridge University Press, Cambridge, 1989)

Andersson, C.J., *Lake Ngami* (Hurst & Blackett, London, 1856)

Arment, C., 'Mystery Reptiles of the Samoan Islands' (*BioFortean Review* [online], no. 10, May 2007)

Armstrong, E.A., *The Folklore of Birds* (Collins, London, 1958)

Armstrong, P., 'The Dodo and the Tree' (*Geographical Magazine*, vol. 57, October 1985), pp.541-3

Ashley-Montague, F.M., 'The Discovery of a New Anthropoid Ape in South America?' (*Scientific Monthly*, vol. 29, September 1929), pp.275-9

Aymar, B. (ed.), *Treasury of Snake Lore: From the Garden of Eden to Snakes of Today in Mythology, Fable, Stories, Essays, Poetry, Drama, Religion, and Personal Adventures* (Greenberg: New York, 1956).

Bailey, G., 'Hens' Eggs and Cockle Shells: Weipa Shell Mounds Reconsidered' (*Archaeology in Oceania*, vol. 26, 1991), pp.21-3

Baker, G., 'Dead, But Not Forgotten' [Peel Street monster] (*Wolverhampton Express and Star*, 9 March 1994)

Balouet, J-C., *Extinct Species of the World* (Charles Letts, London, 1990)

Barloy, J-J., and Civet, P., *Fabuleux Oiseaux de la Préhistoire à Nos Jours* (Robert Laffont, Paris, 1980)

Bartlett, D., 'The Death's Head Hawk Moth' (*Animals*, vol. 2, no. 6, 30 July 1963), pp.150-1

Bassett, M.G., *'Formed Stones', Folklore and Fossils* (National Museum of Wales, Cardiff, 1982)

Beck, J.C., 'The Giant Beaver: A Prehistoric Memory?' (*Ethnohistory*, vol. 19, spring 1972), pp.109-22

Beckford, W.T., *Italy, With Sketches of Spain and Portugal, Vol. 2* (Baudry's European Library, Paris, 1834)

Beer, T., *Poachers Days* (Countryside Publications, Barnstaple, 1985)

Behura, B.K., 'On the Vocal Sounds of Snakes' (*Journal of the Utkal University, Bhubaneswar*, vol. 2, no. 1, July 1962), pp.40-2

Bennetts, J.A.W., 'The King of the Mambas' (*African Wild Life*, vol. 10, 1956), pp.335-6

Bergmann, J., *The Peafowl of the World* (Saiga, London, 1980)

Berridge, W.S., *Animal Curiosities* (Thornton Butterworth, London, 1922)

Birch, M.C., and Smith, D.S., 'The Other Museum: Victorian Fantasy, The Dodo, the Brick the Bishop Dropped, and...the Hope Entomological

Collections' (*Antenna*, vol. 6, no. 3, July 1982), pp.248-50

Bord, J., and Bord, C., *Alien Animals,* revised edn (Panther Books, London, 1985); *Modern Mysteries of the World* (Grafton Books, London, 1989)

Bradshaw, L., 'Trunko', in: Kryptid's Keep website (http://www.angelfire.com/ sc2/Trunko/trunko.html, accessed 13 January 2007)

Brewster, B., *Te Moa: The Life and Death of New Zealand's Unique Bird* (Nikau Press, Nelson, 1987)

Bridges, W., 'Africa's Champion Digger' (*Animal Kingdom*, vol. 61, February 1958), pp.20-2

Bright, M., *There are Giants in the Sea* (Robson Books, London, 1989)

Broadley, D.G., 'The Black Mamba (*Dendroaspis polylepis polylepis*)' (*African Wild Life,* vol. 15, December 1961), pp.299-302

Brock, S.E., *More About Leemo* (Robert Hale, London, 1969)

Buller, W.L., *A History of the Birds of New Zealand* (John van Voorst, London, 1872-3)

Bunbury, A., 'Death's Head Moths and Bees' (*The Field*, vol. 98, 7 December 1901), p.906

Burney, D.A., and Ramilisonina, 'The *Kilopilopitsofy*, *Kidoky*, and *Bokyboky*: Accounts of Strange Animals From Belo-sur-Mer, Madagascar, and the Megafaunal 'Extinction Window'' (*American Anthropologist*, vol. 100, 1998), pp.957-66

Burton, M., *More Animal Legends* (Frederick Muller, London, 1959); *Phoenix Reborn* (Hutchinson, London, 1959)

Burton, M., and Burton, R. (eds), *Purnell's Encyclopedia of Animal Life,* 6 vols (BPC, London, 1968-70)

Burton, R.W., 'The Burmese Wild Dog' (*JBNHS,* vol. 49, 1950), p.300

Campbell, B., and Lack, E. (eds), *A Dictionary of Birds* (T and AD Poyser, Calton 1985)

Carleton, M.D., and Olson, S.L., 'Amerigo Vespucci and the Rat of Fernando de Noronha: A New Genus and Species of Rodentia (Muridae: Sigmodontinae) From a Volcanic Island off Brazil's Continental Shelf' (*American Museum Novitates*, no. 3256, 1999), pp.1-59

Carse, D., 'A Snake's Call' (*The Times,* 5 October 1932)

Cartelle, C., and Hartwig, W.C., 'A New Extinct Primate Among the Pleistocene Megafauna of Bahia, Brazil' (*Proceedings of the National Academy of Sciences of the USA*, vol. 93, 25 June 1996), pp.6405-9

Cartmill, M., '*Daubentonia, Dactylopsila,* Woodpeckers and Klinorhynchy', in **R.D. Martin** et al. (eds), *Prosimian Anatomy, Biochemistry and Evolution* (Duckworth, London, 1977), pp.655-70

Chapman, P., 'Cave-frequenting Vertebrates in the Gunung Mulu National Park, Sarawak' (*Sarawak Museum Journal,* new series, vol. 34, December 1985), pp.101-13

Chapman, S., *The Monster of the Madidi: Searching For the Giant Ape of the Bolivian Jungle* (Aurum Press, London, 2001)

Chippaux, J.P., *et al.*, 'Study of the Efficacy of the Black Stone on Envenomation by Snake Bite in the Murine Model' (*Toxicon*, vol. 49, no. 5, April 2007) pp.717-20.

Clark, L., *The Rivers Ran East* (Hutchinson, London, 1954)

Clausen, L., *Insect Fact and Folklore* (Macmillan, London, 1954)

Cloudsley-Thompson, J.L., *Spiders, Scorpions, Centipedes, and Mites,* 2nd edn (Pergamon, London, 1968); 'Adaptational Biology of Solifugae (Solpugida)' (*Bulletin of the British Arachnological Society,* vol. 4, 1977), pp.61-71

Colbert, E.H., 'Presence of Tubulidentates in the Middle Siwalik Beds of Northern India' (*American Museum Novitates,* no. 604, 30 March 1933), 10 pp.; 'Study of *Orycteropus gaudryi* From the Island of Samos' (*Bulletin of the American Museum of Natural History*, vol. 78, 12 August 1941), pp.305-51

Coleman, L., 'Hunting Hyenas in the US' (*Fortean Times,* no. 187, June 1996), p.42

Coleman, L., and Clark, J., *Cryptozoology A to Z* (Fireside, New York, 1999)

Coleman, L., and Huyghe, P., *The Field Guide to Lake Monsters, Sea Serpents, and Other Mystery Denizens of the Deep* (Jeremy P. Tarcher/Penguin, New York, 2003)

Coleman, L., and Raynal, M., 'De Loys' Photograph: A Short Tale of Apes in Green Hell, Spider Monkeys, and *Ameranthropoides loysi* as Tools of Racism' (*The Anomalist,* no. 4, autumn 1996), pp.84-93

Cordier, C., 'Animaux Inconnus du Congo' (*Zoo,* vol. 38, April 1973), pp.185-91

Corliss, W.R., *Incredible Life: A Handbook of Biological Mysteries* (The Sourcebook Project, Glen Arm - Maryland, 1981)

Cott, H.B., 'Observations on the Life-habits of Some Batrachians and Reptiles From the Lower Amazon ...' (*PZSL,* 1926), pp.1159-78

Cottle, R., *et al.,* '*Euroleon nostras* (Fourcroy, 1785) (Neur.: Myrmeleontidae) Confirmed as Breeding in Britain' (*The Entomologist's Record,* vol. 108, nos. 11-12, November-December 1996), pp.299-300

Cousins, D., 'Ape Mystery' (*Wildlife,* vol. 24, April 1982), pp.148—9

Crichton, J., 'Enigma of the Hula' (*Christchurch Press,* 25 February 1967)

Croke, V., 'The Deadliest Carnivore' [includes giant fossa] (*Discover,* vol. 21, no. 4, April 2000), p.68-75

Curtler, M.S., 'Carolina Parakeet NOT Extinct?' (*Animals,* vol. 7, 23 November 1965), p.532

Davies, N., *et al.,* 'Croc Shock' [Sandwell Valleygator] (*Sandwell Express and Star,* 31 March 1999), p.1

Davy, J., *An Account of the Interior of Ceylon, and of Its Inhabitants* (Longman, Hurst, Rees, Orme, and Brown, London, 1821)

Declercq, N.F., *et al.,* 'A Theoretical Study of Special Acoustic Effects Caused By the Staircase of the El Castillo Pyramid at the Maya Ruins of Chichen-Itza in Mexico' (*Journal of the Acoustical Society of America,* vol. 116, no. 6, December 2004), pp.3328-35

Delmont, J., *Catching Wild Beasts Alive* (Hutchinson, London, 1931)

Demaitre, E., *L'Enfer do Pacifique* (Éditions Bernard Grasset, Paris, 1935)

Denis, A., *On Safari* [book] (Collins: London, 1963).

Denis, A., and Denis, M., *On Safari* [LP] (Pye Records: London, 1962).

Dieterlen, F., 'Über den Haarbau des Andenwolfes, *Dasycyon hagenbecki*

(Krumbiegel, 1949)' (*Säugetierkundliche Mitteilungen,* vol. 2, 1954), pp.26-31

Dinsdale, T., *The Leviathans* (Routledge and Kegan Paul, London, 1966; 2nd edn - Futura, London, 1976)

Dinsmore, J.J., 'History and Natural History of *Paradisaea apoda* on Little Tobago Island, West Indies' (*Caribbean Journal of Science,* vol. 10, 1967), pp.93-100

Ditmars, R.L., *Snakes of the World* (Macmillan, New York, 1931)

Doughty, R., *Feather Fashions and Bird Preservation* (University of California Press, Ewing, 1975)

Duffy, B., 'Howling Beast is Back in Village of the Baskervilles' (*Sunday Express,* 10 September 1989)

Duncan, P.M. (ed), *Cassell's Natural History,* 6 vols (Cassell, Petter, and Galpin, London, 1883-9)

Dunton, J., 'Monster of the Pool Netted After 20 Years' (*Sandwell Express and Star,* 19 July 2003), p.4

Eberhart, G.M., *Mysterious Creatures: A Guide to Cryptozoology,* 2 vols (ABC-Clio, Santa Barbara, 2002)

Éhik, G., 'Jackal or Reed-wolf From Hungary' (*Annales HistoricoNaturales - Musei Nationalis Hungarici,* vol. 31, 1937), pp.11-15

Erickson, C.J., 'Percussive Foraging in the Aye-aye (*Daubentonia madagascariensis*)' (*Animal Behaviour,* vol. 41, 1991), pp.793-801; 'Cues For Prey Location By Aye-ayes, (*Daubentonia madagascariensis*)' (*Folia Primatologica,* vol. 69 supplement, 1998), pp.35-40

Erickson, C.J., *et al.,* 'Percussive Foraging: Stimuli For Prey Location By Aye-ayes, (*Daubentonia madagascariensis*)' (*International Journal of Primatology,* vol. 19, 1998), pp.111-122

Fenell, S., 'Letter' [passenger pigeon] (*Fate,* vol. 19, January 1966), p.132

Fenner, C., *Bunyips and Billabongs: An Australian Out of Doors* (Angus and Robertson, Sydney, 1933)

Figuier, L., *The Insect World* (Cassell, London, 1872); *Mammalia: Their Various Forms and Habits* (Cassell, London, 1892)

Fitzsimons, F.W., *Snakes* (Hutchinson, London, 1932)

Flannery, T., and Schouten, P., *A Gap In Nature: Discovering the World's Extinct Animals* (Heinemann, London, 2002)

Freeman, D., '"Belling Snakes"' (*The Times,* 27 September 1932)

Fresnel, F., 'Sur l'Existence d'une Espèce Unicorne de Rhinocéros dans la Partie Tropicale de l'Afrique' (*Comptes Rendus de l'Académie des Sciences,* vol. 26, 1848), p.281

Fricke, H., and Plante, R., 'Silver Coelacanths From Spain are Not Proofs of a Pre-Scientific Discovery' (*Environmental Biology of Fishes,* vol. 61, no. 4, August 2001), pp.461-3

Fuller, C., 'Bears on Two Legs?' [plus *yokyn*] (*Fate,* vol. 30, May 1977), p.34

Fuller, E., *The Great Auk* (Errol Fuller, Southborough, 1999); *Extinct Birds,* 2nd edn (Oxford University Press, Oxford, 2000)

Gardner, J.B., 'A Ball of Gartersnakes' (*Copeia,* 1955), p.310; 'A Garter Snake "Ball"' (ibid., 1957), p.48

Gervais, P., and Verreaux, J., 'Nouveau Genre de Didelphe' (*L'Institut, Journal Universel des Sciences et des Sociétés Savantes en France et à l'Étranger, Première Section: Sciences Mathématiques, Physiques et Naturelles*, no. 427, 3 March 1842), pp.75-6

Gesner, C., *Historiae Animalium, Liber I qui est de Quadrupedibus Viviparis... (apud* Christ. Froschoverum, Tiguri, 1551)

Gill, B., and Martinson, P., *New Zealand's Extinct Birds* (Random Century, Auckland, 1991)

Gilliard, E.T., *Birds of Paradise and Bower Birds* (Weidenfeld and Nicolson, London, 1969)

Goeldi, E.A., 'On the Rare Rodent *Dinomys branickii* Peters' (*PZSL, 7* June 1904), pp.158—65

Gorman, P., 'Charmed I'm Sure' (*Mail on Sunday – YOU Magazine*, 11 June 1989), pp.24-6.

Gosse, P.H., *The Romance of Natural History, Second Series* (Nisbet and Co., London, 1867)

Gould, S.J., *Hen's Teeth and Horse's Toes* (Pelican, Middlesex, 1983)

Green, K.M., 'Childhood Discovery' [Peel Street monster] (*Wolverhampton Express and Star*, 3 March 1994)

Greenway, J.C., *Extinct and Vanishing Birds of the World,* 2nd edn (Dover, New York, 1967)

Greenwell, J.R., 'Raiders of the Lost Auk' (*ISC Newsletter,* vol. 6, spring 1987), pp.5—7

Greenwood, P.H., and Thomson, K.S., 'The Pectoral Anatomy of *Pantodon buchholzi* Peters (a Freshwater Flying Fish) and the Related Osteoglossi dae' (*PZSL,* vol. 135, 1960), pp.283—301

Griscelli, P., 'Deux Oiseaux Fossiles de Nouvelle-Calédonie' (*Bulletin de la Société d'Études Historiques de Nouvelle Calédonie*, vol. 29, 1976), pp.3-6

Grzimek, B. (ed), *Grzimek's Animal Life Encyclopedia,* 13 vols (Van Nostrand, New York, 1972—5); *Grzimek's Encyclopedia of Mammals,* 5 vols (McGraw-Hill, New York, 1990)

Hadley, P., 'The Passenger Pigeon' (*Science,* vol. 71, 14 February 1930), p.187

Hardy, R.W.H., *Travels in the Interior of Mexico in 1825, 1826, 1827 & 1828* (Henry Colburn and Richard Bentley, London, 1829)

Harris, P., 'The Red Herring is Back After 500 Years' (*Daily Mail*, 1 April 1998), p.3; 'Dog With Two Noses' (ibid., 10 September 2005), p.3; 'Two-Nosed Dogs? We've Sniffed Out Packs of Them!' (ibid., 17 September 2005), p.7

Harrison, T.P., 'Bird of Paradise: Phoenix Redivious' (*Isis*, vol. 51, 1960), pp.173-8O

Hartenberger, J-L., 'La Dent du "Diahot": La Solution n'est pas dans la Poche!' (*La Recherche,* vol. 21, February 1990), pp.240—1

Hartline, P.H., 'Physiological Basis for Detection of Sound and Vibration in Snakes' (*Journal of Experimental Biology,* vol. 54, 1971), pp.349-72

Hartwig, W.C., 'A Giant New World Monkey From the Pleistocene of

Brazil' (*Journal of Human Evolution*, vol. 28, 1995), pp.189-95

Hartwig, W.C., and Cartelle, C., 'A Complete Skeleton of the Giant South American Primate Protopithecus' (*Nature*, vol. 381, 23 May 1996), pp.307-10

Hawkshaw, J.C., 'Tinamu in Hants' (*The Field*, vol. 95, 20 January 1900), p.95

Hayes, I.J., *The Land of Desolation, Being a Personal Narrative of Adventure in Greenland* (Sampson Low, Marston, Low, and Searle, London, 1871)

Hazewinkel, J.C., 'A One-horned Javanese Rhinoceros Shot in Sumatra, Where It Was Not Thought to Exist' (*Illustrated London News,* vol. 93, 23 December 1933), pp.1018—19

Hediger, H., 'Ein Nashorn mit Dürer-Hörnlein' (*Zoologische Garten,* vol. 39, 1970), pp.101-6

Henry, G.M., *A Guide to the Birds of Ceylon* (Oxford University Press, London, 1955)

Heptner, W.G., 'Über das Java-Nashorn auf Neu-Guinea' (*Zeitschrift für Säugetierkunde,* vol. 25, 1960), pp.128-9

Hershey, D.R., 'The Widespread Misconception That the Tambalacoque Absolutely Required the Dodo For Its Seeds to Germinate' (*Plant Science Bulletin*, vol. 50, 2004), pp.105-8

Hershkovitz, P., 'On the South American Small-eared Zorro *Atelocynus microtis* Sclater (Canidae)' (*Fieldiana Zoology,* vol. 39, 24 February 1961), pp.505-23

Hervey, D., '"*Plotosus canius*" and the "Snake-stone"' (*Nature,* vol. 62, 24 May 1900), p.79

Heuvelmans, B., 'Le Problème de la Dentition de l'Oryctérope' (*Bulletin – Museum Royal d'Histoire Naturelle de Belgique*, vol. 15, August 1939), pp.1-30; *On the Track of Unknown Animals* (Rupert Hart-Davis, London, 1958); *In the Wake of the Sea-Serpents* (Rupert Hart-Davis, London, 1965); *Les Derniers Dragons d'Afrique* (Plon, Paris, 1978); 'Annotated Checklist of Apparently Unknown Animals With Which Cryptozoology is concerned' (*Cryptozoology,* vol. 5, 1986), pp.1-26

Hichens, W., 'African Mystery Beasts' (*Discovery,* vol. 18, December 1937), pp.369-73

Hickley, M., 'The Great Croc Hunt' (*Daily Mail*, London, 2 April 1999), p.13

Hodge, W.H., 'The Not So Terrible Mouse' (*Natural History,* vol. 56, September 1947), pp.310-11

Hollman, J., 'A Fruitful Affair' [aardvark cucumber] (*BBC Wildlife*, vol. 14, November 1996)

Hopkins, S.S.B., 'The Evolution of Fossoriality and the Adaptive Role of Horns in the Mylagaulidae (Mammalia: Rodentia)' (*Proceedings of the Royal Society B*, vol. 272, 14 July 2005), pp.1705-13

Hopley, C.C., *Snakes: Curiosities and Wonders of Serpent Life* (Griffith and Farran, London, 1882)

Howl, C.A., 'Mystery is Cleared Up' [Peel Street monster] (*Wolverhampton Express and Star*, 22 March 1994)

Hünicken, M.A., 'A Giant Fossil Spider (*Megarachne servinei*) From Bajo de Véliz, Upper Carboniferous, Argentina' (*Boletin de la Academia Nacional de Ciencias, Córdoba, Argentina*, vol. 53, 1980), pp.317-341

Hutchins, R.E., *Trails to Nature's Mysteries: The Life of a Working Naturalist* (Dodd, Mead, New York, 1977)
Hutchinson, M., 'I Thought I Saw a Huia Bird' (*Birds*, vol. 3, September-October 1970), pp.110—13

Izzard, R., *The Hunt for the Buru* (Hodder and Stoughton, London, 1951)

'Jacamar', 'Birds of Paradise Island' (*The Field*, vol. 231, 18 January 1968), p.106
Jaeger, P., 'A New Species of *Heteropoda* (Araneae, Sparassidae, Heteropodinae) From Laos, the Largest Huntsman Spider?' (*Zoosystema*, vol. 23, no. 3, 2001), pp.461-5
James, C., and Downes, J. (eds), *CFZ Expedition Report 2006 Gambia* (CFZ Press, Bideford, 2006)
James, G.P.L., 'Purring Snakes' (*The Times*, 31 August 1929), p.6
Jensen, A.S., 'The Sacred Animal of the God Set' (*Der Kgl. Danske Videnskabernes Selskab, Biologiske Meddelelser*, vol. 11, 1934), pp.1-19
Jepsen, G.I., '*Tubulodon taylori*, a Wind River Eocene Tubulidentate From Wyoming' (*Proceedings of the American Philosophical Society*, vol. 71, August 1932), pp.255-74
Jordan, J.A., *Elephants and Ivory: True Tales of Hunting and Adventure* (Rinehart, New York, 1956); *The Elephant Stone* (Nicholas Kaye, London, 1959)

Keith, A., 'The Alleged Discovery of an Anthropoid Ape in South America' (*Man*, vol. 29, August 1929), pp.135-6
Kidson, A.L., 'Is the Moa Really Extinct?' (*Christchurch Press*, 18 January 1978); '"Moa Hunters" on Visit' (ibid., 16 February 1978); 'The Moa Hunt' (ibid., 8 March 1978)
King, P.P., *Narrative of a Survey of the Intertropical and Western Coasts of Australia Between the Years 1818 and 1822* (Murray, London, 1827)
Kingdon, J., *East African Mammals: An Atlas of Evolution in Africa, Volume I* (Academic Press, London, 1971)
Kiparsky, V., 'Paradiesvögel im Russichen Schrifttum' (*Arsbok-Societas Scientiarum Fennica*, vol. 39B, 1961), pp.1-18
Knappert, J., *The Aquarian Guide to African Mythology* (Aquarian Press, Wellingborough, 1990)
Knight, C., *Pictorial Museum of Animated Nature*, 2 vols (London Printing and Publishing Company, London, 1856—8)
Knott, J., '"Crowing Snake"' (*African Wild Life*, vol. 16, September 1962), p.170
Koens, J.H., 'Purring Snakes' (*The Times*, 26 August 1929)
Krumbiegel, I., 'Der Andenwolf — ein Neuentdecktes Grosstier' (*Umschau*, vol. 49, 1949), pp.590-1; 'Der "Andenwolf", *Dasycyon hagenbecki* (Krumbiegel, 1949)' (*Säugetierkundliche Mitteilungen*, vol. 1, 1953), pp.97-104

'L., E.', 'Bundles of Snakes' (*American Naturalist*, vol. 14, 1880), pp.206-7
Lamberton, C., 'Contribution à la Connaissance de la Faune Subfossil de Madagascar. Note XV. *Plesiorycteropus madagascariensis* Filhol.' (*Bulletin de l'Académie Malgache*, new series, vol. 25, 1946), pp.25-53
Lawley, D., 'On Pool Patrol To Find Crocodile' (*Sandwell Express and Star*, 1

April 1999); 'Valleygator Puts Bite Into Region's Image' (ibid., 13 April 1999); 'Is This Huge Turtle the Valleygator?' (ibid., 30 July 2001), p.1

Lawrence, R., 'Sun-Spiders' (*Animals*, vol. 6, 27 April 1965), pp.232—5

Lehmann, T., 'Biodiversity of the Tubulidentata Over Geological Time' (*Afrotherian Conservation*, no. 4, May 2006), pp.6-11

Leister, M., *Flying Fur, Fin and Scale* (Stemmer House, Owings Mills, Maryland, 1977)

Leonard, J.A., *et al.*, 'Megafaunal Extinctions and the Disappearance of a Specialized Wolf Ecomorph' (*Current Biology*, published online 21 June 2007)

Ley, W., *The Lungfish and the Unicorn* (Viking Press, New York, 1941); *Salamanders and Other Wonders* (Phoenix House, London, 1955); *Exotic Zoology* (Viking Press, New York, 1959)

Lhote, H., and Weyer, H., *Sahara* (Kummerly and Frey, Berne, 1980)

Llewellyn, I., 'Letter' [passenger pigeon] (*Fate*, vol. 18, September 1965), p.129

Long, J.L., *Introduced Birds of the World* (David & Charles, Newton Abbot, 1981)

Lönnberg, E., 'On a New *Orycteropus* From Northern Congo and Some Remarks on the Dentition of the Tubulidentata' (*Arkiv för Zoologi*, vol. 3, 1906) 35 pp.

Lowe, W.P., *The Trail That is Always New* (Gurney and Jackson, London, 1932)

Loys, F. de, 'A Gap Filled in the Pedigree of Man?' (*Illustrated London News*, vol. 174, 15 June 1929), p.1040

Lum, P., *Fabulous Beasts* (Thames and Hudson, London, 1951)

Lydekker, R. (ed), *The Royal Natural History*, 6 vols (Frederick Warne, London, 1894—6); 'A One-horned White Rhinoceros' (*The Field*, vol. 110, 28 December 1907), p.119; 'Musical Notes in Tortoises' (ibid., vol. 111, 27 June 1908), p.1117; 'Holmwood's Rhinoceros' (ibid., vol. 114, 24 July 1909), p.193

McFarlane, D.A., and MacPhee, D.E., '*Amblyrhiza* and the Quaternary Bone Caves of Anguilla, British West Indies' (*Cave Science*, vol. 16, April 1989), pp.31—4

McIlroy, A., 'Canadian May Hold Key to Chilean Blob' (*Globe and Mail*, Toronto, 10 July 2003)

MacInnes, D.G., 'Fossil Tubulidentata From East Africa' (*British Museum, Natural History, Fossil Mammals of Africa*, no. 10, 1956), pp.1-38

Mackal, R.P., *Searching for Hidden Animals* (Doubleday, Garden City, 1980); *A Living Dinosaur? In Search of Mokele-Mbembe* (E.J. Brill, Leiden, 1987)

McKenzie, A., *Pioneers of Martins Bay*, revised edn (Whitcomb and Tombs, Christchurch, 1952)

Mallinson, J., *Travels in Search of Endangered Species* (David and Charles, London, 1987)

Martin, Y., 'Rare Bird or Flight of Fancy?' [Alice McKenzie's putative moa] (*Press*, New Zealand, 3 February 2007)

Mayrhofer, D., 'Australian Mounds: Birds' Nests or Aboriginal Middens?' (*New Scientist*, vol. 128, 20 October 1990), p.24

Mehta, K.L., 'A Pinkheaded Duck (*Rhodonessa caryophyllacea* (Latham)) at

Last?' (*JBNHS*, vol. 57, 1960), p.417

Mendel, H., '*Euroleon nostras* (Fourcroy, 1785) a British Species and Notes on Ant-Lions (Neuroptera: Myrmeleontidae) in Britain' (*The Entomologist's Record*, vol. 108, nos. 1-2, January-February 1996), pp.1-5

Menzies, J.I., 'Reflections on the Ambun Stones' (*Science in New Guinea*, vol. 13, 1987), pp.170-3

Metcalf, D.W., 'Werewolves in Sussex' [letter re giant grey hill foxes] (*The Countryman*, vol. 55, no. 2, summer 1958), p.357

Meyer, A.B., 'The Rhinoceros in New Guinea' (*Nature,* vol. 11, 4 February 1875), p.268

Michell, J., and Rickard, R.J.M., *Living Wonders* (Thames and Hudson, London, 1982)

Miller, H., 'The Cobra, India's "Good Snake"' (*National Geographic*, vol. 138, no. 3, September 1970), pp.392-409.

Miller, M., and Miller, K., 'In Search of Loys' [sic] Giant Ape of South America' (*World Explorer*, no. 2, spring-summer 1992), pp.18-22

Minton, S.A., and Heatwole, H., 'Snakes and the Sea' (*Oceans,* vol. 11, April 1978), pp.53-6

Minton, S.A., and Minton, M.R., *Venomous Reptiles* (George Allen and Unwin, London, 1971)

Moffat, C.B., 'The Mammals of Ireland' (*Proceedings of the Royal Irish Academy*, vol. 44B, no. 151, 1937-8), pp.61-128

Molamure, A.H.E., 'Pearls From Elephants' (*Loris*, vol. 17, 1970), pp.27-8

Monckton, C.A.W., *Last Days in New Guinea* (John Lane The Bodley Head, London, 1922)

Montandon, G., 'Un Singe d'Apparence Anthropoide en Amérique du Sud' (*Comptes Rendus de l'Académie des Sciences,* vol. 188, 11 March 1929), pp.815-17

Montgomery, G.G. (ed), *The Evolution and Ecology of Armadillos, Sloths, and Vermilinguas* (Smithsonian Institution Press, Washington DC, 1985)

Moriarty, C., *Eels: A Natural and Unnatural History* (David and Charles, Newton Abbot, 1978)

Moritz, R.F.A., *et al.*, 'Chemical Camouflage of the Death's Head Hawkmoth (*Acherontia atropos* L.) in Honeybee Colonies' (*Naturwissenschaften*, vol. 78, no. 4, 1991), pp.179-82.

Morris, R., and Morris, D., *Men and Snakes* (Hutchinson, London, 1965)

Morse, R.A., and Hooper, T. (eds), *The Illustrated Encyclopedia of Beekeeping* (Blandford, Poole, 1985)

Mourer-Chauviré, C., and Balouet, J.C., 'Description of the Skull of the Genus *Sylviornis* Poplin, 1980 (Aves, Galliformes, Sylviornithidae New Family), a Giant Extinct Bird from the Holocene of New Caledonia', in **Alcover, J.A., and Bover, P.** (eds), *Proceedings of the International Symposium "Insular Vertebrate Evolution: the Palaeontological Approach"* (*Monografies de la Societat d'Història Natural de les Balears*, vol. 12, 2005) pp.205-218

Mourer-Chauviré, C., and Poplin, F., 'Le Mystère des Tumulus de Nouvelle-Calédonie' (*La Recherche*, vol. 16, September 1985), p.1094

Mudie, J., *Early Years: The Childhood of Famous People* (Purnell, London, 1966)

Mulligan, J.H., 'Samoa: Government, Commerce, Products, and People' (Consular

Reports, May 1896)

Musser, G.G., and Newcomb, C., 'Malaysian Murids and the Giant Rat of Sumatra' (*Bulletin of the American Museum of Natural History,* vol. 174, 1983), pp.327—598

Nagy, E., 'Der Ausgerottete Ungarische Rohrwolf (*Canis lupus*) war Kein Schakal (*Canis aureus*)' (*Säugetierkundliche Mitteilungen,* vol. 4, 1956), pp.165-7

Netting, M.G., and Wilkes, D., 'Scorpion Stone - a Reputed Cure for Scorpion Sting and Snake Bite' (*Bulletin of the Antivenom Institute of America,* vol. 2, 1929), p.99

Newall, V., *Discovering the Folklore of Birds and Beasts* (Shire Publications, Tring, 1971)

Newton, A., and Gadow, H., *A Dictionary of Birds* (Adam and Charles Black, London, 1896)

Newton, M., *Encyclopedia of Cryptozoology: A Global Guide* (McFarland & Co, Jefferson, 2005)

Nigg, J., *A Guide to the Imaginary Birds of the World* (Apple-wood Books, Cambridge - Massachusetts, 1984)

Nightingale, N., 'The Animal in Question' [Peel Street monster] (*Wolverhampton Express and Star,* 2 March 1994)

Nowak, R.N. (ed), *Walker's Mammals of the World,* 2 vols, 6th edn (John Hopkins University Press, Baltimore, 1999)

Nugent, R., *The Search For the Pink-Headed Duck* (Houghton Mifflin, Boston, 1991)

O'Brien, C., *The Mysterious Valley* (St Martin's Press, New York, 1996)

Oldfield, S., 'Stranger on the Street' [Peel Street monster] (*Wolverhampton Express and Star,* 24 February 1994)

Patterson, B., 'The Fossil Aardvarks (Mammalia: Tubulidentata)' (*Bulletin of the Museum of Comparative Zoology, Harvard University,* vol. 147, 1975), pp.185-237

Penny, M., *Rhinos: Endangered Species* (Christopher Helm, London, 1987)

Philipps, T., 'A Purring Snake' (*The Times,* 22 August and 30 December 1929); '"Belling" Snakes - the Puff Adder's Call to Its Mate' (ibid., 7 September 1932)

Phillipps, W.J., *The Book of the Huia* (Whitcomb and Tombs, Christchurch, 1963)

Picasso, F., 'More on the Mono Grande Mystery' (*Strange Magazine,* no. 9, spring-summer 1992), pp.41, 53

Pickford, M., 'New Fossil Orycteropodidae (Mammalia: Tubulidentata) From East Africa' (*Netherlands Journal of Zoology,* vol. 25, 1975), pp.57-88

Pierce, S.K., *et al.*, 'Microscopic, Biochemical, and Molecular Characteristics of the Chilean Blob and a Comparison With the Remains of Other Sea Monsters: Nothing But Whales' (*Biological Bulletin,* vol. 206, June 2004), pp.125-33

Pitman, C.R.S., *Report on a Faunal Survey of Northern Rhodesia* (Crown Agents, London, 1934); *A Game Warden Takes Stock* (James Nisbet, London, 1942)

Pocock, R.I., 'The Alleged Wild Dog of Mt. Popa, Burma' (*JBNHS,* vol. 39, 15 December 1937), pp.851-2

Poplin, F., '*Sylviornis neocaledoniae* n. g., n. sp. (Aves), Ratite Éteint de la Nouvelle-Calédonie' (*Comptes Rendus de l'Académie des Sciences Paris Sér. D*, vol. 290, 1980), pp.691-4

Poplin, F., and Mourer-Chauviré, C., '*Sylviornis neocaledoniae* (Aves, Galliformes, Megapodiidae), Oiseau Géant Éteint de l'Île des Pins (Nouvelle-Calédonie)' (*Geobios*, no. 18, February 1985), pp.73-97

Powney, N., 'Giant Caterpillar' (*Fortean Times*, no, 225, special issue 2007), p.72

Preston, E., 'More On That Coatimundi' (*Wolverhampton Express and Star*, 14 March 1994)

Reuss, F.A.T., 'Humming Snakes of North America' (*Herpetologica*, vol. 7, 1951), p.144

Rich, P.V., and Tets, G.F. van (eds), *Kadimakara: Extinct Vertebrates of Australia* (Pioneer Design Studio, Lilydale, 1985)

Rich, T.H.V., *et al.*, 'The Supposed *Zygomaturus* From New Caledonia is a Rhinoceros: A Second Solution to an Enigma and Its Palaeogeographic Consequences', in M. Archer (ed), *Possums and Opossums: Studies in Evolution* (Surrey Beatty and Sons, and Royal Zoological Society of NSW, Sydney, 1987), pp.769-78

Richardson, A., [jackal head record] (*The Countryman*, summer 1975), p.186

Richardson, K.C., *et al.*, 'Adaptations to a Diet of Nectar and Pollen in the Marsupial *Tarsipes rostratus* (Marsupialia: Tarsipedidae)' (*Journal of Zoology, Series A*, vol. 208, February 1986), pp.285-98

Ridley, H.N., 'A Visit to Fernando de Noronha' (*The Zoologist*, series 3, vol. 12, 1888), pp.41-9

Ritchie, G.B., 'Letter' [puff adder's bell-like note] (*East Africa,* September 1929)

Roach, J., 'Chilean Mystery Blob Identified as Sperm Whale Skin' (*National Geographic News*, 25 August 2003)

Robey, D., 'TV Quest for a Lost Bird' [moal (*Leicester Mercury,* 4 May 1978)

Rosenberg, H.I., and Richardson, K.C., 'Cephalic Morphology of the Honey Possum, *Tarsipes rostratus* (Marsupialia: Tarsipedidae); an Obligate Nectarivore' (*Journal of Morphology*, vol. 223, 1995), pp.303-23

Sánchez-Villagra, M.R., *et al.*, 'The Anatomy of the World's Largest Extinct Rodent' (*Science*, vol. 301, 19 September 2003), pp.1708-10

Sanderson, I.T., *Abominable Snowmen: Legend Come to Life* (Chilton, Philadelphia, 1961); 'The Dire Wolf' (*Pursuit*, vol. 7, October 1974), pp.91—4

Savage, R.J.G., and Long, M.R., *Mammal Evolution: An Illustrated Guide* (British Museum, Natural History, London, 1986)

Saville, D.B.O., 'Gliding and Flight in the Vertebrates' (*American Zoologist*, vol. 2, 1962), pp.161-6

Schaller, G.B., *et al.*, 'Javan Rhinoceros in Vietnam' (*Oryx*, vol. 24, April 1990), pp.77-80

Schultz, W., 'Zur Kenntnis des Hallstromhundes (*Canis hallstromi*, Troughton, 1957)' (*Zoologischer Anzeiger*, vol. 183, 1969), pp.47-73

Scott, H.H., 'The Story of the Nototheria' (*Australian Museum Magazine,* vol. 3, 1927), pp.24-5

Selden, P.A., *et al.*, 'The True Identity of the Supposed Giant Fossil Spider *Megarachne*' (*Biology Letters of the Royal Society*, vol. 1, 2005), pp.44-8

Selous, F.C., 'On the South-African Rhinoceroses' (*PZSL,* 1881), pp.725-34

Shircore, J.O., 'Two Notes on the Crowing Crested Cobra' (*African Affairs,* vol. 43, 1944), pp.183-6

Shoemaker, M.T., 'The Mystery of the Mono Grande' (*Strange Magazine*, no. 7, April 1991), pp.2-5, 56-60

Shuker, K.P.N., *Mystery Cats of the World: From Blue Tigers to Exmoor Beasts* (Robert Hale, London, 1989); 'A Selection of Mystery Birds' (*Avicultural Magazine,* vol. 96, spring 1990), pp.30-40; *The Lost Ark: New and Redis covered Animals of the 20th Century* (HarperCollins: London, 1993); *In Search of Prehistoric Survivors: Do Giant 'Extinct' Creatures Still Exist?* (Blandford Press, London, 1995); 'Howling Wolf' [New Guinea singing dog] (*Wild About Animals*, vol. 1, November-December 1996), p.72; *From Flying Toads To Snakes With Wings* (Llewellyn, St Paul, 1997); 'Don't Lose Your Head – It's the Waheela' (*All About Dogs*, vol. 2, March-April 1997), pp.54-5; 'Beware – Valleygator!' (*Fortean Times*, no. 126, September 1999), p.48; *Mysteries of Planet Earth: An Encyclopedia of the Inexplicable* (Carlton, London, 1999); 'Making Monsters...' [Peel Street monster] (*Fortean Times*, no. 134, May 2000), p.47; *The Hidden Powers of Animals* (Marshall Editions, London, 2001); *The New Zoo: New and Rediscovered Animals of the Twentieth Century* (House of Stratus, Thirsk, 2002); *The Beasts That Hide From Man: Seeking the World's Last Undiscovered Animals* (Paraview, New York, 2003); 'Living Dinosaurs: 25 Years On Their Cryptic Trail' (*Beyond Magazine*, no. 7, July 2007), pp.14-23

Simpson, G.G., 'Rodent Giants' (*Natural History,* May-June 1930), pp.305-13

Singh, L.P., and Editors, 'The Pinkheaded Duck (*Rhodonessa caryophyllacea* (Latham)), Again' (*JBNHS*, vol. 63, 1966), pp.440-1

Smith, A., *Illustrations of the Zoology of South Africa, Volume I* (Smith, Elder, and Co., London, 1838)

Smith, H.C., 'Peafowl Without a Train', (*JBNHS*, vol. 34, 15 July 1930), pp.583-4

Spittel, R.L., 'The Devil Birds of Ceylon' (*Loris,* vol. 11 supplement, 1968), pp.1-14

Stanbury, P., and Phipps, G., *Australia's Animals Discovered* (Pergamon, Oxford, 1980)

'Stany', *Loin des Sentiers Battus, Volume I* (Table Ronde, Paris, 1951)

Steinberger, A.B., *Report on Samoa* (GPO, Washington DC, 1874)

Stivens, D., 'Has the Huia Gone for Good?' (*Wildlife,* vol. 18, July 1976), p.323

Stone, T., 'Origins and Environmental Significance of Shell and Earth Mounds in Northern Australia' (*Archaeology in Oceania*, vol. 24, 1989), pp.59-64

Stoneham, C.T., *Hunting Wild Beasts With Rifle and Camera* (Hutchinson, London, 1933)

Stracey, P.D., *Elephant Gold* (Weidenfeld and Nicolson, London, 1963)

Swords, M.D., 'On the Possible Identification of the Egyptian Animal-God Set' (*Cryptozoology*, vol. 4, 1985), pp.15-27

Szunyoghy, J., 'Systematische Revision des Ungarländischen Schakals, Gleich zeitig eine Bermerkung über das Rohrwolf-Problem' (*Annales Historico-Naturales - Musei Nationalis Hungarici,* new series, vol. 8, 1957), pp.425-33

Taffs, A. (ed.), *The World of Wonders: A Record of Things Wonderful in Nature, Science, and Art* (Cassell, Petter, and Galpin: London, 1881-2).
Tegeteier, W.B., 'The Tinamu as an English Game Bird' (*The Field,* vol. 63, 23 February 1884), p.276; 'The Tinamou in England' (ibid., vol. 66, 12 September 1885), p.390
Tennent, J.E., *Sketches of the Natural History of Ceylon* (Longman, Green, Longman, and Roberts, London, 1861)
Tennyson, A., and Martinson, P., *Extinct Birds of New Zealand* (Te Papa Press, Wellington, 2006)
TeVelde, H., *Seth, God of Confusion* (E.J. Brill, Leiden, 1967)
Thomas, O., 'Milk Dentition in *Orycteropus*' (*Proceedings of the Royal Society,* January 1890), pp.246-8; 'Name of the Aardvark' (*Proceedings of the Biological Society of Washington,* vol. 14, 2 April 1901), p.24
Thorneycroft, G.V., 'African Palm Civet' (*African Wild Life,* vol. 12, 1958), p.81
Till, H., 'Dead, But Not Forgotten' [Peel Street monster] (*Wolverhampton Express and Star,* 9 March 1994)
Tratz, E-P., 'Ein Beitrag zum Kapitel "Rohrwolf", *Canis lupus minor* Mojsisovics, 1887' (*Säugetierkundliche Mitteilungen,* vol. 6, 1958), pp.160-2
Trivedi, B.P., 'Was Maya Pyramid Designed to Chirp Like a Bird?' (*National Geographic Today,* 6 December 2002)
Troughton, E., 'A New Native Dog From the Papuan Highlands' (*Proceedings of the Royal Zoological Society of New South Wales,* 1957), pp.93-4; *Furred Animals of Australia,* 8th edn (Angus and Robertson, Sydney, 1965); 'The Early History and Relationships of the New Guinea Highland Dog (*Canis hallstromi*)' (*Proceedings of the Linnaean Society of New South Wales,* vol. 96, 1971), pp.93—8
Tudor, K., 'Snapped Up!' [Sandwell Valleygator] (*Sandwell Express and Star,* 6 April 1999)
Tzu-Chiang Chou, 'Chinese Phoenix and the Bird of Paradise - a New Identifica tion of the Ancient Chinese Phoenix' (*Bulletin of the Institute of Ethnology of Taipeh, Academia Sinica,* no. 24, autumn 1967), pp.81-122

Urbani, B., et al., 'La Creación de un Primate: el "Simio Americano" de François de Loys (*Amer-anthropoides loysi* Montandon, 1929) o la Historia de un Fraude' (*Anartia, Publicaciones Ocasionales del Museo de Biologia de la Universidad del Zulia,* no. 16, 2001), pp.1-56
Utton, T., 'Blob From the Deep' (*Daily Mail,* 4 July 2003), p.9

Walker, A.O., 'The Rhinoceros in New Guinea' (*Nature,* vol. 11, 28 January 1875), p.248; 'The Rhinoceros in New Guinea' (ibid., vol. 11, 4 February 1875), p.268
Walker, H.W., *Wanderings Among South Sea Savages* (Witherby, London, 1909)
Wallace, A.R., *The Malay Archipelago* (Macmillan, London, 1869)
Waller, H., *The Last Journals of David Livingstone, in Central Africa, Volume II* (John Murray, London, 1874)

Watling, D., *Birds of Fiji, Tonga and Samoa* (Millwood Press, Wellington, 1982)

Wendt, H., *Out of Noah's Ark* (Weidenfeld and Nicolson, London, 1956)

Wever, E.G., and Vernon, J.A., 'The Problem of Hearing in Snakes' (*Journal of Auditory Research,* vol. 1, 1960), pp.77-83

Wheeler, A., *The World Encyclopedia of Fishes* (Macdonald, London, 1985)

Whitley, G., 'Mystery Animals of Australia' (*Australian Museum Magazine,* vol. 7, 1 March 1940), pp.132-9

Wolhuter, H., *Memories of a Game-Ranger* (Wild Life Protection Society of South Africa, Johannesburg, 1948)

Wood, C.A., and Wetmore, A., 'A Collection of Birds From the Fiji Islands' (*Ibis,* vol. 2, 1926), pp.91-136

Wood, G.L., *The Guinness Book of Animal Facts and Feats,* 3rd edn (Guinness Books, London, 1982)

Wood, J.G., *Illustrated Natural History,* 3 vols (Routledge, Warne, and Routledge, London, 1859-63); *Insects Abroad* (Longmans, Green, and Co., London, 1883)

Woodruff, S., 'The Rattle Snake Disarmed By the Leaves of the White Ash' (*American Journal of Science,* series 1, vol. 23, 1823), pp.337-9.

Wootton, A., *Animal Folklore, Myth and Legend* (Blandford Press, London, 1986)

Young, B.A., 'Morphological Basis of "Growling" in the King Cobra, *Ophiophagus hannah*' (*Journal of Experimental Zoology,* vol. 260, 1991), pp.275-87; 'Snake Bioacoustics: Toward a Richer Understanding of the Behavioral Ecology of Snakes' (*Quarterly Review of Biology,* vol. 78, 2003), pp.303-25

Index of Animal Names

A

Aardvark, common, 17-20, 24-27
    Egyptian, 23-24
    Ethiopian, 18
    Gaudry's, 22
    Ituri Forest, 18
    Madagascan, 21-23
    pygmy, 22
Acherontia atropos, 263-267
    lachesis, 265-266
    styx, 265-266
Acrocinus longimanus,110
Adder, common, 45, 245-246, 248
    night, 40
    puff, 42, 47, 194, 243
Afropavo congensis, 166
Aglais urticae, 114
Alca impennis, 127-128
Alectura lathami, 227
Alopex lagopus, 97
Amarok, 98
Amblyrhiza inundata, 143-145
Ameranthropoides loysi, 49 - 62, 276
Amphicyonids, 98
Anaconda, 48
Anas poecilorhyncha, 124
Anomalurus derbianus, 104
Ant-lions, 108 - 110
Anteater, giant, 19, 26, 219, 282
Apatemyids, 175, 177
Ape, de Loys's American, 49 - 62, 276
    skunk, 256
Aplodontia rufa, 147
Apteryx haasti, 126, 226
Arachnocampa luminosa, 110
Arapaima, 75
Arapaima gigas, 75
Astrotia stokesii, 249
Ateles belzebuth, 50

    paniscus, 53
Atelocynus microtis, 101
Auk, great, 119, 127-128
Aye-aye, 167 - 177
    giant, 173

B

Babirusa, 207
Babyrousa babyrussa, 207
Badak tanggiling, 204 - 205
Bat, common slit-faced, 26
Bear, tailed mystery, 282 - 283
Beaver, giant, 145 - 146
    mountain, 146 - 147
Bee, honey, 267 - 268
Beetle, harlequin, 110 - 113
Bibymalagasy, 23
Big-hoot, 278
Bird, vermilion, 84
Bird of paradise, Chinese, 82 - 83
    Count Raggi's, 82 - 83
    Goldie's, 83
    greater, 83 - 85
    king, 83
    long-tailed sicklebill, 83
    red, 83
Bitis gabonica, 33
    nasicornis, 33
Blackfly, Dundass Island giant, 107
Blob, Chilean, 133 - 136
Boa constrictor, 192 - 193
Bokyboky, 212
Bonytongues, 75, 159
Borophagine, 100
Bothrops (=*Trigonocephalus*)
    lanceolatus, 274
Brecon hebetor, 114
Brush turkey, 227
Bubo blakistoni, 278
    bubo, 278
    nipalensis blighi, 185

Acknowledgements

I wish to express my sincere thanks to the following persons, societies, organizations, and publications for their very kind interest and most generous assistance during my researches for this book and its subsequent preparation.

Within the United Kingdom

Avicultural Magazine; Dr Geoff Bailey; Simon Baker; Dr Michael Bassett; Endymion Beer; Trevor Beer; Birmingham Public Libraries; Lawrence Brennan; British Library; British Museum (Natural History); G.H.H. Bryan; Owen Burnham; Robert Burton; the Centre for Fortean Zoology (CFZ); Philip Chapman; D.N. Clark-Lowes; Prof. John L. Cloudsley-Thompson; the late Tim Dinsdale; Dudley Public Libraries; Excalibur Books; Reginald Fish; Folklore Frontiers; Fortean Times; Richard Freeman; Alan Gardiner; Michael Goss; the late Mary Harvey; Robert Hill; the late Clinton Keeling; my agent Mandy Little of Watson, Little Limited; Lorna Lloyd; Colin McCarthy; Richard Monteiro; Sarah Moran; Dr Desmond Morris; Mark O'Shea; Alan Pringle; Radio WM; Bob Rickard; Sandwell Public Libraries; Paul Screeton; Steven Shipp; Mary D. Shuker; Paul Sieveking; Society For Psychical Research; the late Gertrude Timmins; University of Birmingham; University of Leeds; Uri Geller's Encounters; Walsall Public Libraries; Wolverhampton Public Libraries; Gerald L. Wood; World of Beatrix Potter Attraction; Zoological Society of London.

In addition, I am extremely grateful to John Murray (Publishers) Ltd for granting me permission to include on p. 125 a short excerpt from 'The Adventure of the Deptford Horror', from The Exploits of Sherlock Holmes by Adrian Conan Doyle and John Dickson Carr; to Owen Burnham for permitting me to publish his photograph of a pseudo-three-horned rhinoceros; and to the Zoological Society of London for permitting me to publish their photograph of one of their New Guinea singing dogs.

Overseas

Agassiz Museum of Comparative Zoology, Harvard University (USA); Chad Arment (USA); Bill Asmussen (USA); Dr Graham Baker (South Africa); Lance Bradshaw (USA); Brisbane Courier-Mail (Australia); Juan Cabana (USA); Ceylon Bird Club (Sri Lanka); Carmen Garcia-Frias Checa (Spain); the late Mark Chorvinsky (USA); Arthur C. Clarke (Sri Lanka); Loren Coleman (USA); cryptolist@yahoogroups.com (USA); cz@yahoo.groups.com (USA); Fate (USA); Dr Susan M. Ford (USA); Tonio Galea

(Malta); Bill Gibbons (Canada); the late J. Richard Greenwell (USA); Dr P. Humphrey Greenwood (South Africa); Isabela Herranz (Spain); the late Dr Bernard Heuvelmans (France); Elizabeth A. Hill (USA); T.W. Hoffman (Sri Lanka); Prof. Shoichi Hollie (Japan); International Society of Cryptozoology (USA); Donald Michael Kraig (USA); Gerard van Leusden (Netherlands); Paul B. Lu (USA); Dr Roy P. Mackal (USA); Dr James I. Menzies (Papua New Guinea); Bob Michaels (USA); John Mitchell (USA); Mariano Moldes (Argentina); Dr Ralph Molnar (Australia); Michael Newton (USA); Chris Orrick (USA); Michel Raynal (France); William Rebsamen (USA); Dr Maria F. Rutzmoser (USA); Ron Scarlett (New Zealand); Bobbie Short (USA); Strange Magazine (USA); Nick Sucik (USA); Lars Thomas (Denmark); Larry Tribula (USA); Dr Bruce A. Young (USA).

I am also sincerely grateful to Lance Bradshaw and Bill Asmussen for permitting me to use Bill's Trunko artwork; and to Dr Roy P. Mackal for permitting me to use his artistic representation of the emela-ntouka.

Finally, I extend a particular vote of thanks to Janet and Colin Bord for so kindly writing the foreword to this book's original edition back in 1991, for supplying from their Fortean Picture Library many of the illustrations included in it, and for their ever-willing assistance in locating all manner of extraordinary items of information concerning an array of no less extraordinary animals; and to Jonathan Downes, a longstanding friend and enthusiastic supporter of my work, who has now made it possible via the CFZ Press for this new, 21st Century edition of Extraordinary Animals to see the light of day. Equally, in deep gratitude for their interest, encouragement, and faith in both incarnations of this book, I would like to express my especial thanks to my original publisher, Robert Hale Ltd, and to my new publisher, CFZ Press. I have attempted to obtain permission for the use of all substantial quotations known by me to be from material still in copyright. Any omission brought to my attention will be rectified in any future edition of this book.

My Website

If you have enjoyed this or any of my other books and articles, and have any information or personal experiences/eyewitness accounts relating to any aspect of cryptozoology, animal anomalies, or animal mythology that you consider may be of interest to me and that you wish to share with me, please email me at: karlshuker@aol.com

And for full details concerning my work and publications, please visit my website at: http://members.aol.com/karlshuker (it can also be accessed at: http://hometown.aol.com/karlshuker). Many thanks indeed.

Dr. Karl P.N. Shuker BSc PhD FRES FZS is a zoologist who is internationally recognised as a world expert in cryptozoology, as well as in animal mythology and allied subjects relating to wildlife anomalies and inexplicabilia. He obtained a BSc (Honours) degree in pure zoology at the University of Leeds (U.K.), and a PhD in zoology and comparative physiology at the University of Birmingham (U.K.). He is now a freelance zoological consultant and writer, living in the West Midlands, England. The author of 12 books (translated into over a dozen foreign languages) and countless articles, Dr Shuker is also the official zoological consultant for *Guinness World Records*, and has acted as a consultant and/or contributor for many other publications and television programmes. Dr. Shuker appears regularly on television and radio, has served as a question setter for the BBC's cerebral quiz show *Mastermind*, and has travelled widely throughout the world during the course of his researches. He is a Scientific Fellow of the prestigious Zoological Society of London, a Fellow of the Royal Entomological Society, a Member of the International Society of Cryptozoology, and other wildlife-related organisations, a consultant for the Centre for Fortean Zoology, and is also a Member of the Society of Authors.

THE CENTRE FOR FORTEAN ZOOLOGY

So, what is the Centre for Fortean Zoology?

We are a non profit-making organisation founded in 1992 with the aim of being a clearing house for information and coordinating research into mystery animals around the world. We also study out of place animals, rare and aberrant animal behaviour, and Zooform Phenomena – little-understood "things" that appear to be animals, but which are in fact nothing of the sort, and not even alive (at least in the way we understand the term).

Why should I join the Centre for Fortean Zoology?

Not only are we the biggest organisation of our type in the world, but - or so we like to think - we are the best. We are certainly the only truly *global* cryptozoological research organisation, and we carry out our investigations using a strictly scientific set of guidelines. We are expanding all the time and looking to recruit new members to help us in our research into mysterious animals and strange creatures across the globe. Why should you join us? Because, if you are genuinely interested in trying to solve the last great mysteries of Mother Nature, there is nobody better than us with whom to do it.

What do I get if I join the Centre for Fortean Zoology?

You get a four-issue subscription to our journal *Animals & Men*. Each issue contains 60 pages packed with news, articles, letters, research papers, field reports, and even a gossip column! The magazine is A5 in format with a full colour cover. You also have access to one of the world's largest collections of resource material dealing with cryptozoology and allied disciplines, and people from the CFZ membership regularly take part in fieldwork and expeditions around the world.

How is the Centre for Fortean Zoology organised?

The CFZ is managed by a three-man board of trustees, with a non-profit making trust registered with HM Government Stamp Office. The board of trustees is supported by a Permanent Directorate of full and part-time staff, and advised by a Consultancy Board of specialists - many of whom who are world-renowned experts in their particular field. We have regional representatives across the UK, the USA, and many other parts of the world, and are affiliated with other organisations whose aims and protocols mirror our own.

I am new to the subject, and although I am interested I have little practical knowledge. I don't want to feel out of my depth. What should I do?

Don't worry. We were *all* beginners once. You'll find that the people at the CFZ are friendly and approachable. We have a thriving forum on the website which is the hub of an ever-growing electronic community. You will soon find your feet. Many members of the CFZ Permanent Directorate started off as ordinary members, and now work full time chasing monsters around the world.

I have an idea for a project which isn't on your website. What do I do?

Write to us, e-mail us, or telephone us. The list of future projects on the website is not exhaustive. If you have a good idea for an investigation, please tell us. We may well be able to help.

How do I go on an expedition?

We are always looking for volunteers to join us. If you see a project that interests you, do not hesitate to get in touch with us. Under certain circumstances we can help provide funding for your trip. If you look on the future projects section of the website, you can see some of the pr jects that we have pencilled in for the next few years.

In 2003 and 2004 we sent three-man expeditions to Sumatra looking for Orang-Pendek - a sem legendary bipedal ape. The same three went to Mongolia in 2005. All three members started off as merely subscribers to the CFZ magazine.

Next time it could be you!

Project Kerinci, Sumatra - 2003
In search of the bipedal ape Orang Pendek

How is the Centre for Fortean Zoology funded?

We have no magic sources of income. All our funds come from donations, membership fees, work that we do for TV, radio or magazines, and sales of our publications and merchandise. W are always looking for corporate sponsorship, and other sources of revenue. If you have any ideas for fund-raising please let us know. However, unlike other cryptozoological organisa-tions in the past, we do not live in an intellectual ivory tower. We are not afraid to get our hand dirty, and furthermore we are not one of those organisations where the membership have to raise money so that a privileged few can go on expensive foreign trips. Our research teams, both in the UK and abroad, consist of a mixture of experienced and inexperienced personnel. We are truly a community, and work on the premise that the benefits of CFZ membership are open to all.

What do you do with the data you gather from your investigations and expeditions?

Reports of our investigations are published on our website as soon as they are available. Pre-liminary reports are posted within days of the project finishing.

We also publish a 200 page yearbook containing research papers and expedition reports too long to be printed in the journal. We freely circulate our information to anybody who asks for i

ɔ. Each year since 2000 we have held our annual convention - the *Weird Weekend -* ɥich now takes place in North Devon. It consists of three days of lectures, workshops, ɪd excursions. But most importantly it is a chance for members of the CFZ to meet each ɥer, and to talk with the members of the Permanent Directorate in a relaxed and infor- al setting and preferably with a pint of beer in one hand.

ɐ are hoping to start up some regional groups in both the UK and the US which will have ₃gular meetings, work together on research projects, and maybe have a mini convention their own.

₁nce relocating to North Devon in 2005 we have become ever more closely involved with ɥer community organisations, and we hope that this trend will continue. We also work ɔsely with Police Forces across the UK as consultants for animal mutilation cases, and ɹring 2006 we forged closer links with the coastguard and other community services. ₑ want to work closely with those who regularly travel into the Bristol Channel, so that if ₑ recent trend of exotic animal visitors to our coastal waters continues, we can be out ₑre as soon as possible.

ans are well under way to found a Visitor's Centre in rural North Devon. This will pro-de a museum, a library and an educational resource for our members and for research-'s across the globe. We are also planning a youth organisation which will involve chil-'en and young people in our activities.

ɔart from having been the only Fortean Zoological organisation in the world to have con-stently published material on all aspects of the subject for over a decade, we have chieved impressive results, including:

Disproving the myth relating to the headless so-called sea-serpent carcass of Durgan beach in Cornwall 1975

Disproving the story of the 1988 puma skull of Lustleigh Cleave

Carrying out the only in-depth research ever done into the mythos of the Cornish Owl-man

Making the first records of a tropical species of lamprey

Making the first records of a luminous cave gnat larva in Thailand.

Discovering a possible new species of British mammal - the beech marten.

In 1994-6, carrying out the first archival fortean zoological survey of Hong Kong.

In the year 2000, confirming CFZ theories when an entirely new species of lizard was found resident in Britain.

Proving the existence of giant pike in Llangorse Lake

Confirming evidence of habitat increase of Armitage's skink in The Gambia

EXPEDITIONS & INVESTIGATIONS TO DATE INCLUDE

- 1998 Puerto Rico, Florida, Mexico *(chupacabras)*
- 1999 Nevada *(dog-headed men)*
- 2000 Thailand *(giant snakes called nagas)*
- 2002 Martin Mere *(giant catfish)*
- 2002 Cleveland *(wallaby mutilation)*
- 2003 Bolam Lake *(BHM reports)*
- 2003 Sumatra *(orang pendek)*
- 2003 Texas *(bigfoot; giant snapping turtles)*
- 2004 Sumatra *(orang pendek; cigau, a sabre-toothed cat)*
- 2004 Illinois *(black panthers; cicada swarm)*
- 2004 Texas *(mystery blue dog)*
- 2004 Puerto Rico *(chupacabras; carnivorous cave snails)*
- 2005 Belize *(affiliate expedition for hairy dwarfs)*
- 2005 Mongolia *(allghoi khorkhoi aka death worm)*
- 2006 The Gambia *(`gambo` - Gambian sea monster , ninki nanka and the Armitage's skink)*
- 2006 Llangorse Lake *(giant pike, giant eels)*
- 2006 Windermere *(giant eels)*

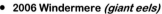

Other books available from
CFZ PRESS

CFZ PRESS

ONLY FOOLS AND GOATSUCKERS
Jonathan Downes - ISBN 0-9512872-3-0

£12.50

In January and February 1998, Jonathan Downes and Graham Inglis of the Centre for Fortean Zoology, spent three and a half weeks in Puerto Rico, Mexico and Florida, accompanied by a film crew from UK Channel 4 TV. Their aim was to make a documentary about the terrifying chupacabra - a vampiric creature that exists somewhere in the grey area between folklore and reality. This remarkable book tells the gripping, sometimes scary, and often hilariously funny, story of how the boys from the CFZ did their best to subvert the medium of contemporary TV documentary making, and actually do their job.

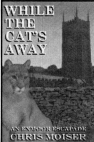

WHILE THE CAT'S AWAY
Chris Moiser - ISBN: 0-9512872-1-4

£7.99

Over the past thirty years or so, there have been numerous sightings of large exotic cats, including black leopards, pumas and lynx, in the South West of England. Former Rhodesian soldier Sam McCall moved to North Devon and became a farmer and pub owner when Rhodesia became Zimbabwe in 1980. Over the years, despite many of his pub regulars having seen the "Beast of Exmoor", Sam wasn't at all sure that it existed. Then a series of happenings made him change his mind. Chris Moiser - a zoologist - is well known for his research into the mystery cats of the westcountry. This is his first novel.

CFZ EXPEDITION REPORT 2006 - GAMBIA
ISBN 1905723032

£12.50

In July 2006, The J.T.Downes Memorial Expedition went in search of a dragon-like creature, known to the natives as 'Ninki Nanka', which has terrorised the area for generations, and has reportedly killed people as recently as the 1990s. They also went to dig up part of a beach where an amateur naturalist claims to have buried the carcass of a mysterious fifteen foot sea monster, and they sought to find a tiny lizard first described in 1922 and only rediscovered in 1989. Here, for the first time, is their story.... With a foreword by Dr. Karl Shuker and introduction by Jonathan Downes.

BIG CATS IN BRITAIN YEARBOOK 2006
Edited by Mark Fraser - ISBN 978-1905723-01-0

£10.00

People from all walks of life encounter mysterious felids on a daily basis, in every nook and cranny of the UK. Most are jet-black, some are white, some are brown; big cats of every description and colour are seen by some unsuspecting person while on his or her daily business. 'Big Cats in Britain' are the largest and most active research group in the British Isles and Ireland. This book contains a run-down of every known big cat sighting in the UK during 2005, together with essays by various luminaries of the British big cat research community.

CFZ PRESS, MYRTLE COTTAGE, WOOLFARDISWORTHY BIDEFORD, NORTH DEVON, EX39 5QR
w w w . c f z . o r g . u k

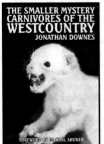

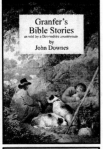

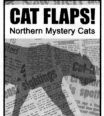

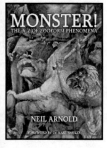

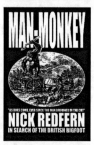